Beyond French Feminisms

Beyond French Feminisms

Debates on Women, Politics, and Culture in France, 1981–2001

Edited by

Roger Célestin, Eliane DalMolin,
and Isabelle de Courtivron

palgrave
macmillan

BEYOND FRENCH FEMINISMS

Copyright © Roger Célestin, Eliane DalMolin, Isabelle de Courtivron, 2003.
All rights reserved. No part of this book may be used or reproduced in any manner
whatsoever without written permission except in the case of brief quotations
embodied in critical articles or reviews.

First published 2003 by
PALGRAVE MACMILLAN™
175 Fifth Avenue, New York, N.Y. 10010 and
Houndmills, Basingstoke, Hampshire, England RG21 6XS.
Companies and representatives throughout the world.

PALGRAVE MACMILLAN is the global academic imprint of the Palgrave
Macmillan division of St. Martin's Press, LLC and of Palgrave Macmillan Ltd.
Macmillan® is a registered trademark in the United States, United Kingdom and other
countries. Palgrave is a registered trademark in the European Union and other
countries.

ISBN 0–312–24019–8 hardback
ISBN 0–312–24040–6 paperback

Library of Congress Cataloging-in-Publication Data
Beyond French feminisms : debates on women, politics, and culture in France,
1980–2001 / edited by Roger Célestin, Eliane DalMolin, and Isabelle de Courtivron.
    p.   cm.
  Includes bibliographical references.
  ISBN 0–312–24019–8 (cloth)
  ISBN 0–312–24040–6 (alk. paper)
  1. Feminism—France.   2. Women—France—Social conditions—20th century.   3.
I. Célestin, Roger.   II. DalMolin, Eliane Françoise.   III. De Courtivron, Isabelle.

HQ1613.B44 2003
305.42'0944—dc21

                                                                    2002072829

A catalogue record for this book is available from the British Library.

Design by Letra Libre, Inc.

First edition: January 2003
10 9 8 7 6 5 4 3 2 1

Printed in the United States of America.

*We dedicate this book
to the memory of
Elaine Marks and Françoise Pasquier,
and to the future of Cassandra, Lara, and Sophie.*

CONTENTS

II. ARTS AND LITERATURE

III. FRANCE—USA

Permissions

We gratefully acknowledge the following organizations and publishers for the permission to reprint the articles listed, which in some cases were modified, updated, and translated for this volume:

Taylor & Francis/Routledge (U.K.), *Sites: The Journal of 20th-century/contemporary French studies, revue d'études françaises* (4.1, Spring 2000, Women/Femmes)
———. "The Turning Point of Feminism: Against the Effacement of Women," Sylviane Agacinski
———. "The Feminization of Professional Names: An Outrage against Masculinity," Benoîte Groult
———. "Body as Subject: Four Contemporary Women Artists," Whitney Chadwick Mariette Sineau
———. "*Parité* in Politics: From a Radical Idea to Consensual Reform"
Taylor & Francis/Routledge (New York) 1998, *Stigmata*
———. "Unmasked!" Hélène Cixous
Centre National de Documentation Pédagogique, 1995, *De l'égalité des sexes,* ed. Michel de Manassein
———. "Symbolic Violence," Pierre Bourdieu
Seuil (Paris), *Pouvoir. Femmes en politique* 82, 1998
———. "Exclusive Democracy: A French Paradigm," Geneviève Fraisse
Découverte (Paris), 1995, *Le foulard et la république*
———. "The Headscarf and the Republic," Françoise Gaspard and Farhad Khosrokhavar
Esprit (Paris), March-April 2001
———. "Sexualities on Parade," Véronique Nahoum-Grappe
Gallimard (Paris) *Le Débat* 87 (November/December 1995)
———. "The French Exception," Elisabeth Badinter
———. "Counting the Days," Mona Ozouf
———. "Vive la différence," Joan Scott. (The version contained in this volume is the original English version; the essay previously appeared in French in the same issue of *Le Débat.*)
Feminist Studies 24.2 (summer 1998), University of Maryland
———. "Made in America: 'French Feminism' in Academia," Claire Goldberg Moses
The Manifesto of the Chiennes de Garde is available as public domain on the Worldwide Web (http://www.chiennesdegarde.org).

Acknowledgments

We are extremely grateful to Margaret Colvin and Audrey Sartiaux for their efficient and always good-humored assistance. At the University of Connecticut, we also thank David Herzberger, Head of the Department of Modern and Classical Languages, for his support of our work in general and for his commitment to this volume in particular. At MIT our thanks go to Philip Khoury, Dean of the School of Humanities, Arts, and Social Sciences, for his generous support of this project. At Palgrave/St. Martin's, we were fortunate to work with Karen Wolny, who initially took on the project, and with Kristi Long, who took over as our editor; Meg Weaver and Erin Chan were superlative production editors, and Annjeanette Kern a no less superlative copyeditor; Roee Raz was, throughout, a patient, efficient, and understanding editorial assistant. We thank them all.

This work, published as part of the program of aid for publication, received support from the French Ministry of Foreign Affairs and the Cultural Services of the French Embassy in the United States.

Introduction

Roger Célestin,
Eliane DalMolin,
Isabelle de Courtivron

From the 1970s to the 1990s

The "beyond" in the title of this book is not meant to indicate that women's issues have been resolved in France, or elsewhere for that matter, and that the concept of feminism is no longer needed and can begin to wither away like the proverbial state. Rather, it aims to stress a number of new phenomena that illustrate the differences between recent debates about women and gender in France and those that took place in the 1970s, which became known in the United States as "French feminisms." What the essays in this collection also reveal, however, are the culturally specific continuities between these recent developments and the French feminisms of three decades ago.

Today, many would agree with the analyses made by Claire Goldberg Moses and by Christine Delphy, among others, that "Made-in-America French Feminism" was in large part a construct of Anglo-American academics during the late 1970s and early 1980s.[1] Indeed, the abstract work of theorists influenced by psychoanalytic theory and literary deconstruction such as Hélène Cixous, Julia Kristeva, and Luce Irigaray did not represent the much broader activities occurring in the French women's movement at the time. This body of work did, however, reflect an original and culturally specific approach to theorizing the effacement of women. The controversial nature of concepts such as *l'écriture féminine* accounted for a great deal of intellectual excitement on some U.S. campuses, in part because academics already steeped in "French theory" were drawn to the philosophical, literary, and psychoanalytical approach of a small but provocative group of writers and intellectuals. These "French imports" also caught the imagination in ways that battles for abortion rights and rape laws did not, insofar as these were more familiar to American feminist concerns and practices. The concrete efforts that were being made to change real—legal, medical, and social—conditions for French women were thus somewhat neglected in academic circles. By the mid-eighties, however, most of the writings about sexual *différence* had fallen out of fashion in France, much sooner, in fact, than they did in the United States. Nevertheless, their impact should not be discounted for they point to a cultural constant that has marked French debates about women historically and that is still very much present in today's discussions among French feminists. In this respect, the arguments around *l'écriture féminine* of the 1970s are not as unconnected as they might seem on face value to the debates over *la parité*[2]—perhaps the single most crucial and emblematic of feminist concerns in France in the 1990s.

By the late seventies, feminist mobilization around social and legal issues had led to a number of important gains. These included the 1975 Loi Veil (the law named after then minister of health Simone Veil), which legalized abortion (followed by the reimbursement of its cost by the national health care system in 1982), the institutionalization of divorce laws based on mutual consent, and the creation of progressive rape laws, among others. Reaching these goals may have contributed to the weakening of feminist alliances between groups whose divergent strategies and values grew from colorful disagreements to serious ruptures. The election of the Socialist Mitterrand government in 1981 and its appointment of a minister for the rights of women may also have further diluted the activism of the previous decade. As had been the case in 1945 when the first wave of feminism in France slowed down after gaining the vote for women, the second wave of the seventies lost steam once the Left came to power and institutionalized parts of this second wave's agenda. The French media in the eighties were therefore quick to relegate feminism to a sort of "historical epiphenomenon."

The various political and economic crises that shook French society throughout the following decade served, for a time, to further draw attention away from specific feminist causes and activism. A phase of quiescence, in certain instances even of backlash, ensued, drawing strength from the growing forces of the extreme Right. Moreover, traditional fears of separatism between the sexes (*la peur de l'indifférentiation*), which plays a particularly powerful role in French culture, helped to relegate feminist concerns to the supposedly "dated" 1970s climate. After undergoing the only period of expansion it has ever known in France, women's studies went underground. Feminist bookstores closed. All of this served to obscure the continuing work of feminists in trade unions and in battered women's shelters as well as the ongoing research and activities of feminist thinkers. In fact, during the eighties and nineties, a number of ground-breaking conferences and publications made significant new contributions to French thought about women. The research of social scientists such as Christine Bard, Christine Delphy, Christine Fauré, Geneviève Fraisse, Françoise Gaspard, Margaret Maruani, Janine Mossuz-Lavau, Michèle Perrot, and Mariette Sineau, among others, helped to refine and deepen the ongoing work of historical and intellectual contextualization. It also highlighted the more negative aspects of certain cultural specificities—the famous *exception française*—which, despite the many gains made during the twentieth century, have caused the continuing exclusion of French women from the public sphere.

THE PARITÉ DEBATES

The precarious economy and the social upheavals centered on unemployment and immigration that characterized the mid-eighties and the early nineties in France ultimately brought feminist concerns back into the public arena. The link between antiracist and antisexist discourse became more explicit as various forces formed alliances in their opposition to traditional political approaches, whether of the Left or of the Right. Tensions between tradition and modernity, between "universal" French identity based on assimilation, on the one hand, and the increasing desire of immigrant groups to retain their cultural specificity, on the other, led a number of politicians and intellectuals to reemphasize the importance of "Republican values." The public controversies over the celebration of the bicentennial of the Revolution in 1989 generated passionate arguments over terms such as "citizenship," "democracy," and "equality," all of which indirectly brought renewed attention to the blatant historical exclusion of women from the public sphere and their jarring invisibility in contemporary politics. Indeed, in the last decade of the twentieth century, France had the dubious honor of claiming the lowest proportion of women in political office of any European country with the exception of Greece. In 1995, only 5 percent of those who held public office in the French political system were women.

At this point, energized by the new idea of *parité* in political elections—initially a grassroots movement—the issue of women's representation in the public sphere became a dominant one. The demand for legislation to ensure women's equal representation in electoral politics gained broad public support after the 1995 elections. In June 1996 a pro-*parité* manifesto, signed by ten prominent women who had held political office in governments of the Right as well as the Left, was published in *L'Express,* the widely circulated news weekly, and was picked up by the subsequent Jospin government, which became a staunch advocate of such constitutional reform. The idea of quotas for women candidates was not a new one. It had been proposed and dismissed several times before, but the demand for a 50–50 proportion of men and women candidates was its most radical manifestation yet. This movement was given visibility and impetus by other phenomena with which it intersected, including activism on the part of the Council of Europe and the World Conference on Women in Beijing. At home it was bolstered by the growing acceptance of women's potential contribution to a much-needed transformation of politics as usual: indeed, in March 1994, amid a series of corruption scandals that reached the highest levels of government, 67 percent of the French had a negative opinion of all political parties. Hence the full participation of women in the governing of their country suddenly appeared as the key to the modernization of French politics.

While the *parité* debates in France (both pro and anti) were given voice and visibility by academics, intellectuals, and politicians, and while they certainly contained their share of complex philosophical arguments and disagreements, they nevertheless became broadly integrated into the fabric of national discourse. Two years after the publication of the manifesto in *L'Express,* the legislation on parity was inscribed on the legislative agenda and, in amending articles 3 and 4 of the French Constitution, it was voted into law in June 2000.

How did France, within a decade, change from one of the most backward societies in terms of women's representation in the political sphere into one of the most progressive in this same area—at least in *theory?* The answer to this question is to be found in a number of convergent factors. On the one hand, it is to be found in the historical paradoxes of Gallic culture, which has always maintained traditional social and cultural aspects of the relation between the sexes while often legislating progressive social measures on behalf of women (as long, of course, as these are within traditionally "feminine" spheres). It is also to be found in the serendipity of timing as politicians in France, equally fearful of losing their electorate, were searching for new ideas and were thus more receptive to the proposition that women would "lead differently." But perhaps most importantly, the *parité* victory was due to the perspicacity of its proponents who increasingly couched their arguments in ways that would be reassuring to French society and would not threaten the primordial values that have always defined the relationship between French men and women.

The *parité* debates initially divided women more than they did men and women, not in terms of traditional Left/Right oppositions, but in terms of philosophical positions. The notion of changing the constitution in order to legislate parity was opposed by Elisabeth Badinter, Irène Théry, Evelyne Pisier, and Mona Ozouf, among other notables, in the name of *l'exception française*, that is, the "natural harmony" between the sexes in Gallic society, as this position has sometimes been caricatured.[3] But they were not alone in being highly suspicious of *différentialisme*—the recognition, beyond Republican universalist identity, of more specific markers of identity; a number of other feminist thinkers also feared a return to a form of "essentialism" in which biology would constitute the determining factor, thus inscribing sexual difference irrevocably in the body politic. The most passionate debates took place between the defenders of the founding principles of the Republican tradition, which does not recognize the specificity of minority group rights, and the pro-*parité* forces whose proposals initially appeared to link individual characteristics to collective group interests. As we will see, this argument, generally considered dangerous for the fabric of French society by the proponents of Republican universalism, was eventually transformed strategically by its advocates.

These "new" battles sometimes rang as a continuation of the old essentialist vs. materialist debates of the seventies, only replaced by a newer version of these binary oppositions: namely, the universalist vs. differentialist arguments (the latter also known as *particularisme* and in some instances *communautarisme*). This controversy, which speaks directly to the complex issues that have emerged since the bicentennial of the French Revolution and have been exacerbated by growing concerns about national identity, immigration, and globalization, was at the heart of larger discussions about French Republicanism. The ideal notion of an indivisible Republic, it was argued, was seriously threatened by social fragmentation if groups seeking considerations as specific communities or categories were allowed to receive special legislation. Pro-*parité* thinkers ultimately developed judicious arguments to demonstrate that their position was absolutely compatible with the popular antiquota approach. Gisèle Halimi, for example, posited that, legally, *parité* was not a quota because it represents "perfect equality" and is therefore not unconstitutional. Sylviane Agacinski, who came late to this debate but had a strong impact, argued that, since the difference between men and women constitutes "the only universal difference," it could not be compared to other demands for special rights and privileges by ethnic, religious, or sexual communities. Thus women could not be said to make up a "category." This stance resonated for many who agreed that since humankind is unarguably male and female, the difference between the sexes is the ultimate difference, and women cannot be compared to a minority, thereby endangering the universalist ideal. While such a position was resisted by gay and lesbian groups who realized that the insistence on sexual difference led to the privileging of heterosexuality, it reassured French society that *mixité* was not in danger, that the traditional coexistence of men and women in all aspects of French life would not be challenged or reconsidered. By countering the "differentialist" rhetoric, *parité* activists made their position compatible with deeply engrained French cultural and Republican values.

Throughout the nineties, the *parité* issue constituted the defining tension within French feminism. It was exacerbated by the important role played by the joining of antifeminist and anti-American forces both on the Left and the Right. In fact, what Jean-Philippe Mathy calls the "signifier 'America'"[4] became one of the most widely used figures in the broad rhetoric of antifeminist discourse. Essentially, the general American cultural and political practice of recognizing the existence of particular identities within its representative democracy was perceived, in this antifeminist rhetoric, as an anti-(French) Republican model, leaving the door wide open to the unraveling of the French state and of its founding principles. According to the logic of this rhetoric, to recognize "woman" as a *particular* identity was equivalent to doing away with the concept of the (abstract) citizen that appeared during the French Revolution. In the words of Olivier Duhamel, "When fundamental principles of constitutional law are concerned, [this French conception of the Republic] knows neither Black nor White, neither tall nor short, smart nor stupid, rich nor poor . . ." and, according to this logic, " . . . neither men nor women."[5] The claims of women to any sort of change in the status quo could then be dismissed as running counter to the very principles of Republican universalism, rather than being libertarian or justified in the context of de facto inequality. Claims to more equitable access to political office could be denounced as the (particularist) attack of a group fueled by its "phobic phantasy of [American] 'political correctness.'"[6] For a while, this practice of equating feminist claims with (American) identity politics leading to the end of (French) republican cohesion made it extremely difficult for feminists in France to make any tactical gains, mocked as they were as followers of Anita Hill and the "P.C. brigades." In short, in the discourse of its opponents, the *parité* road led to the nightmare of American dissolution.

This weapon, combining the celebration of universalism and the menace of a fragmented American social model, was used to oppose a number of other feminist proposals. For example, it structured the virulent exchanges between feminists and the Académie Française (backed by a number of pro-*République* women) on the topic of what can only be called a timid attempt to change some words and titles in the French language to better reflect women's professional roles. What had become the blatant invisibility of women in the political system was suddenly noticed in language as well, where under the guise of the "neutral" nature of French grammar the masculine form has always represented the universal. The proposal to alter, that is, feminize, some professional terms was thus opposed by some for similar reasons as the *parité* reforms.[7] Even as some in the United States were decrying the tyranny of French theory, as exemplified by the Sokal-*Social Text* affair,[8] the French intelligentsia seldom missed an opportunity to castigate the puritanical Anglo-Saxon perversities, which allegedly threatened French definitions of republican citizenship.

The important cultural markers that define French culture and politics historically, and that are foregrounded in most of the essays in this collection, are what differentiate the gender debates in France from those in the United States. These markers apply to gender as well as other (racial, religious, sexual) categories, namely, the emphasis on the prevalence of citizenship and *universalisme* over interest groups and specific identities. Many writers in our collection, however, continue to deconstruct the notion of *universalisme* as one that privileges the masculine and hence excludes women. As Eric Fassin has demonstrated, the strategic use of America as a rhetorical tool in the feminist debate changed only in the late nineties, taking away the last obstacle to a general consensus about the *parité* laws.[9]

In the legislative elections of March 2001, the law on political parity forcing politi-cal parties to offer a slate composed of an equal number of men and women candi-dates in municipal, legislative, and European elections was implemented for the first time. In the elections of September 2001, an additional fifteen women were added to the Senate. Despite the disappointment of some feminist activists, in whose opin-ion the final version of the law did not go far enough ,despite the logistical chal-lenges posed by this complicated reform, and despite some of the more traditionally misogynistic reactions against brand-new women candidates, the idea of equal rep-resentation of both sexes in the public sphere seemed to become an irrevocable fact of contemporary French life.

Meanwhile, French feminists continue to work on a number of fronts, such as employment and reproductive health, against sexism in the scientific disciplines and sexual harassment in the universities.[10] Immigrant women are becoming active in political lobbying as they attempt to bring attention to their double oppression.[11] In-deed, discrimination has not disappeared; glass ceilings and sexual harassment are no longer considered to be exclusively American terms; sexist advertisements are still ubiquitous; salary inequities between men and women continue to exist; and the ef-fort to integrate more women in the public sphere has not yielded a concomitant in-tegration of men in the private, domestic sphere of household tasks, child rearing, and so on. More women are working now than ever (today they constitute almost half of the working population in France, though only 5 percent are senior managers in the largest French companies), but more often than not this still means for many of them a "double shift." For this reason, measures such as paid paternal leaves are being seriously advocated. Indeed, *parité* is now considered to be a concept that can only be successful if it operates in the private as well as the public sphere. The rally-ing cry of many young men and women in feminist groups is *le partage des taches* (the sharing of tasks). After the passage of another progressive law, the PaCS (social civil marriage),[12] questions of "homoparental" adoption and gay marriage have garnered advocates as well as staunch opponents and have led to new debates over "*la filiation*," that is, debates over the issues surrounding legal vs. biological parenthood. Discus-sions continue about whether housework should be paid and whether prostitution should be considered a legitimate profession, often pitting advocates of women's "protection" (difference) against advocates of women's "equality" (similarity). In many ways, the economics and the politics of the family constitute the new frontiers of French feminism. Rethinking terms such as "difference," "equality," "similarity," "neutrality," "complementarity," and "specificity"; avoiding the historical trap of im-prisoning these terms in mutually exclusive definitions; defining new paradigms that concern citizenship and universal values; all of these have led to some of the more interesting discussions among, and writings by, feminist thinkers. It is undeniable that many crucial changes have occurred under the impetus of French feminist ac-tivism and research, as well as through government support boosted by the presence of exceptionally visible and active women ministers in the Jospin government. Con-traception, including the "day-after pill," is now available to minors in high schools. A proposal to extend the allowed length of delay for abortion procedures to twelve weeks is being debated; pregnant women still have four months of paid maternity leave and have access to an extensive day-care system for their children; and in many of the elite schools women are graduating in the top ranks.

Fighting against continuing discrimination, attempting to build an intelligent form of modernity, overcoming the typically French *vertige identitaire,* as Geneviève Fraisse calls it, and retaining the ideal of *une mixité équilibrée* are clear priorities for young French feminists at the beginning of the twenty-first century. Indeed, an examination of often ephemeral and marginal but nevertheless active feminist groups yields interesting information both about the continuities and discontinuities of feminism in France. Groups such as Mix-Cité, Les Sciences-Potiches se Rebellent, Les Pénélopes, and Chiennes de Garde (whose manifesto is published in this collection) are active in the struggle against sexist advertisement, against the harassment of women politicians who face blatant misogyny, against economic and legal discrimination and violence against women. They also integrate these demands into broader national movements, such as rethinking the "culture" of the family in terms of domestic *parité,* as well as within international movements such as the opposition to globalization, or to the treatment of women in fundamentalist cultures. What many of these young militants share are two common tendencies. On the one hand, they tend to distrust the 1970s feminist model as a separatist one and one that was not sufficiently attentive to race and ethnicity, although, paradoxically, most agree that because of the lack of historical "transmission" they in fact know little about these movements and may sometimes be "reinventing the wheel." On the other hand, they staunchly insist on the *mixité* of their organizations, the supreme French value par excellence that always seems to prevail in the end. In their "position papers" these groups all insist on the importance of the alliance between men and women, whether homo-, bi- or heterosexual, and in their common struggle against inequality. They remain adamant about defining their demands and their protests not as actions against men but as a shared struggle of men and women against sexism.

WOMEN IN LITERATURE AND THE ARTS

While the word "feminism" is alive and well among many authors of the historical, political, and philosophical essays in this collection, it is much less salient, sometimes even completely absent, from the essays that focus on a new generation of writers, artists, and filmmakers. But then it is important to remember that historically, and except for the brief *écriture féminine* interlude, French women in the creative fields have always resisted being labeled with categories such as "women writers" or "women painters."

The fact remains that in the past twenty years or so a new generation of women has acquired unprecedented visibility in literature and film in France. This is particularly striking in the field of filmmaking, one that has been, even more so than other fields, notoriously difficult for women to enter. Also unprecedented is the fact that after an initial success—a first novel or a first film, for example—these women have continued, consistently and successfully, to produce literary and cinematic works in a traditionally male-dominated environment.

In literature, the works of women who distinguished themselves in the twentieth century—Colette, de Beauvoir, Duras, and Cixous, among others—were unavoidably concerned with or marked by the feminine and/or the feminist. In contrast, a new generation of women writers is less concerned with feminism—radical or not—than with a shared sense of renewed literary style, subject, and authority. These "new cynics,"[13] these "nieces of Marguerite,"[14] have undertaken to storm the institution of French literature by resisting classifications and labels, adopting new styles, and mixing genres. Among them are Christine Angot, Calixthe Beyala, Catherine Cusset, Marie Darrieussecq, Virginie Despentes, Régine Detambel, Camille Laurens, Marie Ndiaye, Marie Nimier, Amélie Nothomb, Lydie Salvayre, to name only a few. Their language is often violent, direct, and free; their characters torn, disenchanted, and unsettled; their world cold, brutal, and closed off; their humor spicy, iconoclastic, and dark; their style lucid, fragmented, and lyrical. Some of the pillars of "literary" publishing, Minuit, Gallimard, Fayard, POL, have quickly discerned something new in their writing, and the general public has followed suit.

In the 1990s and at the beginning of the twenty-first century, women writers have allowed themselves to tell all, to write all, to be scandalous and provocative, and they have often done so under their own name (unlike what had been the case for Pauline Réage's *Story of O,* to name only one literary predecessor), sometimes with the central character clearly identifiable as the author (Catherine Millet, Annie Ernaux). What disturbs a number of these writers is a certain reductive perception of their work that conspicuously ignores literary merit to fixate on the sexually explicit. It is an old story, but one whose protagonists were, from Sade to Bataille, usually men; a story that Catherine Cusset ironically summarizes as follows: "Women, it would appear, have appropriated for themselves the erotic bastion in order to more easily assassinate the dying novel—and, in passing, to swell the pockets of their publishers, thanks to the commercial visibility of their literary prostitution."[15] What many of these writers claim—like the men who ventured into sexual territory before them—is the freedom and the license to explore not only the limits of sexuality itself, but also the language of that exploration. As novelist and filmmaker Catherine Breillat formulates it: "We are led to believe that talking about sex and sexuality is a sign of lust. By no means. Sex is the territory of an identity."[16]

These contemporary women writers thus expertly handle writing's sharp scalpel across an unpredictable and fully disclosed body, be it that of a man, a woman, or of the writer herself. Sometimes sex appears in the forefront of their writing, sometimes it remains peripheral, as a form of social violence sublimated into the writing itself. For example, sex is diffusely present in Detambel's lyrical and meticulously dissected objects and bodies, in Angot's provocative and abusive characters, and in Salvayre's disturbing inner voices. In other texts sexuality appears as a more central concern, a phenomenon the novelist Marie Nimier has called a "new pornography"—light, audacious, eclectic, beyond traditional social acceptance of sexual behavior, but ultimately ruled by love and trust, and moreover, initiated by women. Authors like Catherine Breillat, Catherine Cusset, Catherine Millet, and Virginie Despentes have also, in their respective styles and with various degrees of violence, opened up the repressed or hitherto mildly exposed domain of female sexuality. It is undeniable that sexuality—not gender—has been one of the primary, perhaps *the* primary theme for many of these writers. The old modernist strategy of using the sexual to subvert the established order proves to be a viable strategy once again, with one major difference: this time, it is being used by women. Some argue that this practice has created a fissure in the old paradigm and that, through it, appear new figures, new metaphors, new ways of seeing and representing. Others object that this reversal of the gaze does not seriously destabilize the traditional ideology of representations. Nonetheless, the domain of sexuality is undeniably a powerful strategy used by contemporary women writers to challenge the literary imaginary as well as to make a place for themselves in the world of publishing.

Perhaps more than women writers, women filmmakers have inherited the burden of operating in the borrowed world of male myths and images. They also acquired from their predecessors the desire to react to the normalized voyeuristic impulse that characterizes the representation of women and has even been implicitly accepted by them, ultimately defining the way women perceived themselves. A (New Wave) pioneer of cinema, Agnès Varda, speaks of the distorted female gaze always defined by those (men) looking at a woman's body and soul, and she calls for a "feminist gesture" that implies that a woman must now look at herself without the tutelage of men.

One cannot address questions of representation of women in contemporary cinema without reviewing the scandals generated by two controversial women filmmakers in the late nineties: Catherine Breillat and Virginie Despentes. Both women stirred up the press and moviegoers when, picking up from Varda's idea, they attempted, in extreme and often graphic fashion, to bring it to cinematic fruition by destroying abruptly what critic Anne Gillain calls the traditional masculine "tits-and-ass romance" film. Despite radically different aesthetic principles, both directors offered to a stunned public an anarchistic vision rendered in intensely intimate and violent images of women's sexuality. If their films did not achieve the feminism Varda had imagined a few years earlier, they did manage to short-circuit the typically masculine images of sexual representation, thus clearing the field for their successors. Films like Breillat's (sardonically titled) *Romance* and *À ma soeur* have not only given free visual range to hitherto unspoken aspects of female sexuality while avoiding the simply pornographic, they have also brought to the cinematic scene images of the male sex, erect or not, and thus eliminated the comfortable platitudes and repetitions of man-made representations of woman's sex alone. Coralie Thrin-Thi, co-director with Virginie Despentes of the film *Baise-moi,* an eponymous adaptation of the latter's notorious novel, summarizes this idea thus: "In my view, an art film is one of those pain-in-the-ass French films where nothing happens, and porno is like masturbation. Our film is neither one nor the other."[17]

Bringing together an unparalleled display of female violence while at the same time presenting a strong view of female friendship, Despentes and Thrin-Thi have gone where nobody had quite gone before. On the surface, it seems that the brutal and abusive sexual scenes alone in *Baise-moi* presented the film-rating commission with an unprecedented situation. But it has also been argued that the strong bond between the two criminal women may have in fact (unconsciously?) disturbed the commission more deeply than the sex and the violence per se. In other words, was it the image of violent young women that French society could not accept? Or was it the deep solidarity and shared critique of the male world that carried their friendship throughout the film that shocked its viewers? First released as a film "interdit aux moins de seize ans" (no one under sixteen allowed), it subsequently received an "X" from the rating commission under pressure from conservative groups. This decision was rejected by a group of leading artists who gathered support in the name of civil liberties. The solution ultimately adopted was to bring back the "Interdit aux moins de dix-huit ans" rating (no one under eighteen admitted), one that had disappeared from the French rating system and required an amendment to the existing law. In the end not everyone was satisfied. Civil liberties were respected and adolescents could not see the film, but the violence of the unmediated sexual scenes generated by women made the general public uncomfortable and, despite the acts of friendship that brought the two main characters together, the film gained only limited feminist support.

However shocking and controversial these particular films by Breillat and Despentes have appeared, they may turn out to be short-lived *succès de scandale* (similar to the publication of Marie Darrieusecq's notorious *Truismes* in 1996). If profuse sex and unadorned representations of female—and male—genitalia have made of Breillat and Despentes the talk of Paris in the late nineties, other less provocative filmmakers have been actively engaged in the demystification of male representations of woman, and they have done so in domains that are not always as strictly delimited by sexuality and violence. This is a cinema Geneviève Sellier calls a "hybrid art form," gathering its varied inspiration and themes from often neglected or taboo cultural and gender issues: Agnès Merlet's representation of the traumatic world of children left to grow up without a mother in *Le fils du requin* (1992); Sandrine Veysset's perspective on the simple love and profound despair of motherhood in *Y aura-t-il de la neige à Noël?* (1996); the discomfort of sexually and esthetically ambivalent characters played and directed by Josiane Balasko, whose *Gazon Maudit* (1995) was an enormous success across the board; the even greater success of Agnès Jaoui's first main feature *Le goût des autres* (2000), which successfully mixes sociocultural concerns with gender issues in order to question the patriarchal order that the film simultaneously condones and defies. In the nineties, an unusual number of women directors have challenged a growing sense of "uneventfulness" pervading contemporary French cinema. They have put excitement back in cinema by representing women in ways that certainly point to a clear sense of social independence and artistic autonomy.[18]

In the arts, fewer women have taken the lead in dissipating man-made concepts of beauty and the coding of sexuality itself. However, despite their small number, some have become important and recognized artists as they turned the perfectly orchestrated world of aesthetics on its head. Female artists like Nikki de Saint-Phalle and Orlan have focused their talent on radical representations of the female body. As with the cinema of Breillat and Despentes, the controversial Orlan represents a spectacular if isolated example of ways in which art by women has dealt with the body. Using her own body secretions as well as her body itself, Orlan demonstrates that the concept of corporeal beauty as we know it may still be obtainable on the thinnest edge separating and joining the beautiful, the artistic, and the grotesque. Her documented and broadcast "surgical performances" have allowed millions to witness the actual transformations of her own body at the hands of thoroughly prepped plastic surgeons asked by Orlan to perform specific surgical interventions on her body under local anesthesia. Today, young artists may not be flooding the artistic scene, but they are continuously and systematically challenging traditional views of woman's body. Recognizing the centrality of this concern but also acknowledging its generic quality beyond an exclusively female or feminist gesture, art critic Whitney Chadwick concludes her essay on French women artists in this volume by stating: "Interest in rethinking the body in ways that renegotiate its materiality and its boundaries characterizes much contemporary art by women in France today."

In contrast to film directors and artists, the larger contingent of women poets has remained more peripheral to questions of sex and of women's bodies. They have not openly claimed a specifically female territory in the particularly exclusive domain of French poetry. For some, the femininity in their poetry has become synonymous with contemporary lyrical poetry, a revamped and active contemporary genre reflecting the idea that all poets, men and women, have a strong tendency toward the feminine regardless of the author's sex. For others more inclined toward the literal and the objective, the act of poetry has simply come to mean a "systematic" search in the subjectless field of mathematical and logical thinking. This state of affairs does not mean that women poets have unilaterally obliterated all questions related to the representation and redefinition of women posed by other female writers and artists. Bound by poetic rules but also freed by a certain sense of universalism, some women have nonetheless found a way to express gender-specific concerns in their poetry. For example, in this collection poet Marie Etienne explains how some women poets have transformed and sublimated the usually coercing concept of domesticity into a poetic place of female power and identity.

Francophone authors offer a reversal of the configurations noted above. Indeed, they have tended to use their writing mostly to express a feeling of loss with regard to their country of origin while also partaking of a new type of freedom as women living in the West. For them the challenge is to retain or rebuild their sense of female identity outside any form of acceptable "home." They may appear as the homeless victims of postcolonial times, but their writings have in fact challenged and disturbed the very premises of the French literary tradition. For example, immigrant African women in Calixthe Beyala's novels see coming to France as an opportunity to break away from the traditional and sometimes oppressive domestic sphere that they left behind. In other novels by recent writers such as Nathalie Etoké, Sandrine Bessora, and Fatou Diome, more general issues regarding the legal and civic status of African immigrants in republican France are raised for both men and women. For Franco-Maghrebi women writers such as Leila Sebbar and Assia Djebar questions of bilingualism and biculturalism have become central. Caribbean writers like Gisèle Pineau and Maryse Condé have become mainly preoccupied by questions of nomadism and exile for their female characters torn between their native island and the postcolonial *metropole*. Thus it seems that for Francophone women writers the constant questioning and challenging of the concept of "home" is the central concern.

In discussing the situation of contemporary French women, we note that there often seems to be a marked gap between the laws that govern their lives and the representations that govern their imaginary, a phenomenon that points to an interesting divergence between real-life reforms and creative constructs. Whether the new creative "female gaze" in literature and film is a radically new one or whether it repeats in new ways some of the traditional tropes; whether these young women creators have had to "shock" in ways that are both provocative and reassuring in order to be seen, heard, and read and will move in new directions as their numbers and visibility become established; these are open-ended questions. It is likely that, encouraged by this growing number of successful writers and filmmakers, more women will take up writing and filmmaking in a context that appears more favorable to women today than it did twenty-five years ago.

Back to the Future

Despite the fear of ridicule and the supposed obsolescence that made it go underground for a while, it would seem that the demise of feminism in France has been greatly exaggerated. Today much is indeed changing, especially for a new generation of women. In the same way that France is exploring ways to take advantage of its diverse ethnic composition without falling into fragmented communities, it is attempting to define gender equality in ways that will be consonant with its historical and cultural traditions. Will it achieve either of these? We cannot answer this question, of course. All we can do in this book is to signal certain directions and outline the accomplishments as well as the contradictions. What we can conclude, however, is that despite the persistence of a number of traditional continuities, women's roles and representations are being rethought and reshaped in light of the many debates and transformations that have taken place in French politics, society, and culture at the end of the twentieth century.

As the long bibliography at the end of this volume attests, abundant research on women and gender continues in France, though not much of it has been translated into English. And, increasingly, there are conferences, colloquia, seminars, and even timid attempts at degrees on a variety of subjects in women's studies. During the past twenty years or so French women may have moved away from some of the issues that once characterized "French feminisms." Yet they are in the forefront of the cultural and political scene at the beginning of the twenty-first century, promoting a broad array of new concerns, debates, and creative productions that the eclectic but representative collection of essays in this volume seeks to present.

Postscript (June 2002)

The timespan covered by this volume begins with the election of Mitterrand in 1981 and ends as the elections of the spring of 2002 approached. Its emphasis is clearly on the decade of the 1990s. Our bibliography covers the years 1985 to 2001, when most of the substantive new works on French women appeared.

As this volume was going to press in the spring of 2002, a number of important developments shook France and, although these extend slightly beyond the years covered by this collection, we consider that they merited a brief update.

It was a tremendous shock to the French political system, and a disaster for the Left, when Jean-Marie Le Pen, leader of the far right National Front, became Jacques Chirac's opponent in the presidential elections in April 2002. After bursts of mass political activity on the part of the French, Chirac was roundly elected to the presidency in May. The following month, the legislative elections were held and the French, breaking with the trend of "cohabitation," voted to give the majority in the National Assembly to Chirac and his new political party, consisting of Gaullist and non-Gaullist politicians.

One of the great losers in this national electoral drama was the *parité* law, passed in June 2000 and discussed in several articles in this volume. Indeed, the strongest and largest political parties, also the richest, could afford to pay the fines imposed on all parties that did not meet the requirements of the law. By contrast, the small and financially strapped parties (such as the Greens and the Front National) avoided such fines by presenting a much larger slate of women candidates. Chirac's new majority party presented 20 percent women candidates and even the Socialist party could only muster up 36 percent. As a consequence, only 12 percent of the current French National Assembly is made up of women—not much of a change from the pre-*parité* days.

The larger political parties offered several justifications for this dismal record, mostly based on the shock of the Le Pen vote, and the various electoral strategies that had to be promulgated in order to block the Far Right. Would the scenario have been different if the elections had gone more routinely? This is a difficult question to answer; all we can conclude is that despite one of the strictest laws in the world in terms of political equality, the situation de facto in France is radically different from what it is de jure.

In spite of this serious setback to the progress made by feminists in the 1990s, all the news is not grim. While the Chirac government does not have as many visible women in important positions as did the Jospin government, it has made some unusual appointments including, for the first time, a woman as Minister of Defense (Michèle Alliot-Marie). Other women in significant positions include Roselyne Bachelot, Minister for Ecology and Sustainable Development; Tokia Saifi, Secretary of State for Sustainable Development (the first "Beur" in a French government); Claudine Haigneré, Minister Delegate for Research and New Technology; Nicole Lenoir, Minister Delegate for European Affairs; and Nicole Fontaine, Minister Delegate for Industry. While a Minister Delegate for Parity and Equality in the Workplace has also been appointed (Nicole Ameline) not much has been heard from this minister or about her goals and responsibilities. Moreover, as Geneviève Fraisse convincingly explains, being *appointed* to govern is symbolically very different from being *elected* to represent.

Thus we should perhaps conclude this postscript with Pierre Bourdieu's warning, also in this volume, that we should neither overestimate "the transformations of the feminine condition" nor underestimate "the permanence of its gains."

NOTES

1. Claire Goldberg-Moses. "Made in America: 'French Feminism' in Academia," in *Feminist Studies* 24:2, Summer 1998. See also, for example, Christine Delphy, "The Invention of French Feminism: An Essential Move" in *Yale French Studies* 87, 1995.
2. Basically: concrete, legislatively, and constitutionally enforced equality in respective numbers of men and women who run for political office, leading to more "gender-equitable" political representation.
3. Philosophical differences among anti-*parité* writers (as well as among pro-*parité* ones), while they may sometimes appear esoteric, should not be minimized. Pisier, for example, proposes a critique of *parité* from a universalist perspective while Théry bases her opposition on the idea of sexual difference.
4. See Jean-Philippe Mathy's essay *infra*.
5. Cited in ibid.
6. See Pierre Bourdieu's essay, *infra*.
7. The debates around "linguistic *parité*" echoed those concerning political *parité*, and their resolution took a parallel course. After years of widespread and sometimes

virulent exchanges, an official *circulaire* was passed by the Jospin government, inviting all government administrations to feminize the official terminology of ranks and professions. It published a "grammatically correct" *Guide d'aide à la féminisation des noms de métiers, titres, grades et fonctions* to help establish these changes and render them uniform. Within a very short time, the government, educational institutions, and the media, had all begun to use this new terminology and very little was heard again on the subject.

8. Alan Sokal, a New York University professor of physics, submitted a bogus essay on "postmodern thought and science," filled with critical jargon, clichés, and scientific errors to *Social Text,* a high-profile journal of critical theory and cultural studies. The essay was accepted and published. A few months later, Sokal revealed the hoax in an article published in *Lingua Franca,* a review read mostly by academics and education professionals. A debate, some called it a scandal, followed, involving, among other topics, a questioning of the (deleterious) influence of "post-structuralist French thought" in the United States. For a good overview of the "Sokal-*Social Text* Affair," see Jean Philippe Mathy's *French Resistance: The French-American Culture Wars* (Minneapolis: University of Minnesota Press, 2000) and David F. Bell's essay "Text, Context: Transatlantic Sokal," in Ralph Sarkonak ed., *France/USA: The Cultural Wars,* spec. issue of *Yale French Studies* 100 (Fall 2001), ed. Ralph Sarkonak.

9. Eric Fassin, "The Purloined Gender: American Feminism in a French Mirror," in *French Historical Studies,* 22:1, Winter 1999.

10. As recently as February 2002, the issue of sexual harassment was brought to the forefront, this time in higher education. Although a law punishing sexual harassment had been passed in 1992, it had not often been activated, and was never applied to universities. In late January 2002, a petition was circulated asking university administrators to take the leadership in dealing with the sexual abuse that sometimes accompanies the relationship between a professor and a student but that has always tacitly been accepted. Shortly thereafter, a suit was lodged by a female graduate student against a male professor at the prestigious Ecole des Hautes Etudes Pratiques, alleging that her academic future had been jeopardized when she refused to have an affair with her thesis director. Although *Le Monde* and *Libération* gave both the petition and the particular suit ample coverage, it must be noted that *Libération* could not resist subtitling its concluding paragraphs "Dérive à l'américaine." See *Libération,* February 19, 2002, and also Eric Fassin's very thoughtful essay on this matter in *Le Monde,* February 21, 2002.

11. See "Dans les quartiers, un féminisme en gestation," in *Libération,* January 28, 2002.

12. For more on PaCS, see Eric Fassin's essay, *infra.*

13. See Dominique Viart, *Le roman français au XXe siècle* (Paris: Hachette, 1999).

14. See Catherine Cusset's essay, *infra.*

15. Ibid.

16. Quoted from Anne Gillain's essay, *infra.*

17. Ibid.

18. The success of women's films is confirmed by the growing popularity of the Festival de Films de Femmes de Créteil, which will celebrate its twenty-fifth year in the spring of 2003. This international week-long festival has become a vibrant site for film screenings, forums, performances, and prize giving. It offers a striking exception to French women artists' frequent refusal to be identified and grouped by their gender.

PART I

Politics and Society

CHAPTER 1

The Turning Point of Feminism
AGAINST THE EFFACEMENT OF WOMEN

SYLVIANE AGACINSKI

In France today women are in the process of taking feminism to a turning point. By demanding, with *parité,* the de facto sharing of political responsibilities, they are clearly rejecting the *nondifferentialist* ideology that, despite equal rights, preserves the ever-persistent male monopoly of power. *Parité* is not a way of letting nature "dictate law" (we know full well that nature itself never "dictates"); rather, it is a way of giving meaning to human existence characterized by sexual difference (*sexué*). Nature has never founded anything: neither the past hierarchy of the sexes, nor the present demand for their equality. *All this is political through and through.* Nevertheless, the fact that human beings are characterized by their sex (*sexué*), that they are born boys or girls, that they can become fathers or mothers (but not both at the same time: such is the constraint of the dichotomy of the sexes) is not political—despite what Judith Butler and some others have said.[1]

Moreover, contrary to what we spontaneously think, it is not the natural *difference* between the sexes that has legitimated their *inequality,* rather it is a denial and a reduction of this difference. Throughout our history, women have not been considered "different" beings embodying humanity on the same grounds as men. They have been defined as *incomplete* and *inferior* men. From Aristotle to Freud, woman was always lacking something in order to be a man "like any other." She has been humanity's weak figure, its minor form, and not one of two legitimate forms. It is time to understand that this logic of lack and inferiority is not the logic of difference. Woman alone *differed* from man, and not he from her. She has not been recognized as half of humanity but as its exotic and "particular" part. We can see this androcentric logic at work all the way up through Kant's *Anthropology.* Abstract universal thought, from the eighteenth century to the present, is in keeping with this logic, whether it structures political thought or grammatical law. It seems to me that Joan Scott[2] does not sufficiently explain that it is this same paradoxical logic, according to which the universal is masculine and the particular is feminine, in which French feminists have found themselves caught and that has led them to demand their rights sometimes as women, sometimes as human beings, condemned to oscillate between the "particular" and the "universal." The "paradoxes" of feminism have simply been the counterpart to the paradoxes of androcentrism, which identifies the universal with the masculine. Consequently, we can break out of these paradoxes by showing that universal humanity is not *singular,* but *double,* and that it must be understood as the humanity of both man *and* woman.

We can then understand why *conceptualizing sexual difference is a new development,* since to do so one must finally acknowledge that the human race is "mixed," and that its existence is characterized by sexual difference *(sexuée)* from the outset, without a singular model. By acknowledging the *universality of difference,* we can escape the aberrant logic of androcentrism that relegates all demands made by women to "particularism."

The impasse of abstract universalism, which neglects sexual difference for the benefit of the sole "human being," has already been pointed out by Simone de Beauvoir in the introduction to *The Second Sex.* It is surprising that we don't remember this. Indeed, she warns us against the temptation, which she believes to be above all *American* (!), to erase the meaning of the word "woman," while she mocks the "highly irritating" *("fort agaçant")* work of Dorothy Parker who declared: "All of us, men as well as women, should be regarded as human beings."[3] This is an abstract declaration according to de Beauvoir, who adds: "It's obvious that no woman, without being in bad faith, can pretend to situate herself beyond her sex."[4] And why is a woman tempted to erase "her" difference, while a man is not? It is because she feels "in the wrong" being a woman, while a man is "in his right" being a man. The author of *The Second Sex* is thus quite conscious of the androcentric trap of abstraction (even if, all too often, she herself falls into it, notably when she cannot keep herself from scorning all female traits, maternity in particular) and makes it clear that human beings' "inauthentic flight"[5] into abstraction originates in . . . the rationalism and philosophy of the Enlightenment. Here we are, then, back in Europe to verify, if necessary, that the effacement of sexual difference tempts both sides of the Atlantic equally. Certain Franco-American disagreements on the question of women are perhaps less simple than they appear.

As we indeed know, certain fiercely anti-*paritaire* French women who take refuge in abstraction and refuse to claim their rights *as women,* pride themselves in universalism and accuse American women of *differentialism.* We must not let ourselves get caught up in this false dichotomy, for in reality it masks two harmful ways of erasing sexual difference and of not acknowledging its universal character.

The "French" effacement proceeds by engulfing both sexes in an abstract humanism, from which only the singular model of a sexually neutral human being can surface. (In reality, as Françoise Héritier[6] has shown, neutrality is not possible within this model, since *one* of the two sexes takes the place *of both* according to an implacable androcentric logic.)

The "American" effacement proceeds by drowning women in a systematic particularism in which minorities of all sorts (ethnic, religious, cultural, etc.) are grouped together, and both sexes end up being considered pure "constructions" when they are not the result of a "heterosexual matrix," as Judith Butler puts it.

Today, the new French feminism simultaneously challenges both these types of sexual neutralization in affirming sexual duality as the only *universal difference* within humanity. This is why it was able to conceive of the *parité* ideal in politics.[7]

So, yes, obviously, to the extent that differentiation of the sexes characterizes every human being a priori, and is therefore universal, it can be called *natural.* In spite of the historically and culturally variable values and interpretations applied to male/female difference, this difference structures human existence and, beyond that, most living beings. Granted, there are *only uses* of nature—social, political, etc.— and these uses are always interpretations without *ultimate* truth. Yet the differentiation of the sexes, with its history, remains nonetheless something that we can neither create nor invent, and that we cannot simply deny through a peremptory decision. Our corporeal existence is given to us as such; just because the experience of the body and of death is from the outset historical in nature does not mean that we can surmount or get around it, even spare ourselves from thinking about it. Like the other beings on this earth, we must eat to survive, we are destined for reproduction and corruption (as Aristotle would have said), and we need both sexes to create life. Claude Lévi-Strauss reminds us that the *most undeniable* characteristic of man is that he is first and foremost a *living being.*[8] In the name of what idealism should we forget or deny our membership in the world of the living? What would be the use of economies or politics without the needs and passions of the finite beings that we are? Cultures treat death or the duality of the sexes differently according to their beliefs, their rites, or their institutions, and individuals in modern societies are all confronted with the question of the meaning of their sexually differentiated (*sexuée*) and mortal existence. These questions are not matters for ordinary political science, but require anthropological and philosophical reflection. Sexual difference is a reality at once natural and instituted: necessary for life, male/female differentiation is a natural given, but the taboo that marks incest and the building of kinship and filiation establishes sexual difference socially.

A hasty reading of Sartre often leads us to condemn every allusion to nature in the name of the opposition between nature and freedom. But Sartre uses the expression "human nature" in the philosophical and classical sense of *essence:* he thereby asserts the incompatibility between the idea of "human nature," that is, the idea of an *essence* of man imposing *a priori* his behavior, and the idea that man is free, that is, that he must conceive of his life's purpose without any possible recourse. The principle whereby "existence precedes essence" means that each person must "choose his/herself" and by him/herself give meaning to his/her existence. This does not mean that we can invent our existence and determine the particular or universal conditions in which we must exercise our freedom as individuals.

Today, blinded by the mirages of technical power, we would like to defeat old age and death, even surmount our condition by changing our sex or by creating embryos in the laboratory with genetic material taken from individuals. Those who, on both sides of the Atlantic, advocate the effacement of sexual difference no doubt congratulate themselves for this "progress" and for the new liberties that such "progress" offers *individuals.* The fact that each person can give life *on one's own* and become at the same time father and mother, thanks to the techniques of medically assisted procreation, seems to them to mark progress toward individual autonomy. Even Robert Badinter sees nothing problematic in this, not even the recourse to surrogate mothers, which, in his opinion, is tantamount to "simple adoption by anticipation."[9] In fact, those who, out of fear of a "naturalism," challenge the recognition of sexual difference in the law, are blindly throwing themselves into the arms of applied science, as if from now on science alone could become the basis of the law. With a certain legal consistency, the same people who condemn *parité* also legitimize the right for couples of the same sex to have "biological or adopted" children.[10] To these people, universal difference between men and women is not worthy of involving the law, while biology carried out in laboratories is justification for all rights. Tomorrow, biology will give us the means, if not to abolish the difference between men and women, at least to make it so that they no longer need each other. "Biological" children will no longer be born of men and women, but will be manufactured with genetic materials, like any hand-crafted or even industrial product. This possibility does not signal progress, but rather a disturbing mutation of the species. It should make us conscious of the fact that human societies are not founded on conglomerations of independent atoms.

The existence of both sexes confronts each sex with its finiteness and prevents each from considering itself alone to be the incarnation of "man," forcing the one to coexist with the other (but not necessarily to define oneself as heterosexual). This duality presupposes nothing about the essence of "man" (in the generic sense) nor about the essence of man or woman: it simply confronts each person with the heterogeneity of the human race and leaves the trace of the other in our bodies and in our minds.

Feminism today, like feminism yesterday for Simone de Beauvoir, cannot therefore consist in denying the sexually marked (*sexué*) character of existence—unless we want a feminism without women—but should instead overthrow, theoretically and practically, the old hierarchy of the sexes. To do so we need a critique of androcentrism wherever it subsists, particularly in political life—a point to which I will return.

If we can speak of a *turning point* in relation to the trail blazed by the first wave of feminism and Simone de Beauvoir, it is because de Beauvoir did not seem to realize the equality of the sexes that women could not simply move into the world as it was but had to transform it, deconstruct it. She did not see that it was not enough for a woman to become a professor, a philosopher, or a citizen for theoretical or androcentric political constructions to collapse. Women's practical and political problems, regarding their place and status, could not be solved by their "assimilation," by their accession to a world built and thought by men, for the *male/female hierarchy was still there* in this world, still present, efficient, theorized.

For my part, this is what I discovered when I became a professor of philosophy. Teaching Plato or Kant, I became aware that I was not dealing with speculations on universal and neutral subjects, but with sexually marked (*sexué*) philosophical subjects, whose very concepts were penetrated by the male/female hierarchical structure. Without imagining *a priori* a systematic divergence of male and female points of view—which does not always exist—we must be able to analyze the androcentrism of theoretical constructions whenever it appears. Why are so many of the current innovations in philosophy and the social sciences the work of female theorists? It is because they shift attention to the *very basis* of their discipline—from Nicole Loraux to Arlette Farge, from Françoise Héritier to Elisabeth de Fontenay, from Sarah Kofman to Blandine Kriegel (I name these thinkers at random, there are many others . . .).

It is necessary, for example, to challenge philosophy's age-old exclusion of the question of procreation. I have tried to do so in my book[11] by asking why, beginning with Plato's *Banquet,* the *male* philosopher must choose between the love of ideas (and the soul *of boys*) and the desire for progeny (therefore women). Built on a "virile" rejection of flesh and women, metaphysics has left traces in all its conceptual constructs, all the way up to modern oppositions of subject and object or activity and passivity. It is always the feminine that philosophers have *depreciated,* along with the body, matter, and nature. If we do not see the relationship between certain conceptual hierarchies and the hierarchy of the sexes, we are applying classical concepts without critical thinking and we remain inside systems marked by androcentrism.

In France, this project has always been hindered by women as well as men by the constant temptation to sacrifice the question of difference to the question of a deceptive universal or abstract legal equality.

Also called "republican," this equality, which implies that the citizen is *neither man nor woman* since both are equal in the eyes of the law, in fact prohibits women from making any demands *as women,* and forces them to put up with the persistence of the androcentric order. This universalist trap was able to seduce feminists who, early on, were eager to identify with men in order to better emerge from their condition.

After all, this identification has not been only negative: it has allowed women to break with the models in which their mothers had been imprisoned. But, as it rejected any "feminine" legacy, *feminism has fed on misogyny.* Most women of my generation for whom freedom took precedence over everything—and it is in this sense *that we were passionately Beauvoirians*—opted first for this identification with men and repudiated "maternal models" in every sense of the phrase, since it was in the family that the subordination of women was still being institutionalized. The choice of economic independence and the critique of marriage very often characterized the way girls of my generation saw things (and the very word "girl" retains the flavor of that era).

Nevertheless, the "feminine" made a come-back, particularly in the body and in sexuality. In the 1960s and 1970s, the success of contraception and the struggle for abortion rights made clear the dissymmetrical reality of the sexes and caused women to become conscious of the specificity of their own liberation. The discourse of women *as women* was no longer taboo, especially since discrimination of all sorts continued to run rampant, despite supposed equality and the dream of the indifferentiation of the sexes. The ideal was therefore no longer to become a man "like any other," but to assert difference in equality.[12]

The control of reproductive rights also allowed us to rethink maternity in a new light: as a strength, as the satisfaction of an essential desire—thus as a freedom—and finally as a privileged experience of responsibility. On this point, we could not be guided by de Beauvoir, who wrote that procreation includes "no project" and for whom childbirth was only a "natural function," devoid of meaning and essentially alienating.

Freely chosen and emancipated from the male point of view, however, maternity became not only a freedom but also a privilege to such an extent that men today find themselves, in a certain way, deprived of the power that patriarchal domination had guaranteed them for so long: the mastery over progeny. The conditions necessary for men and women to establish new relations, founded on respect for their difference and equality, are perhaps now in place.

On the political scene, the idea of *parité* has represented, since the beginning of the 1990s, a way of giving new content to political equality. In a representative democracy, save for cases of referendum, representatives normally exercise the sovereignty that belongs to the people as a whole. In both governmental assemblies, the National Assembly and the Senate, 90 percent of the seats are held by men (without even mentioning other governmental bodies), and thus a male quasimonopoly of power deprives women of their *right to exercise sovereignty.*

This deprivation does not exist because French women do not want to become candidates, nor because people do not vote for them, but because political parties, traditionally male or even "macho" territory, do not nominate them as candidates. They perform a *constant positive discrimination* toward *men*, prolonging the legacy of a Republic long ago inspired entirely by ancient models. So the question of what a democracy that includes women should be—which has never been addressed—is particularly urgent in France today.

Until now, the Constitutional Council (*le Conseil constitutionnel*) has always considered that the Constitution of 1958 did not allow the law to distinguish between men and women in matters, for instance, of electoral lists. The law was thus supposed to remain neutral with respect to the sexes, even though society was not neutral.

Conversely, if we grant that *both* sexes constitute humanity *universally*, it is legitimate to rethink the sovereignty of the people by taking into consideration the double composition of the people. In this case, women should not only be able to elect representatives, but should also be able to represent the people on the same level as their fellow male citizens. (It is obviously not a question of men's and women's *separate* representation.) Women must therefore have increased access to the status of political candidate, which they do not have in political parties today. What is at stake in modifying the Constitution today is the ability to break free of a false universal by acknowledging that men and women must have equal access to mandates and elective office and by allowing the law to correct the effacement of women in our democracy.

Translated by Mary Schwartz

NOTES

1. Judith Butler, *Gender Trouble* (New York: Routledge, 1990).
2. Joan Scott, *Only Paradoxes to Offer* (Cambridge: Harvard UP, 1996).
3. Quoted in Simone de Beauvoir, *The Second Sex,* trans. H. M. Parshley (New York: Vintage Books, 1989), xx.
4. T.N.: "Il est clair qu'aucune femme ne peut prétendre sans mauvaise fois se situer par-delà son sexe." (*Le Deuxième Sexe* [Paris: Gallimard, 1976], 13). This sentence is curiously missing from Parshley's English translation of *The Second Sex.*
5. T.N.: "fuite inauthentique." De Beauvoir, *Le Deuxième Sexe* 13.
6. Françoise Héritier, *Masculin/féminin: la pensée de la différence* (Paris: Odile Jacob, 1996).
7. See in particular Blandine Kriegel, *Philosophie de la République* (Paris: Plon, 1998).
8. Claude Lévi-Strauss, *Structural Anthropology,* trans. Claire Jacobson and Brooke Grundfest Schoepf (New York: Basic Books, 1963), 47–48.
9. T.N.: "une simple adoption par anticipation." Robert Badinter, *Le Débat* 36 (1985): 10.
10. See Evelyne Pisier's "PACS et Parité: du même et de l'autre," *Le Monde* (October 20, 1998).
11. Sylviane Agacinski, *La politique des sexes* (Paris: Seuil, 1996).
12. This change was set in motion in particular by Antoinette Fouque. See *Il y a deux sexes: essais de féminologie, 1989–1995* (Paris: Gallimard, 1995).

CHAPTER 2

Symbolic Violence

PIERRE BOURDIEU

People act as if the feminist revolution were a fait accompli. They enumerate women's victories, the formerly inaccessible social positions they now occupy. They feign uneasiness about the threat this new power poses for men and even go so far as to form movements for the defense of male interests.

The dominant always tend to overestimate the victories of the dominated and to give themselves credit for that which was actually wrested from them by force. Today, a neo-machismo overestimates the transformations of the feminine condition even as it underestimates the permanence of its gains. It can even use these changes to reinforce the status quo. For example, some may use the pretext that the protest movements of blacks, homosexuals, and women (with their phobic fantasy of "political correctness") pose a threat to the freedom (of white male heterosexuals) as a means of contesting the very principles of feminist claims; whereas others may turn "sexual liberation" into an argument/instrument of imperative seduction. Intellectuals, so eager to think of themselves as liberators, are actually not the last ones on the block to place the prophecies of liberation at the service of new forms of domination. I have in mind, for instance, those who invoke psychoanalysis to denounce the repression of an allegedly innate, universal desire for pleasure and the "desexualization" of women, hence the passivity and frigidity from which they must be freed. Or take, for example, those like Bataille, Klossovski, Robbe-Grillet, or Sollers, who reproduce—disguised as an aesthetics of transgression-cum-radical subversion and snugly wrapped in the assurances provided by the irreality and irresponsibility of literary fiction—masculine fantasies of omnipotence, which are easily sustained given the total control exerted over female bodies reduced to passivity.

That having been said, where do the changes in relations between the sexes really stand? There can be no doubt that masculine domination can no longer be assumed. It has become something that must be defended or justified, either something to refrain from or not be caught practicing. There is no doubt that what we call the "liberation" of women, of which "sexual liberation" is merely the most striking component, has profoundly modified the surface appearance of things. This questioning of the most obvious has gone hand in hand with the far-reaching transformations of the feminine condition: for example, a growing access to secondary and higher education and salaried employment, and thus to the public arena; and the tendency among women to distance themselves from reproductive functions, a trend especially evident in postponed pregnancies and shorter absences from the workplace following childbirth.

Yet these visible changes mask a permanence, both in objective structures and in the obvious and visible. If we are to assume that access to schooling at the secondary and higher levels represents not only one of the most important changes in objective relations between the sexes but also one of the most decisive factors in the transformation of these relations, we cannot allow this apparent equality of access to mask the inequalities that impact the distribution of women in various academic disciplines and, by extension, career opportunities. More girls than boys obtain the *baccalauréat* and go on to study in universities, but they are far less represented in the most prestigious fields: the percentage of girls in the sciences remains very low, whereas there is a steep rise in the percentage of girls with the "A" *baccalauréat* (liberal arts). The same phenomenon can be observed in the technical highschools: girls gravitate toward the less-qualified fields traditionally considered "feminine" (staff in professional organizations or business enterprises, secretarial work, the health sector). The same inequality persists in preparatory classes for the *grandes écoles scientifiques* (prestigious public institutions of higher education in the sciences) and in the schools themselves. In the medical schools, the proportion of women declines the further up the hierarchy of specializations they climb; some fields—surgery, for example—are practically off-limits to women, whereas others, such as pediatrics and gynecology, are more or less reserved for them.

A similar logic governs the access to various professions and the positions within each of them. For example, while it is true that more and more women are represented in the public sector, they are relegated to the lowest-level, most precarious positions. (There are large concentrations of them among untenured and part-time staff; in local government, for instance, they are placed in subaltern and service jobs—cleaning, cafeteria, day-care assistants, etc.) All factors being equal, women almost always receive—at no matter what level of the hierarchy—positions and salaries inferior to those of men. Positions of leadership, which more and more women have begun to assume, are usually in sectors under government control; that is, the production and circulation of symbolic goods (publishing, journalism, the media, education, and so on).

This permanence, which can hide behind an undetected shift in the border separating the sexes, as in the case of education, can only be grasped if an element altogether different from the effects of external force and masculine will is introduced. Yet it would be no less naïve (and scandalous) to assign responsibility, as has been done, to women themselves, although they can appear, in a number of instances, as contributing to their own exclusion. In questioning adolescent girls about their academic experience, one cannot help but be struck by the "collective expectations," (*"attentes collectives"*) to borrow an expression from Marcel Mauss, and by the powers of inducement, both positive and negative, that parents, teachers (especially guidance counselors), and peers exert by explicitly reminding them what the traditional view considers their proper calling. The result is that many of them notice teachers in the sciences calling on girls more than boys; that parents as well as the teachers or guidance counselors steer them away "for their own good" from certain careers deemed masculine ("When your own father tells you: 'You'll never be able to do this job,' that really hurts"), while encouraging their brothers to enter those professions. These calls to order, however, owe their effectiveness in large part to a whole series of earlier experiences, especially in the realm of sports, where they have often experienced discrimination, that prepared them in advance to accept all these injunctions, and led them to internalize the prevailing perception: these girls "cannot imagine themselves" "on a construction site" or "giving men orders," or simply occupying a traditionally male job. The sexual division of labor, rooted in objectivity and spontaneously generated statistics by which each one of us forms an image of what is normal, taught them (in a magnificent tautology that accounts for what is socially obvious) that "these days, you don't see many women in male occupations," or, to be more precise, mechanics are almost always men and therefore the career track of this trade (a technical *baccalauréat* with a specialization in mechanics) is not for them. Should by chance they forget this despite all the ill-intentioned interference from teachers and peers, they are reminded by the difficulty—and they all say this—of being alone, or just a handful, in classes consisting completely, or almost completely, of boys. ("People don't understand what it's like being a girl alone in a class of boys. Often I cry in my father's arms when I come home.")

In short, through the experience of a social order in which the division of labor is fairly rigorously enforced according to sex, and through explicit calls to order from their parents, their teachers, and their peers (armed with a vision and a *di*-vision developed through similar social experiences), these adolescent girls have adopted the dominant viewpoint in the form of perceptual and evaluative patterns deeply embedded and almost inaccessible to the conscious mind—a viewpoint that inclines them to accept as normal, even natural and obvious, the social order as it is. Research has shown that the masculine viewpoint continues to assert itself visibly (even if young people consider themselves less "sexist" than adults), especially in their habits. This is evident, for example, in the fact that the age gap between partners of a couple continues to favor the male (most women preferring a male partner taller and older than they are).

It then follows that women contribute to their own domination, in a certain sense, by harboring tendencies that, as a product of the established order, incline them to submit to this order, in the absence of conscious, voluntary consent and under no direct duress. In order for the symbolic domination of which they are the victims to function—as with all other forms of behavior by which they choose their destiny, in a way, refusing the academic tracks or careers from which they are excluded, embracing those to which they have been assigned—women had to have incorporated, as do all victims of symbolic violence, the structures by which the domination they submit to is implemented. Furthermore, their submission cannot be the result of a conscious, voluntary act (as in "voluntary servitude"). To understand symbolic domination and its permanence, we must break with the philosophies of consciousness to which critical theories, such as Marx's theory of social domination or feminist theories of sexual domination, remain attached. Consciousness has very little hold at the level of physical predisposition. This is true in the case of sexual domination, a symbolic form of domination that is practiced with the complicity of the woman who submits to it: or, more precisely, with the complicity of internalized structures that the dominated individual acquired in prolonged confrontation with the objective structures of domination.

We would do well to enumerate all the instances in which the best-intentioned men (symbolic violence does not operate in the register of conscious intent) engage in *discriminatory* acts: excluding women from positions of authority without even questioning their action; trivializing their claims and demands as mere whims, which a conciliatory word or a pat on the cheek is supposed to fix, and so on. There are so many infinitesimal, unconscious "choices," which, taken together, make profoundly unfair the situation to which women everywhere are reduced. Statistics on feminine representation, especially in politics, periodically take stock of this.

Masculine domination, which turns woman into a symbolic object whose being (*esse*) is one of a perceived being (*percipi*), effectively puts women in a permanent state of physical insecurity, or, to use a better term, of symbolic alienation. Endowed with a being that is appearance, she is tacitly called upon to demonstrate—by the way she holds her body and displays it (clothes, make-up, posture, etc.)—a kind of availability (sexed, if not sexual) in regard to men. The a contrario proof of the truth of this analysis, which obviously risks appearing rather excessive, is the transformation of subjective and objective experiences of the body that intensive engagement in sports can work in a woman. From the woman's viewpoint, a sport profoundly changes her relation to her own body. No longer existing only for others or—what amounts to the same thing—for the mirror (not an instrument that facilitates "seeing," as is commonly assumed, but that lets us see how we are seen by others), the body becomes a body for its own sake: from a passive body acted upon, it becomes an active, acting body. From a male perspective, women who in a sense reappropriate their physical image, severing the tacit relationship of availability, are considered to be "unfeminine," or even lesbian—the expression of intellectual independence, which also has physical manifestations producing very similar effects.

In closing, it would be well to evoke what certain feminist analyses characterize as "feminine masochism"; that is, the sort of eroticization of social relations of domination whereby, in Sandre Lee Bartky's words, "dominance *in men is exciting*."[1] Suffice it to say that the seduction that powerful men and power exert draws its principle not from a sort of deliberate perversion of consciousness, but from the submissiveness ingrained in bodies, in the form of unconscious tendencies, by all the silent injunctions of the social order as masculine order. Since the foundations of symbolic violence reside not in a mystified consciousness that needs to be enlightened, but rather in tendencies adjusted to the structures of domination of which they are the product, the symbolic revolution that the feminist movement seeks cannot be reduced to a conversion of consciousness. We cannot simply wait for a severing of the complicitous relationship that the victim of symbolic domination allows the dominant. Only a radical transformation of social conditions can predispose the dominated to adopt a viewpoint toward the dominant and toward herself that is none other than the viewpoint of the dominant.

Translated by Margaret Colvin

NOTES

1. Sandra Lee Bartky, *Femininity and Domination, Studies in the Phenomenology of Oppression* (New York: Routledge, 1990). In English in the text.

CHAPTER 3

The Politics of PaCS in a Transatlantic Mirror

SAME-SEX UNIONS AND SEXUAL DIFFERENCE IN FRANCE TODAY

ERIC FASSIN

1989 was not only the year the Berlin Wall finally collapsed. In France, 1989 was primarily the year of the Bicentennial of the French Revolution—that is, at long last, the Revolution was over (at least, according to François Furet[1]). This meant that, henceforth, instead of opposing 1776 to 1789, a (good) liberal Revolution to a (bad) radical Revolution, French "neo-liberals" could invoke de Tocqueville to denounce the perils of democracy in America—thus turning around the transatlantic mirror: in contrast to a French tradition of civility fortunately inherited from a happy combination of the Old and New Regimes merging in the *"République,"* "democratic passions" (meaning the immoderate love of equality) jeopardized the American nation. This became intellectual common sense in Parisian circles in the following years, in response to American (so-called) political correctness, and shortly thereafter, to (so-called) sexual correctness.

In France, 1989 was also the year of the *affaire du foulard:* should young Muslim women be allowed to wear a veil in public schools? The political choice was generally presented as an alternative between the principle of *laïcité* (secularism) and a (somewhat unprincipled) cultivation of cultural difference. Language notwithstanding, this debate was not so much about religion: in fact, it reflected a growing concern about the "integration" of immigrants, or rather, second-generation immigrants, in French society. The defense of a national model against the perils of ethnic fragmentation was elaborated by public intellectuals such as Elisabeth Badinter, Régis Debray, and Alain Finkielkraut—in the name of the "République." Resisting *ghettoïsation,* they identified the French nation with what they defined as a universalist model of individual integration. In the process, they too drew on a transatlantic contrast: American differentialism (that is, the *communautarisme* of identity politics) was the mirror image of French universalism (that is, the *individualisme* of Republican politics).

In France, 1989 may then have been the moment when "liberal" intellectuals (*à la Furet*) and defenders of the "nation" (*à la Finkielkraut*) united under the banner of the French "République" against the American countermodel, as they identified the critique of egalitarianism with the critique of identity politics. After the final collapse of Communism, America became the new Other. (Or should one say that America was, yet again, the other Other?) This political alliance largely defines the intellectual climate of the 1990s in France—for the beauty of this rhetorical construct of a contrast between national political cultures is that it applies equally well (or poorly, depending on one's perspective) to extremely diverse issues: not only ethnicity, but also gender and sexuality.

Indeed, not only does the "Republican paradigm" define French public debates in the recent period about "immigration" (with the transatlantic contrast generally presented as one between the French "melting-pot" and American "multiculturalism"), but it has also been used to discuss the politics of feminism (for example, in Mona Ozouf's essay *Les mots des femmes*), and the politics of homosexuality (in particular, in Frédéric Martel's essay *Le rose et le noir*).[2] In each case, the authors define, in contrast to the "disuniting of America," the so-called *modèle républicain*. For example, gay counter-culture is rejected in the name of individual integration: the yearly Gay Pride demonstration is according to this view but another example of "Americanization."[3]

Given this universalist framework, one would expect French "Republicans" of all stripes to embrace wholeheartedly the issue of same-sex marriage: it would seem to be the culmination of a universalist agenda. Or at least, so it has been recently, in the United States—precisely where French universalists look not for a model, but rather for a counter-model.[4] This is how Hannah Arendt's "Reflections on Little Rock" could be recently updated for contemporary American purposes—from the Civil Rights movement to the Gay Rights movement, from the late 1950s to the late 1990s: "The right to marry whoever one wishes is an elementary human right compared to which . . . nearly all other rights enumerated in the Constitution are secondary."[5] Indeed, whereas the Supreme Court of the United States started racial desegregation in schools with *Brown v. Board of Education* in 1955, it did not complete its work until desegregation applied to marriage as well, with *Loving v. Virginia* in 1967: only then was the old logic of *Plessy v. Ferguson* in 1896 finally and completely overturned—races could not any longer be deemed equal while they remained separate. Desegregation can be the most powerful weapon against discrimination—especially within marriage.

One essential question remains—whether the shift from race to sexual preference is legitimate. Does the same logic apply in both cases? Can one extend the argument—from one kind of discrimination to another, from one minority to another? Paradoxically, the answer may be easier to provide in France than in the United States: since 1985, French law (in contrast to American federal law) has explicitly rejected discrimination based on "sexual orientation" (or rather, literally, "mores"), alongside other forms of discrimination—based on race, sex, national origin, religion, and so on. The parallel between miscegenation laws and the issue of same-sex marriage should thus be even more obviously convincing in France than it is in the United States.

Of course, as many have pointed out, not every legal distinction can be considered a form of discrimination: equal treatment only applies to comparable situations. For example, we find it obvious that children and adults should not be entitled to the same rights—in France as well as in the United States. The legal distinction only reinforces that which we usually consider to be an acceptable social distinction. However, not every social distinction is given legal reinforcement. For example, class differences or religious differences are not legally established—neither in France, nor in the United States. Thus, giving legal status to a social distinction does require powerful justifications; otherwise, it is appropriate to call such legal distinctions a form of discrimination. Women are a case in point: in France, women are entitled to a pregnancy leave: they are the ones who give birth to children. However, parental leave is not for mothers only—women do not have a monopoly over prime education. In a word, although the legal system may legitimately distinguish between different categories of citizens, it may only do so for good, strong, or (to use the language of American law) "compelling" reasons; otherwise, the law only serves to justify what could be called (to use the language of the French political tradition) "privileges."

Homosexuality is indeed different from heterosexuality; but is the difference such that they should be legally distinguished—with different rights attached to each? And in this case, what are the "compelling" reasons that could justify maintaining homosexuality outside of marriage laws, especially once discrimination against homosexuality is illegal, as is the case in France (contrary to the United States)? Or, conversely, why should the political principle of equality not apply within the family—why should it not extend to marriage law? And how can one say that this not about homosexuality, but about marriage, and the family—and not see that marriage and the family do have something to do with discrimination against homosexuals?

Indeed, the family as an institution is not merely the last bastion of discrimination against homosexuals in France; it is also at the heart of this discrimination. Not only because all families play a primary role in socialization—in families, values are taught, as well as prejudices—but also because while this institution is defined as heterosexual by nature, it remains legitimate to exclude homosexuals from their families. It is no wonder that even today parents should reject their own child, and children their own father or mother, when they first discover his or her homosexuality—in both cases ensuring that homosexuality stays out the family. It is no wonder that in France courts should deny custody of a child to the gay parent after a divorce, or reject adoption demands by single homosexuals, even though the law says nothing about a person's sexuality for purposes of divorce or adoption. In all these cases, judges, parents, and even children simply draw a logical conclusion from a general principle: if the family is defined as heterosexual, then homosexuals do not belong in the family.

How can one not see this? The answer, of course, is simple. Not that discrimination is invisible. Actually, people do not see what they do not want to see—they are blind to what they refuse to acknowledge. In the same way, in 1980, the French Constitutional Council, reviewing laws that go back to Vichy establishing a different age of consent for heterosexuality and homosexuality, refused to invalidate them. The argument was that "for the sake of minors, the law may distinguish, without disregard for the principle of equality, between sexual acts based on whether they involve persons of the same sex or not." Within two years, the National Assembly was to repeal this law: discrimination was then in full view. Today, many in France argue that toleration for homosexuality should not lead to its inclusion within the family: but

discrimination may soon cease to be invisible. Or so it would seem, given the contemporary emphasis, among intellectuals, on universalism as a defining feature of
French political culture.

Logically, both "liberal" and "national" Republicans should have applauded as same-
sex marriage became a public issue. Indeed, a bill granting some kind of a (limited)
legal status to same-sex couples originated in the early 1990s with political figures
claiming a universalist logic—such as Jean-Pierre Michel, a gay assemblyman politically affiliated with the arch-Republican minister Jean-Pierre Chevènement. However, once the PaCS (Pacte Civil de Solidarité, formerly known as Contrat d'Union
Sociale, or Contrat d'Union Civile—CUS or CUC) was under attack, for the most
part, Republican intellectuals either remained silent or joined in its denunciation.
Politics has its own logic, which may not always coincide with intellectual logic—and
this is also true of intellectual politics.

Those who are willing to grant a certain number of social rights to same-sex couples in France today, through something like the minimal *concubinage,* often reject
more legitimate forms of domestic partnership, such as the PaCS. The real issue, beyond the PaCS (even though the bill currently discussed in Parliament makes no reference to the topic whatsoever), is in fact access to adoption as well as reproductive
technologies—both of which currently legally exclude same-sex couples in France.
The real problem is that, while not objecting to gays and lesbians as individuals, nor
even as couples, many refuse the perspective of gay and lesbian families.

It is not exactly surprising that this should be a problem on the Right—
traditionally, the Right has defined the family in a traditional fashion, indeed, as the
bulwark of tradition. The question is then: why should this also be a problem on the
Left—as evidenced by the embarrassing absence of most left-wing *députés* when the
PaCS was first put to the vote on October 9, 1998? Two answers then come to mind.
The first is "cultural"—and not altogether surprising. While the persistent misogyny
of politicians is more frequently discussed today, in light of the *parité* debates, homophobia is hardly absent in either of these circles, and should not be overlooked. And
it is only in the last few years that in France what might be called (in comparison
with the United States) the Old Left has started opening somewhat to the (French)
New Left, in order to consider not only class but also minority issues—both inequality and discrimination. And there is yet a long way to go.

The second answer is "historical," and it probably requires a longer explanation.
When the Left returned to power under the leadership of Lionel Jospin in 1997, the
idea expressed by the new government was to reclaim the family in the name of a
politique familiale de gauche: whereas, according to an opposition inherited from the Republican tradition, the French Left had always been suspicious of the (private) socialization that takes place in families, and preferred to rely on the (public)
socialization of schooling, now at last the phrase "left-wing family policies" (or "politics," for that matter) would not be an oxymoron. This means that the image of the
family had to be transformed: instead of opposing legitimate to illegitimate families,
one should extend the definition of a legitimate family. These "brave new families"
rehabilitated by left-wing politics are complex families, composed and recomposed
("blended"), but not decomposed, through marriage, divorce, and remarriage—not
to mention unmarried couples with children. The left-wing modernization of the

family was in fact the acknowledgement of complexity in contemporary family life, as analyzed, for example, in the work of sociologist Irène Théry.

The Left thus opened up the definition of the family. But how open should it be—that is, how far should one go in the direction of complexity? For all throughout the 1990s, the issue of same-sex couples had been raised on the Left: should these couples be granted a status? And if so, since the question was not any longer merely of toleration, but actually of recognition, should one not go a step further and grant legitimacy not only to same-sex couples, but also to gay and lesbian families? This was the new question raised when the Left regained power in 1997, as gay and lesbian organizations joined in support of (beyond the much more moderate version of the PaCS) same-sex marriage itself—not only the APGL (Association des Parents et futurs parents Gays et Lesbiens), but also the Centre Gay et Lesbien, AIDES, and even Act-Up Paris.

The Socialists in government then tried to resist this pressure by occupying a political position that might be defined as *juste milieu*.[6] This "middle ground" logic applies both to family and to homosexuality issues (and indeed, to others as well, such as immigration). On the former front, the idea is that one should open up the definition of the family—but not go too far: marriage need not be stable for the family to survive; but in order to preserve stability for the children, at least, the principle of sexual difference should remain at the foundation of the family. On the latter front, the idea is that discrimination against homosexuals should be opposed. It is true that this had already been established by the Socialists in the early 1980s, after the election of François Mitterrand. But in the 1990s, they argue, it is possible to go further, though not too far—halfway between toleration and recognition, halfway between homosexual individuals and gay and lesbian families: a semi-recognition for same-sex couples.

Only one problem remains. The middle ground strategy is clearly a politically shrewd choice, as it may gain support in the center, and thus remain popular: this is why the French Socialists define their position in a contrast to both "extremes"—in simultaneous opposition to homophobic militants, and homosexual militants. But obviously, the risk is that framing this contrast as an equivalency may also have a political cost: the center may not be on the left, after all. How could the *juste milieu* characterize the Left? And then, how can the French Socialists still claim to be on the Left?

This is the point where intellectuals play a crucial part: they provide arguments to justify this political choice. Not that this is very new: in France, the relative power of intellectuals also implies that they tend to be closer to power—their influence in public space is sometimes purchased at the expense of independence from public opinion. This is the key function of public intellectuals in France: they provide arguments for public debate. But the easiest way for intellectuals to influence politics is to use the language of politics—their political language is more likely to be reflected in the public sphere if this language itself reflects preexisting positions in the political world.

What is remarkable in this case, is that French opponents of same-sex marriage, especially on the Left, shift from the political language of universalism to other languages, in order to justify their position: universalism can hardly justify the *juste milieu* as a left-wing position. Given the difficulty of coming up with a political justification, the first solution is to look for a foundation outside of politics—hence the recourse to the social sciences; hence the importance of "experts." Sociologist Irène Théry, in particular, first through an article published by the (*juste milieu*) think tank Fondation Saint-Simon, and then through a report on family reform ordered by the Socialist government, provided arguments to establish the intellectual legitimacy of middle ground politics.[7]

In her work, "sexual difference" (*la différence des sexes*) is not presented as a political issue, but rather as an anthropological foundation: this *ordre symbolique* (a notion that combines French intellectual traditions in social anthropology and psychoanalysis) is not open to political negotiation—it is a given. Of course, one can dispute the anthropological data: as anthropologists have known for a long time, "sexual difference" is hardly the universal definition of marriage and the family. One can also dispute the idea that anthropology (or psychoanalysis, or any other "science") should predetermine our political choices—as if marriage and the family were outside of the political realm, beyond the democratic pale of public debate. But the political choice of the middle ground is still granted more legitimacy when intellectual discourse resonates with conventional wisdom in order to establish sexual difference at the heart of marriage and the family.[8]

Scientific legitimacy in and of itself is not sufficient to justify the *juste milieu*. Political justifications are required to show that "sexual difference" is not only a scientific necessity, but also a political imperative. And this is where the debate about *parité* comes in: it contributes the left-wing aura of feminism to the politics of the middle ground.[9] In order to avoid the stigma of Americanization, the inventors of *parité* in politics were willing to say that it had nothing to do with (American-style) "quotas": women were no minority, since sexual difference was no ordinary difference, like class or ethnic differences; it was an essential, universal difference. This potentially essentialist argument served a strategic purpose: at first, it worked powerfully in the direction of equality—between men and women. But in the context of the debate surrounding gay and lesbian couples and families, it could also work, quite powerfully too, against equality—between heterosexuals and homosexuals. This is what Prime Minister Lionel Jospin's wife, philosopher Sylviane Agacinski, suggested in a book on "sexual politics," whose gender politics has consequences on the politics of sexuality: according to her, Simone de Beauvoir notwithstanding, "sexual difference" is not merely a social construct—it is, through motherhood, a biological reality. This philosophical argument translates politically: "sexual difference" is a political necessity for the women's movement; therefore, it should not be given up for the sake of gay and lesbian families.[10]

The paradox is that this reformist view of feminism (progressive in terms of gender, conservative in terms of sexuality) finds echoes in France among radical feminists and radical lesbians. Of course, it is not altogether surprising: these radical critics of patriarchy find it difficult to fight a political battle in favor of marriage and the family—even if it means the inclusion of gays and lesbians in these institutions. The fact that gay leaders should support same-sex marriage does not always help, as the gender tensions have obviously not vanished in a gender-neutral politicization of homosexuality. The result is that radicals may be tempted by the arguments of women like Irène Théry and Sylviane Agacinski—not because they want to preserve a "symbolic order" that excludes homosexuals from marriage and the family, of course, but because they advocate (from the outside) a counter-cultural vision of ho-

mosexuality. Middle-ground reformists prefer "disorderly conduct" among homosexuals: as long as homosexuality remains subversive, it will not subvert the "symbolic order" of heterosexuality.

The symmetrical paradox is of course the price that intellectuals have to pay for
this *juste milieu:* they now have to oppose, and sometimes in the name of Foucault, the
"assimilation" of homosexuals within society, through marriage and the family. In
order to provide an intellectual and political justification for the *juste milieu,* they have
to recant, both intellectually (by invoking *la différence des sexes*) and politically (as they
reject the logic of equality), their professed universalism.

These debates raise numerous questions. We may conclude with a political one.
Today, in France, "universalism" is the name of the game. This means that the question of being in favor of or opposed to universalism is politically irrelevant: universalism is the common language within which disputes about "minorities" take
place—this is obvious in the case of *parité,* and it is becoming visible in the case of the
PaCS. The relevant question is then: how can we make use of this rhetoric to contribute to social change? How can we appropriate it in a politically satisfactory fashion? My suggestion is that today in France it is possible (though difficult) to
articulate the claims of the women's movement and of gay and lesbian liberation by
using the language of equality, instead of sexual difference—for sexual difference is
today the language with which the interests of women and homosexuals are pitted
against each other. Paradoxically, when French Republicans are forced to abandon
the language of universalism in order to resist minority claims, it may be wise to appropriate this rhetoric in order to fight for equality—not for homosexuals, not for
women, but for all.

(February 1999)

POSTSCRIPT (OCTOBER 2001)

Two years after the PaCS finally became law in France, the perspective is quite different. It is not that events contradict the analysis developed above, and earlier, in
the midst of the battle. On the contrary, the final defeat of intellectual and political
opponents of the PaCS only confirms what was then claimed: resisting rights for gay
and lesbian couples could hardly be successful in a political culture defined by its
universalist claims. In late 1990s France, universalism proved a potent weapon in the
battle for minority rights: this paradox should not come as a surprise to the reader
of this text. What remains to be seen is whether the universalist logic stops at the
PaCS, or follows its course, *beyond* the PaCS, thus leading to a redefinition of laws on
"filiation"—that is, access to adoption and reproductive technologies.

Occasional homophobic outbursts notwithstanding, homophobia proved illegitimate in France—both politically, and intellectually. Indeed, in the wake of the vote,
an anti-homophobic bill was even sponsored by UDF leader François Léotard, while
RPR candidate Philippe Séguin soon tried to reclaim the gay and lesbian vote in his
(unsuccessful) mayoral bid for Paris: right-wing parties thus attempted to repair
their image, somewhat damaged by the anti-PaCS crusade they had launched not

only within the National Assembly and the Senate, but also nationally, in the streets and through petitions.

It is not that homophobia does not exist, of course, especially on the Right; but rather, thanks to the debate, it became clear that it does not pay, politically, when the ideology of the "République" prevails. According to this rhetoric, gays and lesbians (just like Jews at the time of the French Revolution) should be granted nothing as a community—but everything as individuals. Even Catholic bishops had to refrain from using the Bible, and were confined to the same arguments about the so-called symbolic order.

Equally revealing has been the reaction of the Left. Among Socialists and their allies, the initially tepid support was belatedly replaced by a warm endorsement: Prime Minister Lionel Jospin now proudly claims the PaCS (even more than *parité*, which was not opposed by the Right) as one of his main accomplishments. How can one account for this sudden reversal?

First, the humiliating defeat of October 1998 exposed Socialists to the accusation of hypocrisy—how could they initiate a bill they did not support? The Right then seemed more coherent and honest in its frank opposition than the Left in its half-hearted support. For the Socialist representatives, the only way to avoid ridicule was to claim that their absence had no meaning: they insisted it was purely accidental. And the only way they could prove this was by embracing whole-heartedly the PaCS.

Second, this forced strategy soon transformed into a deliberate one: whereas on sexual (especially homosexual) matters representatives (especially on the Left) had assumed that they were far ahead of the population they claimed to represent, they started realizing that they were far behind. Public opinion turned out to be more progressive than intellectual and political elite—and as time went by, more and more so. The Enlightenment model was thus turned upside down: leaders certainly did not lead the way; at least, they felt that they could follow it. This is true of intellectuals no less than of politicians: whereas many had invoked the authority of anthropology to oppose the "butoirs indépassables de la pensée" ("insurmountable buffers of thought") to same-sex "filiation," Collège de France professor Françoise Héritier now explains that the "impensable" has (or will soon) become "pensable," thanks to the evolution of public opinion.[11]

This is why it is important now to consider PaCS not so much any longer as a reflection, but rather for its role in the *production* of French culture—thus approaching culture in terms of *change,* rather than tradition. All the more so since the reality of PaCS, just like the reality of *parité,* is no longer that of an ideological debate: both are now practices, as same-sex and different-sex couples have become *pacsés,* and more women were elected in the municipal elections of March 2001. No one opposes either law today. No one suggests that they could or even should be repealed. Both have become part of the social and political landscape. This should not suggest that the debates are over—the logic initiated by the two laws will continue, but perhaps on different grounds, both beyond the PaCS, and beyond *parité.*

This is (as could be anticipated) because reproductive rights loomed on the horizon after the PaCS (adoption rights or access to reproductive technologies for gay individuals or couples), or because *parité* would prove an unfinished revolution (How many women did indeed become mayors, at least in major cities? How many will be elected deputies in 2002? How many will even run for the presidency in the same year, especially among the major candidates?) These issues are just a continuation of the previous debates—and their development may owe as much to European as to French social logic: for example, with the recent laws in the Netherlands opening marriage and adoption rights to gay couples, or with the imminent decision of a European court on adoption by a gay individual.

But there is more. PaCS and *parité* initially appeared as radically different debates. One focused on gay and lesbian rights, the other on women's issues. The former had to do with private life, the latter with the public sphere. However, both oppositions were soon to collapse. On the one hand, "sexual difference" could be invoked as an argument while debating both sexuality and gender—both gay and lesbian rights and women's issues. On the other hand, whereas PaCS involves the public recognition of private arrangements, the new political participation of women encouraged by *parité* has domestic consequences. It becomes difficult to think of PaCS and *parité* without elaborating on their links to each other.

This has two consequences. Both PaCS and *parité* have to do with discrimination, and both are "minority" issues—and, as has been argued here, both have been framed in universalist terms. This convergence explains that in combination, the two reforms have reframed political debates beyond their actual contents. In theory, *parité* is only about political representation. But the absence of women on the boards of major companies simultaneously became visible, as well as the lower pay of women at all levels: economic participation also became an issue. *Parité* goes beyond *parité*. In theory, PaCS has to do mostly with the discrimination endured by gay and lesbian couples. But racial or ethnic discrimination immediately became more visible, both in the PaCS (in the case of immigrants) and outside the PaCS (for example, the absence of "visible minorities" on French television, their exclusion in housing and employment, and so on, became issues). PaCS goes beyond the PaCS. The confusion of identity politics and minority politics that had prevailed under the hegemony of the rhetoric of the "République," opposed to *communautarisme*, finally came to an end after the joint success of PaCS and *parité*. This may signal the end of what I have suggested calling *l'épouvantail américain* (the American scarecrow)—at least for minority issues.

The other consequence is more specific. It has to do with the revival of feminism in France, at the same time as gay and lesbian issues found a new prominence—say, from the Chiennes de garde to Act-Up. Two pessimistic readings prevailed during the debates. First, *parité* exacerbated tensions among feminists, between those who supported and those opposed the reform. Indeed, feminist critics of *parité* feared that the political gain came at a great cost: were a few political positions worth the naturalization of gender? Was not the essentialization of womanhood lurking behind the updated version of "sexual difference"? Second, the tensions between feminists and supporters of gay and lesbian rights were displayed in full sight, and possibly reinforced: not only could sexual difference be simultaneously invoked for *parité* and against same-sex "filiation," but also feminists often felt that advocates of the PaCS were oblivious to their critique of marriage.

Though justified, these negative assessments cannot fully account for what eventually amounted to a double victory, both for feminist *and* for gay and lesbian politics. This one can measure through unexpected consequences. On the one hand, far from reinforcing the (traditional) "symbolic order" opposed by feminists, PaCS did undermine it: in the wake of the debate, for the first time in France, the imposition of the patronym was questioned in a bill that grants the same symbolic rights to the father's and the mother's names. This only confirms the hope expressed by some (in the United States and in France) that same-sex marriage could help "dismantle the gender structure of marriage." On the other hand, abortion rights were simultaneously expanded, against the opposition of medical experts whose role paralleled that of social science experts in the PaCS debate.[12] Feminists could both gain and learn from the PaCS. Conversely, supporters of gay and lesbian rights did profit from the experience of feminism—not only from its critique of marriage, but also from its denaturalization of gender roles.

At the same time, even the tensions—within feminism as well as between feminists and advocates of gay and lesbian rights—can be interpreted more positively, because they produced a dynamic. Early initiators of *parité* (in particular, Françoise Gaspard and Claude Servan-Schreiber) had to take more seriously the risks involved in their arguments when "sexual difference" was invoked against same-sex couples and families (the two women, both feminists, were to announce and celebrate their PaCS publicly). In the process, they found new common ground with some of their feminist opponents—universalist critics of *parité* (such as political philosopher Evelyne Pisier) and critics of the naturalization of sex (such as anthropologist Jeanne Favret-Saada). The evolution of *Les temps modernes* is revealing: whereas the journal first presented in 1998 the arguments on PaCS of lesbian skeptics or critics (Marianne Schulz and Marie-Jo Bonnet) alongside those of a gay initiator of PaCS (Gérard Bach-Ignasse),[13] in 2000, feminists joined gay rights advocates (Evelyne Pisier and Daniel Borrillo, Liliane Kandel, and Marcela Iacub) joined in a denunciation of the new "symbolic order" established with the joint authority of psychoanalysis and anthropology.[14]

As a consequence of this redefinition of feminism, alongside gay and lesbian rights, a new generation of activists has come to light during these years who did not then, and do not now, differentiate between the two battles—for example, associations as diverse as Mix-Cité and Pro-Choix. Both signed (alongside a range of feminist as well as gay and lesbian associations and personalities) a manifesto entitled *Pour l'égalité sexuelle*, that is, both for gender equality and for equality in terms of sexuality, both for *parité*, and for PaCS.[15] This new generation is not trapped in the oppositions of the recent past (feminists inspire and are inspired by Act-Up). But this generational renewal should not be reduced to a generational opposition: Jeanne Favret-Saada writes in ProChoix's magazine, which also claims French classic figures of feminism of the earlier generation Colette Guillaumin and Nicole-Claude Mathieu as founding influences. Nor should it even be reduced to generational questions: the renewal can be more accurately described in terms of interests and issues. Feminist and gay rights figures, Françoise Gaspard and Didier Eribon, could now join forces to teach jointly about "homosexualities" at the prestigious École des hautes études en sciences sociales.

The simultaneous debates and victories of PaCS and *parité* have thus contributed to redefining the political landscapes of both feminists and gay and lesbian activists. Their simultaneous marginalization in the 1980s and their simultaneous demonization in the early 1990s gave way to a simultaneous revival after 1997—precisely as the American countermodel collapsed along with the rhetoric of the "République." PaCS and *parité* have jointly contributed to reformulating the dominant "republican" ideology. These social and political events should not be understood as mere reflections of Frenchness—instead, they shape French culture in its new form.

1. Furet, who died suddenly in 1997 shortly after his election to the Académie française, was considered, both in France and North America, a leading expert on the French Revolution. He was the author of numerous books on the subject.

2. Mona Ozouf, *Les Mots des femmes, essai sur la singularité française* (Paris: Fayard, 1995). Some of the reactions are to be found in a dossier published by *Le Débat:* "Femmes: une singularité française?" 87 (November-December 1995). See also Frédéric Martel, *Le rose et le noir, les homosexuels en France depuis 1968* (Paris: Seuil, 1996).

3. On this recent history of French intellectual (and political) history, I have published two pieces in English: "'Good to Think.' The American Reference in French Discourses of Immigration and Ethnicity," *Multiculturalist Questions,* ed., Steven Lukes and Christian Joppke (Oxford: Oxford University Press, 1999), 224–41; and "The Purloined Gender. American Feminism in a French Mirror," *French Historical Studies,* 22:1, (Winter 1999): 113–38. They expand on what is only sketched here.

4. For a more fully developed comparison of the French and American debates, see Éric Fassin, "Same Sex, Different Politics: 'Gay Marriage' Debates in France and the United States," *Public Culture* 13.2 (2001): 215–32 (and a forthcoming volume with Duke University Press).

5. Hannah Arendt, "Reflections on Little Rock," *Dissent* 6.1 (Winter 1959), excerpted in Andrew Sullivan's reader: *Same-Sex Marriage: Pro and Con* (New York: Vintage, 1997), 144.

6. I have developed a political history of these recent developments in "*PaCS Socialiste:* la gauche et le 'juste milieu,'" *Le Banquet* 12–13, dossier "Mariage, union et filiation" (October 1998): 147–59.

7. Irène Théry, "Le contrat d'union sociale en question," *Esprit* 10 (October 1997): 159–87, and the report *Couple, filiation et parenté aujourd'hui. Le droit face aux mutations de la famille et de la vie privée* (Paris: Odile Jacob/La Documentation française, 1998).

8. I have developed a critique both of the arguments (what I call *l'illusion anthropologique*) and of the intellectual stance (what could be called *l'illusion de l'expertise*) in two articles: "L'illusion anthropologique: homosexualité et filiation," *Témoin* 12 (May 1998): 43–56; and "Le savant, l'expert et le politique. La famille des sociologues," *Genèses* 32, September 1998, 156–69. By contrast, I have tried to sketch the counterfigure Foucault called for: "'L'intellectuel spécifique' et le PaCS: politique des savoirs," *Mouvements* 7, "Savoir c'est pouvoir: expertise et politique" (January-February 2000): 68–76.

9. For an intellectual as well as political history of the two debates, see Michel Feher and Éric Fassin, "Parité et PaCS: anatomie politique d'un rapport," *Au-delà du PaCS: l'expertise familiale à l'épreuve de l'homosexualité,* ed. Daniel Borrillo, Éric Fassin, Marcela Iacub (Paris: PUF, 1999, 2001), 13–43.

10. Sylviane Agacinski, *La politique des sexes* (Paris: Seuil, 1998); see also, for example, her interview (and the critical review by Michel Feher) in the gay and lesbian magazine *Ex Aequo* (July 1998): 22–25, and her later (controversial) article on the front page of *Le Monde,* February 1999, against "l'effacement des sexes."

11. Françoise Héritier, "Les hommes peinent à accepter que les femmes soient leurs égales," an interview with Blandine Grosjean, *Libération,* August 18–19, 2001: 30–31. "Quand les choses deviennent pensables, c'est-à-dire acceptables, de façon majoritaire, elles peuvent se réaliser: on l'a vu pour le Pacs, pour la parité politique. L'homoparentalité, apparemment, n'est pas encore pensable dans notre société pour être réalisable en termes de lois, ça viendra, mais ça ne l'est pas encore" (30). This is a far cry from the anthropologist's controversial arguments on "insurmountable" limits, expressed in the heat of the PaCS debate in a Catholic daily ("Aucune société n'admet

de parenté homosexuelle," interview by Marianne Gomez, *La Croix,* November 9, 1998: 16).

12. I made this argument in the conference organized by the feminist association Pro-Choix at the Senate on January 5, 2001: "L'avortement sous expertise (entre la France et les États-Unis)," *Avortement, droite de choisir et santé* (Paris: ProChoix éditions, 2001), 61–70.

13. Articles by M.-J. Bonnet, M. Schulz, G. Bach-Ignasse, *Les temps modernes* 598 (March-April 1998): 85–170.

14. "'Différence des sexes' et 'ordre symbolique,'" a dossier with articles by E. Pisier, D. Borrillo, M. Iacub, L. Kandel, as well as Patrice Maniglier and Michel Tort, *Les temps modernes* 609 (June-July 2000): 155–306.

15. "Pour l'égalité sexuelle" (collective text), *Le Monde,* June 26, 1999: 17.

CHAPTER 4

Women's History after the Law on Parity

CHRISTINE FAURÉ

It may at first seem incongruous to link the recent law on parity of June 28, 1999, which reorganizes the French electoral landscape, with an essentially methodological question, that of writing women's history.

The French law on parity seeks to remedy an anachronistic democratic deficit in Europe: the weak percentage of women elected in its representative institutions.[1] It unsettles the old intellectual equilibrium; it breaks with a system that favored compensatory attitudes: in women's history, for example, the depreciation of politics and the valorization of social issues and group mentalities. The history of ideas meets with equally significant obstacles: critically aligning works by major authors with works by women whose impact was minute, asserting a common measure[2] without sufficient research on context and intertexuality. In order to encompass a long history and identify influences and transmissions, it is necessary to understand what each of us knows about our respective periods. Without such investigative work, the validity of specific examples remains an open question.

What most undermines women's history, however, is the persistence of a strong discrimination against women in French political life. This is reflected in the choice of subjects, in the historical perceptions one can form about them and that, in the end, and over the course of many years, has created a total blackout concerning the political history of women. The actions of women have been buried in the sands of cultural history. The contour of their initiatives has faded due to a diminishing of agency that is reinforced by the illegitimacy of women historians in their own discipline. In other words, the attempts to appropriate politics, which was risked by women over the course of centuries, have been devalued in deference to themes thought to better delimit the condition of women: the study of religious archetypes for example,[3] or the study of spaces such as the space of the salon.[4]

The law on parity in France concludes a series of events that from the eighteenth to the end of the twentieth century spans the entire formation of our democracy. The occasionally metaphysical character of the debates should not mask, however, the profound adjustments made between French constitutional history and this law that, as we shall see, focuses on the erasure, the absent inscription, of the political rights of women. This decision, the first in France to be taken with the support of

women—which was not the case with the right of suffrage in 1944—and which benefited from an unprecedented response in public opinion, allows us to open a new
chapter in the history of women.

DISTINCTIVE ASPECTS OF CONSTITUTIONAL CONSTRUCTION IN FRANCE

Human rights, those principles that Western societies so often invoke, did not specifically include equality between the sexes until the twentieth century. More than a
century and a half was needed before the rights of man recognized the rights of
woman as the right of any individual. In 1789, 1793, and finally in 1795, Revolutionary France made the effort to redefine these famous rights of man, but there was
never any question of the rights of women in the declarations and preambles of the
different constitutions. For the political personnel of the various assemblies (Constituent, Legislative, and Convention), women's suffrage was a subject to avoid. On
rare occasions, contemporaries even voiced their fear of the rioting power of women.
Without any hesitation, the revolutionaries of 1791 took on the monarchical prejudices concerning the incapacity of women to govern, in other words, Salic law.[5]

Condorcet, although editor in 1790 of a text on the admission of women to the
rights of citizenship,[6] did not integrate the political rights of women into the
Girondist Constitution of February 15 and 16, 1793. He strongly supported equality
of the sexes, however, as his final work, *Sketch for a Historical Picture of the Progress of the
Human Mind,* testifies.[7]

The Declarations of the Rights of Man and Citizen, elaborated in the eighteenth
century, constitutes a moral pillar still in force, and marks French political culture
with their prejudices in regard to women. For the equality of the sexes to be constitutionally guaranteed, one must wait until after World War II and the Constitution
of October 27, 1946, which states: "The law guarantees to women in all domains
rights equal to those of men." The ordinance of April 2, 1944, had accorded women
the right to vote and eligibility for public office, though not without difficulty if we
consider the preliminary debates to this decision, which took place in the Provisional Consultative Assembly of Algiers (Dec. 23, 1943-Mar. 24, 1944). From the so-
called technical arguments put forth by the Radicals (a moderate Republican party
that participated in numerous governments of the Third and the Fourth Republics),[8] to the opposition manifested by certain Gaullists like René Cassin, opponents of women's right to vote appeared numerous in the Assembly. Without the
active leadership of Robert Prigent, the Christian syndicalist, and the communist
Jean Grenier,[9] the right to vote of women would have been put off indefinitely. But
in this solemn moment of return to the Republic, one had to avoid subjects of discord that could compromise the future and weaken the union in the eyes of the English and American Allies who had long ago settled this question.

Let us take a closer look at the points argued by the heads of the three principal
parties (Radical, Socialist, and Gaullist). Eligibility for political office appeared as
the lesser evil to these opponents to women's right to vote because it was culturally
improbable, and politically nonexistent.

Monsieurs Giacobbi, Cassin, Auriol underscore the happy transaction which permits
women to be elected though they have not been accorded the right to vote in these first

provisional elections. We thus avoid the following: a disproportion between the number of female and male voters, a considerable loss of time that would result from the compilation of electoral lists comprising women; the risk of being premature and impulsive, and thus a loss in consideration for the female vote if it takes place in poor conditions. And through their eligibility, women themselves will be able to take charge of matters with which they are particularly familiar.[10]

In reality, the enthusiastic spirit of the liberation period having passed, and the memory of the heroism of female Resistance fighters forgotten, the number of elected women would decrease: 1.9 percent in the Senate in 1958 and 1.5 percent in the National Assembly that same year.[11]

In the Constitution of October 4, 1958, the formulation concerning the equal rights of men and women was abandoned and replaced with a reference to the Constitution of 1946, and to the Universal Declaration of Human Rights of 1948 whose preamble affirms equal rights between men and women.

THE LAW ON PARITY AS CONSTITUTIONAL REPENTANCE

The constitutional law relating to equality between men and women, otherwise known as the law on parity, seeks to modify article 3 of Title I of the Constitution defining national sovereignty and article 4 on the role of the parties and political affiliations.[12] This law was adopted on June 28, 1999, by the Congress of the Parliament, in other words by the National Assembly and the Senate combined, a solemn procedure meant to demonstrate the general consensus of parliament members on this issue.

The debates in the National Assembly as well as in the Senate were heated and the appeal to history failed to mask the absence of juridical precedence. The situation was novel and since there was no law to refer to, one evoked figures from the feminist pantheon: "I think first of Olympe de Gouges who in 1791 drew up the Declaration of the Rights of Woman which proclaimed in article 10: 'Women have the right to mount the scaffold, they should equally have the right to mount the rostrum.' She was guillotined on November 3, 1793, five days before Manon Roland."[13]

In response to attacks by proponents of republican universalism, the history of women was invoked to lend the enterprise a legitimacy it sorely needed. It was a rhetorical approach that drew on the heroism of women rebels who in their time dared to accomplish what they were not permitted, the eccentric Olympe de Gouges, the convict Louise Michel, the abortionist Madeleine Pelletier. In sum, not very commendable women! Such dubious morality was not disturbing, however; for present-day parliament members, time has rounded off the perception of their misdeeds.

OPPOSITION TO PARITY

The most organized opponent of parity was Robert Badinter, senator of the socialist majority, former Minister of Justice and famous advocate for the abolition of the death penalty. He saw in the government's proposed law a drift toward "communitarianism" that would render republican universalism void by defining the sovereign people in purely sociological or even biological terms. "Sovereignty, like the Republic, is one and indivisible, and so . . . when I hear . . . that this sovereignty shall be embodied by the two halves of humanity, by women and by men, I admit that I cannot follow this argument. I cannot conceive what a sovereignty embodied in two parts would be . . . universalism is universalism, period!"[14]

> The most important contribution in my mind that France has made to this idea of democracy is the invention of a republic that is one and indivisible, which I would qualify, why not, as universal. A Republic composed of citizens who all enjoy the same rights without distinction among them, whether it concerns of course the physical distinction that has been evoked and which is quite evidently the common lot of humanity, but also all others: race, opinion, religious opinions or beliefs. . . . Such are the founding principals of our Republic. It has never been a mosaic of communities, or a juxtaposition of different components. It has not and never will recognize anything but individuals, human beings and citizens, without any discrimination at all."[15]

To this ideal Republic one can oppose numerous refutations: not only discrimination between men and women in the matter of civil and political rights, but also between women themselves after the obtainment of the right to vote: Muslim Algerian women were deprived of it between 1945 and 1958. This rejection of the law on parity prolonged for Robert Badinter the decision of the Constitutional Council of November 18, 1982, which had annulled, in the name of the indivisibility of the electoral body and the principle of equality, the following clause of the Electoral Code: "The list of candidates may not comprise more than 75 percent of the same sex." This clause had been declared unconstitutional according to article 3 on national sovereignty and article 6 of the Declaration of Human and Civil Rights: the equality of all before the law. Robert Badinter made no direct comment during the debate on parity about this episode, a deeply unpopular one among the majority of women whatever their political affiliation. His opposition to any positive discrimination was affirmed a number of times. The doubtful circumstances surrounding the decision of the Council added to the scandal and the incomprehension. The power of the court to take on a case of its own seisin, which it had used concerning the measure of the electoral code on quotas, was not disputable, however this measure had not been an object submitted by either the Parliament nor the government, as certain observers as Yvette Roudy have remarked. The Constitutional Council has long claimed the power to examine conformity of all measures contained in a law to the Constitution, even if this measure is not explicitly contested.[16]

Badinter's persistent rejection of the law on parity reveals a legal conservatism common to old democracies often incapable of institutional reform. For France, this conservatism is called the "republican tradition" and its sanctuary is the Senate. This political stance, brilliantly defined by Odile Rudelle, is rooted in a century-long history whose founding myth was the Dreyfus affair and around which, once the revolution had been accomplished, the whole symbolism of the Republic would be built.[17] These values of a "secular, parliamentary liberalism, but also a military and colonial patriotism" were hardly propitious for the emancipation of women and their integration into political representation

Heir to an exclusive conception of democracy, Robert Badinter used arguments in accord with the past. In 1932, the danger represented by the vote of women focused on a threat from abroad where the right to vote had already been granted, giving rise to xenophobic arguments; in 1999, the law on parity introduced a form of communitarianism reminiscent of America, incompatible with our French traditions.

REPUBLICAN UNIVERSALISM AND THE FRENCH EXCEPTION

For republican universalism, the introduction of foreign concepts into its tradition would distort the Republic and falsify its history. A historian of the French Revolution, Mona Ozouf, anticipated the movement by celebrating the French exception, in her portrait of ten women, through a cultivated lifestyle condensed within the space of the *salon*.[18] Ten resumes of lives like so many allegories where the good luck of being female challenges the restraints and vicissitudes of this state. It is the civilizing talent of each to make her own world bear fruit that Mona Ozouf underscores. These women knew how to accept their destinies through writing, to endure despite adversity, and to emerge pacified from such trials. The complaints, the demands, which could sometimes turn into recrimination, have no place in the lives or works of these women. Yet despite this the author shows fortitude by integrating into this garland of women Hubertine Auclert and Simone de Beauvoir, figures of militant radicalism whose intransigence can provide material for caricature: "It is thus the radicalism of French conceptions and not their timidity that explains the postponement made in matters of female suffrage."[19]

Republican egalitarianism, too removed from the lives of women, did not permit intermediate and gradual solutions, unlike those produced by Anglo-American utilitarianism. Such was the explanation suggested by Mona Ozouf, who dismissed the accusation of anti-Americanism others had made against her.[20] Yet her glorification of the French democratic model, forgetful of the political fate of women during the Third and especially the Fifth Republics, rests upon a patriotism which is certain of its history and little open to criticism. Exactly at a time when the comparison with other European countries decisively undermined national arrogance, Mona Ozouf wanted to keep giving us reasons to believe in the French myth.

"Republic: the word is inseparable from the Revolution," writes Pierre Nora in *A Critical Dictionary of the French Revolution*.[21] In this *Dictionary*, the insensitivity of republican ideology to the question of women is reflected in the representation that the chief editors, François Furet and Mona Ozouf, make of the Revolution: the critical assessment of the French Revolution does not include women and none of the thematic areas concerning them are treated. They are not seen as "actors" of the revolutionary movement, their entrance onto the public scene is not considered an event.[22] Only three lines of Mona Ozouf's article "Equality" is dedicated to the political exclusion of women during the Revolution. From the Republic to the Revolution, the demands of women who refused to be passively robbed of all political power, their virulent protests, are overshadowed.[23]

FEMALE PROTESTATION IN HISTORY OR THE RECRIMINATING WOMAN

It has often been remarked that in France the cause of women can hold no comparison to the mobilizing capacity of groups organized around demands for reparations in the industrial domain—worker's movements,[24] ecological movements—or around an attempt to take over power.[25] Is this social over-cautiousness a French exception linked to a weakness in communal life and to the scarcity of convivial places where meetings preliminary to any collective effort can take place? Could it be the darker side of this civilization where men and women lead the good life together? These questions remain unanswered. The cultural affinities between Western countries should facilitate the exit from national history in which studies of women's movements are too often enclosed. It would also allow us to focus on the modes of action too often judged irregular, exceptional, or individualistic and thus unable to be categorized from a sociological viewpoint. Indeed, the question for us is to overcome, in terms of women's history, the opposition between individual and collective action, which corresponds to a major epistemological division between the social and the psychological sciences.

The sociologist Luc Boltanski has proposed, on the basis of a sample of letters received over a period of three years by the newspaper *Le Monde,* an analytical scale to characterize public denunciation. "A denunciation establishes a system of relations between four protagonists: 1) the person who denounces; 2) the person in whose favor the denunciation is made; 3) the person to whose detriment it is made; 4) the person to whom it is made."[26] Boltanski's proposition seeks to apply an analogical treatment to acts by nature very different, emanating from a variety of sources, and collected arbitrarily. He wishes to extract the rules that determine the success of an action, its recognition or its disqualification.

The connection made between women's history and public denunciation may initially appear disconcerting. Still, describing the position of the subject in the act of denunciation with the aid of other protagonists resolves, from a theoretical viewpoint, the difficulty of apprehending these overly individual actions of women. Whether these women decide to give their names, to remain anonymous, to state their qualifications, whether or not they express themselves in the name of a group, all these variations of self-referentiality that enlarge individuals and reinforce their stature are to be taken into account. But the decoding of the position of the subject is not sufficient without an erudite knowledge of context: locating the use of existing forms and the diversion of juridical performativity. We offer two examples here, which could be developed into a systematic and comparative study of the actions of women taken through the mediation of language.

First example: the *Declaration of the Rights of Woman* (September 14, 1791) by Olympe de Gouges. The author presents an individual request to the Queen in the best tradition. What is Olympe de Gouges's approach? The Declaration of the Rights of Man need in her eyes to be reattributed to women in order for them to acquire humanity and the rights which the representative assembly wants to deny them. Hence the numerous structural similarities between her text and the Declaration of the Rights of Man. Between the speaking subject and the catalogue of these forgotten and scorned rights, the self-referential connection with the Declaration of 1789 is maintained. In the preambles of the two texts, mention is made of a declaration being prepared, which lends them a performative value comparable to a contractual engagement: "I here and now promise" writes the author of a contract. A similar act is found in Olympe de Gouges's text: by this declaration "mothers, daughters, and sisters . . . have resolved to set forth in a solemn declaration the natural rights of woman . . . the superior sex that is as superior in beauty as it is in courage . . . recognizes and declares . . . under the auspices of the Supreme Being, the following Rights of Woman and of female Citizens."[27]

The appeal to the divine confers to the declarative act a threatening solemnity in the case of the non-accomplishment of the promise made. Against whom is this Declaration of Rights made? As in the Declaration of the Rights of Man, the Declaration of the Rights of Woman is aimed at "governments" and not at male power. A balance between the power of the two sexes should be preserved for the "happiness of all" and toward this end she imagines a "form for a social contract between man and woman." Addressing the queen, the government she thinks of is the legislator whose complete dishonesty concerning women she mentions in her afterword. Such searing phrases should have assured her the understanding of all, but Olympe de Gouges published her Declaration of Rights in a rather unfavorable context. She appealed to the Queen to right the wrong done to women by the members of the Constituent Assembly just after the flight of the royal couple, recaptured in Varennes in June 1791. It was a moment of great tension and one that Olympe de Gouges, against all expectation, saw as propitious for an intervention of her own. Between June and September, she was never so prolific. Thus she signed a small work entitled *Sera-t-il roi, ne le sera-t-il pas?*[28] followed by *Projet adressé à l'Assemblée Nationale le jour de l'arrestation du roi,*[29] in which she proposes "to change the Queen's house, to restore it completely like the kingdom." She also requested the establishment of a female national guard to watch over the queen. In July 1791 *Observations sur les étrangers*[30] appeared, in which she criticizes the extravagant trust the French place in foreigners and the tolerance that permitted their participation in the work of the National Assembly. After this came *Repentir de Mme de Gouges*[31] where she defends herself against accusations of aristocratic behavior (September 5, 1791) and finally, on September 15, she published *The Declaration of the Rights of Woman and the Woman Citizen.*[32]

The Declaration of the Rights of Woman and the Woman Citizen, so popular in the twentieth century, was not understood in the eighteenth century, for the conditions of its drafting deprived it of any chance for success. Emanating directly from the imagination of Olympe de Gouges, the text found no social resonance, as would be the case two centuries later. *The Declaration of the Rights of Woman and the Woman Citizen* remained an isolated act: in a period when the cause of women had no part in contemporary political issues, the denunciation of the collective injustice imposed on them was not admissible.

Second Example: Women's Petitions in France, post-revolution. The right to petition has been seen as a residual genre: "petitions as the only means of expression left to women, the example of the Restoration," writes the archival historian Odile Krakovich.[33] Yet this constitutional right is an important one whose procedure of reception was taken up for debate several times by the Assemblies. The right to petition was considered a barometer of local opinion, having the principal merit of warning the authorities of existing dissatisfaction. It was open to everyone—even those who did not enjoy political rights—and it compensated for the restrictions on the right to vote.[34] Women took advantage of this freedom; they were sometimes ardent petitioners although their numbers were well inferior to those of their male peers.

After 1814, petitions had to be presented in writing. This transformation of the act of petitioning into a signed text that required of each the ability to read and write was a decisive stage in the evolution of this democratic right. The open genre of the petition—no generic form exists—thus inscribes itself in the history of correspondence.[35] The epistolary manuals of the nineteenth century, which propagated stylistic norms of usage among popular classes, classify the petition as a letter to the authorities. It was important not to mistake the titles of the people one was addressing, to draft short texts, and, especially, to avoid "flowery language" that uselessly lengthened the petition.[36] Attention to writing, to spelling and style, signs pointing to a level of instruction, appear as the unavoidable step for whomever wants to evaluate this mode of expression, vehicle of personal ambitions and of the political hopes of citizens of both sexes.

It is difficult however to consider the contents of a petition without taking its reception into account. A petition is basically worth the welcome it is shown by the constituent bodies. Only two articles were devoted to the petitions of women during the Restoration and the July Monarchy;[37] the only study of the petitions submitted under the Restoration concerns itself with their reception, focusing on the institution's response and leaving aside the whole verbal dimension of the procedure. Women's petitions were rarely sent to the ad hoc commissions and "The Order of the Day" is what is most often cited, which is the same as a deferred dismissal. Yet this order of the day has the merit of providing us with the reactions of the Assembly and informing us about the appropriateness of the procedures undertaken. We have chosen the year 1837 because it includes, besides the usual civil and military pension requests made by women on behalf of their husbands, petitions of more general import made by women who chose, in Boltanski's words, a mode of subjective "aggrandizement" susceptible of giving legitimacy to their request. This attention to rhetorical forms, to modes of presentation used by petitioners for themselves and their cause, to manifestations of the self, constitute the raw material of a renewal of the methodology of women's history.

In this year 1837, which we take as example without wanting to generalize our observations, we find six petitions signed by M. Poutret de Mauchamps, managing proprietor of the *Gazette des femmes* (Petitions n. 18, 262, 713, 751, 752, 753). These numbers correspond to their inscription in a register that listed them with a summary of one or two lines.[38] The petitions in question deal twice with the modification of the Civil Code, the Penal Code, the restoration of divorce, the right of women to be jurors and, finally, the right to vote for the electoral colleges. They comprise two handwritten pages and a printed copy of the *Gazette des femmes,* a newspaper of legislation and jurisprudence (1836, 1838). Of the six petitions, only two were noted in the order of the day including Petition 262, devoted to the suppression of article 213 of the Civil Code: "The husband should protect his wife, the woman should obey her husband." It triggered open laughter (May 20, 1837).[39]

Still in 1837, petition no. 101 presented by Louise Dauriat failed to retain the attention of the legislator for long; the petitioner requested the abrogation of articles in the Civil Code contrary to the right of women, which evoked laughter and scornful comments from the reporter. He merely saw "the summary of those eternal controversies, the usual fodder for provincial conversation."[40] In this text composed of nine pages fluently written with irreproachable spelling, Louise Dauriat presents herself to the legislator in the name of the rights of women:

> Gentlemen, I come before the present legislature to request the revision of the Civil Code, in other words the abolition of articles in this Code that are in opposition to the dearest, the most sacred rights of women and, consequently, to fairness, to morality, even to religion for they are the cause of all domestic and social calamities. And this has

nothing to so with Saint-Simonism whose precursor was the famous Mary Wole-stonecraft, the same Saint-Simonism that would perish at birth like all movements that produce misdirected passions, like everything that arises from untruth or error. Often enough I have been seen during my public teachings to speak out against dangerous di-visions, against all systems of corruption and perversity.

This right of women stands here in opposition to Saint-Simonism in which she places Mary Wolestonecraft and which she designates as the origin of evil. She re-quests the abolition of the offending articles of the Civil Code in the name of the right of women. The urgency of the situation she evokes justifies her action and le-gitimizes her interventions. She opposes the law of another political age. Her de-mand for a revision of the Civil Code becomes a way to adjust it to contemporary mores. Louise Dauriat, a woman of letters—for this is how she signs her petitions— pursues her protest by printing her petition with an introduction in which she can-not avoid a diatribe against the members of the Chamber of Deputies.

O representatives of men and not of women, you whom they have not charged to rep-resent them, who dispose of the fortune and fruits of these other taxpayers; you who in such great number hasten to the so-called National Assemblies out of ambition for sta-tus and money.[41]

In 1846, Louise Dauriat was the untiring commentator of the Rambuteau report on the situation of institutions and pensions of young women of the Seine. In 1849, she addressed a new petition to the Assembly on the subjects of indigence, begging, pub-lic assistance, and labor organization. A barrage of slanderous lampoons taunted Louise Dauriat like all those who preceded her. Though cited in the *Dictionaire Uni-versel* of 1826, Louise Dauriat was soon condemned to obscurity. Her determination to denounce injustices against women in civil and political life garnered her no posthumous notoriety. But this activity, in which she and many other women whole-heartedly engaged, is a mode of democratic appropriation characteristic of a stage prior to political decision making that the history of women in France has refused to consider.

The petitions of women in the eighteenth century are known thanks to the cu-mulative work of male and female historians of the French Revolution. On the other hand, the study of the 131 years of petitions, from 1814 to 1945, the year when women first exercised their right to vote during municipal elections, should consti-tute an irreplaceable addition to the political history of women.

Translated by Lucy McNair

NOTES

1. *Mappemonde: Women in Politics 2000.* Situation in March 2000 according to official data of the Organization of the United Nations, Department of Information, New York; Inter Parliamentary Union, Geneva, December 1999.
2. Geneviève Fraisse, "Les deux gouvernement: la famille et la cité," *La démocratie en France,* ed. Marc Sadoun, vol. 2 (Paris: Gallimard, 2000), 14.

3. "La bonne catholique, de la femme protestante, la femme juive," Georges Duby and Michelle Perrot, *Histoire des femmes, XIXème Siècle* (Paris: Plon, 1991). The English edition is: *A History of Women in the West,* ed. Georges Duby and Michelle Perrot (Cambridge, MA: Belknap Press of Harvard University Press, 1992–1994).

4. Mona Ozouf, *Les mots des femmes, essai sur la singularité française* (Paris: Fayard, 1995).

5. Chapter II, section I of the Constitution of 1791: Christine Fauré, *Des droits de l'homme aux droits des femmes, une conversion intellectuelle difficile,* in *Encyclopédie politique et historique des femmes* (Paris: PUF, 1997), 205–207; *Political and Historical Encyclopedia of Women* (Chicago: Fitzroy Dearborn Publishers, Routledge 2003).

6. *Sur l'admission des femmes au droit de cité,* Condorcet, Journal of the Société de 1789, n. 5, July 3, 1790. *Paroles d'hommes (1790–1793),* presented by Elisabeth Badinter. (Paris: P.O.L., 1989); and *Condorcet: Selected Writings,* ed. Keith Michael Baker (Indianapolis: Bobbs-Merill Company, 1976).

7. *Esquisse d'un tableau historique des progrès humains,* presented by Yvon Belaval (Paris: Vrin, 1970); English edition: *Sketch for a Historical Picture of the Progress of the Human Mind,* trans. June Barraclough (Westport, CT: Hyperion Press, 1979).

8. "It would be materially impossible, given the short time available, to proceed toward a regular constitution of the electoral lists." Session of March 24, 1944, Supplement of the *Journal Officiel,* debates of the Provisional Consultative Assembly of March 30, 1944.

9. William Gueraiche, *Les femmes politiques de 1944 à 1947: Quelle libération?* In: *Clio, Histoire, Femmes et Société,* "Résistance et libération, 1944–1945" (Toulouse: Presses Universitaires du Mirail, 1995), 165–86.

10. Commission for legislation and reform of the State, testimony given Thursday, March 2, 1944 at 3 p.m., eighteenth session, Archives de l'Assemblée Nationale, 1049.

11. *Women in Parliaments, 1945–1995,* global statistical study, Reports and Documents series, n. 23, Geneva, Inter Parliamentary Union, 1995, 128.

12. To articles 3 and 4 one must add the following two lines: "The law favors equal access for women and men to election mandates and elective office." "[The parties] contribute to the realization of the principle stated in the last line of article 3 in the conditions determined by the law" (*Journal Officiel,* Congrès du Parlement, March 9, 1999).

13. Elisabeth Guigou, Minister of Justice, December 15, 1998, Assemblée Nationale n. 18, 10496.

14. Robert Badinter, Senate session of January 26, 1999, n. 4 S (CR), 279.

15. Ibid. 280.

16. Danièle Loschak, *Les homes politiques, les "sages" (?) et les femmes; à propos de la décision du Conseil Constitutionnel du 18 novembre 1982, Droit Social,* n. 2, 1983, p. 133.

17. Odile Rudelle, *La tradition républicaine, Pouvoirs 42,* (1987), 32.

18. Mona Ozouf, *Les mots des femmes, essai sur la singularité française,* 377. English edition: *Women's Words: Essay on French Singularity,* trans. Jane Marie Todd (Chicago: University of Chicago Press, 1997).

19. Ibid. 377.

20. Mona Ozouf, "Le compte des jours," in *Le Débat 87* (November-December 1995): 141.

21. François Furet, Mona Ozouf, eds., *Dictionnaire critique de la révolution française* (Paris: Flammarion, 1988), 832. English edition: *A Critical Dictionary of the French Revolution,* trans. Arthur Goldhammer (Cambridge, MA: Belknap Press of Harvard University Press, 1989).

22. Patrice Higonnet, professor of history at Harvard, is alone in noting this presence of women in his article on the *sans-culottes,* but this observation remains isolated and receives no further comment in the work.

23. Same offhandedness in Patrice Gueniffey claiming that Sièyes, like Condorcet, would have pleaded in favor of woman's suffrage. Nothing of the sort exists in Sièyes, unless we are tricked by a flowery clause that nothing later confirms and which is employed in France up until 1944 to postpone women's suffrage: "Women at least in the present state, children, foreigners, should have no direct influence over public affairs." ("Préliminaires de la Constitution, reconnaissance et exposition raisonnée des droits de l'homme et du citoyen" by Abbot Sièyes, in Christine Fauré, *Les Dèclarations des droits de l'homme de 1789*, Paris, Payot, 1992, p. 103.) These public comments, which can appear ambiguous, should be completed by his archives originally not meant for publication and in which he embraces the misogyny of his time. "Sur l'amour du vrai . . ." in: *Des Manuscrits de Sièyes, 1773–1799*, Christine Fauré (ed.). Paris-Geneva: Champion Slatkine, 1999, p. 360.

24. Madeleine Rébérioux, *La culture au pluriel, in: Histoire de la France*, ed. André Burguière and Jacques Revel (Paris: Seuil, 1992), 477.

25. Pierre Rosanvallon, *Le sacre du citoyen, histoire du suffrage universel en France* (Paris: Gallimard, 1992), 411.

26. Luc Boltanski, *L'amour et la justice comme compétences* (Paris: Métailié, 1990), 267.

27. Olympe de Gouges, *Ecrits politiques, 1788–1791*, prefaced by Odile Blanc (Paris: Coté Femmes, 1993), 206. The English translation of The Declaration of the Rights of Woman can be found in *Women in Revolutionary Paris, 1789–1795*, trans. Darlene Gay Levy, Harriet Branson Applewhite, and Mary Durham Johnson (Urbana, Chicago, London: University of Illinois Press, 1979).

28. Translator's note: *Will He Be King or Won't He?*

29. Translator's note: *Proposition Addressed to the National Assembly on the Day of the King's Arrest.*

30. Translator's note: *Observations on Foreigners.*

31. Translator's note: *The Repentance of Mme de Gouges.*

32. This chronology was established by Odile Blanc because the dates are not all identical at the end of Olympe de Gouges's texts.

33. In: *Femmes dans la cité, 1815–1871*, ed. Alain Corbin, Jacqueline Lalouette, and Michèle Riot-Sarcey (Crane: Créaphis, 1997), 347.

34. Léon Duguit, *Traité de droit constitutionnel*, vol. V (Paris: De Boccard, 1925), 443.

35. *La correspondance, les usages de la lettre au XIXème siècle*, ed. Roger Chartier, Alain Boureau, and Cécile Dauphin (Paris: Fayard, 1991). English edition: *Correspondence: Models of Letter-Writing from the Middle Ages to the Nineteenth Century*, trans. Christopher Woodall (Princeton, NJ: Princeton University Press, 1997).

36. *Le nouveau secrétaire de cabinet, extrait de Nouveau secrétaire française contenant des modèles de lettres sur toutes sortes de sujets, suivi de modèles de billets à l'ordre, précédés d'une courte instruction sur le cérémonial épistolaire* (Metz: Grosclaude, 1813).

37. Michèle Riot-Sarcey, "Des femmes pétitionnent sous la Monarchie de Juillet." In: *Femmes dans la cité*, 389.

38. Archives nationales, C* 2417.

39. Ibid., vol. III, Paris, 1905, 460.

40. Ibid., vol. 107, Paris, 1903, 395.

41. Louise Dauriat, *Demande de révision du code Civil*, Paris 1837, 8.

CHAPTER 5

Exclusive Democracy
A FRENCH PARADIGM

GENEVIÈVE FRAISSE

When we talk about French democracy and the political exclusion of women, two vectors inevitably intersect: history, using the Athenian model, and geography, as reflected by the United States. We will look at each of these vectors. In order to lay bare the mechanisms of the exclusion, as well as the inclusion, of women, in political life, we must acknowledge that the history of relations between men and women is not merely a series of contingencies, but rather a construct of thought and will.

In the course of interpreting this paradox of democracy that is the exclusion of women, we must also put aside moral history, that is, history that explains this exclusion in terms of psychological or social prejudice, the morals of the country, or the contingencies of a revolution. Since the history of the sexes belongs to political history (and some still doubt it), then we must try to work within its logic: the unexpected turn of events, as well as the pressure of a nation's morals, may be historical determinants, but they do not provide adequate explanation (of the *reasons*).

Let me begin by affirming that the exclusion of women from democracy was a deliberate process. This in no way means that it can be explained in terms of a political theory based on some element inherent to the democratic system itself, and thus is definitive. Rather, exclusion is a principle in the sense of a driving principle, a dynamic.[1] Our task is, then, genealogical: rather than identifying an origin or a source, it is to understand the origin of the present situation, beginning with its initial establishment.

The revolutionary hysteria of women, archaic and reactionary religiosity, egalitarian *libertinage,* a mixing of the sexes for the benefit of the republic, Napoleonic machismo, and so on: these provide the underpinnings of what I choose to call moral history—all of it interesting, but inadequate. In the same way we must refuse interpretations that are timid due to too much benevolence. In the opinion of Pierre Rosanvallon, for example, the exclusion of women is an established fact (a thesis that was still treated with a certain reserve at the end of the 1980s), but this fact is interpreted as an unaccomplished possibility, as unrealized democratic potential.[2] Inclusion is thus received as intrinsic to a simple unfurling of the democratic dynamic. Bronislaw Baczko has much the same idea: exclusion, in his view, is caused by

the clumsiness of nascent democracy, gradually corrected and set straight by contemporary history.[3]

What I propose is slightly different, for I look at the determinant character of exclusion, the constituent aspect of this exclusion within the democratic epic. This
type of approach does not posit a theory of deliberate exclusion, but it does recognize the existence of a political will, of a decision.

EXCLUSION

It is impossible to render in English "*démocratie exclusive,*" the initial subtitle of my
book *Muse de la raison* (1989). "Excluding," that is, omitting or keeping out, or "exclusive," that is, selective, are two possible if distinct literal translations. When *Muse de
la raison* appeared in English, therefore, I understood why the ambiguity of the adjective "exclusive" was essential when defining the relation between democracy and
female citizens. "Exclusive" certainly does carry a double meaning, and an exclusive
democracy points both to exclusion and choice, exclusion *by* choice.

Such is modern democracy: it does not explicitly formulate exclusion; it produces
it without spelling it out. Article 8 of the Napoleonic Civil Code specifies that a citizen is one who benefits from the entire body of civil laws; it fails to mention, however, that only human beings of the male sex benefit from those civil rights. Women
are thus omitted by this fact alone without any article of the Code having to spell it
out. Modern democracy is forgetful. It loses coherence somewhere between what it
says for everyone and what it *does* for some. This commonplace of contemporary
democracy deserves to be brought to our attention at this juncture, for it is what
constitutes the very definition of exclusive democracy.

Several categories, including women, are excluded from basic citizenship. In fact,
contrary to democracy in antiquity, which was explicitly exclusive and officially masculine, democracy in our time excludes women from citizenship through a series of
mechanisms internal to its own operation. Exclusion is not an explicit principle, but
rather an implicit product. Yet a definite echo can be detected between the ancient
and the modern states.

According to Nicole Loraux,[4] the Greek state was constructed "upon" the exclusion of women, the defeat of women being linked, however, to a victory of the feminine, since the notion of exclusion was not carried through to its conclusion. For
Joan Landes,[5] modern public space was built "against" women; it is a space from
which they have been "expelled"—a fact that Jürgen Habermas, to whom she responds in her book, completely ignored. In the opinion of Michèle Riot-Sarcey,[6]
modernity reproduces a democracy based "on" women but, unlike the Greek state,
feminists have subverted this exteriority. These three analyses can be summed up as
follows: women are beneath, or outside of, democracy.

In my view, modern exclusion seems to have been constructed "with" *and*
"against" women, that is, within the democratic space itself. The interpretations referred to above thus seem inadequate for the subject we wish to address: "on"
means the exteriority of the "class of women" and assumes this exteriority in its necessity as an external support of the state. "Against" on its own points to a deliberate intention to exclude, a pure and simple rejection. By contrast, "with" and
"against" indicates that women are simultaneously associated with and dissociated

from the democratic process. Hence the coupling of the adjective "exclusive" with "democracy."

Exclusion is produced, not expressed; manufactured, not theorized. This is precisely how inclusion was made possible by democracy itself: each mechanism of exclusion was turned into its opposite in the nineteenth and twentieth centuries,[7] enabling both a possible emancipation and an inevitable feminism. The other explanations for contemporary political exclusion do not, in my view, allow us to understand this obvious dialectic.

This leads us to an essential observation: there is no model for the political exclusion of women within democratic space. Whereas they were positioned outside Greek political space along with the other categories, notably the slaves, women in contemporary democratic life are excluded from within. That is the nature of exclusive democracy: a refusal of active citizenship within the space of a generally passive citizenship. As opposed to ancient times, every male and every female is henceforth labeled a citizen. This is no official, declared exclusion, but rather a series of mechanisms implicit in the thinking of modern democracy.

GENEALOGY

Three elements of our tradition play a role in our evaluation of the history of the exclusion of women: what becomes of democracy after the 1800s; how the republic is conceived by political theorists beginning with the end of the Ancien Régime; and how the French monarchy has persisted in the imaginary of political power. These three elements, like three wellsprings, intertwine and bestow upon France its specificity: a founding event of democracy, a political theory of the Republic, a survival of monarchic rule in the collective imagination.

Democracy is based on an image of identity, of resemblance and similarity among individuals. This makes the great giddiness of the 1800s easier to understand: what can be done about the difference between the sexes if the identical prevails over the different? This fear is existential: suppressing sexual difference by giving women the same thing men possess is out of the question. The democracy of the rights of man is universal only on the surface, hiding exclusions necessary to society and to a fundamental sexual connection. This is the price for the survival of love: friendship and competition, which would lead to democracy between the sexes, must be banished.

Democracy assumes the identical, the similar—and it assumes these qualities for everyone, one by one. The men of postrevolutionary France recoiled from such a radical position. Under the monarchy, the existence of a few brilliant, emancipated women did nothing to open the way to the continued extension of their acquired freedom and virtual equality. In short, under the Ancien Régime, the exception did not make the rule. On the contrary, democracy implies that the exception can be the rule; it announces a *new* rule. That is why democracy's potential shift—from identical to equal—stopped short at the difference between the sexes; male domination required this.

The republic, however, was not unduly troubled by any original reflection on the subject of the difference of the sexes. Rousseau summed it up when he described women as "the precious half of the republic,"[8] out of a simple respect for difference. To be sure, women partook of the republic, but once again, *exclusively*. Granted, they

constituted a half. But first and foremost they were "precious": and their "price" was
to be responsibility for the fabrication of morals, not laws. As everyone knows,
morals are established first and foremost in the home, whereas laws are made outside the home, in the Assembly. All women establish morals, but only some men
make laws. Clearly, women were citizens by their role as mothers who educate, but
they left to men the symbolic task of law and the function of representation.

Representation always implies mediation; that is its basic symbolic strength. And
representation was a new, a modern figure: the res publica. Citizenship today is divided between participation in and representation of public matters. The passage
from the citizen's participation to representation is far from evident and in fact
seems to be more of a qualitative than a quantitative leap. It is also an important element of the exclusion of women and must be examined.

THE SYMBOLIC

For quite a long time, I believed that the rupture made by the Revolution and the
gradual establishment of the republic clearly accounted for exclusive democracy. In
fact, the phenomenon of exclusion at the level of citizens' participation is under-
standable within the context of the very mechanisms of democratic and republican
thinking. This was, of course, the simple logic of the new political regime. Yet this
logic is subject to another level of reading—that of the long history of male domination. The fact that it is ubiquitous does not preclude our isolating its role at the
level of political institutions; nor does it stop us from examining the way in which
political systems overlap.

Such an analysis of overlapping political representations, which is capable of
shedding light on the persistent tendency in France to exclude women from political life, was rendered necessary in my view when I realized the following fact not too
long ago: fifty years of the right to vote had not in the slightest modified the weak
participation of French women in political representation.

This realization was actually twofold. It revealed, on the one hand, the paradox
constituted by a real implication of women as voters—women in no way different
from other citizens—and, on the other, simultaneously the absence of women from
the space of representation, of power exercised by a few. Women's interest in public
matters did not in the least empower them to represent the people and the nation,
to exercise political power. Yet nothing in the mechanisms of exclusion common to
democracy explains this discrepancy between participation and representation of
women in the state. To participate means only to represent oneself. Are women then
relegated to a restricted citizenship?

The republican division between laws and morals sheds some light on the question. As I already noted, the fabrication of morals was the power accorded to
women; men, on the other hand, were granted the power to make laws. These two
distinct powers originated in a single tradition during the period of patriarchal mon-
archs: that of the definition of "government." Political government and domestic
government were two forms of power that overlapped, complemented each other,
and were constantly compared. Rousseau declared unequivocally that they had to be
separated, and it is easy to understand why: the novelty and modernity of republican
government lies in its representative nature. Political power was henceforth to be di-

vided between the representational role and the governmental role. Now, there would be *two* ways of exercising power, *two* places to which women would not easily gain access.

But important nuances arose between the functions of being *elected* to represent and being *appointed* to govern. I would just like to note quickly that the symbolism inherent in the fact of being delegated by a part of the people or the nation, on the one hand, and the symbolism inherent in being appointed because of special expertise or by the decision of the prince, on the other, are not the same. Yet, Eliane Viennot reminds us[9] that women have always governed, and they were recognized—albeit seldom, albeit often reluctantly—for their domestic as well as their political government. That the notion of women as government leaders was either rejected or disputed was a clear indication that the imaginary link between women and government was possible, thinkable. Government designates not only the exercise or the practice of power, but also the sovereignty, the strength of power. This is how symbolic strength was introduced.

As for representation, it is not only the exercise of power, but also the symbolic expression of power. This expression is twofold: by the mediation of representation between those represented and those representing; and by the very function—which is making laws—of those representing. It is obviously essential to pause for a moment and note the symbolism inherent in power, for there is a huge difference between the fact of *governing* and the fact of *representing*: the way in which the person holding the power is symbolized is not the same.

Yet in both instances, we are talking about power, and about symbolic power, for there is also the symbolic nature of government, which is one of sovereignty.

PARADIGM

The monarchy preceded the republic. The central concept of the monarchy, besides that of sovereignty, was that of government. In a patriarchal society, political government and domestic government are superimposed, like two images, one macroscopic, the other microscopic. The French monarchy added two specific characteristics to this model: divine right and the transferal of power through males. The monarchy of divine right implied that the king, through coronation, had a direct link to the transcendent, to God. This was symbolic power at its strongest. We should add to this a law that became a part of French law, Salic law, which imposed the transferal of power through males. This law was not a principle of the monarchy, but rather a mechanism to enable it to function. Initially a law covering all aspects of the transferal of property, it was later invoked to avoid certain alliances between nations. It was not a principle, but rather an instrument of the monarchy. Yet its role, real and imaginary, was important to the reinforcement of the masculine symbolic of power. What is even more remarkable, even strange, is that this law assumed its full empirical and legal reality at the very moment of the Revolution, in a decree of October 1789, in the first Constitution of 1791.

Far from identifying merely the survival of a regime (the monarchy) in a new regime (the republic), Salic Law welded national history to the longstanding history of male domination. This was implicit and more or less official under the monarchy; it became clearly explicit later on, both in the Constitution of the Revolution as well as in the bill introduced by Napoleon III during the Second Empire. Why, then, should we be surprised at this very French persistence of male political power, at this holdover of a feudal practice in the twentieth century? We already know the consequences: a heavily masculinized image of symbolic power, whether it be the power of government, of representation, or of sovereignty.

Let us remain specific, however: even if the tradition of the transferal of masculine power persists to this day, we cannot necessarily assume that we are dealing with a patriarchal society. The *brothers* of the republic have supplanted the *father* of the monarchy, in spite of his imagined tenacity. Thus, according to Françoise Gaspard,[10] we live in a "fratriarchy."

We can henceforth discern that heterogeneous elements, scattered among a variety of institutional strategies, converge in the construction of male power in politics. In my view, this is the genealogy of our political modernity. It is a genealogy whose reconstruction indicates a paradigmatic situation rather than an exception (in contrast to a rule) or a singularity (in contrast to something generally widespread). A paradigm is not a model, but it obeys the explicative rules of logic.

If, therefore, there is a French specificity, it would be that of providing a paradigm by which to understand exclusive democracy. National history goes hand in hand with, in the present case, an emblematic history: one that involves a meeting between a founding event (the French Revolution), French political thinking about the Republic, and a strong monarchic tradition.

In this regard, France seems to me to offer a paradigmatic situation, rather than a singular or an exceptional one. France is not an exception, a political singularity isolated in a vast group, a singularity whose positive aspects are to be proclaimed with satisfaction—or masochism. Mona Ozouf reflects this comparatist current.[11]

But what comparison are we talking about? That between a dominant model, Anglo-Saxon history and its explicative norms, and a French non-model that would constitute an exception? It seems to me clearly more fruitful to construct the comparison between an Anglo-Saxon model and a French model rather than to play the French exception against a norm imported from elsewhere. This would have the immediate advantage of deepening the gaze that falls on France: French exclusive democracy is not an exception, but a paradigm.

For norms do not originate elsewhere. We must rid ourselves of all value judgments in order to avert (and it does not matter which country we are talking about) the fruitless deadlock over the important thing at stake: the political equality of the sexes. France is exemplary in its elaboration of the exclusion of women: hers is not a model that other countries have imported, but rather a kind of *reasoned* elaboration of exclusion, one that could contain explicative value for another national situation and serve as an interpretative hypothesis. That is a paradigm.

POWER OF THE SUBJECT

It still remains to be seen where the place of politics is in this scheme, or even how power is defined other than as a myth, a mythical word. The distinction between governing and representing is not only a means of honing the understanding of the mechanisms of exclusion of women from power, but also one of understanding power itself. No doubt because I was tired of hearing broad generalizations about the power of men and the powerlessness of women, I found it necessary to address the question again at its very base—the power of the modern individual, of the citizen-subject. Let us recall that in the 1830s, feminists insisted that King Louis-Philippe cease being the king of France and became king of the French. These women hoped in that way to make women visible.

The modern French individual unavoidably possesses several identities: man or woman, militant citizen and/or salaried worker, child and/or parent, husband or wife, etc. The modern individual, gradually defined by his/her autonomy, has the power to be him/herself, to "govern" him/herself. I therefore read the modern construct of private and public spaces after Rousseau: when we talk about the "separation of spheres," we must primarily understand this as the "separation of governments." This idea, already mentioned earlier, can now be examined in a different light, that of the autonomy of each one of us, which is implied in the government of the self. From this vantage point, modernity offers a completely new situation compared with the model of antiquity: the individual maneuvers between two separate, distinct spheres. During the period in which exclusive democracy was being established, two other movements became visible: the civil rights and the labor movements.

For the past two centuries, the civil autonomy of woman has steadily increased in terms of her power to be herself. Elisabeth Sledziewski has shown how the French Revolution created a civil subject rather than a civic subject:[12] the "civil capacity" of women was expressed beginning with the law authorizing divorce in 1792. The Napoleonic Code, in its desire to place the wife under guardianship, also ensured the equality of brothers and sisters in matters of inheritance. In short, the civil rights of women, daughters, or wives gradually developed two distinct characteristics: independence and equality. They continued to increase from 1800 to the present against a backdrop of representation of the individual and his autonomy. Let me offer a symbolic anecdote: the Divorce Law of 1975, which put mutual consent at the heart of this right, that is, and at the farthest possible remove from the "wrongdoing," was finally as radical as the law of 1792!

The significant participation of women in the public space as a result of salaried labor is the second movement that affects the government of the self. French women were remarkably present as workers beginning in the early 1800s. This was a particularly important phenomenon in France, as the 1900s underscored and the current situation continues to confirm. Margaret Maruani goes so far as to refer to the "spectacular growth of feminine activity" since 1960.[13] Who would deny that economic independence alone brings true autonomy?

The real blossoming of the civil rights for women and their economic participation account for the reality of their citizenship. To be a citizen is to be an autonomous member of society. The power of the citizen is thus here, too, in civil and economic life. It seems hard to continue to analyze the political inclusion of women without taking into account these two dimensions of citizenship—even if they are far from showing that women have had an easy time of it: the civil individual, as Irène Théry says, is often caught up in a "malaise of filation,"[14] and women live their independent lives only at the price of a double workday. Democratic autonomy carries a heavy price for women. But in no case are they ready to give it up.

I must add that this is the *sole* reality capable of confronting the symbolic male hold on power. The rock crushes the paper, some might say: unless, thanks to civil and economic realities, women introduce a doubt as to the validity of the masculine symbolic of power. What more can women do to bridge the gap that exists between the autonomy of every individual and political representation with its masculine symbolic? They can bring to bear the weight of economic and social reality. Thus, we must once again tie together that which Rousseau sundered: the two halves of the republic, domestic government and political government. Women are capable of re-creating this bond; their lives are deployed as one entity in the private and public spaces. No doubt this image of citizenship—a utopia wherein self-government and the government of others (in the family or in the state) would be compatible—will be slow in gaining currency.

Parity also becomes a utopia in this instance; and that is my conclusion. Utopia is not a *negative* word; it signals a horizon from which the possible can become thought. But my version of parity is not a very orthodox one.

Starting with the practical effect of parity joined to the theoretical problem of its philosophical justification, I have proposed here a reversal of Kant's famous saying: "Parity is true in practice and false in theory." And in fact, as much as the idea of parity remained a great exposer of political inequality and of general inequality between the sexes, it seems to me that this idea cannot not have a philosophical basis. We will never be able to deduce the political from the biological. In contrast, the movement for parity has left an exciting imprint on the history of the last two centuries. The idea of parity is a mixture, a melange of two political currents of the modern period: by its demand to be expressed as law, it is an idea related to democratic universalism, hence to a representation of man in the abstract; by its desire to designate visibly the two sexes of humanity, it is an idea belonging to the utopian and revolutionary tradition, which, since Fourier and the Saint-Simonians, regards humanity in terms of its sexual reality. Parity is at the crossroads of these two political currents, and therein lies its utopia—and mine, as well: parity is an interesting notion only if it also means economic and domestic parity. Parity seeks the sharing of power; but power must be shared in *every* domain: domestic, civil, economic, and political.

If power is once again rooted in reality to the detriment of its symbolic standards, government and representation will finally become modern functions.

Translated by Margaret Colvin

NOTES

1. I demonstrate this in my works *Muse de la raison: la démocratie exclusive et la différence des sexes* (Aix-en-Provence: Alinéa, 1989); reedited with a postface, Folio Collection (Paris: Gallimard, 1995); and *La raison des femmes* (Paris: Plon, 1992).
2. Pierre Rosanvallon, *Le Sacre du citoyen. Histoire du suffrage universel en France* (Paris: Gallimard, 1992).
3. Bronislaw Baczko, "Egalité et exclusions," *Le Débat* 87 (November-December 1995).
4. Nicole Loraux, *Les enfants d'Athéna. Idées athéniennes sur la citoyenneté et la division des sexes* (Paris: Maspero, 1981).
5. Joan B. Landes, *Women and the Public Sphere, in the Age of the French Revolution* (Ithaca: Cornell University Press, 1988).
6. Michèle Riot-Sarcey, *La Démocratie à l'épreuve des femmes. Trois figures critiques du pouvoir, 1830–1848* (Paris: Albin Michel, 1994).

7. See *Muse de la raison* and *La raison des femmes*, cited above.

8. *La raison des femmes*, introduction.

9. Eliane Viennot, "Les femmes d'Etat de l'Ancien Régime, un enjeu capital pour le partage du pouvoir en démocratie," in *La démocratie "à la française" ou les femmes indésirables*, Eliane Viennot, ed. (Cahiers du CEDREF, Paris-VII, 1996).

10. Françoise Gaspard, "La fratriarcat: une spécificité française," *Après-demain. Journal mensuel de documentation politique* 80 (January-February 1996).

11. Mona Ozouf, *Les Mots des femmes: essai sur la singularité française* (Paris: Fayard, 1995). This book is discussed in *Le Débat* 87 (November-December 1995), with the contributions of Bronislaaw Baczko, Elisabeth Badinter, Lynn Hunt, Michelle Perrot, Joan Scott, and Mona Ozouf herself. It is also analyzed, remarkably, in its political epistemology, by Eric Fassin in "The Purloined Gender: American Feminism in the French Mirror," in *French Historical Studies* 22:1 (1999).

12. Elisabeth G. Sledziewski, *Révolutions du sujet* (Paris: Méridiens Klincksieck, 1989).

13. Margaret Maruani, "L'emploi féminin à l'ombre du chômage," *Actes de la recherche en sciences sociales* 115 (December 1996).

14. Irène Théry published a dossier "Malaise dans la filiation," *Esprit* (December 1996).

CHAPTER 6

The Headscarf and the Republic[1]

FRANÇOISE GASPARD
AND FARHAD KHOSROKHAVAR

As far as the issue of the veil is concerned, feminists are unanimous in condemning the oppression that it signifies. But they are just as divided as the other social spheres when it comes to finding a solution to the question that has been put to us—should the schoolgirls who wear it be expelled from school or not?—and they are better aware of the dimension that, at the beginning, was very much secondary in the eyes of the case's protagonists: the question of equality between men and women. This principle *must* be taken into consideration. But, once again, this must be done in the French national sphere: in the neighborhoods to which housing politics has confined immigrant workers on the one hand and in a country that fears the institutionalization of "minority communities" on the other.

Adolescent girls are being forced to wear the veil by their Muslim families: some of them because their father is a militant fundamentalist, others simply because they are recent arrivals and they are attached to what they consider to be the custom. There is no question for these girls of going to school or out in public without the headscarf. Other constraints that are at least as heavy, and that are certain to influence their futures, weigh these girls down: learning to be modest starting at a very young age, not being allowed out of the house, living with the threat of being sent back to their home country or the possibility of an arranged marriage, and so on. Can forbidding the headscarf constitute pressure on the fathers and save these adolescent girls from the yoke it represents? It does for those families who see the school as the means through which their children will hopefully go up the social ladder. However, these are generally not the families who impose the veil. Those who tend to do so are found among the relatively recent immigrant families, mostly Moroccan or Turkish, where the idea of an eventual return to the home country is prevalent, the idea of integration is refused, and it is deemed unacceptable for girls to emancipate themselves from tradition. And even if these girls were to leave the house without the veil, where is the guarantee that by this fact alone they would escape all the other constraints that their father, their brothers and male cousins, and sometimes even the women in the family impose upon them? At the very moment when all of France was debating the suitableness of the Bayrou directive, the case of a Turkish family was unfolding before the court. With the agreement of the mother, a brother, and a male cousin, a man had killed his younger sister because she had dared to "emancipate" herself. This tragedy served to remind us that integration is not a phenomenon that is accomplished by the sole act of taking off the veil in public. It causes incomprehension, a lack of ability to communicate, and even conflict between generations. Among members of the second or third generation, where the signs of integration or even of assimilation are readily apparent, it can also lead to a desire to return to the very roots that the immigrant parents or grandparents had tried to hide because they were stigmatized by the society around them. And finally, it presupposes a complex process that takes time and plays itself out in the interaction between the newly arrived immigrants and the society that receives them. It is not solely up to the immigrants to make an effort to adapt; the local population who receives them, too, must assist the newcomers in understanding the norms of the society in which they will henceforth live so that they might accept these norms.

What these "cases," which led to several girls being expelled from schools in Mantes, Lille, Strasbourg or Goussainville, have contributed to revealing is that in reality, oftentimes the headscarf is not imposed by the families, but is the result of a free choice, and it is not lived as a submission, but rather as a self-affirmation. These girls—especially the veiled high-school and university students—are the product of a society that for ten years has been persecuting North African immigrants, their parents: a society that resorts to all pretexts in order to stop the construction of mosques, thus running the risk of seeing the number of underground mosques multiply, a society that tolerates racism. The education that these youths have received has hardly been adequate: young males as well as females ignore the fact that an Islam other than the version offered by the fundamentalists, which is the one primarily discussed in the French media, even exists. They do not realize that the veil can have political implications that go against the interests of women; that it can enslave them by separating them from men, thus leaving the men as the only ones with the opportunity to freely move about in the public space while women's right to appear in public is allowed only when the freedom of their bodies is limited; that the veil imposed upon the women who do not wish to wear it in Muslim societies on the road to modernization is the repressive expression of a sexist and antidemocratic political system.

If the girls who veil themselves here do not know all that, this is because in France, equality of the sexes has never been considered to be a political cause and has never been a clear priority of any government. This is only because of the pressure applied by the various feminist movements, and also for pragmatic reasons (primarily economic). Equality in the eyes of the law has been attained. In everyday life, by contrast, the situation leaves much to be desired, as it fails to provide these girls with a model of equality and does hardly anything to obligate the brothers of these girls to respect their autonomy. Manifest in the discourse of these veiled girls there is, in fact, not only the desire to display signs of their Muslim identity, but also the expressed need to protect themselves and, paradoxically, to free themselves. Since they have taken to wearing the veil, they say, the neighborhood boys respect them and their brothers allow them to go out. The fact that young suburban Muslim girls in France choose to wear the veil (an act that in fact often bothers their parents, who are trying hard to show how well they are integrated into French society) in order to feel secure on the street is something that those responsible for urban politics, as well as all those fearing that France could disintegrate into a patchwork of communities closed in on themselves, should consider. Moreover, the only prescription stated in the Koran that concerns these girls as women and with which they are familiar is the wearing of the headscarf. What is more, they are quite firm in their position that no father and no husband will dictate their future, their choice of career, or the sharing of domestic duties.

COED YOUTHS

Civic equality of the sexes is a recent phenomenon and civil equality even more so, a fact that we tend to forget too often. French society has yet to understand all the consequences of this. The fact that "today, girls outperform boys in all four stages of education"[2] must be understood in the context of a secular history that has contributed to substantially transforming relations between men and women. And, as Christian Baudelot and Roger Establet point out, "there are few social changes that take place at such a sustained pace: only the rate of growth of the availability of television in the 1960s is analogous. This last phenomenon has caught the attention of several sociologists. Spread over almost an entire century, the advances that have taken place in the education of girls have gone practically unnoticed." The model of coeducation that all school children today take for granted has in fact existed for barely more than thirty years. Because of pressure applied by the Catholic Church, the separation of boys and girls (a situation that, for a long time, led to girls being poorly educated, if at all) was carefully organized throughout the nineteenth century. The first text concerning primary education, the edict of February 29, 1816, states: "Boys and girls will never be taught together."[3] Material conditions, however, made it necessary, here and there, for girls and boys to share the same school building. No matter! The solution was to separate them while class was in session. Various ministerial directives of the time are devoted to this delicate question. They have to do with the dimensions of "the separating partition wall" that must be installed between the two classes and the necessary interval between the dismissal times of the boys and the girls so as to prevent them from meeting—the recess courtyards being separate, of course. The republicans were secular, but they brought into being an educational structure that separated the sexes and provided boys and girls with programs that were different.

In our towns and villages we find reminders of this separation inscribed in the very architecture: in the middle, we usually see a higher building serving administrative purposes and housing the teachers; this building is flanked on both sides by wings in which classrooms are located and each of which is surmounted by a pediment: "Girls School" on the one side, "Boys School" on the other. Jules Ferry's letter during the Third Republic defines secular education. It is couched in the ideology of the times. Although it alludes in passing to the reality that female teachers do, in fact, also exist, it is addressed to "Monsieur l'instituteur." This (male) teacher must conduct himself in such a way as to earn the confidence and the gratitude of the families; he must "appeal to the reason of the father and to the heart of the mother." Reason is a male domain while those of the female are sensitivity and intuition. It was only in 1962, and because of demographic pressures much more than a concern for co-education, that the decision was finally made to open only coeducational schools[4]: to build just one school is less costly than to build two of them. It was not until the mid-1970s that the entire system became coeducational at last and that the *grandes écoles,* such as the Polytechnique or Saint-Cyr, until then reserved for men, finally opened their doors to women. This victory of equality is not taught, but rather is presented as a fact. Lionel Jospin's directive—just as Bayrou's—states that boys and girls have equal rights when it comes to education and that no infringement on this equality is acceptable. But since coeducation was chosen above all else out of economic necessity rather than because it was seen as a basic principle of our social organization, it has yet to be analyzed in terms of real equality. For students who are entering the university today and whose entire schooling took place in a coeducational setting, the battle for equality, of which they know nothing, is ancient history. They are completely taken aback when told that, until 1965, French women were obliged by law to seek their husbands' permission in order to work outside of the home!

If we therefore think in terms of the equality of all human beings, is not the expulsion of girls from school today tantamount to fighting the wrong adversary, using the wrong method in the wrong era? In this atmosphere of confusion, it amounts to singling out adolescent girls as the enemy, while in fact they are the victims. They are the victims of cultural systems in which the separation of roles and of status remains under the influence of tradition, under the cover of respect for religion. They are also the victims of a modern society that has not yet fully completed its modernization in the area of male-female relations. Is adopting this law, then, not tantamount to adopting a sexist measure of a sexist nature since it leads to a breakdown of equality between boys and girls when it comes to obligatory schooling? By excluding the girls while their brothers, who have significant powers of control over them, remain free to continue to take advantage of the state school system—and, if they wish, to wear the unruly beard of the Fundamentalists while doing so—we are, in fact, sending the girls right back to the very fathers whose obscurantism we denounce. Is this not giving up on the pedagogy of conviction, the democratic conviction that would allow girls and boys to understand that secularism means not only the acceptance of the other and the other's private beliefs, but also the construction of a society in whose leadership both sexes share equal powers and receive equal representation, both in the public and the private sphere?

CONCLUSION

Examining the veil—or the headscarf, since we have, for the sake of convenience, used these terms interchangeably throughout this analysis—worn by young adolescent, preadolescent, or postadolescent girls has shown us just how far from unequivocal it is. The veil, as worn by these girls, does not at all convey the same meaning in all cases. There is the veil imposed by the parents, but there is also the one chosen, demanded even, by the young postadolescent women. Finally, there is the veil worn as the expression of a religious experience that cannot simply be reduced to respect for the commandments of Islam.

Furthermore, we have seen that this veil paradoxically translates the desire to become integrated among young girls who are unable to find other means of taming and negotiating the distance that separates the community in which their parents live from French society. And finally, the veil of the young postadolescent women who claim for themselves a "veiled identity" must not be understood as a rejection of French citizenship, but rather as a desire for integration *without* assimilation, a desire on these women's part to be simultaneously French *and* Muslim.

Other phenomena of a circumstantial nature can be added to these facts: Islamic or Islamist fundamentalist organizations—and these are not synonymous—hold influence over some of these girls, and do so partly because of the French society's virulent rejection of France's Muslim population. However, this phenomenon is, for the time being at least, still marginal—in the same way as the current Algerian situation only minimally changes their attitude.[5] The vast majority of the girls expelled from the high schools and junior high schools in the fall of 1994 were actually not of Algerian, but rather of Moroccan or Turkish, origin, which is a fact that was not emphasized.

If the veil is a sign of dissymmetry between boys and girls, then it is time to ask ourselves whether we attach sufficient value to the equality of men and women and whether our schools reflect this equality as more than just a mere formality in the content of the school curriculum. The historical roots of these girls are rarely studied as part of this curriculum. Many of them are made to feel inferior because of their social and ethnic background, and for those among them who choose to wear it, the veil is the expression of their recovered dignity at least as much as it is a symbol of their Islamic purity. They strive to become pure because they often find themselves in a doubly inferior position: in French society where, as "*beurettes*," they are devalued; and in their neighborhoods, where a new community vision reigns, in which a woman is anything but a man's equal.

The headscarf is henceforth a French phenomenon. Any attempt to portray the headscarf as an exterior phenomenon amounts to a misunderstanding of this reality. This French headscarf, as opposed to an Islamist one, tolerates diversity. These veiled girls have nonveiled friends, and neither one side nor the other harbors any feeling of superiority or inferiority concerning this reality. There now exists a *French veil,* which is a sign of a specific life experience that cannot be reduced to any foreign influence, be it that of Algeria, Morocco, Tunisia, or Iran. It does not matter that French Islam does not possess its own formal institutional framework; what French Islam does have are specific modes of expression in the framework of everyday life.

The negative reaction to the veil by a large part of French society is a sign of its refusal of this Islam, a refusal that is not entirely anchored in its fidelity to secularism. Rather, it is a refusal that reacts against the sudden appearance in France of a Muslim population whose stay was to be temporary, but which has, in less than three decades, settled in France permanently and formed France's second largest religious tradition. Too little time has passed since this unforeseen arrival of a permanent new population and with it the emergence of this foreign religion for French society to be able to take clear note of its existence and not resent its presence in France as a threat to its own identity. The migrants from the Muslim world have put down roots. The children are not as docile as their parents and a minority among them is eager to publicly display its Muslim identity.

If to this we add the memory of the decolonization process (especially in Algeria) and of the rise of political Islamism along the south shore of the Mediterranean, we will understand the difficulty with which many French people accept the veil within the borders of their national territory. In Germany, in Great Britain, and in other European countries, the same veil, and sometimes a more political veil than the French one, does not create such fear and anxiety. The disproportion between the phenomenon of the headscarf in schools and the passionate reactions to it raises the question of whether France can continue to practice integration by assimilation or whether we must now accept a certain distance between these two processes. Can one be a loyal citizen of France and still wear a *kippa,* a turban, or other religious symbols in the public space? Can a woman be a loyal citizen if she covers herself with a veil? France's integration with Europe and the difficulty of blending its secular identity with the intermixing of diverse identities in a changing world makes it urgent to answer the question of the image that France has of itself. Instead of hiding behind vestmental fetishes, instead of crying wolf each time a young woman wearing a headscarf or a young bearded man appears on the horizon, we should try to figure out what the limits of tolerance should be and ask ourselves how capable of managing identity differences a society can be. Such differences will surely crop up in societies that increasingly lack a central plan or a collective vocation.

In an everyman-for-himself society, is it not logical that we create our own identities with the material available to us in order to escape the absence of meaning with which we are faced? Do we not create new identities, sometimes "tribal" ones, in order to deal with anomie? Above all, is it not necessary to create a more just and less inegalitarian society if we want to be safe from the drift of identities, and if we want everyone to care about the res publica? The role of voicing protest on behalf of the public ["*fonction tribunicienne*"][6] used to belong to political parties, associations, and unions on the left wing of the political spectrum. At the present moment, a total vacuum reigns in the public sphere.

In France, the veil is one of the signs of a new type of identity cobbled together in a world where nothing but consumerism and individual advancement make sense, a world in which nothing compels us to work together on a common plan of existence. Young women and girls who wear the veil are not prepared to experience this dilution of meaning in the collective desert as the heady freedom that it is for some, who are no doubt more protected than they are from its consequences, both materially and existentially. The ground they stand on is too shaky because they belong to an in-between space: on the one hand, the devalued and often humiliated universe to which their parents belong; on the other, the French one, often inaccessible and always disdainful vis-à-vis youths from immigrant families. Living in this double space is quite literally wearing. On one side lie the demands of a society in which we are all supposed to resemble each other in the public space, even as each of us must constantly prove his/her "competitive" originality in an invasive and corrosive marketing sphere. On the other, there is a world where, in total contradiction with the republican credo and the supposed neutrality of the market, there is broad racism, disdain for immigrants, and the refusal to give them equal recognition within the French Republic. The veil is an ambiguous reaction on the part of many young women who have made a choice to be different in order to affirm their existence, an existence trapped in this in-between space.

In the modern world of collective nonsense, France is particularly vulnerable. In contrast with other societies, France has, until quite recently, maintained its centralized cultural homogeneity without making any attempts to institutionalize its peripheral, minority or intermediate cultures in the various "niches" of civil society. For a large part of the working classes, this homogeneity was, in addition, inseparable from the ideological plan of the Left. This plan fell apart and no other has taken its place. Fear and anxiety have substituted themselves for utopian expectations. All particularism is now being interpreted as a menace to the integrity of the Republic. But what alternative identity could now cement together our collective existence?

Translated by Eva Valenta[7]

NOTES

1. Editors' note: this article refers to the controversy that began in September 1989 when three young women students attended their high school in the town of Creil wearing Islamic headscarves (often erroneously called a "veil") and were expelled for challenging the secular nature of public schools in France. This highly debated event galvanized, and divided, immigrant groups, feminists, politicians, and intellectuals, and led to a number of official compromises by successive ministers of education.
2. Christian Baudelot and Roger Establet, *Allez les filles!* (Paris: Seuil, 1992).
3. Quoted by François Jacquet-Francillon, "Le problème de la mixité scolaire au XIXe siècle," in *Egalité entre les sexes, mixité et démocratie,* ed. Claudine Baudoux and Claude Zeidman (Paris: L'Harmattan, 1992).
4. Prisca Bachelet, "La fausse évidence de la mixité dans l'enseignement élémentaire et primaire," in *Egalité entre les sexes,* ed. Baudoux and Zeidman.
5. Editors' note: during national elections in Algeria in 1992, the Islamic Salvation Front appeared to be winning. Fearing that the Front would impose an Islamic state, the army-backed government annulled the election, leading Islamic extremists to wage guerilla warfare that targets officials, soldiers, journalists, and the general civilian population. Sixty thousand people have died as a result of what has become a civil war in Algeria.
6. That of institutionalized protest against the ruling order—Georges Lavau coined the phrase. See *A quoi sert le parti communiste français?* (Paris: Fayard, 1981).
7. Editors' note: the translator of this essay is responsible for the translation of all of the French quotations into English.

CHAPTER 7

The Feminization of Professional Names
An Outrage against Masculinity[1]

Benoîte Groult

The French generally think that their language, formalized by Vaugelas as early as 1647, then constantly rectified by successive grammarians and brought into line by that guardian of the French language, the Académie française, is a treasure to be protected. However, as sociolinguistics has demonstrated, language is not only a tool or a means of communication. Vocabulary is not neutral. It holds up a mirror to society and reflects its prejudices, taboos, and fantasies, perpetuating its structures and hierarchies. Language is power.

One should therefore not be surprised to find a subtle network of discriminations tending toward the effacement or marginalization of women in the French vocabulary, just as discrimination in the law has tended to make them into second-class citizens. Society's patriarchal structures are equally operative in speech.

Some claim that this particular aspect of women's oppression is secondary and insignificant. But that would mean forgetting the fundamental role of language in the constitution of identity—be it national, cultural, or social. How women speak, how they are spoken to, how they are spoken about: all of this determines the image they project in society and, even more so, the image they have of themselves.

Besides, such linguistic discrimination is not a new phenomenon. In the fifth century B.C. Herodotus already remarked that in several of the African and Eastern countries he had visited there existed distinct speech patterns for men and women, be they in phonology, syntax, or vocabulary. With the passing of the centuries and regardless of the regime (always exclusively masculine), the situation has hardly improved. In the seventeenth century, for example, we recall the irony with which Molière showered *Les femmes savantes* and *Les précieuses ridicules,* whose crime was— already!—their desire to have access to the same language as men. For a long time a learned woman was considered to be a "blue-stocking," a term that has a no masculine equivalent, whereas a learned man was a "gentleman," (*un honnête homme*), a term that has no feminine equivalent! (The phrase *"une honnête femme"* only referred to a woman's morals.) By the same token, a cultivated man was a respected scholar, whereas an educated woman was no more than "a hag seeking to imitate her master" (Proudhon). Language is yet another means of putting woman in her place.

Moreover, we should feel some gratitude toward the *précieuses,* for they represented women's first attempt to speak up and appropriate linguistic elegance, *"le beau langage."* This attempt was later severely repressed by implacable means; the basic principle in the education of girls right until the end of the nineteenth century was the refusal of instruction. During the French Revolution a member of the parliament, Sylvain Maréchal, even made a proposal to "prohibit the teaching of reading to women."

And yet the feminization of professional names had never been a problem. So few women had occupied such positions in the past. In the Middle Ages, for example, names were feminized without any problem. One used the words *"tisserande"* (weaver woman) and *"venderesse"* (woman seller; a word still used in legal vocabulary). Even the Church feminized: deaconess, prioress, mother superior, abbess, and so on.

The blockage first appeared in the twentieth century, when the increasing numbers of women acceding to professions hitherto reserved for men began to threaten the male monopoly. Every possible response was called for: girls were denied access to the *grandes écoles,* prohibited from independent professional practice, and refused the right to vote or be elected (and this until 1945!). The prohibition of the feminine from appearing in language was therefore a logical consequence of this. If they persisted in invading the male professions, they would be obliged to renounce the feminine!

There is no doubt that this is a power issue, since the acceptance of feminine names becomes inversely proportional to the prestige of the profession! The examples speak for themselves: telephone operators, computer technicians, and other operators take the feminine in French according to the conventional rules and without shocking the Académie française. On the contrary, as soon as high-level professions are involved, adding a silent "e" to the masculine, changing the suffix "teur" into "trice," or using a feminine article such as "la" or "une" (for example *la* ministre, *une* députée) is tantamount to an outrage against the masculine. This abuse of power has been attributed to feminists though it is simply a question of applying a rule of elementary grammar: "The noun generally agrees with the gender, masculine for the male, feminine for the female. In French the neuter noun of Latin has disappeared" (*Grammaire Hamon*). One is almost ashamed of having to recall this evidence.

The obstacles are not to be found in words, however, but in people's heads, as the following incongruous examples demonstrate. If you reach the age of a hundred you have the right to be called a *doyenne.* But if you preside over a university faculty you'll be called Madame *le doyen.* If you work for a director, you're *la secrétaire.* But if you enter the government you'll be called Madame *le secrétaire d'état.* You can call yourself *directrice* if you're the headmistress of a primary school. But if you work for the government's scientific research program you will be called Madame *le directeur.*

And what about all those professional names ending in a silent "e" that might therefore apply to either sex, such as *ministre, juge, peintre, poète?*[2] Why refuse them a feminine article when numerous words ending in a silent "e" are unproblematically used with either gender, such as *photographe, concierge, téléphoniste,* and many others? But men do not take umbrage at these professions. And so we come back to the question of prestige. . . .

Such resistance to the normal evolution of language is even more unacceptable insofar as grammarians agree unanimously on the repudiation of "the awful *Mme le,* which spoils so many of our texts." These are the words of Ferdinand Brunot uttered as early 1922. And in 1955 in the *Guide du bon usage*, another eminent linguist affirmed:

> When women have been persuaded that the feminine is not a weakness, but the opposite, the ground will have been cleared of a heavy mortgage. . . . The woman who prefers the masculine to the feminine for the name of her profession admits by that very claim an inferiority complex that betrays her legitimate protests. To hide one's gender behind the opposite gender is to betray it. To say *Mme le directeur, Mme le docteur* is tantamount to proclaiming the superiority of the male of which the masculine gender is the grammatical expression.

Damourette and Pichon, authors of the essay *Des mots à la pensée,* went even further: "The capacity of the French language to form differential feminine nouns should dissuade women taking on hitherto masculine professions from making a mockery of their own laudatory efforts by adopting sickening and grotesque masculine terms which blight the genius of the language."

Finally Robert le Bidois, an authority in language matters, approved of feminization, opting for the *eure* form of the feminine, which exists in Quebec, (*proviseure, docteure, ingénieure*) in order to give users every encouragement to use the feminine determinant.

The situation remained blocked in spite of everything; the Minister for Women's Rights in François Mitterrand's 1981 socialist government, Yvette Roudy, decided to create a "Working Commission for feminization of professional names, ranks, and status" in order to propose changes that might prove acceptable to the majority of users. In the 1980s numerous committees for terminology were appointed to adapt the French vocabulary to new realities in the medical, scientific, and technical domains. Words such as *stimulateur cardiaque* were created to replace pacemaker; *logiciel,* and *ordinateur* for computer hardware and software, and many other neologisms. The struggle was waged against the invasion of American terms that often seem more prestigious than their French equivalents. A considerable number of these words, proposed by specialists in each discipline, have today entered general usage. But in addition to forms of linguistic alienation due to snobism, there is a linguistic alienation that is due to sexism, such as occurs when masculine terms appear more honorable than their feminine equivalent. Furthermore it is with the very pretext of not debasing their profession that these women refuse to feminize it. They consider *avocat* more respectable than *avocate* and think it more prestigious to be called *Mme le docteur:* a sorry state of affairs since it shows to what extent women have internalized the feminine as inferior.

Equally lamentable is the attitude of the Académie française whose only gesture in favor of the feminine since its creation in 1634 insisted, let us recall, on refusing to receive women beneath its venerable dome. And when finally in 1980 Marguerite Yourcenar was elected, the 39 members of the Académie greeted her with the barbarism "Madame l'Académicien!" Then when she died a few years later, the press release read "the death of our dear *fellow-member* Marguerite Yourcenar" ("le décès de notre chère confrère Marguerite Yourcenar").[3]

This linguistic anomaly accentuates the anomaly of a woman's presence in such an august place as an academy. All this is part and parcel of what Luce Irigaray called the "strategy to efface the feminine."

Yet very recently we have seen cracks in the ice bank of French traditionalism. In the government that Lionel Jospin formed in 1999 five new ministers announced to the press that henceforth they wished the feminine form to be used to designate their office: *Mme la ministre* (Madame minister), *Mme la Garde des sceaux* (Madame Attorney General), and so on.

The Académie, cut to the quick, then sent a solemn message to President Jacques Chirac, protector of the said Académie, through the intercession of three of its members: Maurice Druon, permanent secretary, Hélène Carrière d'Encausse, "*directeur*," and Hector Biancotti, chancellor. The Immortals affirmed in all seriousness that such an impetuous decision endangered the French language. This is an even more indefensible position for those who consider themselves the guardians of linguistic purity in that the formula *Madame le* constitutes a grammatical contradiction in addition to testifying to thoughtless elitism. The members of the Académie nevertheless agree that the use of feminine forms "is now established for shopkeepers, e.g., *boulangère, charcutière, épicière* . . . but that it is not desirable to form new ones." Is there a clearer admission that the feminine can be tolerated in the service industries but not in the higher professional spheres?

Happily the days are gone when the Académie laid down the law and held the French people in awe. They are beginning to notice that they are the last of the Francophones to accept that their language should follow changes in society! Already in 1990 the European Council published a circular on "the elimination of sexism in language," recommending that all member states "adapt their vocabulary to accord with the autonomy of both sexes, the fundamental principle being that the activities of each should have the same social visibility."

This is no feminist torch bearing; one cannot suspect the Council of Europe of being a hotbed of female firebrands. But public opinion had not progressed sufficiently and the circular recalling "the interaction between words and behavior" and remarking that "the use of the masculine gender to designate both sexes often generates awkward uncertainties" was greeted by silence in the press.

Following the European recommendation, Francophone Belgium issued an edict for the feminization of professional names, statuses, and offices in all administrative documents on the instigation that "Language constitutes a sexist instrument of power which prevents women from becoming fully integrated in society."

Only France refused to listen. Worse, Maurice Druon, considering himself the sole proprietor of the French language, sharply called the Belgian community to order, declaring their decision to be misguided and shocking.

At the same time, the Grand Conseil in Switzerland, arguing that the refusal to feminize "obscured the existence of women, who are half of humanity," decided to bring up to date the text of official documents.

Finally, we know that Quebec, for whom safeguarding the French language is a proof of identity, feminized all professional names a long time ago, opting where words ending in "eur" are concerned (a difficult case since there is no rule for the formation of the feminine here) for the addition of a silent "e." It is quite common to read *une auteure, une docteure, une professeure, une ingénieure,* following the model of *prieure.* The commission I presided was tempted by that solution, if only as a way of harmonizing French usage in different countries, but in 1986 we were reminded that words ending in *eure* has been formed from comparatives and one could therefore not add a silent "e" to words like doctor or engineer that were not comparative! It is a fact that grammarians are finicky people. They added that the French did not consider themselves obliged to follow the example of their peasant cousins in Quebec, whose origins did not predispose them to legislate the French language. So usage will decide, given that in all cases those professional names are preceded by a determinant in the feminine: *une professeure* or *une professeur*.

In 1996, however, there emerged a new and encouraging factor: a certain number of professions appeared in the Larousse dictionary in the feminine. The French daily *Le Monde* applauded "these felicitous feminizations enabling us to escape from the enforced masculine." For the first time we read *la juge, la ministre, la sculptrice,* and a few others. Let me point out *factrice* and *inspectrice* have been in the Littré since 1967 and *agricultrice* since 1982.

The restrictions surrounding the entries concerning female judges or ministers speak volumes about the weight of the prejudice that had to be overcome. The Larousse moves forward here with extreme caution. At the end of the entry and in parenthesis, we read "the feminine is sometimes used in a familiar register," or even, "the spelling *députée* would be unacceptable." After two years of attending, in my capacity as president of the commission, in debates between linguists, I can easily imagine the anguishing discussions that produced those careful, almost shameful formulas. But the essential thing is to have crossed the threshold into the Noble Book, even through the back door.

To conclude, I would like to review in a different light the question of feminization over which so much ink has been spilt in the past ten years, that of French singularity.

Why, when we compare French feminism to the forms it takes under other skies, does it seem to have such a measured, even timid character—often deplored by Anglo-Saxon feminists?[4] Why is it never aggressive or combative? Why does it lack the militant dimension that transforms individual recriminations into positive struggle, giving rise to active solidarity and tangible progress?

That effacement, that submission on the part of women, belongs to an old tradition in France. It goes back to the sixteenth century, when Henry IV disinterred the Salic law dating from the year 511, which established codes for land inheritance that excluded women.[5] He made a law prohibiting women from inheriting land in the French kingdom. As a consequence, we have never had a queen as a monarch, but only royal wives, regents during their son's childhood, or even favorites and courtesans. In 1789, in spite of there being two feminist members in the Convention, Condorcet and Goyomar, Salic law was reactivated by the French Revolution. And in May 1870, Napoleon III had it reinscribed in the Constitution!

Insofar as power depends upon the Sacred (the monarchy was transmitted by divine right), it is evident that Salic law still functions today since, in spite of democracy, women have still not succeeded in reaching high-level positions or in putting pressure on the government. The most striking example: French women only obtained the vote in 1945, after Indian and Turkish women, and the second to last in Europe. As for representation in the parliament, they again lag far behind: less than 10 percent. Only Greece fares worse.

French women have been handicapped by their education, the "good education" given to young girls that makes women polite to the point of the ridiculous. They show politeness by remaining silent, never insisting on anything, ignoring French *gauloiseries* and dirty jokes, and worse, even finding them funny. The greatest fear of

French women is to lose their powers of seduction, to appear aggressive—or non-feminine. The Parisian, the seductress, are pillars of the masculine imaginary. In contrast to the United States, there is no hostility toward men in France. They are not considered collective oppressors, nor are women considered victims. A far cry from the almost maniacal codification of relations between the sexes in America, in France there is a long tradition of social exchange between men and women that was inaugurated in the Middle Ages with courtly love. It continued until the eighteenth century with the renowned Salons, which one would be wrong to take for boudoirs, and where Enlightenment philosophy was debated between equally cultivated men and women (Mme de Staël, Mme du Deffand, Mlle de Lespinasse, Mme du Chatelet, a physicist and Voltaire's companion, and so on).

The result is that there is not such a breach between the sexes as in the United States but by the same token there is a rampant misogyny that keeps women in subaltern positions far from political, economic, or religious centers of power.

Where do we stand in 1998? Let us recall that our terminology commission concluded its work in 1986 with an order signed by Prime Minister Laurent Fabius, which appeared as an official government publication. It established that the feminine exists by right and must be defined if not by a different word form, at least by a feminine determinant. That proposal has only been followed by courageous individual initiatives. Calling oneself an *écrivaine* still solicits pitying smiles. But the recent decision by women ministers, taken at the highest level, is changing the climate. I cite as proof the recent circular addressed by Amnesty International to its worldwide bureaus, announcing that the formula *Droits de l'Homme* (Rights of Man) be replaced by the more inclusive *Droits de la Personne* or *Droits Humains,* inspired by "Human Rights," the object being to eradicate sexism in language and to conform to the French Order for feminization.

So it seems that the effort of numerous women doctors, chemists, lawyers, and members of parliament is beginning to bear fruit. In France, women are most audacious when it comes to their bodies and for a long time now they have not thought twice about baring their breasts. Why should they be ashamed of baring their feminine?

Translated by Anne-Marie Smith

NOTES

1. Editors' note: Groult's article for this volume was written in the midst of heated debates about the "feminization" of language. While feminists, Groult foremost among them, fought hard for "linguistic parity," traditional groups such as the Académie française objected vehemently to any proposed changes, citing the universal nature of the French language. This most recent of the many *querelles de la langue* (language debates) led Prime Minister Lionel Jospin, citing the importance for the government to take the lead in combating the ideological resistances reflected by language, to name an official commission. Its charge was to suggest grammatically correct changes in women's professional titles. In March 1998 an official document was published: *Femme, j'écris ton nom . . . Guide d'aide à la féminisation des noms de métier, titres, grades et fonctions.* This guide included a 120-page list of suggestions for the appropriate way to feminize

the titles of government functions, most of which were quickly integrated in the fabric of French life and discourse.

2. These are words having the same form in the masculine and the feminine.

3. Editors' note: As of May 2002, there were three women among the 37 (normally there are 40) members.

4. See Mona Ozouf's *Les mots de femmes: essai sur la singularité française* (Paris: Fayard, 1995).

5. As decreed by the Salians.

CHAPTER 8

The Politics of Reproduction

JEANINE MOSSUZ-LAVAU

At the beginning of the 1990s, reproductive Rights in France were regulated by several laws, some of them longstanding. The first law, called the Neuwirth law after the parliamentary member who prepared it, dates from 1967. This law legalized so-called modern contraception and permitted access, at last, to the diaphragm, the pill, and the intra-uterine device (IUD). Other laws concerned abortion. The Veil law was established on January 17, 1975, and allowed abortions to be performed by the medical profession during the first six weeks of pregnancy, but it required parental consent for minors, and residency in France for at least three months prior to such services for foreigners. This law, which weathered a particularly stormy debate, was given only a five-year period of validity;[1] in 1979, it was voted in again. In 1982, a new law established that abortions would be reimbursed by the state health-care system.

In the 1980s, the "French sexual landscape" was changed by the presence of several new elements. Above all there was the advent of AIDS. In January 1982 the French media began to speak of a "gay cancer" in America and reported a case in France. Soon the epidemic took on the proportions we now know and preventative campaigns aimed at condom use were mobilized. This, in some ways, eclipsed pregnancy prevention. Many women abandoned the pill, thinking, "we'll have to use a condom anyway"; since condom use proved to be less than systematic, they found themselves pregnant. Another modern aspect was introduced with the development of fertility treatments and medically assisted pregnancies. The first test-tube baby, engendered through in vitro fertilization, was born in France in February 1982, although artificial insemination through donors had been in practice since the beginning of the 1970s. Reproduction was thus no longer automatically linked to sexuality, which raised lively discussions, as did debates on the ultimate power of science. On February 23, 1983, the National Consulting Committee on the Ethics of Life and Health Sciences was formed. Various colloquia dedicated to these questions sprang up over the following years.

The 1990s were marked by other changes in reproductive legislation, instigated by antiquated laws ill adapted to reproduction in the modern day and age or brought on by the absence of laws altogether. But there has been resistance to these new laws. Later we will examine an example of this resistance in the case of the newly proposed abortion law.

It is important to note that these changes came about during political changes of a more general nature in France. The Left (which had come back into power in France in 1988) lost its majority in the National Assembly in the 1993 legislative elections, and a Right-wing government came to power. The presidential election of 1995 brought a Rightist, Jacques Chirac, into office. For two years, then, both the National Assembly and the President were on the Right. In 1997, Chirac dissolved the National Assembly, and the Left gained back the majority in the new election. Thus began a period of cohabitation. But with a new, Leftist National Assembly, progressive reforms became possible, and several laws concerning reproductive Rights came up for a vote.

The Question of Emergency Contraception, or "The Morning-After Pill"

Emergency contraception, which consists of taking two Norlevo pills (over an interval) as soon as possible after unprotected sex, was made available in France on June 1, 1999. (Another product, Tetragynon, had been available since March 1998, but it was much less effective.) This decision was made, in part, to help staunch the 6,500 abortions undergone by minors (out of 10,000 who become pregnant) each year. But public access to the new method did not stop at that. A few months later, Minister of Education Ségolène Royal announced that school nurses could administer these pills to students "in distress." An official document on public school health care and emergency policy distributed on December 14 stated that "the nurse may administer Norlevo to the student in question in cases in which sexual contact has occurred less than 72 hours previously, in order to, through emergency contraception, avoid an unwanted pregnancy at an early age."[2] These resolutions concerning minors were issued with a number of stipulations: the nurse must try to convince the student to speak to her parents and to go to a family planning center; yet if she refuses and exhibits "marked distress," the two pills are to be provided. For students of legal age, if a visit to a family planning center is not possible, the nurse is to inform her that Norlevo can be bought at a pharmacy, and "in exceptional cases, notably, in cases of geographic distance," the nurse can provide the pills. This protocol appeared on January 6, 2000, in the Official Bulletin of National Education.

This decision came up against a number of criticisms, notably by family Rights groups opposed to abortion, who filed an appeal with the Council of State (*Conseil d'Etat*). The press made this appeal public on June 6, 2000. On June 30, the Council of State annulled Ségolène Royal's decision, stating that Norlevo, as a hormonal contraceptive, was not covered under the law of January 17, 1975, regarding abortion, in application of the provisions of article 3 of the law of December 28, 1967, and could not therefore "be prescribed by anyone other than a doctor or distributed anywhere except in a pharmacy or, by the conditions suggested in article 4 of the law, by a family planning or education center."

Since the document permitting school nurses to distribute emergency contraception was declared against the law of 1967, the only course of action was to change the law, which was done, all things considered, quite quickly. On October 5, 2000, a new article was added to the public health code, voted in by the National Assembly, specifying that emergency contraception does not have to be prescribed by a physician and that such a pharmaceutical product can "be administered to minors or adults in the school setting." In the course of the debate, the Right's standard arguments were voiced, with contentions such as "human life begins at conception," or that "the fatal blow" had now been dealt to family values. Yet some members of the Right voted for this amendment. When the text arrived in the Senate, a new proposition was instigated: that the morning-after pill be made available free of charge to adolescents on weekends and during school vacations.

The law of 1967 was accordingly modified so that it was now possible to obtain the morning-after pill in pharmacies without a prescription, and, for students, from school nurses. Hence another method for managing unwanted pregnancies was made available, especially to young people. At the same time, other mechanisms were put into place toward the same goal.

A New Abortion Law

Five thousand women are compelled to leave France every year to seek abortions abroad (in the Netherlands, England, or Spain), because they have exceeded the legal term for abortions in their own country, the famous ten-week limit, which is the shortest in all of Europe. For several years, a number of groups (primarily feminist organizations) have been demanding the legalization of longer-term abortions so that some of these women might be able to undergo the procedure in France. In addition, they have asked for the cancellation of parental consent laws for minors.

After the Left's return to power, a number of specialists were asked to give reports on the scope and nature of unwanted pregnancies. (Professor Michele Uzan's report, "The Prevention and Management of Adolescent Pregnancy," was submitted in April 1998; Professor Israel Nisand's report, "Abortion in France," was submitted in February 1999.) Public debate grew. On July 27, 2000, Minister of Employment and Solidarity Martine Aubry announced the decision to reform the Veil law of 1975 on abortion and the Neuwirth law of 1967 on contraception. She proposed that the legal delay for abortions be moved from 10 weeks to 12 weeks, and that minors not wanting or unable to obtain parental consent be accompanied by an "adult reference" of their choice.

Debate on this proposal began in the National Assembly on November 29 and 30, 2000. The two propositions (lengthening the legal delay, jettisoning parental consent) were passed. The members also decided that a visit to a family planning center prior to abortion would no longer be obligatory for adults. Other amendments proposed the legalization of voluntary sterilization, and, in very limited cases, the sterilization of mentally handicapped adults "when absolutely no other contraceptive methods are medically possible or it is established that such methods cannot effectively be put into place." Abortion was finally decriminalized. (It would no longer figure in the penal code, but would be covered exclusively under the public health code.) All members of the Left voted for these amendments, as did a dozen members of the Right. The Senate, considering the new laws on March 27, 2001, rejected the legalization of abortions in the twelfth week, but accepted the adult "reference" under the condition that they not only "accompany" the minor but also that they "be present." In addition, the Senate proposed that voluntary sterilization be possible only for those over 30 years old.

The modified text has not yet been returned to the National Assembly, but the Assembly has the final say, and since a majority is in favor of the original proposition, the amendments will most likely be voted in without changes.

Medically Assisted Reproduction[3]

The numbers of cases of medically assisted reproduction in France have become considerable. In 1999, 40,000 babies were born with the aid of in vitro fertilization and almost as many with artificial insemination. Animated debates on filiation, the family, and the status of the embryo were quickly generated. Tales of widows and women past menopause becoming pregnant, as well as questions on the ethics of surrogate mothers and embryonic research gave rise to the fear of a society run adrift and to a broad demand for new laws. Government agencies again sought expert advice.

A fairly liberal law was initially adopted by the National Assembly in November 1992. But in the spring of 1993, a Rightist majority was elected to the National Assembly, and the 1992 law was immediately put into question. Three new laws were voted on in 1994 and promulgated in July of that same year. The first of these posited several broad principles concerning the respect of the human body. As Dominique Mehl writes, Title I of this law "affirms the dignity of the individual, the inviolability of the human body, and its integrity. It condemns eugenics. It guarantees that donors be anonymous and that donations be free. It forbids surrogate maternity."[4] In Title III, it is stipulated that "in cases of assisted reproduction with a third-party donor, paternity may not be established between the donor and the child who is the issue." In other words, the mother is the woman who gives birth, and the father is the husband or companion of the mother.

The second law states the conditions that must be met in order to benefit from medically assisted reproduction. "Both the male and female parent must be living and within reproductive age; they must be married or capable of proving that they have lived together for at least two years; and they must have consented to embryonic transfer or artificial insemination." There is a provision for "exceptional cases" by which a couple can consent in writing to having their spare embryos given to another couple. The "donation" of an embryo is thus rendered possible. On the other hand, "all *in vitro* fertilization of human embryos for the purpose of study, research, or experimentation is forbidden." Yet, in "exceptional cases" once again, "the couple may authorize research on their embryos," as long as it is done in writing. It is stipulated, however, that "this research must have a medical purpose and must not injure the embryo."

These laws were voted in for a five-year period, and "ordinarily" should have been voted upon again in 1999. In 2001, this vote had still not taken place. Given the recent evolution in the debates, the laws call for a veritable revision, but on points that will once again instigate confrontation. The questions and concerns that have arisen primarily pertain to couples desiring reproductive assistance. Is it legitimate to control it, as it is now controlled, with such strict criteria? Why not, for example, allow postmortem insemination? Must all donated gametes remain anonymous? Yet the greatest divergences of opinion seem to center around the embryo. According to

Dominique Mehl, "The prohibition of research poses a real problem. All those concerned, when consulted about legislative revision, are more or less for a relaxing of the law, even for an utter liberalization of this aspect of the law."[5] But there are partisans of absolute protection of the embryo who are poised to protest if things are taken in that direction. This debate is linked to the debate on abortion, as we shall see; for the question on the status of the embryo, if it is taken up, can also be used by opponents of abortion.

In any case, animated debates take place, often in the media, on the dangers of letting science go too far, on the research that might lead to the genetically perfect child, on the child's Rights, and on what has relentlessly been called "procreation." The recent achievement of animal cloning has given rise to even more polemics, with a distinction being made between procreative and therapeutic cloning. It is apparent that these new methods of reproduction will continue to fuel discussions in France for a long time to come.

A CHANGE UNDERWAY:
PROVISIONS FOR HOMOSEXUAL PARENTS

We come now to a question that may constitute one of the next great social debates, a demand made by homosexuals and lesbians: the possibility of becoming parents through adoption or assisted reproduction.

A single person has the right to adopt a child in France today, but if authorities learn that he or she lives with someone of the same sex, approval is not (or is extremely rarely) accorded. Therefore, if a gay man or a lesbian wants to adopt a child, he/she must lie about his/her sexuality. Additionally, a single woman does not have the Right to artificial insemination from a donor. Lesbians wishing to become natural parents often go to Belgium, where single women can receive artificial insemination.

More and more frequently, homosexuals and lesbians have been demanding an end to this discriminatory treatment. Thus, the Association of Gay and Lesbian Parents and Future Parents (APGL, l'Association des parents et futurs parents gays et lesbiens) was created in 1986. In 2000, its members numbered more than one thousand, and member parents were in the process of raising more than 400 children. The association demands equality for all citizens, and "equal protection for their children," regardless of sexual orientation. It is a purview they hope to establish legally, with judicial ties between children and what are called their social parent or coparent, that is, those who, along with the biological or adoptive parent (currently the only recognized parent), are raising the child. In June 1997 the APGL organized a preliminary colloquium for "gay and lesbian families of Europe," whose proceedings were published. Over the next year, they ran a multidisciplinary group to work on the issues of homosexual families. A second colloquium, "Kinship and Sexual Difference," took place in Paris in October 1999, gathering more than 500 people.[6] This second colloquium focused more specifically on parents, sexual difference, and gay parenthood. More recently, the APGL organized a petition, collecting over 2,000 signatures, to protest the law that forbids women in homosexual relationships from adopting a child. There are other organizations and individuals besides the APGL struggling for gay and lesbian parenting Rights, too, but they do so through other methods. The jurist Daniel

Borillo, for example, has been fighting for the legalization of same-sex marriages, which would take care of this particular point of discrimination. If same-sex marriages were legalized, gays and lesbians would have the Right to adopt as well as to seek assisted reproduction.

We are thus facing a new debate in France, one that questions the relationship between sexuality and reproduction and that calls for advances in reproductive politics. But there is no lack of adversaries. Rightist parliamentary member Renaud Muselier recently organized his own petition, signed by nearly 100,000 people, "against adoption of a child by two persons of the same sex." It is not the only item to which one finds resistance. During the fall 2000 debates on abortion, the opposition to change was, as we shall see, extremely virulent.

II. THE DEBATE ON ABORTION IN THE FALL OF 2000

October and November 2000 witnessed the unfurling of a new abortion debate, first in the media and then in the Assembly, where the law was examined on November 29 and 30. Was it a new debate? In certain respects, yes; in others, no. The outcome was a return to rather conservative arguments that one might have hoped buried with the debates of 1974, 1979 (when definitive abortion laws were passed), and 1982 (when the law for state reimbursement of abortion was put into effect).

Eugenics

This was one of the points most argued by the opponents of a longer delay (moving from 10 to 12 weeks of gestation) for legal abortions. They pointed out that, slight deformities in the fetus being detectable between the tenth and twelfth weeks of pregnancy, women would request an abortion even if they were not in a dire situation because the desire for a "perfect fetus" would become a factor. Women who wanted a girl and learned that they were carrying a boy might be tempted to abort as well. What one wants is a perfect child.

Philippe de Villiers (Movement for France, a Rightist party) announced to the National Assembly on November 29: "History will remember that, incited by the National Socialists, you have introduced state-sponsored eugenics into our country." He positioned himself as the defender of "the most vulnerable, those without voice, those with small hands, who do not yet have a lawyer." He continued: "We have reached the state of sorting out the unborn. A new Right emerges: the Right to prenatal euthanasia."

It is hardly a new argument. In the debates that took place in the 1970s, it was employed time and time again. It was said then that a life must be respected at all costs, as soon as it begins, that we must disallow the destruction of an embryo, for we will never be able to stop what follows: first we will kill the fetus, then the child, then the old man, the handicapped, all "undesirables," anyone who is "useless." There was talk of "genocide."

During the fall 2000 debates, a new rider grafted itself onto the old argument. It contended that, if offered, a greater margin of maneuverability (two more weeks) would give rise to incertitude: women would begin to imagine that the infant *might* be affected by this or that condition, and, not being sure, they would abort.

Medical and Technical Considerations

Medical and technical considerations were proposed primarily by Jean-Francois Mattei (Liberal Democracy, a Rightist party) during his presentation to the National Assembly on November 29, 2000. These arguments hinged on the fact that after 10 weeks of pregnancy, "intervention requires general anesthesia and the fragmentation of the fetus," which above all would require doctors to employ different procedures.

> The operation is different after ten weeks because the embryo has become a fetus. . . .
> Up to ten weeks, a simple vacuuming with a delicate nozzle is sufficient because the embryo is of a liquid or gelatinous consistency. After ten weeks, the fetus has begun to become bony and thus a surgical intervention with general anesthesia and fragmentation of the fetus is necessary before vacuuming out the uterus with a larger nozzle. The jurisdiction is different because the act potentially has more serious consequences and the patient must be informed of these.

This is not a new medical argument. Already in 1967, when the question of legalizing "modern" contraception arose, one heard members of the parliament evoking the risk of cancer aggravated by the pill or the dangers of the IUD. The pill was accused of deregulating the feminine libido. As for abortion, they claimed, it would have heavy consequences on women's health because it would be used repeatedly.

Listening to the medical and technical arguments against abortion in the fall of 2000, one cannot help wondering why French doctors cannot use methods that most other European doctors (Italians, for instance, in whose country the legal delay is 13 weeks) employ. Might French doctors be struck with a certain inaptitude from which most of the European Union does not suffer?

The Irresponsibility of Women

According to opponents of the proposed law, we must not lengthen the legal delay because, as we all know, women are irresponsible. All through the debates, a number of public figures made presentations to further the case against women. Roselyne Bachelot-Narquin, one of the few Rightist parliamentary members who supported the new law, declared to the National Assembly, "We were treated like irresponsible children who must be given tutelage. In this day and age, this process of infantilism is abetted by all those who would like to subordinate a woman's access to abortion to the authority of a committee of experts or to collective medical opinion." On the Right of the political spectrum, opponents are prepared to "help" thousands of women who are obliged to leave the country for abortions (beyond the legal delay) on condition that the decision to do so be made by a commission whose composition varies according to different cases. One does not see them proposing a new Right, one by which they might decide only by their own conscience and mind. This, for example, is what Françoise de Panafieu (Assembly for the Republic, a Rightist party) proposes, conferring all power to doctors and experts: "Jean-Michel Dubernard, Richard Cazenave and myself propose enlarging the conditions under which abortion is accessible, by considering situations of grave psychological distress. The requests will be examined case by case by a multidisciplinary body." In the same debate, another Rightist member spoke of "unaccountability and laxity."

In fact, to some, the idea that women might make their own decisions on all that concerns them is still unbearable. It brings tiresomely to mind one of the points used in the debate against *parité*. The argument ran then that women were still in the process of learning, still in the process of development, and one wondered if they would be competent, and so on. In fact, suspicion arises whenever there is question of a woman's autonomy or the Right to make important decisions for herself. Elisabeth Sledziewski, an academic who was in favor of *parité*, declared (in *Le Monde* on October 6, 2000) that the narcissism of women might run amok, if the abortion delay were lengthened, that a woman would be able to act even more at her own *convenience*, each one becoming "a mad subject, her own will an object of idolatry."

To sum up the gist of many of these arguments, then: since women are irresponsible and can only follow the easiest path available to them, abortion will become rampant and even ho-hum. That would, indeed, be an abortion based on convenience. It is an old discourse: a member of the Right, Mr. Delande, had proclaimed back in 1979 that "There are more abortions in January because no one wants to ruin her summer vacation. People decide to abort because it is not the right time, because they are moving or getting a new car" (*Journal Officiel*, AN, November 30, 1979).

Thus, we inevitably reach the next stage: that abortion laws will incite women to abort.

The Compulsion to Abort

Women will feel under pressure to abort; this is part of the argument developed in the National Assembly, especially by Rightist member Marie-Therese Boisseau, who wants to do everything possible "to give women the Right to keep their children" and who accused the majority Left of encouraging them toward abortion: "I am unbelievably shocked at how you're throwing out everything that might allow a woman to keep her child. . . . Not every woman who goes to the first interview has already decided to abort." These are her words against the Left's proposition to get rid of the preabortion interview for all but minors. About pregnant women in distress, she adds: "Their freedom of choice should be treated with the greatest respect. With this law, you no longer leave them a choice. You assume that they have already chosen to abort."

Christine Boutin (a Rightist), taking her turn in the Assembly to talk about the pressure that proabortion support puts on pregnant women seeking an abortion declared: "By offering only the possibility of ending their pregnancies, France refuses to consider the real reasons for some pregnant women's distress and in the end adds to their troubles." Then she raised her new battle cry: "post-abortive suffering." "Over the past 25 years, post-abortive suffering has hardly been admitted or acknowledged. Nevertheless, women are beginning to talk about it. Some confide that if they had known what they would have to go through, they never would have aborted. How much longer will we refuse to hear this silent suffering?"

Along the same lines, once again at the National Assembly, Jean-Francois Mattei (of the Liberal Democracy Party, already quoted above) called to mind the sterile couples who have consulted him (he is also a doctor) or those parents who have given birth to a handicapped child, adding: "It is in such cases that an abortion from several years before, buried in these parents' minds, rises to the surface and evokes new feelings of guilt and regret." Clearly, one could not do better than to attempt making sterile couples or parents of handicapped children feel guilty.

When all is said and done, the argument goes, women would be compelled to abort, which would lead them to suffer for the rest of their days, and it would have all been avoidable. This process is all the more shocking to the Rightist opposition since abortion is not even a right in their eyes. Speaking of the Veil law, Marie-Therese Boisseau declared in the National Assembly in November 2000: "The proposed legislative provisions were presented as a measure of exception to a human Right [to live], not in the least as a universal right that must then be recognized."

The Ongoing Problem of Evading the Issue

This argument reminds us of the fact that only 40 percent of the women beyond the delay could seek abortions in France if the law were adopted. This raises the question: what will become of the rest? The opposition protests that soon the laws will be pushed to 14-, 16-, "even 22-week" delays, waving this progression of numbers in the air like a threatening stick. The following was repeated over and over by a Rightist member who was not hoping to propose it, but instead to make the parliamentary members tremble: "And why not, then, a delay of 14 or 20 weeks?"

Fear tactics, a problem in earlier decades as well, were promulgated through other methods. In 1979, a right-wing parliamentary member announced: "The law, in accepting abortion when it should be instead considered a last resort, has removed any sense of reproach and has rendered it a potentially normal form of birth control, which it is not. Women already demand the right to abort when and how they want, even to be reimbursed for it by the state" (*Journal Officiel* 112 1N, November 28, 1979).

There was yet another argument waiting in the wings.

Questioning the Family

This argument concerns the provision for minors undergoing abortions who choose to have an "adult reference" if they cannot or do not want to obtain parental consent. This provision would cast the family into question. The opprobrium provoked by this new ordinance revealed a ready-made vision of the family as an idyllic unit in which parents and children speak honestly and openly about sex. One knows, however, that in many families it is quite the contrary. The opposition proposed a commission that would decide for the minor, "together with the parents."

One proponent of the opposition declared to the National Assembly: "Rather than a reference, we propose a team consisting of a physician, a psychologist, and a social worker to help the young woman. In addition, family support will be offered as a part of the effort to help strengthen family ties and give the young woman a positive vision of the family."

How do you give a young woman who is the victim of incest "a positive vision of the family" when she is trying precisely to undo what has been done by one of the men in her family? Neither this problem, nor that of the numerous abuses some young women experience within their families, seems to have been taken into consideration. Yet opponents insist that the family must always be informed. Another Right-wing member of the Assembly put it in these terms:

I admit that the conditions for a sensible dialogue between adolescents and their parents cannot always be met and that in such cases the presence of a third-party adult reference might be useful. But even in such cases, the family should not be circumvented. For my part, I would have them informed in all cases. You have decided otherwise, at the risk of further disrupting the family unit and taking even more power away from parents.

How would such "information" be received in families belonging to cultures in which virginity is enforced until marriage? Have they thought of what might happen to a young woman of such a family when it is learned that not only has she been sexually active, but that she is pregnant as well?

In spite of some outbursts, and although too many of these arguments hark back to the 1970s and 1980s, the current debate on reproductive rights is more restrained (except as evidenced in Philippe de Villiers's statements) than in the preceding era, when the very right to have an abortion was not recognized. In December 1979, for example, a senator shouted at his colleagues: "As so many of us, alas! I have seen men die on the field of battle and have often heard them call out for their mothers. . . . Would we have—this is the question we must ask ourselves—the same respect for our mothers if we knew they could have aborted any one of their children?" (*Journal Officiel*, S, December 21, 1979)

Today, the enforcement of the Veil law survives and proves that an irreversible trend was in the works. The nonsense is less abundant now, and even if the Right-wing opposition does all it can to stop amendments to the law, it does not question the basic principle itself, and has not attempted to rescind the statutes now in place.

In the final count, the end of the 1990s and the beginning of the new millennium were marked by liberal advances in the judicial system that regulates sexuality. The options for handling unwanted pregnancies were increased, even if more should have been done in the area of legal delays for abortion. What remains to be done is to imagine parenthood as something much more diverse than today's model and to conceive of assisted reproduction in an equally versatile manner. But let us not forget that legislative and presidential elections in France are to take place in 2002, and a Right-wing majority will certainly not make any efforts in this direction.[7]

Translated by Eleni Sikelianos

NOTES

1. For more on the debates on reproductive Rights, see Janine Mossuz-Lavau, *Les lois de l'amour, Les politiques de la sexualité en France (1950–1990)* (Paris: Payot, 1991).
2. See the statement presented at the Institute of Political Studies in Paris in September 2000, "L'introduction du Norlevo dans les collèges et lycées," by François Lainé.
3. For further discussion, cf. Dominque Mehl, *Naître? La controverse bioéthique* (Paris: Bayard Editions, 1999).
4. Ibid., 357.
5. Ibid., 287.
6. The notes, *Homoparentalités, états des lieux, Parentés et différence des sexes* (Paris: ESF Editeur, 2000) were published under the direction of Martine Gross.
7. See the postscript to introduction, *infra*.

CHAPTER 9

Sexualities on Parade

VÉRONIQUE NAHOUM-GRAPPE

Taking a walk is a delicate enterprise in which each step moves toward forgetting. Occasionally, at a turn in the road, an improbable visual encounter occurs. So when in one of our contemporary cities, such as London, Paris, or Hamburg, the *flâneur* stumbles upon the Gay Pride parade, the urgency of seeing, up until that moment numbed by walking, holds her transfixed; on the edge of this procession of proudly claimed homosexualities she is open to everything. From the sea of sexualized figures before her arises the astonishing spectacle of collective imagination working on the presence of the human body at the risk of submerging her like a small pebble whipped up in waves of bodily images. Whatever her political views and the degree of intellectual intimacy she maintains with her own sexuality, distracted and wide-eyed, the ordinary passerby slows down her pace in accordance with the spectacular impact of the event. What is at stake in this demonstration is *the aesthetic nature of the link between politics and sexuality.*

Wandering about aimlessly to the beat of the techno base, astounding figures become increasingly mysterious the more they occupy one's field of vision. Is this a political demonstration; a hilarious and terrifying masked carnival, the sort Bakhtine might analyze; a great multicolored parade; a street bash for young people with the appropriate jokes and noisy behavior; an explosive bacchanalia with Dionysus designed by Andy Warhol; a hip publicity clip for a trade name in nightclub amplifiers? A tract here, a mask there, an erect phallus somewhere else, and everywhere the sort of technical paraphernalia that would help an ethnologist, but not a passerby. The latter has a passing contact with profiles, bare flesh, lace, nails, and curves and indolently takes in the ever-increasing opacity of all that bodily expression. The ignorant passerby does not see things from the same perspective as the committed ideologist, who wants to produce a particular effect, nor as the study-bound historian who resolves the enigma of the present spectacle through a written historical account. Between the choice of bodily appearance and the choice of sexuality, oblique signs proliferate and what they lose on the level of signification they gain in expressiveness: these disguised, masked, travestied figures become more unreadable as one gets closer. Behind the political banner of excess lies a complex, irresolute amalgam of features. Before a masked ball the sociologist stands equipped, the ethnologist can read the subversions of carnival, but faced with the Gay Pride parade the passerby remains silent.

First of all, one cannot really say "faced with"; you cannot confront something all-enveloping that traverses by you and then turns away before you have really caught a glimpse. The passerby's whole body becomes a resonance box for noises and a mirror for images before any perspective is achieved. To what particular register of interpretation can we refer what is going on here? The identificatory references for such body images remain enigmatic; why that mauve lace on that collarbone? Of course this is a travesty of gender, but in what sense? What is the sex of that angel with the big bottom? What sex are those anonymous buttocks? The play of travesty produced as nature would have it (as culture would have it) by the militant politicization of the homosexual question is not an adequate tool of interpretation here in the face of all those possible poses of the human body; the frontier between genders is obviously crossed mimetically and drag queens are the stars of the party such as occurs in the classic fashion of festive subversions when the street world, here the aesthetic prostitution of both sexes, becomes the crux of the spectacle and occupies the center of the stage. But furthermore, it is the limits between the species themselves, insects, octopuses, and even animate and inanimate beings, real and unreal, and finally between all possible figurations and defigurations of the human presence, historic or fictional, which are here transgressed.

Small bare-calved marquesses cross paths with gray and mauve octopuses, knotty muscle and wobbly flab perturb the conventional scale of beauty and ugliness, the beautiful crosses paths with the bizarre—each equally radiant, like in those "space bars" we have seen in cartoon strips and contemporary science-fiction movies for about the last 20 years. (The first famous "space bar" in which beings of all imaginable species cross paths is no doubt the one in *Star Wars*.) If the passerby has had the opportunity, during some chance encounter while shopping, to daydream about the iconography on the record covers of those music groups deriving from the punk and hard-rock movements, she will be able to recognize the same family of disparate, off-beat, bold figures: it's us, we are like that. The same signs are no doubt in circulation between different contemporary fabrications of the human appearance from the 1970s to today: sexual difference is muted to the profit of other types of difference, precisely such differences as gender or behavior. Pink legionnaires and hairy angels, insect wings on white bellies, cruel features and hanging flab, all that meeting on the same body and between bodies to the point of producing an indubitable impasse when eyes meet. The first glance, which in normal circumstances is always in search of identificatory signs in the encounter with a new body, is here hindered, entangled, mixed up in all senses of the word. And the first difference immediately perceived on a normal walk, the difference between the sexes, is here an object of extreme complication.

The overstatement, the concentration on individual style, the playful appendages ultimately leave scope for the sensitive question of skin, its solitude as it hangs on the bone. The passerby shudders in spite of frenetic audacities. Her desire to see is both quenched and increased tenfold at each moment as the formal enigma of the human body she brushes against increases.

SEEN IN PROFILE

The passerby's perspective is our choice of perspective here: the passerby does not occupy center stage; she is in the background, even if she is ensnared. Her scale of vision is the blurred horizon of things close up. She is not attached to them. She is not a militant: she takes advantage of a visual windfall. She daydreams unemphatically. She is looking for nothing in particular and remains in disharmony with what she encounters. A double gratuitousness hits her path, that of chance encounters around the corner, and then the contingency of all sudden appearances. A mild disaffection for the surrounding world emerges during her walk.

Looking on from the wave's edge, the *flâneur* asks herself: what's going on here? She returns to her question: what separates a political demonstration from an artistic celebration, a cultural event from the cultural scene? The exhibition of a social project and the reverie of a pure present of which the forthcoming reality is announced in this global clip? "True life," that oneiric and political legacy of May '68, of the militant feminism of the 1970s, spewed out in advertising images of the period, is it finally going to produce the long-awaited social revolution? Would May '68, that 30-year-old tree stump, be able to produce new leaves amid the flushed excesses of the sexualized bodies here exhibited? Or is it rather some kind of bewildering hazing in which the bewildered freshman is the passerby himself, frayed and floating at the pavement edge like a shred of yellow foam, left on the shore by a colored wave?

That is, unless the great floats, those masters of the world of sound, deafening producers of industrial and cardiac rhythm, are the true motors of this action. The beat of the base, vibrating through one's intestines in double blows, produces this frenetic throbbing in the great wave of collective motion occurring almost in place behind the enormous engine, without transition or melody. This recognizable rhythm, also beating through the Techno parade that has recently begun to cross through our towns, commercial and perverted sister of the great gay demo, brings together the political question of sexualities and the mute question of desire, throbbing faster between the legs of those it arouses, no matter the object.

There's more than galoping creatures, there are also jumping-jacks, gliding, majestic, and sculpted on the platforms of the terrible trucks, the hip-swaying, those in profile, fading survivors of the great tremor, able to squeeze nearer to the shocked, gaping passerby. Little by little, however, the rough outline becomes perceptible.

The role-playing goes far beyond a simple problematic of inversion and travesty: the famous drag queens who caricature femininity at its most hackneyed are not the only heroines of the scene, but they are the egeria, the emblems of the whole performance. They push the signifying boundaries of "femininity" to their very limit; their heels are so high that they pitch laterally, their false eyebrows so long that they go past their noses, their use of colors so strange that they seem phosphorescent. They are beyond beauty or ugliness, they carry glamour to its utmost apogee, where make-up borders on the carnivalesque mask. A top model's most astounding extravagance seems pale and insignificant beside a drag queen. The fading of the difference between masculine and feminine is not achieved by the effacement of the feminine, but by the fact that its hyperbole is submerged in the infernal circle of other mimetic caricatures. Extreme virility sometimes encounters extreme femininity in the same body, always that of a man, whatever his sexual choices. In the middle of this urban crossroads, as in the heart of our grammar, the masculine crushes all other genres. The phallus is definitely more present in the Gay Pride parade than the clitoris, and the banner of feminization carried by the men is far more spectacular than the austere masculinization of homosexual women. They are neutral when they "act like men"; they wear jackets, have cropped hair and no make-up—and the butch woman does not provoke laughter as does the effeminate man in the sphere of appearance. On the stage of the spectacular event constituted by this procession, women are eclipsed. Why? They are scarcely visible, have to be searched out. As a physical presence they are no longer women nor men. In the sphere of appearance they have been defeated by the male homosexuals who appropriate both the feminine and the masculine, with their excessive high heels and knotty muscles. They do not construct a three-meter-high clitoris for their enormous floats; if they were to do so, it would not be as easily recognizable as the phallus.

The regime of visibility of the feminine, so exploited in everyday advertising, is here overthrown. The feminine in the stereotyped sense of the word—"effemininity," one might say—turns out to be the extremely caricatured instrument of a militant theatricalization of masculine homosexuality. But those emblems of the woman's body that are not the object of grotesque emphasis are excluded from this circle of imaginable sexes. The Gay Pride parade accords to the phallus the central solitary place it already occupies in Freudian psychoanalytic theory, for example, as it accords to male homosexuality the biggest place in the image production of the sexualized body. As in society in general, this carnival of alternative sexualities continues to eliminate women as visible actors but also as a body emblematic of difference. It achieves this by appropriating the visibility of chosen emblems of farcical femininity nonetheless submerged in the infernal superlative of all imaginable aesthetics of the body. The result is the loss of the distinct visibility of binary sexual difference, the absence of the ordinary female body from action and cultural event. Gay pride effects an excessive masculinization of the place it occupies, and the condition for this is the mimetic devouring of all alternative thinkable identities.

THE REPRESSED IN THE EXTRAVAGANCE

The leaflets are few. The proposition, the message, is nonverbal. The passerby traversed by the ambient thudding, splashed with human flesh on the edge of the flux, must be led to wonder about the link between politics and sexuality and its closeness to her own intimate desire. Faced with a dissymmetric explosion of sexual references around the masculine body, the only true actor in the unbridled mimetic work, the passerby, if it is a woman, experiences the secret exclusion of the feminine as if she were watching a military parade, even if in principle the latter amounts to a political opposite of the Gay Pride parade. In the latter there are only bacchants who borrow recognizable characteristics from all other beings—octopuses, ectoplasms, or also the military—no longer only from feminine women; and the phallus is alone in a world that it occupies entirely, through the whole chain of being, "from the oyster to the angel" (according to Mme du Deffand's expression).

It seems to me that therein lies the source of a particular contemporary reverie that involves straining the eyes of the *flâneur,* and her distance from the scene. A reverie even more full of promise when we consider that the ordinary regime of banal images at the corner of contemporary urban streets, on the screens, and at newspaper kiosks, are indeed the bodies of both sexes showing off their form and their frolicking, their nudity and their simultaneously torrid and glacial sexualities. Such ravishing faces of feminine women on magazine covers, even those that are not

concerned with women! Such well-formed virile bodies in our ads! In normal circumstances the visibility of sexualized bodies is already uncannily dominant, not to
mention novels and films telling us how to do "it." If a society can be defined by what
it pastes on its walls, then the golden, stripped, dazzling figures of femininity and
virility make up the common matter of our other social dreams. But that galoping
demography of images of the sexualized body, so prevalent in contemporary decor,
remains binary. The masculine and the feminine are locked together or in flight one
from the other, face one another or stand in profile, be it against the background of
a coffee cup or on the beach, in all possible contexts, and the promise of their first
meeting, their first kiss, which the whole film keeps in suspense, constitutes the key
scene, the narrative, the final cause.

The use of the human body as a dominant aesthetic form in a given culture is
partly due to the status of sexuality in that same culture. Does that amount to a sul-
phurous sin, an athletic performance, a libertarian experience, a sacred ecstasy, a sane
habit, a duty of the psyche? Is its failure thought of in terms of asceticism, illness,
pathology, a political or moral error? The insult *"mal baisée"* (that is, sexually frustrated) is aptly used to describe the political error made by an ugly old hag who con-
fuses her pathetic frustrations with the world order. The idea is often illustrated at
the movies, where the wicked man or woman is frustrated, impotent, and sadistic.
On the contrary, "true life," belonging to the dazzling beauties on the posters, full of
successful spasms and orgasms, is defined implicitly in that imagery as morally and
politically correct—and politically "liberated"—the ultimate chic.

Gay pride also uses the aesthetic of the sexualized body, but how? And what becomes of the face to face? back to back? side to side? male/female binary divide? The
difference between the sexes as a parameter always forces us to think in terms of
symmetry, inversion, and inequality. Where do we stand in relation to the fight between sexual signs in our sexualized procession? In the army, as in society in general,
the masculine is always the winner; the question of the link between politics and sexuality as aesthetics is a palpable reminder of this. The struggle for freedom of sexual
choice, which constitutes the explicit stakes of this event, nevertheless demands a
tacit acceptance of the disappearance of the ordinary feminine. And with the pretext of abolishing the reign of fascist heterosexuals, of standing against the imposition of one single binary sexual difference between male and female, the parade of
sexualities offers only one icon, a single pillar around which the world's merry-go-
round turns, the male member in all senses of the word.

Translated by Anne-Marie Smith

CHAPTER 10

Chiennes de garde of the World, Unite!
THE BITCH MANIFESTO,
MARCH 8, 1999[1]

We live in a democracy. There is freedom of speech, but not all debates are equal.

Any woman who asserts herself or puts herself forward, runs the risk of being called a "whore." If she is successful, she is suspected of having played couch politics. Every woman in the public eye is judged on her appearance and labeled "motherly," "the maid," a "dyke," a "bimbo," etc.

ENOUGH IS ENOUGH!!

We, members of bitches, have decided to bare our teeth.

Sexist remarks about a woman in the public eye insult all women. We undertake to show our support to women in public life who are insulted as women. We contend that all women must be free in both action and choice. Bitches defend something of great value: the dignity of women.

WARNING

We intend to place the debate on a higher level!
Together! For there is strength in unity. March 8th 1999
No More Sexist Violence!

Every woman in French politics today has received sexist insults, such as "stupid cow," "slag," "bitch," etc., scrawled on their campaign posters and shouted in public or over the telephone: insults in a country that is proud of its tradition of gallantry (which could be viewed as the polite face of sexism) any woman taking an initiative is likely to be treated in this way. (The word prostitute originally meant "exposed.")

When Simone Veil defended a French law on abortion, the key to women's freedom, in 1974, she was insulted; then other women in the public eye, such as Yvette Roudy in 1983 when she wanted to pass an antisexist law, Edith Cresson, who was Prime Minister in 1991, and, more recently, Nicole Notat, the general secretary of one of France's largest trade unions, were all subjected to sexist attacks whose violence was directed at their womanhood.

Recently, machos made sneering remarks such as "vaginal verbosity" when Roselyne Bachelot, a member of parliament, stood up to make a speech, and others told the "Green" minister Dominique Voynet to "take her panties off."

Women politicians—and indeed most other women—are not judged on their capabilities, but too often on their physical appearance alone (adjectives such as "sultry," "charming," "portly," "sensible," etc. are bandied about) and assimilated with a sexual function: ("motherly," "big sister," "dyke," "slag," etc.)

The very rare women in politics before 1974 were not treated with such violence. Most of those in politics shortly after World War II had been active in the Resistance, which probably contributed to the respect they received. The feminism of the seventies, with slogans such as "our bodies ourselves" and "the personal is political" caused a backlash in the antifeminist current, which has always been virulent in France. Now, as in the past, and in France, as elsewhere, those who cannot accept the legitimacy of female participation in decisions on a par with men use violence as a method of reducing all women to invisibility and silence.

In other developed countries, women politicians are not attacked with such machismo. Why is France an exception? Is it because women were originally excluded from the French Republic? It was only on April 21, 1944, that French women obtained the vote, 96 years after the French Republic declared so-called universal suffrage. Unlike in neighboring countries, the number of women elected to the parliament is still ridiculously small.

The Caillaux case in 1914 and the suicide of Roger Salengro in 1936 are two examples of how violent insults and public mud-slinging between male politicians could, in the past, be used to gun down enemies. Evolving attitudes and a growing trend toward lawsuits encouraged a measure of self-control in democratic debate among men in politics. But what about women? Well, from 1981 to 1986, the then Minister of Women's Rights Yvette Roudy accomplished great work, but failed to obtain an antisexist law along the lines of the antiracist law of 1972.

Today, it is up to us, women and men, to make our voices heard in the name of *liberté, égalité, fraternité,* and tolerance. We demand a law against sexism. We demand an in-depth analysis, educational resources, and preventive measures. We want to live in a society in which we can act freely, respecting others and being respected by them.

It would probably be wiser to "be thrifty with one's contempt, for there are so many in need of it," but is it reasonable to hope that mentalities will change uniquely of their own accord, under the beneficial influence of civilization? What if we gave civilization a helping hand?

A sexist insult to a public woman insults all women. It is time we said no and bared our teeth.

Contact us at: bureau@chiennesdegarde.org. Sign the Manifesto! Join our organization! Men welcome.

NOTES

1. Editors' note: The Chiennes de garde (Watch-bitches) was originally created in 1999 in response to sexist insults aimed at women in public office. This manifesto was

signed by a number of prominent French men and women, shocked by the growing verbal violence against women politicians in particular and supporters of the Chiennes de garde's actions. The English translation in this volume can be found at http://www.chiennesdegarde.org/englishmanifesto.html.

CHAPTER 11

New Gendered Mosaics
THEIR MOTHERS, THE GAULS

MIREILLE ROSELLO

In 1999, Valérie Dumeige and Sophie Ponchelet published a volume of interviews with six women whose photographs appear on the cover of the book as six rectangles of equal size. Each one is the subject of one of the six chapters.[1] The short summaries provided before each testimony reveal that two of the young women were born in Senegal, one in Vietnam, one in Algeria, and two in Romania. The status of their nationality varies but they all reside in France permanently and some of them have been in the country for more than 20 years. Across the obviously multiethnic and multicultural collection of portraits, the title stands out, in triumphant, perhaps defiant tall bold letters: **FRANÇAISES [FRENCH WOMEN]** (Dumeige and Ponchelet, 1999).

The fact that the cover and title intertwine nationality, gender, and ethnicity is obviously worth noting as a sign of the times and perhaps as a symptom of the changing relationship between a historically universalist French tradition and two categories (gender and ethnicity) that challenge, in different ways, the utopian ideal of a genderless and, even more persistently, raceless Republican subject. French Feminists of the seventies had loudly called into question the illusory representativity of a supposedly genderless but often male subject. But they had perhaps not as successfully solved the difficulties of what Christine Delphy calls "the management of multiple and irreducible forms of oppressions" that cut across other types of economic or ethnic identification (Delphy 2001, 361). As Delphy puts it in her recent book *L'ennemi principal*, "The smallest common denominator, the 'universal' feminine condition on which the feminist movement based its analyses, has too often been that of the prototypical woman who was often implicitly white, explicitly heterosexual, and some would add 'bourgeois'" (Delphy 2001, 360).[2]

The reduction of women to a "prototypical" heterosexual bourgeois white woman denounced by many feminists now appears as a historically dated proposition, as one specific and nonrepresentative combination of identification markers (Spivak 1992, 1999). Today, it would sound conservative, even old-fashioned to ignore the increasingly audible voices of women who emphasize the diverse national, cultural, or ethnic heritage of all the women who live and work in France.

But which rhetorical and narrative tactics do cultural agents use when they seek to address the issue of multicultural gender within a traditionally but evolving universalist context? Which strategies of representation must contemporary authors invent or adapt once they have decided to pay attention to types of identification markers that were traditionally ignored by Republican discourses?

This essay proposes to focus on two types of narratives generated by individuals who seek to recombine the categories of gender, ethnicity, and nationality. In the first part, I focus on contemporary reconfigurations of what is perceived as France's multiculturalism: descriptions of today's encounters between gender and race belong to the same regime of truth, and they invent the present as much as describe it. A French gendered mosaic gradually emerges, complete with proposals about what is and what should be, what is politically and ethically desirable or undesirable. These visions of the present are only possible because of a reevaluation of the national past, and especially of the last years of the colonial era. The second part of this essay is therefore devoted to what we could call the reinvented genesis of the gendered mosaics. Women whose present and past were assumed from their visible (or invisible) minority status are adding their voice to the mosaic. Their narratives are fascinated by the figure of the mother, or rather by a very specific type of ethnicized and politicized motherhood. These autobiographies participate in the construction of the contemporary gendered mosaic by highlighting aspects of the past that radically changed the mythical perception that the public had of the relationship between typical "French" feminists of the seventies and ethnicity. The factor that remarkably unites both perspectives (in the present and in the past) is that the new parameters affect both "minority women" and women who have always been constructed as "French feminists" and whose ethnicity was considered irrelevant.

I. Contemporary Gendered Mosaics

The presence of new critical parameters appears in new types of arguments or tropes of representation (they are not a function of the speaker's opinion): the same rhetorical tools serve to produce pessimistic as well as optimistic visions. While Dumeige and Ponchelet obviously celebrate what they perceive as the unmistakable existence of new multicultural encounters, others denounce the French resistance to ethnic integration, their racism, and their xenophobia. *Françaises* has a pessimistic counterpart in Calixthe Beyala's *Lettre d'une Afro-Française à ses compatriotes,* an angry denunciation of the limits of universalism (Beyala 2000). The book was written in the wake of the public controversy started in February 2000, when the famous novelist of Cameroonian origin staged a well-calculated interruption of the twenty-fifth annual "night of the Césars," the highly ritualized equivalent of the American Oscars. Accompanied by Luc Saint-Eloy, a Caribbean playwright, comedian, and director,[3] she interrupted the live ceremony attended by a large audience of media celebrities and also by political and administrative decision makers.[4] They both read from a prepared statement critiquing the lack of adequate representation of "visible minorities" in French television programs, and demanding "a genuine representative of France's multiracial reality in all the medias."[5]

Both speakers presented themselves as two "black" people. For Saint-Eloy and Beyala, origin was obviously less significant than blackness, itself presented as a metaphor for other historically marked races.[6] In the book, Beyala (more or less accurately) remembers the content of their speech:

> During the Césars' ceremony, on February 19 2000, Luc Saint Eloy—a director—and myself read the following statement:
> Imagine a world where television and movie screens would only show you stories exclusively about blacks, for blacks with blacks, and no other color. Imagine a country where billboards only display products made by blacks for blacks with blacks.[7]

The Collectif Egalité, an organization founded by Beyala, Saint-Eloy, and others in 1998, had started a public debate that resonated long after the unexpected event. They triggered predictably hostile responses (as well as some interesting initiatives and comments) because they advocated a form of affirmative action that was interpreted as un-French and typically American. They recommended what Beyala calls "QDD" (*quota à durée déterminée*), a temporary system of quotas that would increase the representation of minorities in the media. Even if many commentators opposed the notion, the whole episode generated a French discussion about a type of identity politics that theorizes ethnicity and race as components of the Republican subject.

Interestingly enough, neither Beyala nor Saint-Eloy mentions gender. And yet, Beyala's spectacular performance and her subsequent public interviews make it impossible to erase that variable of the equation especially since their argument is about "visibility." Beyala makes it clear that she wants to be a spokesperson for a whole community, which reverses the typical assumption that the masculine stands for the group. Her female body cannot be interpreted according to historical constructions that treat men as nonmarked. Whether it was formulated or not, a famous black woman who insists that she is an "Afro-Française" embodies the ideas of the Collectif Égalité.

And clearly, the issue of how visibility is articulated is one of the major questions raised by the new debate: recognizing that what was once invisible is now culturally relevant is only a beginning. Examining *how* gender, ethnicity, and nationality intersect remains to be done. For example, we could ask to what extent Ponchelet and Dumeige's book or Beyala's desire for better representation of "visible minorities" correspond or not to what Delphy calls an anti-imperialist approach. Both parties are obviously making a point about the definition of "Frenchness" as marked by ethnicity as well as gender. Ponchelet and Dumeige are not treating the six "Françaises" as a remarkable collection of individuals worthy of study because they are marginals. This mosaic is not to be read as an exception to the rule of Frenchness although the very design of the cover may be interpreted as a provocative statement.

In *Françaises,* a gendered and ethnicized Frenchness is presented as an absence of shared attributes, an *unimagined* community to adapt Anderson's phrase (Anderson 1991): what the six women have in common is that they have no predictable or stereotypical French quality and no strictly hexagonal French past in common. In other words, their "ancestors" or foremothers cannot serve as guarantee. Besides, they are the exact opposite of the (obsolete but still recognizable) *béret-baguette* icon, especially if, under the *béret,* we visualize a white man.

But are we expected to judge the book by its cover, and French mentalities by *that* cover? For even if we agree that this kind of verbal and visual statement can be treated as an emblem of what is going on in France today (a representation both of

French society and an example of the French people's discourse on their own culture), the picture remains a complex and multilayered text. It would therefore be dismissive to automatically celebrate it as anti-imperialistic without first formulating exactly what constitutes desirable progress in the discursive, political, and cultural universe where gender, ethnicity, and nation meet. Suspicious cultural critics may point out that the gathering of different races under the same flag is not to be unconditionally celebrated. If unacknowledged invisibility is most often a form of disempowerment, visibility as such is no guarantee of enfranchisement, even if the book invites us to consider the women's mere presence—their being-there as visibly ethnic female subjects—as the main point of the image.

We know that a racially encoded portrait on a cover or on a flyer can serve a number of political purposes and that colonial history books contain their share of multicultural posters used to publicize imperial projects. There was a time when the representation of several races would have been a form of colonial propaganda, a vision of the Greater France spreading from Dunkerque to Tamanrasset. For colonial visual art was not systematically male-centered either: even if posters used to recruit colonial subjects into the French military did address an exclusively male audience by representing only men,[8] even if some iconic representations of male faces allegorized the presence of all human races in the colonies, some (male) artists such as Jules Cheret or David Dellepiane chose to symbolize the multiracial nature of colonial exhibitions by drawing black or brown women dressed in traditional costumes. Of course, colonial representations of women were not necessarily feminist either, as exoticism was also a form of voyeuristic consumption.[9] In the real world, the encounter portrayed by Dellepiane would have been unrealistic and the women he represented would have had no opportunity to meet each other. And in the absence of a common or at least compatible project that links all its elements together, a mosaic can remain a meaningless collection of self-contained solitudes.

It is historically significant that Beyala, Ponchelet, or Dumeige do not need to distance themselves from that type of representation: between 1922 and 1999, the issue of visibility and culturalism, of racialization and republicanism, has shifted so radically that today, conservative (and antifeminist) discourses are more likely to be found on the side of radical universalism than on the side of multiculturalism (Wiewiorka 2001). The lack of self-consciousness exhibited by the proud mosaic of faces of *Françaises* is already a comment on the fact that the authors are not afraid of being misread as the uncritical heirs of past colonial thinkers. And it is interesting to note that their cover inherits the traces of but also moves away from this colonial heritage: here multiracial encounters are not *only* a reminder of France's imperial history, although there is no attempt to erase it either. The Algerian (Naïma Kouadria), Senegalese (N'Deye Binta Dia and Oumy Dia), and Vietnamese nationals (Anne N'Guyen) have chosen France as their land of emigration partly as a consequence of the traces left by colonization, but two of the young women are outside of that postcolonial logic. Livia Cristina and Silvia Viana, both refugees from Romania, modify our perception of the direct relationship between immigration and colonization. As a result, their story has an impact on our stereotypes about the definition of majority and minority ethnicity: here, two of the "immigrants" are Eastern Europeans and they are also white women. This is the type of mosaic that popular culture as a whole is also beginning to represent.[10] In other words, whiteness now appears as a visible "color" and the definition of "ethnicity" is shown not to overlap with origin. If

France cannot be assumed to be uniformly white, whiteness does not have to be un-remarkably French either. The vindication of one's origin, the preservation of one's cultural memory, cannot be reduced to the issue of visibility and both ethnicity and origin have to be part of the narrative.

2. MOTHERHOOD AND ETHNICITY

When this new multicultural approach involves a reevaluation of the past rather than a description of the contemporary French mosaic, other types of texts obtain: a remarkable collection of autobiographical filmic or literary narratives are adding his-torical depth to works anchored in the immediate present. As Delphy puts it: "Many feminists' re-discovery of their own cultural history marks their opposition to that underlying imperialism" (360).[11] These autobiographies are written by women who are either perceived as "women of minority origin" or known as "French feminists" but their texts precisely undermine this opposition: when they look back on their past, many authors tell a story that either subverts the difference between the two categories or demonstrates that our assumptions about some women's origins were misconceptions.

This recombination of identification markers works both ways: on the one hand, some women's investment in the future of (hexagonal) France forces their public to rethink the significance that it implicitly attributes to their ethnicity and foreign origin; but on the other, some famous French feminists, whose origin was never under scrutiny, now emphasize their colonial past by telling the story of their non-hexagonal childhood. The vast majority of these autobiographical quests could be described as an interest in and search for foremothers: most revolve around the fig-ure of the mother or of the grandmother, whose pivotal influence has left indelible cultural marks.

One of the most visible representatives of the former category is Yamina Ben-guigui whose work deals with the memory of the (male and female) Algerian immi-grant community. A successful journalist, author, and filmmaker whose popular documentaries have been shown on television and in movie theaters, she is also a very modest and unheroic public figure who describes herself as a facilitator, not as a liberator or a Pelean poet like Aimé Césaire in Martinique. Yet, her goal was to "liberate" the voice of many other daughters of Algerian immigrants and of their mothers. Although her work can been seen as a point of discontinuity that separates a before and an after, a silence and the possibility of storytelling, she makes no great claim, and does not advocate a revolutionary poetics: instead, she collects life stories and she films members of the Algerian immigrant community. Her mission is to a help the French public (including that community) discover or remember the tra-jectory of Maghrebi women who came to France to live with their husbands at the time when the vast majority of (male) migrant workers still lived in shantytowns around French cities. Thanks to the widely successful *Mémoires d'immigrés*, the "moth-ers" of the so-called first generation of immigrants recognized their own untold story as they listened to the women interviewed by Benguigui.[12]

The life of middle-aged women of North African origin has apparently not been radically transformed by a decade of "Beur" literature and cinema that put their (often male) children in the limelight. Benguigui worked as a historian but

also embarked on a process of autobiographical self-discovery: through the montage of a series of interviews with women who were her mother's age (but not her
own mother, precisely), she was able to discover what her parents had gone
through. They had not been able to transmit their story directly to their off-
spring.[13] And if Benguigui's first documentary (*Femmes d'islam*) focuses mostly on
women, her subsequent *Mémoires d'immigrés* is capable of taking into account the difference made by gender in two generations of migrants: when she interviews her
elders, the filmmaker feels the need to distinguish between the "fathers" and the
"mothers" whose experience was historically distinct.[14]

The most striking feature of her role as a historian is that rather than speak for
her community, Benguigui works at modifying the relationship between the author
of documentaries and her public, that is, between herself as a daughter and all the
mothers with whom she has a chance to interact when she presents her work. During an interview shown on Canal + (*Nulle part ailleurs*), she explains that her public is
often composed of Maghrebi families and that during the time normally reserved for
"questions," after the show, her audience tends to switch to another genre and to establish a new type of relationship with her. Instead of asking the type of questions
that a journalist would ask a professional filmmaker, the mothers typically tell their
own life-story and a sort of collective exchange of memories starts spontaneously.
Benguigui both talks about her past and liberates the mothers' words.

To explain how they launch into the story of their own arrival in France, Benguigui quotes them as they address her: "*Ah ma fille, moi*. . . ." If a journalist or a bourgeois male spectator had asked the question, they could obviously not have addressed
Benguigui as "*ma fille*" (daughter). It would be meaningless at best, even disrespect-
ful. When Benguigui appears on television as the author of her films, she is a French
professional filmmaker and a historian, an artist and an intellectual. But for the
mothers, she has another function as well, she is a catalyst: the "*ma fille*," is not a reference to biology, it is not exactly the equivalent of "my daughter" although the generational gap and the existence of a type of symbolic filiation is also marked in that
way. For Benguigui and for the spectator, the intimate "*ma fille*" is a reference to the
fact that both the mothers and this filmmaker belong to a community that uses
French in a special way. But it also insists on the role of "motherhood" in the creation of historical discourses. The daughter ventriloquizes the mother's tongue, so
that her French public can hear it.

Here, the "daughter" engenders. Just as Assia Djebar points out that, in certain
cases, the mother must learn her daughter's language instead of always trying to rediscover her foremother's linguistic roots (Djebar 227). Benguigui's mothers listen
to her way of telling stories, discover her narrative before being able to speak about
and for themselves. The mother's tongue does not preexist the daughter's language.
And once the symbolic filial link is recognized, the "mothers" as mothers can start
telling their stories to themselves, to their real daughters, and, ultimately, to the public at large. Their story adds new layers to the cultural figure of the "mother" and
complicates the reference to fictional mothers who have appeared in the autobiographies produced by the first generation of Beur authors of the 1980s.

Naturally, just as Ponchelet and Dumeige's cover is haunted by the ghosts of colonial images, Benguigui's work sometimes encounters old fault lines between and
within communities. Her sometimes unpredictable alternance between "we" and
"you" when she talks about "the French," "France," or the immigrant community

complicates the reception of her discourse. For some, she probably occupies the ambiguous place of the native informant, or of the mediator who builds bridges between a white French Christian majority and the immigrant community of other "mothers." But it is becoming more difficult to categorize her as the exceptionally hybrid other: she is only one of the voices that talk about the mothers of contemporary French citizens. A whole other collection of new portraits suggests that ethnicity and cultural difference were always already a reality that some did not know how to factor into the cultural French equation: we cannot simply assume that Benguigui's "mothers" are from Algeria and therefore exceptional. Although she tends to say "we" when she talks about the community of Algerian immigrants, she always insists that what happened to the Maghrebi community that immigrated to France after World War II is an integral part of French history, a history that each French citizen (of any origin) should be taught if France is to invest in a common future.

When asked to review *Vivre au paradis,* a film made by Boualem Guerdjou from Benaïcha's autobiographical novel,[15] she states: "That film is not exclusively made for Maghrebis or for the Algerians who lived in shantytowns. October 17, 1961, is your problem, it is for you, it is part of your history, a page of France's history that has been completely erased by society and by us but we can no longer . . . we cannot invest in the future today without this resurgence of memory."[16]

And it is clear that women who have recently let their ethnic, religious, and national origin organize the narrative that they make of their identity are not necessarily newcomers or recently immigrated individuals. Nor are they always female bodies that the media would identify as ethnically marked. And their feminism is theoretically very different from that of the seventies: they are less focused on patriarchal realities, on the opposition between the feminine and the masculine. They no longer attempt to theorize the female body as a different type of "mechanics" (as Luce Irigaray did in the 1970s); they no longer make specific claims regarding the specificity of a feminine voice or "écriture" (Irigaray 1974, 1977, Marks & de Courtivron). Their discipline of predilection is the intersection between history and testimony, a discursive space that allows them to blend together textual or visual elements culminating in the *mise en scène* of bodies that are both very strongly gendered (male or female) and ethnicized. This rhetorical and ideological choice illuminates their vision of the present but also of the past: as they look back on their own cultural antecedents, they create a gendered (rather than or as well as gynocentric) narrative that retrospectively illuminates the obscured aspects of their heritage. The "Gaullois" ancestors mocked by postcolonial thinkers slowly reemerge as gendered and ethnicized bodies, as a generation of mothers slowly emerges from the colonial fog.

At least two of the feminist figures whose voices have been historically associated with French feminism are involved in the engendering of a long overlooked colonial past, and in the ethnicization of their own French history. For Gisèle Halimi and Hélène Cixous, the mother's body is constructed as a complex puzzle of ethnic and gendered elements, and their stories, like Benguigui's memories, acknowledge France's relationship with the African continent.

On the cover of Gisèle Halimi's *Fritna* (Halimi 1999), a tall, barefoot, dark-haired woman looks at the reader: she is the author's mother. Halimi's selection of the picture is reinforced by the words she uses to describe it. She focuses on the "black light of her Jewish Spanish eyes . . . [her] Bedouin's clothes, her long dark hair sliding all the way down to her loins, enormous dangling earrings, a clay pot on her back, attached by a piece of string around her forehead—we called it 'gargoulette' . . ." (Halimi 1999, 15–16).[17]

Halimi's public persona has not always foregrounded those specifically ethnic or cultural parts of her heritage. The internationally famous French feminist is best known for cofounding the association Choisir with Simone de Beauvoir and for her successful legal struggles in favor of women's reproductive rights in the 1970s.[18] And at present, she is involved in the political battle for parité, of which she is one of the earliest and most determined advocates (Martin 1998, Corbett 2001). One significant stage of her activist career did however have a strong North African component since it was directly motivated by the war of Algeria and anticolonial struggles in the 1960s: historians remember that Halimi was Djamila Boupacha's lawyer when the young Algerian woman was tortured by the French military.[19] Neither censorship during the war nor the subsequent years of amnesia alienated her from the past that Benguigui's public needs to (re)discover. If Benguigui wishes to help children of immigrants recapture a past that no one transmitted to them, interestingly enough, Halimi's work could be said to be part of that legacy.

And yet, another version of that same past would tend to perceive the two women as the representatives of the two sides: "France" and "the Maghreb." In some constructions of the real, Halimi's activism could be constructed as a typically hexagonal venture, a fight for universal rights that a "French" woman fought with a small cohort of French intellectuals such as Jean-Paul Sartre, Simone de Beauvoir, Pierre Vidal-Naquet, or Paul Maspero. From that perspective, Halimi's anti-imperialism predates what Delphy analyzes as a more recent phenomenon (the "rediscovery" of cultural roots) and the current proliferation of memoirs on the Algerian war. But the Boupacha case story can be seen as a symbolic alliance between the West and the East, a woman from the "West" and a woman from the "Third World." The deliberate and almost theatrical ethnicization of the mother's figure makes a different point that the reader must interpret or reflect upon even before opening the autobiography.

The image of Fritna as bédouine does not so much blur national and ethnic boundaries as encourage us to acknowledge our assumptions about such frontiers: readers who are surprised by the portrait would have to admit that they had, unconsciously, entertained other fantasies of what Halimi's mother looked like. Familiar conventions are at work here: the costume, the pose, and the grain of the old photograph evoke the atmosphere of those exotic postcards that Malek Alloula had decided to send "back" to the colonizers in The Colonial Harem (Alloula 1981). At the same time, the trajectory of such a picture is much more complicated than a simple "return to the sender" and the layers of identification provided by the costume, the props, the body, as well as by the paratextual apparatus of the book cover propose a recombination of the concepts of origin, ethnicity, and politicized visions of femininity. After the mother's death, Halimi paints a portrait that provocatively underscores the contradictory nature of Fritna's political opinions.

For it would of course be an error to conclude, from Fritna's appearance, that she simply belonged to the "other side." The picture does not pretend to finally give access to a long hidden truth: Fritna may physically resemble Benguigui's mothers, but this newly found "origin" does not explain why Halimi and Benguigui's feminist positions are politically or ideologically similar at the beginning of the third millennium. If Benguigui's mission is to reconstitute a broken link with her own mother(s), Halimi's narrative emphasizes discontinuities between Fritna and herself. In both cases, the mother's legacy is problematic and sometimes painful, and in both cases, exile, migration, cultural and religious otherness play an important role in the construction of an ethnicized and nationalized motherhood. Benguigui, whom a stereotypical perception would construct as the native Algerian informant, was precisely not born in the Maghreb and has to rediscover her mother's heritage. On the contrary, Halimi's Tunisian roots are clear childhood memories, but readers will need her testimony in order to reethnicize her mother's body and to understand what was transmitted by Fritna. Halimi's feminist work has to be replaced in the context of a colonial childhood: she grew up in Tunisia, the daughter of a Jew of Spanish origin married to a "Berber Bedouin [whose] . . . ancestors lived under a tent" (Halimi 1999, 50).[20]

From a political point of view, Fritna is the ultimate countermodel: the book describes an unsupportive and sometimes downright hostile mother. The daughter's anticolonial sentiments cannot be said to have been simply inherited or strengthened by a rediscovery of the past. One chapter reveals that Fritna even used her daughter's political activism as the ingredient of a little family myth that served to encode her as a bad mother: after Fritna's death, the daughter and/as narrator must fight the power of insidiously transmitted narratives. Halimi's own sons apparently believe the grand-mother's version that Gisèle Halimi neglected her children: "Yes, as she kept repeating, 'your mother prefers to defend Arabs rather than look after you'" (79).[21] And as in Benguigui's documentary, each use of "you" and "them" both underscores the constant risk of separation, fragmentation, and exclusion, and provides the place of a mediation where each social agent can participate in the overall picture. Fritna's beautifully ethnicized portrait is also that of a fervent colonialist, and her construction of "Frenchness" excludes the types of bodies that we think we have recognized when we see her photograph on the cover.

> Fritna was never a political genius, and that is an understatement. Her passionately expressed opinions owed much to other people's tales, to others' choices, to stereotypes . . . My mother always remembered all of the racist clichés imported by colonization: dirty, thieves, lazy, "they" would never be able to lead a country. If they had power, what would they do to us those "natives" (my mother sometimes used the word to sound more chic and more objective at the same time)? And the "we" included the French, the Jews, the Italians. In a nutshell, the Whites. Civilized vs. Barbarians. (70)[22]

Like politically ambivalent multicultural mosaics, the rediscovery of one's historical roots and the mother's ethnic and culturally hybrid heritage explains nothing: the narrator must interpret, transform the past into a legible legacy. In 1999, Fritna's opinions are clearly identified as mistakes that "they" (the colonialists) made: different "we" and different "they" now exist that have to be reconciled with the "we" of communities constructed by other French women such as Benguigui. The "us" as conceptualized by Halimi's mother is sealed off by quotation marks and explicitly repudiated. The novelty is not so much that Fritna's daughter never agreed with her mother but that her text gives us an opportunity to view the "mothers" as the pieces of another, earlier mosaic. Fritna and Benguigui's interviewees are different facets of the same past. Mother-daughter relationships are envisaged through the filter of a very specific history: the relationship between France and the Maghreb at the time of the protectorate. The specificity of the female condition does not disappear and divergences among women are here highlighted: Halimi's autobiography seeks to correct the mother's narrative and she reiterates a feminist position that contemporary thinkers will most probably take for granted: caretaking does not have to be incompatible with political and anticolonial work. But *Fritna* also warns us against any idealization of the ethnic mother's figure.

Hélène Cixous's recent work also emphasizes the role of the mother, of colonialism, and of ethnic and cultural identity, but it offers a unique recombination of the factors that we have seen at work in Benguigui's and Halimi's work. In *Rêveries de la femme sauvage*, Cixous focuses on her Algerian childhood and more specifically, on the role of her mother as a woman and (subtle) political figure during the war of independence. The mother portrayed in this autobiography occupies and defines a more optimistic (although utopian) position where universalism and local politics are recombined and woven into what we could call a politics of international motherhood.

Like Halimi, Cixous looks back on a childhood that took place away from Parisian circles, those supposedly ethereal spheres that critics of French feminism suspect of elitism and Eurocentrism. Long associated with the "laugh of the Medusa" and the first wave of "écriture féminine," Cixous joined a more recent cultural movement when she started exploring her North African roots, her multicultural and Jewish upbringing in colonial Oran and Alger. Her recent autobiographical texts are marked by what she calls her "Algeriance," a process of always deferred arrival or departure, the impossibility to ever be from an Algeria severed from itself by the violence of colonialism. Like Benguigui and Halimi, Cixous must interrogate the highly unstable "we" that unites or separates members of always rearranged communities.

Cixous, whose father was stripped of his civil rights and professional identity during World War II, knows that Fritna's civilized "we" was illusory and deceptive (Cixous 1999). As a Jew, the immigrant father and French citizen could not count on the stability of universalist principles. For Cixous, no "we" is ever a given. No solidarity between any members of any (gendered, religious, national) group seems possible, yet, no separation is possible either: she is, herself, "*inséparabe*" (89). Fragmentation, racism, and anti-Semitism come first, like a disease. What is "foundational" is racism, which the narrator equates to a pillar, the base of French society, (43) and to which "one must add anti-semitisms whose forms, naturally, add up" (43).[23] The Father is not "French," he is an "arabizarre" (46).

And yet, in this text, the figure of the mother constitutes a most unexpected allegory of hope capable of transcending the violence of a diseased country. If Fritna is perceived as the mother who expects her daughter to choose between family and politics, between, in a sense, (a simplistic notion of) ethnicity and (a conservative definition of) gender, the mother of *Rêveries* strangely reintroduces a sort of always defeated yet admirable universalism.

If Benguigui's mothers help the daughter learn about cultural differences that the daughter's French identity may have masked, Cixous's trajectory is almost reversed: as a little girl, Cixous perceives her native land as an impossible origin, a place from which she was always excluded. Benguigui's hope is that the discovery of a distinct past will be the precondition to some sort of imaginary investment in the national hybrid (French) future, while *Rêveries* presents the past as always already doomed: as if to deny the possibility of either closure or progress, the book begins and ends with the same sentence: "as long as I lived in Algeria, I dreamed of once arriving in Algeria."[24] The child's pessimism is absolute: in colonial Algeria, relationships between communities are tragic: they can only lead to unspeakable violence. No mosaic, no *métissage* is even imaginable. The metaphor of land as mother is powerfully reinterpreted and the multicultural colonial city becomes a "nest" whose eggs already contain the seed of disasters to come. Alger is described as a "a giant and multicolored egg-holder shaped as a hen hatching eggs of war" (41).[25] Arabs, Jews, *pieds-noirs,* men, women and children are instantaneously transformed into "guilty or contaminated accomplices victims" (41).[26]

In Cixous's work, the lucid vision of catastrophic colonial cohabitation is not redeemed by hopes in a decolonized *métissé* future. The mosaic breeds hatred. And the only positive reconfiguration of differences is presented as the vision, the dream of a quietly idealistic mother who is bent on ignoring gender, nationality, and ethnicity. In that inextricable knot of hostilities, only the character of the mother is (at least temporarily) capable of creating another type of imagined communities: after her husband's death, Cixous's mother decides to train as a midwife and the daughter's book describes her new profession as a stubborn, fragile enterprise of political resistance to colonialism.

The narrator neither embraces the tactics nor condemns the mother's idealism and although she does relate the tragic end of the experiment, she carefully documents its implausible triumphs over hatred. The mother refuses to acknowledge that she is surrounded by "eggs of war" and creates her own nest, the "Clinique" where she delivers babies: "One would come here to be born, naked. A unique place and time where humankind has no other goal than to, extraordinarily, come to life" (41).[27]

The mother is not interested in hybridity and unlike Fritna, she does not draw any comfort from the illusions of identification. Her strategy is described as a form of selective blindness to violence, to ethnic and racial categories: "From the top of a tree or the roof of Clos-Salembier, from 1946 to 1956 we saw everything that my mother, down in her nest, did not see" (43).[28] The mother actively refuses to think in terms of nations, not because she is convinced, like Fritna, that she is "French" or that she is on the side of civilization but because she is capable, as her daughter explains, to rebuild "a nest within exile itself" (58).[29] "As a midwife, I have always been international on my own side. The baby is an international newborn. At the Clinic, there were always two doors and they were always open" (107).[30]

In this text, the mother is not simply the biological body who gives birth to her children: she treats motherhood as a professional responsibility. Even if her intervention is ultimately defeated by other forces—including a narrow interpretation of nationalism—her definition of motherhood links the clinic to the foundation of a borderless state. The mother's body as metaphor of the first frontier, of the "door" that children must cross in order to step into their identity as citizen of a nation is here replaced by the two doors of the clinic, which are always open.

Of course, the "international" midwife's personal tragedy and the pessimistic message of the autobiography as a whole is that Cixous's mother cannot deliver her own children who remain trapped between warring communities. The clinic's two "open doors" are closed to them and she cannot give them access to this egalitarian world that she wishes to construct from naked international newborns. If Halimi could rebel against her mother's clearly stated xenophobia, Cixous's mother's children cannot inherit her blindness, her internationalism: "Once born at the Clinic, that is, in our own house, all those children stepped into Algeria, whereas we, who had been born there (yet not at the Clinic) we could not follow them, we were not admitted" (58).[31]

CONCLUSION

Daughters who liberate their mothers' words, mothers who learn the daughters' language instead of rediscovering the mother's tongue, mothers who reject nationalism and invent utopian forms of motherhood, mothers who fantasize themselves as *Françaises de souche* [native-born French women] in spite of their daughter's narratives: contemporary figures of motherhood invite the reader to formulate a de-universalized reinterpretation of gendered filiations. In *Fritna* and *Mémoires d'immigrés*, motherhood is not a biological fatality, the source of women's subjection that all feminists must rethink through their fight for reproductive choices or their repositioning of female civic role. It is defined by the politics of a given historical moment and by the ways in which a generation defines race, community, and ethnic identity in general. Even Cixous's *Rêveries de la femme sauvage*, which could be said to propose a unique re-universalizing of the mother's position as international anticolonialist, is presented as poetic utopia.

Added to new gendered visions of a contemporary French mosaic, these texts invite us to try out recombinations of the concepts of gender, nationality, and ethnicity that sometimes overlap or compete with each other, and sometimes ignore each other. As the controversy triggered by the Collectif Egalité demonstrates, the spectacular encounter between one word, "*Françaises*," and many images of "*Françaises*" proposed by recent cultural events is no evidence that the entities known as "France," "feminism," and "multiculturalism" have suddenly and for the first time reorganized into a happy French multicultural feminism. But the way in which new images and cultural events define the terms of the debate invites us to try a recombination of elements that we can no longer legitimately isolate or subordinate to studies on gender, nationalism, or ethnicity. They suggest that the relationship between each "*Française*" and her past is to be discovered rather than presupposed.

Such texts also invite the readers to redraw the disciplinary boundaries of "feminism": they suggest that it is not productive to construct "minority women" or "women of immigrant origin" as a coherent object of study that could be analyzed separately from the rest of "French gender studies." It is no longer unproblematic to assume that ethnic or national identities are "visible" or that they will tell us much about priorities or discursive strategies. Because certain "affairs" (the headscarf affair, the issue of excision, the debate on polygamy) continue to be perceived as issues concerning only a small (ethnic) minority of women, while others (the issue of "*parité*") seem to exclude a discussion of ethnicity, alliances remain mostly unformulated between agents involved in different types of struggle. Yet, I would suggest that the most remarkable elements of the different types of discourses generated by the women of the *métissé* Hexagon are their points of often unformulated convergence.

The existence of similar nodes of divergences and disagreements within discourses that otherwise ignore each other may provide the observer with an image of the various trends of new contemporary gender discourses, whether or not they affect the majority of French women or a given minority: some version of the differ-

ence between "republicanism" and "communitarism" (Wiewiorka 2001, 9) or "egalitarian" vs. "differentialist" (Servan-Schreiber 36) feminism reappears in most of the
texts analyzed in this essay. It is more difficult today to assume that such "minority
women" or "women of color" would collectively author a certain type of minority
feminist discourse. The view that "French feminisms" is a unique (albeit multiple)
discursive formation within which we can study a subcategory identified—or imagined—as the feminism of women of immigrant or ethnic minority origin might soon
be obsolete since a gendered and ethnicized mosaic has started operating according
to other logics of fragmentation.

NOTES

1. Scholars interested in Beur culture will remember that Sophie Ponchelet and Aïcha
   Benaïssa published a book entitled *Née en France: histoire d'une jeune Beur* later turned into
   a television film, *Leïla born in France.*
2. "Le plus petit dénominateur commun, la situation féminine 'universelle,' sur lequel le
   mouvement a construit ses analyses, a été trop souvent en réalité celui d'une femme
   prototypique implicitement blanche, explicitement hétérosexuelle, certains
   ajouteraient 'bourgeoise.'" (360) Although Delphy's position may sound relatively
   compatible with the critiques generated in an Anglo-Saxon context, it is worth noting that she considers "French feminism" to be a "product made in the USA" (325), a
   deceptive corpus of short disparate texts that have allowed Anglo-American academics to systematically misread, misunderstand, and distort the reality of "féminisme
   français" (from which she excludes, for example, Hélène Cixous and Julia Kristeva).
   See also "France, Amérique: regards croisés sur le féminisme," *Nouvelles questions femi-
   nistes* 17. 1 (1996).
3. Beyala and Saint-Eloy are two of the cofounders of the Collectif Egalité, an association created in 1998 and whose goal is to promote the recruitment of actors and journalists of color in the media.
4. The Minister of Culture, Catherine Trautman and Hervé Bourges, president of the
   National Council of the Audiovisual (CSA) with whom the Collectif had already had
   discussions, were in the audience.
5. "Une véritable représentation de la réalité multiraciale de la France dans tous les médias" See Jane Freedman and Carrie Tarr 2000. The authors refer to an article published in *Télérama* in 1999: "En France l'égalité se fait attendre" (Delassale 1999). The
   Collectif Egalité's activities had already been mentioned several times in *Le Monde*, especially in one of the weekly supplements devoted to "métissage" in the media (see
   Humblot and Labe 1999).
6. For example they made no allusion to Africa or the Caribbean.
7. "Lors de la remise des Césars, le 19 février 2000, Luc Saint-Eloy—metteur en scène—
   et moi-même, lisions ces phrases:

   Imaginez un monde où les écrans de télévision et de cinéma projetteraient exclusivement des histories de Noirs, pour des Noirs avec des Noirs, à l'exclusion de toute autre couleur. Imaginez un pays dont tous les murs seraient
   habillés exclusivement de produits fabriqués par des Noirs, pour des Noirs
   avec des Noirs. (70)

8. Note that today, the exclusively male focus would not go without saying even in an
   equivalent context. (See the national police recruitment campaign shown on French
   television in 2000 to encourage people of color and women to apply.)

9. See especially the poster he made for the "Exposition Coloniale" held in Marseilles in 1922 where two young women seem to symbolize Sub-Saharan Africa and the former "Indochina."

10. If the first "banlieue films" of the 1980s concentrated mostly on young men and on the "black blanc beur" trio (where the "blanc" character was often Jewish as in *La Haine*), the cinema of the 1990s is more varied and less systematic. See for example the almost exclusively female cast of Mehdi Charef's *Marie-line*, which tells the story of a team of female characters who have come from the Maghreb, from Sub-Saharan Africa, or from Eastern Europe.

11. "C'est le refus de cet impéralisme sous-jacent que manifeste la redécouverte par beaucoup de feminists de leur spécificité culturelle."

12. *Mémoires d'immigrés* was also published as a book of interviews. See Durmelat and Rosello in Freedman and Tarr (2000). Since then, Benguigui has directed *Inch Allah Dimanche* (2001), in which the main protagonists are the "mothers" interviewed in the second part of *Mémoires d'immigrés*.

13. See *Nulle part ailleurs,* a television program devoted to Yamina Benguigui on the evening preceding the presentation of *Mémoires d'immigrés* on Canal + (May 29, 1997). Benguigui must regularly answer questions about her own father from whom she has been estranged for many years.

14. In their introduction to *Women, Immigration and Identities in France,* Jane Freedman and Carrie Tarr suggest that specifically gendered issues among a growing immigrant population were at first often downplayed due to the overwhelming majority of male migrant workers. Family reunion, which was a by-product of the closing of borders to migrant workers, altered the sociological and demographical realities after 1974 (Freedman and Tarr 2000, 1–10). Benguigui's decision to separate men and women is not systematic: she does not make the same distinction between the "sons" and "daughters" (the last chapter of the documentary deals with "the children") but she makes sure to select both male and female interviewees in that part. Given her meticulous attention to gender, this decision constitutes a historical statement.

15. *Vivre au paradis: d'une oasis à un bidonville* is the story of a boy who spent his childhood in the Algerian *bidonville* of Nanterre (Benaïcha 1992). "Le journal du cinéma du mercredi," Canal + (February 4, 1998).

16. "Ce film-là, il n'est pas que pour les Maghrébins ou les Algériens qui ont vécu dans les bidonvilles, le 17 octobre 61 ça vous concerne, c'est pour vous, c'est un pan de votre histoire c'est un pan de l'histoire de France qui a été entièrement occulté et par la société et par nous, mais on ne peut plus . . . on ne peut pas pas investir le futur aujourd'hui s'il n'y a pas ce retour de mémoire."

17. " . . . la lumière noire de ses yeux de Juive espagnole, . . . ses cheveux sombres glissant jusqu'aux reins, d'immenses anneaux aux oreilles, une jarred (on disait une gargoulette) de terre attachée au dos, tenue par une coredellet sur la tête . . ."

18. One of the most famous cases tried by Halimi is the so-called Bobigny trial during which she defended a young woman, Marie-Claire Chevalier, accused of having sought an illegal abortion after being raped (1972).

19. See *Djamila Boupacha,* prefaced by Simone de Beauvoir, originally published in 1962.

20. "Bédouin, berbère . . . ses ancêtres vivaient sous la tente."

21. "Oui, comme elle le répétait souvent, 'Votre mère préfère défendre les Arabes que de s'occuper de vous!'" (79)

22. "Le moins qu'on puisse dire c'est que Fritna n'a jamais été une tête politique. Ses opinions, assénées avec passion, tenaient aux récits des uns, aux choix des autres, beaucoup aux idées reçues. . . . De tous les poncifs racistes que la colonisation avait importés, ma mère n'en oubliait aucun. Sales menteurs, voleurs, paresseux, 'ils' seraient bien incapables de tenir un pays. Ces 'indigènes' (ma mère utilisait quelquefois le terme, pour

faire plus chic et plus objectif à la fois), s'ils avaient le pouvoir, que feraient-ils de nous? Ce 'nous' englobait Français, Juifs, Italiens. Blancs, en un mot. La civilisation contre la barbarie." (70)

23. "Il faut ajouter les antisémitismes, lesquels naturellement s'additionnent entre eux."(43)

24. "Tout le temps que je vivais en Algérie, je rêvais d'arriver un jour en Algérie. . . ." (Cixous 2000, 9–168)

25. "Un coquetier géant et bigarré en forme de poule qui couve des oeufs de guerre."

26. " . . . victime complice coupable ou contaminé." (41)

27. "Ici on entrait pour naître nu. Unique lieu et moment où il n'est point d'autre but pour l'humanité que venir, chose extraordinaire, au jour." (41)

28. "Perchés sur un arbre ou sur le toit du Clos-Salembier de 1946 à 1956 nous voyions tout ce que ma mère en bas dans son nid ne voyait pas." (43)

29. " . . . un nid dans l'exil même. . . ." (58)

30. "En tant que sage femme j'ai toujours été internationale de mon côté. Le bébé est un nouveau-né international. A la Clinique il y avait deux portes qui étaient toujours ouvertes." (107)

31. "Une fois nés à la Clinique, donc dans notre maison, tous ces enfants entraient en Algérie tandis que nous qui y étions nés, mais pas à la Clinique, nous ne les y suivions pas, nous n'y étions pas admis." (58)

WORKS CITED

Alloula, Malek. *Le Harem Colonial.* Paris: Garance, 1981.

Anderson, Benedict. *Imagined Communities: Reflections on the Origin and Spread of Nationalism* (2nd edition). London: Verso, 1991.

Benaïcha, Brahim. *Vivre au paradis: d'une oasis à un bidonville.* Paris: Desclée de Brouwer, 1992.

Benguigui, Yamina. *Mémoires d'immigrés.* Paris: Canal + Editions, 1997.

Beyala, Calixthe. *Lettre d'une Afro-Française à ses compatriots.* Paris: Mango, 2000.

Cixous, Hélène. "My Algeriance, in Other Words: To Depart Not to Arrive from Algeria." Translated by Eric Prenowitz. In *Stigmata: Escaping Texts.* New York: Routledge, 1998. 153–72.

———. *Les rêveries de la femme sauvage.* Paris: Galilée, 2000.

Corbett, James. "Cherchez la femme! Sexual Equality in Politics and Affirmative Action in France," *The French Review* 14.5 (April 2001): 882–90.

Courtivron, Isabelle de, and Elaine Marks. *New French Feminisms.* New York: Schocken Books, 1981.

Delassale, N. "En France l'égalité se fait attendre," *Télérama* 2597 (October 20, 1999): 98.

Delphy, Christine. *L'ennemi principal.* Paris: Editions Syllepses, 2001.

Djebar, Assia. *Oran langue morte.* Arles: Actes Sud, 1997.

Dumeige, Valérie, and Sophie Ponchelet. *Françaises.* Paris: Nil, 1999.

Durmelat, Sylvie. "Transmission and Mourning in *Mémoires d'immigrés: l'héritage maghrébin:* Yamina Benguigui as 'Memory Entrepreneuse,'" trans. John Ryan Poynter. *Women, Immigration and Identities in France.* Ed. Jane Freedman and Carrie Tarr. New York: Berg, 2000. 171–88.

Freedman, Jane and Carrie Tarr, eds. *Women, Immigration and Identities in France.* New York: Berg, 2000.

Freedman, Jane, and Carrie Tarr. "Introduction," *Women, Immigration and Identities in France.* Ed. Jane Freedman and Carrie Tarr. New York: Berg, 2000. 1–10.

Halimi, Gisèle. *Fritna.* Paris: Plon, 1999.

———. *Djamila Boupacha.* Paris: Gallimard, 1962.

Humblot, Catherine and Yves-Marie Labe. "La télé monochrome en question," *Le Monde,* October 18, 1999, supplement.

Irigaray, Luce. *Speculum de l'autre femme.* Paris: Minuit, 1974.

———. *Ce sexe qui n'en est pas un.* Paris: Minuit, 1977.

Martin, Jacquelin, ed. *La Parité: enjeux et mise en oeuvre.* Toulouse: Presses universitaires du Mirail, 1998.

Ponchelet, Sophie, and Assia Benaïssa. *Née en France: histoire d'une jeune Beur.* Paris: Payot, 1990.

Rosello, Mireille. "Gender, Hospitality and Cross Cultural Transactions in *Les Passagers du Roissy Express* and *Mémoires d'immigrés.*" *Women, Immigration and Identities in France.* Ed. Jane Freedman and Carrie Tarr. New York: Berg, 2000. 135–52.

Servan-Schreiber, Claude. "La parité, histoire d'une idée, état d'un débat." *La parité: enjeux et mise en oeuvre.* Ed. Jacqueline Martin. Toulouse: Presse universitaires du Mirail, 1998.

Spivak, Gayatri. "French Feminism Revisited: Ethics and Politics." *Feminists Theorize the Political.* Ed. Judith Butler and Joan Wallach Scott. New York: Routledge, 1992. 54–85.

———. *A Critique of Postcolonial Reason: Towards a History of the Vanishing Present.* Cambridge: Harvard University Press, 1999.

Wiewiorka, Michel. "Préface." *De l'égalité formelle à l'égalité réelle: la question de l'ethnicité dans les sociétés européennes.* Ed. Manuel Boucher. Paris: L'Harmattan, 2001. 7–11.

CHAPTER 12

Parité in Politics

FROM A RADICAL IDEA
TO CONSENSUAL REFORM

MARIETTE SINEAU

*"Nous [les femmes] sommes
le Tiers-Etat de la République.
("We [women] are the Third
Estate of the French Republic.")*

—Edith Cresson, France 2 Radio, June 9, 1996

"Hemiplegic," "one-legged"—the metaphors are not lacking to qualify the French version of democracy and the monopolization of political power by males. In the spring of 2002, France still ranks next-to-last among the countries of the European Union in terms of percentages of women elected to the lower house (10.9 percent). If France seems inept, most notably compared to Scandinavian countries, at feminizing its political establishment, it owes this to certain historical burdens. The Salic law, which under the monarchy prohibited women from succeeding to the throne of France, was resumed by the Revolutionaries of 1789. As a consequence, political equality among all citizens has adapted itself to the exclusion of women from all political rights. This sidelining of women would last more than a century and a half, until the ordinance of April 21, 1944, made women full-fledged citizens. To the weight of these historical factors are added institutional checks. For example, certain characteristics of the Fifth Republic (such as a uninominal voting system for the election of deputies, the widespread practice of multiple elected posts, and so on) blocked the entry of women into the electoral or parliamentary scene.

To break the deadlock, a radical idea blazed a trail during the 1990s: the idea of political parity. Defined as "l'égalité quantitative garantie pour l'accés à certaines fonctions électives" (guaranteed quantitative equality for access into certain elective functions),[1] *parité*[2] marked an unexpected return to the legal battle. The concept of *parité*, which was presented both as "une demande d'égalité" (a demand for equality) and as "la reconnaissance d'une altérité socialement construite" (the recognition of a socially constructed alterity),[3] provided an escape from the classic dilemma presented by the citizenship of women in democracy: the dilemma of choosing between equality and a recognition of sexual difference. This is why the notion of *parité* has had the beneficial effect of making everyone rethink abstract universalism and analyze differently the question of the political representation of women.

A number of groups have taken up the cause, thereby increasing public awareness of the invisibility of women in the arena of political decision making and helping remobilize a feminist movement that was previously disinterested in electoral issues.[4]

I. PARITÉ UNDER DEBATE: UNIVERSALISTS VERSUS DIFFERENTIALISTS

An analysis of the debates that have taken place as a result of the battle for *parité* reveals the presence of tensions caused by different concepts of equality and democracy. On the one hand, universalist Republicans oppose *parité* today just as they opposed all categorical rights in the past. In the opposing camp are all those (both women and men) who emphasize the limits of formal egalitarianism, who distance themselves from any fixed interpretation of the law, and who refuse to characterize as "democratic" any democracy without women.

A Universalism Indifferent to Differences

If numerous legal experts and male politicians are opposed to *parité*, it is because, they say, of their attachment to the principle of universality set forth in the French Declaration of the Rights of Man and the Citizen of 1789, which does not recognize any sexual distinction among individuals. Hence, the enactment of a democracy organized on the basis of *parité* would bring harm, in their view, to the Republican principle of national sovereignty, which does not lend itself to any fragmentation among voters or any distinction of these voters by category.

Qualified by legal experts as an infringement of the right to impartiality, *parité* is expressly denounced by a number of acting "Republican" politicians as a breach that imperils democracy. Thus, François Mitterrand, during his second term as president, declared he was shocked that anyone could want to "découper la démocratie en tranches" (cut up democracy in slices). The former president of the Constitutional Council, Robert Badinter, also counted himself among the unconditional universalists, and viewed the enactment of *parité* as an intolerable threat of "communitarianism."[5]

The tenants of Republican universalism have often been supported by militant feminists in their opposition to the idea of *parité*. Some women saw it as a way to reintroduce, or even essentialize, gender differences in politics. It is from this perspective that Eleni Varikas denounced a "solution magique qui prétend traiter l'exclusion des femmes par des mesures qui perpétuent et institutionnalisent la répartition sexuée qui fonde leur exclusion" (magical solution that proposes to deal with the exclusion of women using the same measures that perpetuate and institutionalize the sex-based distribution upon which their exclusion is founded).[6] Other women, notably on the extreme Left, criticized the relevance of an alliance of all women under the banner of *parité*, for it included no reference to a societal undertaking that would raise the question of social inequalities and the division of labor according to sex.

In the media, journalists, analysts, and essayists from all sides tirelessly denounced the malice behind the idea of *parité*. They pointed out its inherent dangers or the aberrations to which it might lead. Olivier Duhamel, for example, perceived *parité* as a veiled menace to democracy, the destructive effects of which (ethnicism, nationalism, and a reversion to difference) would not fail to have an impact. He held that "l'acte de parité est parfois indispensable, mais que le principe de parité serait déplorable" (the *act* of *parité* is sometimes indispensable, but the *principle* of parity would be deplorable) (*L'Express,* November 1993). Echoing her husband, Elisabeth Badinter decried the idea that "les paritaires ne proposent rien moins que de changer de système politique et d'imposer la démocratie communautaire des quotas importée des Etats-Unis" (proponents of *parité* propose nothing less than to change political systems and to impose the communitarian democracy of quotas imported from the United States) (*Le Monde,* June 12, 1996). Finally, in an editorial bearing the revealing title, "La violence des faibles" (The violence of the weak), Jacques Julliard exclaimed that the principle of *parité* in politics would place women "dans une situation d'assistance perpétuelle c'est-à-dire d'infériorité réelle" (in a situation of perpetual assistance, that is, of real inferiority): "A force d'insister sur l'identité au détriment de l'universalité, les faibles ou les minoritaires scient la branche sur laquelle ils prétendent s'asseoir: leur appartenance à un droit commun valable pour tous" (As a result of their insistence on identity at the expense of universality, the weak or the minorities are sawing off the branch upon which they claim to be seated: their eligibility for a common right that is valid for all) (*Nouvel-Observateur,* June 27-July 3, 1996).

Women as a danger to democracy: this is a frequently recurring theme of the French political debate. Under the Third Republic, radicals and radical Socialists refused to grant women full political privileges, arguing that their vote would threaten the fragile Republic, which was at that time under royalist attack. Today, universalists, whether they lean toward the Left or the Right, often exaggerate the potential deviations introduced by the principle of *parité*, drawing the same conclusions as their forefathers: women, by claiming *parité*, are going to destroy the foundations of the Republican, democratic ideal.

Here is a case in point: partisans of the legal status quo invoke the judicial precedence of the Constitutional Council. They remind us that supreme jurisdiction, in a decision approved on November 18, 1982, overruled the article of municipal law instituting a maximum quota of representation according to sex (75 percent) on lists of candidates in municipal elections (in communes of more than 3,500 inhabitants). It was overruled in the name of equality of all citizens before the law, guaranteed both by article 3 of the Constitution of 1958 and by article 6 of the Declaration of the Rights of Man and the Citizen. In the name of principles ensuring formal equality, the constitutional judge in essence opposed a measure aimed at ensuring real equality in municipal assemblies. Hence, as a means of obstructing a policy of women's rights founded on the principle of positive action, he cited the concept of universalism and the philosophy of the rights of man.

Adversaries of the principle of *parité*, try as they might to entrench themselves in legal precedence, cannot bury the debate on democratic *parité*. They invoke rights and the Constitution to reject voluntarist policy as a means of nominating and electing more women to office.

Unequal Rights for Unequal People

Other authors have adopted a different interpretation of the law—one, moreover, that goes hand-in-hand with another concept of the right to and principle of equality. This reading most often comes from activists engaged in the fight for *parité*, but it has also rallied some legal experts. It affirms that there would be no constitutional obstacle barring the enactment of a law on *parité* and even emphasizes that there might be concrete textual elements to support this interpretation. The generators of this interpretation base their argument mainly on a sentence in the preamble of the Constitution of 1946, which is reiterated in the Constitution of 1958: "La loi garantit à la femme, dans tous les domaines, des droits égaux à ceux de l'homme" (The law guarantees women, in all domains, rights equal to those of men). Following this line of argumentation, there would be no reason to revise the Constitution to impose *parité*. It would suffice to lay claim to this equality of legal status, as guaranteed by the legislature of 1946, in order to draft a law on *parité*. Such a law, they argue, would be a measure of real equality, whose existence has its basis in the formal legal equality posited by the Constitution.

Other interpreters of the law have pushed even further by affirming that national legislation does not respond to the legal norms contained in the Constitution. This is Gisèle Halimi's position (she is founder of the feminist movement, Choisir-La Cause des Femmes), who has stated: "Plus qu'un constat, plus qu'une déclaration, voire une proclamation, il y a garantie, obligation du passage de la liberté formelle au droit réel" (More than a realization, more than a declaration or even a proclamation, there is a guarantee, an obligation, to progress from formal liberty to real rights) (*Le Monde diplomatique*, October 1994). These authors emphasize that the principle of *parité* is quite different from the principle of quotas, and that the judicial precedents of the Constitutional Council thus do not apply. While a quota, by opposing equality, is unconstitutional, the notion of *parité*, which advocates perfect equality, is constitutionally necessary. Although they see no legal obstacle to the enactment of *parité*, many supporters of the reform nonetheless consider that a revision of the Constitution is absolutely imperative for political reasons.

Defenders of *parité* are supported by philosophers and political scientists intent on questioning the very principles of current Republican citizenship. To show that the notion of *parité* has a valid basis, the political scientist Jean Vogel has questioned the structure of democratic universalism and recalled that "l'institution de la citoyenneté procède d'une auto-définition arbitraire du corps politique" (the institution of citizenship proceeds from an arbitrary self-definition of the political body).[7] He continued, "Ainsi la décision de limiter, au siècle précédent, la composition du corps électoral aux électeurs censitaires, ou celle de considérer pendant des décennies le suffrage universel masculin comme identique au 'suffrage universel' tout court, étaient des faits arbitraires, dont aucun juriste n'arguera cependant jamais pour démontrer l'illégitimité des lois adoptées par les représentants élus par les électeurs de l'époque" (So the decision in the nineteenth century to limit the composition of the electoral body to eligible voters, or the decision, [which was in place] for decades, to consider universal masculine suffrage as identical to "universal suffrage"—these were arbitrary facts. But no lawyer would have ever attempted to demonstrate the illegitimacy of the laws adopted by representatives elected by the voters of that period). From that moment on, something that is arbitrary can be changed at any time, and the body politic can, in light of new values (such as *parité*), decide to redefine, to open itself.

Some women philosophers, including Jeannette Colombel, are happy to remind us that the notion of *situation*—which is at the core of the Sartrian concept—has come to "dérégler, la première, l'universalisme en philosophie comme en politique . . . Sartre évite le piège du repli communautaire ou d'affirmation identitaire tout en parlant de différences—'l'Autre en Histoire'—espérant cependant en des 'universels concrets', des 'universels singuliers' " (be the first thing to upset universalism in philosophy as in politics . . . Sartre avoids the trap of communitarian refuge or of identity affirmation, all the while speaking of difference—"The Other in History"—placing hope nonetheless in "concrete universals" or in "singular universals") (*Libération,* December 31, 1995). In a similar vein, Françoise Collin has pointed out that the time has come to "penser l'un en même temps que le deux, ou que le plusieurs, et non en dehors l'un de l'autre" (think the one at the same time as the both, or the several, instead of separating them one from another). In this sense, *parité* in politics would permit [the French people] to "sortir de la logique des contraires" (escape the logic of opposites), to counter universality and specificity "selon une pensée dichotomique d'héritage cartésien" (according to a dichotomic idea of Cartesian heritage). ("Les hommes ont toujours été à la fois des êtres humains, et des êtres masculins, sans que cette double qualification leur apparaisse comme un dilemme") (Men have always been both human beings and masculine beings at the same time, without this double qualification appearing as a dilemma to them).[8] Finally, in response to the article by Elisabeth Badinter, the philosopher Sylviane Agacinski examined the value of universalist abstraction in these terms: "Si l'universalisme consiste à ignorer absolument la différence sexuelle, l'essentielle mixité du genre humain, alors, il faut faire la critique philosophique et politique de l'universalisme" (If universalism consists in absolutely ignoring sexual difference, the essential mixture of the human race, then the philosophical and political critique of universalism must be made) (*Le Monde,* June 18, 1996).

French universalists have also been taken to task by certain legal experts. In a long, theoretical work, Eliane Vogel-Polsky engaged in an elaborate critique of the legal theory on the equality of the sexes, which constitutes in her view an "inaboutissement programmé" (programmed nonoutcome). This is shocking evidence, though rarely denounced: "L'égalité des sexes est la seule qui ait été et qui soit encore conjoncturelle, fragmentaire et diachronique, c'est à dire qu'elle a été intégrée dans les systèmes juridiques contemporains par une succession de textes séparés visant des domaines spécifiques: l'égalité des hommes et des femmes n'a jamais été consentie, reconnue et accordée en une seule fois pour tous les domaines de la vie en société . . ." (Equality between the sexes is the only kind that has been and that still today is related to economic fluctuations that are fragmentary and diachronic; that is, it has been integrated into contemporary legal systems by a succession of separate texts targeting specific domains: the equality of men and women has never been consented to, recognized, and granted once and for all in all the domains of life in our society . . .). In her view, legal systems that recognize "l'égalité des citoyens et des personnes de manière abstraite et neutre en l'assortissant de l'interdiction de discriminations fondées sur le sexe, la race, la couleur . . ." (equality of citizens and of people in an abstract and neutral manner, by adding it to the prohibition of discrimination based on sex, race, color . . .) necessarily lead to an impasse. To get out of this rut, it is necessary to switch tools and to adopt a legal system that "reconnaisse le droit fondamental autonome—existant per se et non par incidence—de l'égalité de la femme et de l'homme. Et ce droit fondamental doit se traduire par la *parité*" (recognizes the fundamental, autonomous right—existing per se and not incidentally—of the equality of woman and man. And this fundamental right must be translated through *parité*).

Specialists in social legislation note that this branch of the law "articule volontiers égalité et différence" (willingly articulates equality and difference) and emphasize that "le discours juridique de l'égalité a longtemps été le discours de l'égalité formelle qui n'est pas refus des différences mais plutôt indifférence aux différences" (the legal discourse on equality was for a long time the discourse of formal equality, which is not the refusal of difference, but rather indifference to differences).[9] Jean-Jacques Dupeyroux, for one, does not hesitate to say "non au principe d'égalité" (no to the principle of equality) if it leads to rich and poor alike having the same claims to state-allocated family benefits (*Libération,* November 10, 1995).

To some observers, these remarks demonstrate that the best argument to support the claim to *parité* may be to say, "For unequal people, there must be unequal rights"; or, on the contrary, to say, "To grant to women and to men the same legal treatment leads to denying justice to women." This critique of formal equality, moreover, has some illustrious antecedents. It is the logic of the criticisms that Marx was already leveling at the agenda of German Socialists. Using this logic, Guy Braibant has recalled in a timely manner that, if the principle of inequality has constitutional value, it also has political value. He writes, "Les assemblées juridiques ne sauraient s'opposer aux évolutions nécessaires et entraver la marche vers l'égalité réelle au nom d'une conception de l'égalité juridique. . . . Des discriminations considérées aujourd'hui comme justifiées ne le seront peut-être plus demain—par exemple à l'égard des étrangers. D'autres seront au contraire considérées comme fondées pour mieux assurer l'égalité des chances et des conditions" (Legal assemblies would not be able to oppose the necessary changes and hinder progress toward real equality in the name of one conception of legal equality. . . . Some types of discrimination that today are considered justifiable may not be so tomorrow: for example, with respect to foreigners. Others will, to the contrary, be considered as founded to better assure equality of opportunity and of conditions).[10]

This "instrumentalist" vision of the law—in the service of an equality that is up to the politicians to define—is shared by Francine Demichel. In her view, "Sans intervention sur le terrain même du droit, les femmes sont condamnées, pour très longtemps encore à n'être désignées par celui-ci qu'à la condition d'être assimilées aux hommes, conjuguées au masculin. La *parité* est seule à même de remplacer cette identification unilatérale d'un sexe à l'autre par une réelle égalité des rapports entre les sexes." (With no intervention in the arena itself of law, women, for a long time to come, will be condemned to be designated under the law only on condition that they be assimilated with men, conjugated with the masculine. *Parité*, and only *parité*, can replace this unilateral identification of one sex with the other by a real equality of relationships between the sexes). Demichel, a legal expert, insists that the concept of abstract citizenship, as represented by the Constitutional Council and the majority of jurists, is excessively "dogmatic" or "absolutist." In her view, sex must be taken into account in the theory of representation, because it contributes to defining "l'identité même de l'individu et du corps social" (the very identity of the individual and of the social body). Did we have to wait for a woman lawyer to intervene and write an editorial for the *Recueil Dalloz* in order to read such conclusions?[11]

La parité as a Stake in Politics: Taking Back the Idea

Political figures have not remained indifferent to the debate on *parité*. Witness the multiplicity of reform proposals that have succeeded one another since 1994. Over the course of time, the number of both Right- and Left-wing male politicians to seriously consider the principle of *parité* has been on the rise.

Electoral preoccupations are no stranger to this state of affairs. In the midst of a crisis in political representation, political leaders understood that it was time "d'entendre la société sous peine que bientôt celle-ci ne les écoute plus" (to hear society, lest it soon stop listening to them).[12] Moreover, opinion is shown to be more and more favorable to the feminization of political decision makers, even at the top.[13] Thus, the IFOF survey published in *L'Express* of June 6, 1996, revealed that a strong majority of French people of both sexes approved of a whole series of reforms that would be taken to achieve male-female equality in the political arena: 84 percent of those surveyed were in favor of an "interdiction pour les hommes politiques d'occuper plusieurs postes à la fois" (restriction prohibiting politicians from holding several political offices simultaneously); 82 percent responded favorably to the "organisation d'un referendum sur les mesures permettant d'atteindre l'égalité hommes-femmes" (organization of a referendum on measures permitting male-female equality to be reached); 79 percent said yes to the "nomination d'autant de femmes que d'hommes aux postes importants qui dépendent de l'Etat et du gouvernement" (appointment of as many women as men to high-level State and governmental positions); and 77 percent were in favor of a "[modification de] la Constitution afin d'introduire la *parité* hommes-femmes comme principe général" (modifying the Constitution in order to introduce male-female *parité* as a general principle).

In 1994 numerous reforms were proposed. This was because *parité* was on the agenda in the European elections in June in the form of several lists composed of equal numbers of male and female candidates (including the Socialist and the Ecologist lists). Simone Veil, the incumbent Minister of Social Affairs, Health, and Urban Affairs in the Balladur administration (RPR[14]), proposed a reform aimed at the institution of a progressive quota for female representation in municipal, regional, and European elections (all of which employ a list system of proportional representation, which lends itself better to the application of numerically perfect *parité* than does a uninominal system[15]). In addition, six bills (of parliamentary origin) were put forward. One of them, drafted at the initiative of the association Choisir-La Cause des Femmes and presented by three deputies of the Mouvement des Citoyens (Citizens' Movement), had as its objective a modification of article 3 of the Constitution by the addition of the following clause: "L'égal accès des femmes et des hommes aux mandats politiques est assuré par la *parité*" (Equal access for women and men to politically elected posts is guaranteed by *parité*).

In 1995—a presidential election year—three new legal proposals saw the light of day. One of the more surprising outcomes of the campaign was that the main competitors addressed the question of the division of power between the sexes. Several candidates explicitly addressed the issue of *parité* and proposed reforms in order to achieve it. Dominique Voynet, on behalf of the Green Party, rallied support to modify the Constitution and drafted a legal proposal to that end. The Communist Party candidate, Robert Hué, declared himself in favor of a referendum to implement *parité*. The Socialist Party candidate, Lionel Jospin, made several proposals in order to "faire avancer cette grande idée de la *parité*" (further this great idea of *parité*), including a limitation on the accumulation of mandates and a reform of the ballot system used in legislative elections. "Un scrutin mixte en France (majoritaire et proportionnel) serait la manière de réaliser une meilleure égalité hommes-femmes" (A mixed ballot system [using both majority rule and proportional representation] would be the only way to attain better male-female equality) (*Le Monde*, March 10, 1995). On the Right, Edouard Balladur declared himself in favor of the implementation of quotas for women ("disons 30 pourcent pour base") (let's say 30 percent to start) and promised to organize "dans les cent jours" (within the first hundred days), if he were elected, a constitutional revision by referendum. Jacques Chirac, for his part, declared his desire to link party financing to the feminization of each party's list of election candidates and promised to create a National Observatory of *parité*.[16]

In 1996, six new legal proposals relating to *parité* were tabled. In June, an article entitled the "Manifeste de dix" (Manifesto of Ten) was published in *L'Express*. The article was signed by ten former women ministers—Left-wing, moderate, and even Right-wing—all of whom were ready to rise above partisan politics in order to achieve *parité*. The publication of this text, which had the impact of a bombshell in the wading pool of politics, accelerated a shift among those in charge of the question of *parité*. On the Right, incumbent Prime Minister Alain Juppé (RPR) declared himself clearly in favor of revising the Constitution. On the Left, the unconditional conversion of Michel Rocard to the idea of *parité* marked a milestone. For the former prime minister, only this radical, yet not "undemocratic," solution would allow for an end to the prevailing situation by which it was "la communauté des mâles qui gouverne" (the community of males that governs) (*L'Express*, June 20, 1996). The Socialist Party Secretary himself, Lionel Jospin, also made great strides on the issue of *parité*. In 1996, he recognized that "le temps de la contrainte est bel et bien arrivé" (the time for constraint has finally arrived). This willingness to change things was reflected in the text ("Les acteurs de la démocratie") (The players in democracy), which was adopted by the Socialist Party during the National Convention on Democracy, held in Paris on June 29 and 30, 1996. There, activists pronounced themselves in favor of a revision of the Constitution that would establish the principle of male-female parity. The Socialist Party also affirmed its determination to at least double the proportion of women elected over the course of the elections, and decided to apply a quota of 30 percent to the number of female candidates in the next legislative elections.

The legislative elections were held as scheduled in May and June 1997, after the decision of President Jacques Chirac to dismiss the French National Assembly. In the course of the election campaign, Lionel Jospin made renovation and feminization of the political arena one of the central themes of his platform. He firmly declared himself in favor of *parité* between women and men in the political arena. After the victory of the Socialists—who presented a list containing nearly 30 percent women, of whom some 17 percent were elected—Jospin, the new prime minister, renewed his promise. In his statement of general policy on June 19, 1997, he proposed to the French a new Republican pact founded on the modernization of France's democracy: "Il faut d'abord permettre aux Françaises de s'engager sans entraves dans la vie publique. . . . Une révision de la Constitution, afin d'y inscrire l'objectif de la *parité* entre les femmes et les hommes, sera proposée" (We must first of all enable French women to engage in public service without obstacles. . . . A revision of the Constitution will be proposed, with a view to inscribe in it the objective of *parité* between women and men).

This promise was kept, even though revision of the Constitution in a period of "cohabitation"[17] was considered a difficult exercise, for it required cooperation between the two chiefs of the executive branch. This time, the chief of state did not oppose revision: not wanting to alienate half the population, he took up as his own theme the need to feminize politics.

The Time of Reforms

On June 18, 1998, the government brought before the office of the French National Assembly a bill for constitutional reform. First presented to the National Assembly on December 15, 1998, the proposal was unanimously adopted by the French deputies on March 10, 1999. Having triumphed over the Right-wing opposition and the Senate (which, faithful to its tradition of misogyny, had swept the project aside after a first reading), the measure required only a vote by both Chambers at the Congress of Versailles on June 28, 1999.[18] Voted into law with 741 parliament members in favor and 13 against (with 48 abstentions), the bill became "constitutional law number 99–509 of July 8, 1999, regarding equality between women and men." The new version of article 3 of the Constitution (concerning sovereignty and universal suffrage) states that "la loi favorise les conditions dans lesquelles est organisé l'égal accès des femmes et des homes aux mandats électoraux et fonctions électives" (the law favors the conditions under which is organized equal access of women and men to electoral mandates and elective functions). To the contrary, article 4 specifies that political parties "contribuent à la mise en œuvre du principe énoncé au dernier alinéa de l'article 3 dans les conditions déterminées par la loi" (contribute to the enactment of the principle set forth in the last clause of article 3 under conditions determined by the law). The term *"parité"* appears nowhere in the wording, although it is the very object of the reform. Why is this? The reasons, we are told, relate to the practical difficulties of its realization. *Parité,* which evokes the idea of perfect equality, "renvoie à un déterminisme mathématique impossible à mettre en œuvre" (implies a mathematical determinism that is impossible to put into action).[19] The motives were also clearly political. The term *parité* was carefully avoided and replaced by the term *égalité* in the text of the bill—at the express demand of the Elysée Palace, after Jacques Chirac had persuaded deputies that the Right would resist voting for a reform that authorized quotas of 50 percent.

The revision of the basic law was criticized as being an empty shell. Georges Vedel, a former member of the Constitutional Council, was the most severe, qualifying the project as "marivaudage législatif" (legislative banter): "Et voilà aujourd'hui que le pouvoir constituant, ce souverain, dans un débat fondamental dit qu'il n'a rien à dire, que c'est au législateur de se débrouiller et au Conseil constitutionnel de prononcer le dernier mot" (And we see here today that in a fundamental debate, the constituent assembly, that sovereign power, has nothing to say, that it is up to the legislature to find its way and up to the Constitutional Council to say the last word) (*Le Monde,* December 8, 1998).

On the Left and the Right, a number of women politicians expressed a rather critical view, from Gisèle Halimi (Choisir-la cause des femmes) to Roselyne Bachelot (RPR) and Yvette Roudy (Socialist Party), not to mention Muguette Jacquaint (Communist Party). They all emphasized that the revision would not have any real meaning until the articles of its application were adopted; many of them feared that these articles would pose serious difficulties, notably because the uninominal voting system makes for an awkward fit with the principle of equal access to men and women.

In reality, this reform is both *minimalist,* restricted to affirming that formal equality needs to be implemented through deeds, as well as *fundamental,* because of the breach in the symbolic order it has caused. A redefinition of the sovereign people, in effect, took place with the new wording of article 3. How can we fail to notice, in the words of Geneviève Fraisse, that "ce sont deux siècles d'abstraction démocratique, d'abstraction masculine [qui] se referment. Et que s'ouvre une ère nouvelle, celle de l'incarnation du souverain par les deux sexes." (Two centuries of democratic abstraction, male abstraction, are sealed shut. And let a new era begin, an era of the embodiment of the sovereign by both sexes) (*Libération,* December 29, 1998). A paradigmatic shift had taken place. And that is why some, including Leftist members, were critical of the revision, beginning with Robert Badinter, a Socialist senator and the former president of the Constitutional Council. So was his spouse, Elisabeth Badinter, who saw it as "a regression," leading to the enshrinement in the Constitution of "the right to difference . . . after 20 years of working toward equality of the sexes" (*L'Evénement du Jeudi,* February 3, 1999).

The new constitutional order promptly led to voluntary measures designed to achieve the goal of *parité.* Starting on December 8, 1999, the Council of Ministers approved a government bill establishing *parité* between men and women in politics. The text of the bill obliged parties to present 50 percent of women on ballot lists but does not provide any guidelines in terms of the position occupied by women candidates on those lists. For legislative elections, which are uninominal ballots, the bill provided incentives to parties in the form of state financial aid to respect candidate *parité.* The government's bill found favor well beyond the ranks of the majority. The president himself did not fail to show interest, and many of the leading voices on the Right were heard in favor of *parité.*

The initial text was heavily amended by the National Assembly in an effort to tighten the law, since the principle of *parité* of women candidates in large part gave precedence to *parité* of women elected to office. According to the provisions of law number 2000–493 of June 6, 2000, "tendant à favoriser l'égal accès des femmes et des hommes aux mandats électoraux et fonctions électives" (tending to favor equal access of women and men in elective mandates and positions), parties are obligated, under pain of having their candidates' lists invalidated, to present 50 percent of the candidates from both sexes (with a maximum difference of one) for all elections by ballot list. Moreover, the alternation between a woman and a man or a man and a woman is obligatory from the beginning to the end of the list for elections of only one round (European Union elections and senatorial elections in the most heavily populated *départements*). For elections with two rounds (regional elections and municipal elections for communities of more than 3,500 inhabitants, and the Corsican Assembly), *parité* must be respected in six-candidate segments. For legislative elections, *parité* is not obligatory, but the law calls for financial penalties for parties and political groups that have not presented 50 percent of the candidates from both sexes (within a 2 percent margin). The state aid they receive in accordance with the number of votes obtained in the first round of the legislative elections is reduced "d'un pourcentage égal à la moitié de l'écart entre le nombre de candidats de chaque sexe rapporté au nombre total de candidats" (by a percentage equal to half of the disparity between the number of candidates of each sex compared with the total number of candidates). For example, if a party's list consisted of 35 percent women and 65 percent men, the disparity would be 30 percentage points. State aid would thus be reduced by 15 percent.

This law is clearly a useful tool—"constraining" as some critics say—to produce a mix in elected bodies without delay. In fact, at the outcome of the municipal elections of March 11 and 18, 2001, which served as a sort of test case of the law, local assemblies had a different profile. On the evening of the second round, more than 38,000 women were elected to municipal councils of towns with more than 3,500 inhabitants in metropolitan France, that is, 47.5 percent. The increase, when compared with the municipal elections of March 1995 (with 25.7 percent women elected), is clear: the number almost doubled!

The spirit of *parité* had little effect, however, on mayoral elections. (Mayors are elected through indirect suffrage by members of the municipal council, and the law made no provisions for this.) Only 181 women were elected mayors of towns of more than 3,500 inhabitants. This is not much, even considering progress made since 1995: 6.9 percent, compared with 4.9 percent six years ago (40.8 percent). While the French put great hope in the feminization of town halls,[20] no egalitarian dynamic came to redistribute public offices in cities. Forced to cede seats to municipal councilors, they were all the more able to hang on to the control of towns in which they benefited from more political capital (name recognition, length of office, partisan experience . . .). The presidencies of urban communities—a sort of regrouping of communes that will be the structures of the future—dropped even more—and almost exclusively in favor of men.[21] Martine Aubry may well govern Lille-Centre, but Pierre Mauroy is president of the urban commune. In Strasbourg, the same division of power occurred between Fabienne Keller and Robert Grossmann. In other words, the feminization of towns is hierarchical: 47.5 percent of municipal councilors are female; this compares with 6.9 percent female mayors and 5.4 percent women presidents represented in intercommunal structures.

The division of responsibilities is still far from attaining *parité* when compared with men. Yet a real dynamic is in gear, and nothing seems to be able to stop it. The law of June 6, 2000, the so-called law on *parité,* has rung in the end of the "French exception" as we know it: a unique nation, reserving for men the legitimate political monopoly. The time of "women as exceptions" or "token women" is over; it belongs to the past. In the new millennium, the *parité* generation is taking over.

Translated by Heidi Kyser Genoist and Margaret Colvin

NOTES

1. Francine Demichel, "A parts égales: contribution au débat sur la parité," *Recueil Dalloz* (Paris: Dalloz-Sirey, 1997), 95.
2. Translator's Note: In France, the movement that has grown up around the concept of political parity as it is defined here, and which has involved the efforts of politicians, activists, scholars, writers, and journalists, has itself come to be known as "*parité*." The varying translations of "parity" and "*parité*" herein have attempted, respectively, to account for the concept as such, at its most objective, versus the school of thought at large, along with its products, although there is always necessarily some measure of overlap between the two.
3. Françoise Gaspard, "De *la parité*: genèse d'un concept, naissance d'un mouvement," in *Nouvelles questions féministes*, 15.4 (Paris), 31.
4. Different stages have punctuated the increase in power of this claim: September 1, 1989, the European Council organizes a Seminar on Democratic Parity; 2. Spring 1992, the release of a work, *Au pouvoir citoyennes! Liberté, Egalité, Parité* contributes to the diffusion of the idea of *parité* in France; November 3, 1992, the Declaration of Athens is adopted on the occasion of the premier European summit on "Women and Power"; November 4, 1993, the Manifesto of 577 for Democratic Parity is published in the daily newspaper *Le Monde;* May 5, 1996, the Charter of Rome is signed promising the promotion of "la participation égale des femmes et des hommes à la prise de décision" ("equal participation of women and men in decision-making") on a European level.
5. In an interview with the daily newspaper *Le Figaro* of March 9, 1995, he stated his position with perfect clarity: "Nous entrons dans un monde où. nous verrons s'opposer deux conceptions de la démocratie. L'une est celle dans laquelle les citoyens se pensent d'abord en termes de communautés, considérées comme des composantes structurelles de la nation. L'autre vision qui, elle, me paraît véritablement républicaine, fidèle aux pères fondateurs, est celle de la nation française, de tous les citoyens français, quels que soient leur origine, leur sexe, leurs affinités culturelles, leur religion, leur race" (We are entering a world where . . . we will see two conceptions of democracy at odds. One is that in which citizens think of themselves first in terms of communities, considered to be like the structural elements of a nation. The other vision, which I myself see as truly republican, loyal to the founding fathers, is that of all French citizens, regardless of their origin, their sex, their cultural affinities, their religion, or their race).
6. Eleni Varikas, "Une représentation en tant que femme? Réflexions critiques sur la demande de parité des sexes," in *Nouvelles Questions féministes,* 16.2 (1995), 118.
7. Jean Vogel, "La citoyenneté revisitée," in Eliane Vogel-Polsky, Les femmes et la citoyenneté européenne, European Commission, European Network, "Les femmes et la prise de décision," (Brussels: Direction Générale V, multigraphié, 1994), 43.
8. Françoise Collin, "La raison polyglotte ou pour sortir de la logique des contraires," in *EPHESIA, La place des femmes, L'enjeu de l'identité et de l'égalité au regard des sciences socials.* (Paris: La Découverte, 1995), 675.

9. Antoine Lyon-Caen, "L'égalité et la différence dans l'ordre du droit," in *EPHESIA, La place des femmes, l'enjeu de l'identité et de l'égalité au regard des sciences sociales* (Paris: La Découverte, 1995).

10. Guy Braibant, "Le principe d'égalité dans la jurisprudence du Conseil constitutionnel et du Conseil d'Etat," in *Conseil constitutionnel, La déclaration des droits de l'homme et du citoyen* (Paris: PUF, 1989).

11. Founded in 1824, the *Recueil Dalloz* is a publication exclusively devoted to legal matters. It is the work of reference for scholars, members of the law profession, government officials, and so on.

12. National Assembly, Report 1240: Rapport fait au nom de la Commission des lois constitutionnelles, de la législation et de l'administration générale sur le projet de loi constitutionnelle (985) relatif à l'égalité entre les femmes et les hommes (December 1998), 45.

13. Mariette Sineau, "La féminisation du pouvoir vue par les Français(es) et les hommes politiques: images et représentations," in *La parité. Enjeux et mise en œuvre*, Jacqueline Martin, ed. (Toulouse: Presses universitaires du Mirail, 1998), 61–81.

14. Translator's note: "RPR" stands for "Rassemblement pour la République" (usually translated as "Rally for the Republic"), the Republican Party, or the Right, as it is called, of France.

15. In France, two assemblies are elected by ballot in a uninominal system consisting of two rounds: the French National Assembly and the General Councils (or departmental assemblies).

16. By a decree of the President of the Republic dated October 18, 1995, an "Observatoire de *la parité* entre les femmes et les hommes" (Observatory of *La parité* Between Women and Men) was instituted. On January 15, 1997, the Observatory gave Prime Minister Alain Juppé a report, drafted by Gisèle Halimi, that proposed various solutions to arrive at *parité*. Subsequent to this report, a debate on the presence of women in the political arena took place at the French National Assembly on March 11, 1997. This debate did not result in a vote.

17. Periods of "cohabitation" occur when the President of the Republic must confront a majority opposition in the parliament.

18. According to the stipulations of the Constitution of 1958, in order for a constitutional reform to be adopted, it must be voted on in the same terms by the National Assembly and the Senate, then ratified by a majority of three-fifths by both Chambers of Congress together.

19. Report of the National Assembly 1240.

20. According to the results of a survey of October 25 and 26, 2000, conducted by CSA/*Lunes*, an absolute majority of French people (65 percent) indicated a preference for a woman mayor. *Lunes* 14 (January 2001).

21. Before the election, only 54 electoral jurisdictions (districts, communities within communes, and communities within cities and urban centers) out of a total of 1,672—that is, 3.2 percent—had women mayors. (40 of those 1,672 jurisdictions had less than 15,000 inhabitants.)

WORKS CITED

Conseil d'Etat. *Rapport public 1996. Sur le principe d'égalité.* Paris: La Documentation française, 1996.

Demichel, Francine. "A parts égales: contribution au débat sur la parité." Recueil Dalloz-Sirey. Paris: Recueil Dalloz-Sirey, 1997.

Femmes en politique. Spec. edition of *Pouvoirs* 82 (September 1997).

Gaspard, Françoise, Claude Servan-Schreiber, and Anne Le Gall. *Au pouvoir, citoyennes! Liberté, Egalité, Parité.* Paris: Seuil, 1992.

Halimi, Gisèle. *Rapport de la Commission pour la parité entre les femmes et les hommes dans la vie politique.* Paris: Multigraphié, 1996.

Jenson, Jane and Mariette Sineau. *Mitterrand et les Françaises. Un rendez-vous manqué.* Paris: Presses de Sciences Po, 1995.

La parité "contre." Special edition of *Nouvelles questions féministes,* May 1995.

La parité "pour." Special edition of *Nouvelles questions féministes,* November 1994.

Martin, Jacqueline, ed. *La parité. Enjeux et mise en œuvre.* Toulouse: Presses universitaires du Mirail, 1998.

Mossuz-Lavau, Janine. *Femmes/Hommes pour la parité.* Paris: Presses de Sciences Po, 1998.

Sineau, Mariette. *Profession: femme politque: sexe et pouvoir sous la Cinquième République.* Paris: Presses de Sciences Po, 2001.

Vogel-Polsky, Eliane. "Les impasses de l'égalité ou pourquoi les outils juridiques visant à l'égalité des femmes et des hommes doivent être repensés en termes de parité." *Parité-Infos,* supplemental edition to the series. Paris: Parité-Infos, 1994.

PART II

Arts and Literature

Chapter 13

Francophone Women Writers in France in the Nineties

Odile Cazenave

Following a shift from testimonial narrative to more openly rebellious voices in the eighties, critical of postcolonial, sociopolitical African societies,[1] a new generation of young women novelists has emerged in the nineties. In an article reviewing African women's writing in the past two decades,[2] I asked the following questions: would the Senegalese Mariama Bâ still write the way she was writing in 1980? What has changed since then? What are these new voices expressing? Is it still adequate and meaningful to talk of a "gendered writing"?

In this article, I would like to focus on Francophone women writers writing *within France* in the nineties. How does their location affect their writing? How do gender, identity, space, and postcolonial creative writing intersect? To what extent can these works be characterized as immigrant narratives?[3] How much do the works by Francophone women writers reflect their national origins? How much do the issues addressed pertain to the experience of (im)migration, of acculturation, of the authors' perception of otherness? These are the questions I would like to address here.

AFRICAN WOMEN NOVELISTS

In the eighties, most works by African women were written from within the African continent; women novelists, often in their mid-thirties to late forties, were also writing poetry, theatre, and children's literature. Today, two-thirds of the novels written by African women are by those living in France. All of these writers are in their early twenties and thirties. While some were born in France, most writers are first generation and immigrated to France as (young) adults. These new voices privilege the novel as their genre. In terms of market and readership, the situation has remained pretty much the same: like their male peers, they are published in France and the cost of the book makes it difficult for the African reader from the African continent to have access to their works.[4]

Among the writers who actively contributed to a change of form and voice in African literature during the eighties, Calixthe Beyala is the only one who was already living in France. With a prolific production—ten novels and two essays since the mid-eighties—and numerous literary awards, including the Grand Prix de l'Académie française in 1996 for *Les honneurs perdus,* she has certainly become one of the most visible African woman writers at work today.[5]

Her first three novels focused on Africa and initiated a change of textual practice and social setting.[6] With *Le petit prince de Belleville* (1992) and its sequel, *Maman a un amant* (1993), Beyala shifted her gaze in the nineties to the African immigrants in Paris.

In these "Parisian novels" (as they are often called), she began to focus on the women and the men who are part of the African community in Belleville. More than a geographical shift, this also meant an attempt at a new dialogue between man and woman, a search for new sexual ethics.[7] Beyala has been looking at immigration in terms of the positive changes it can potentially bring about for women. Typically, her female protagonists (single or married, young or middle-aged) come to Paris in order to become something new. Not surprisingly, the author portrays sharp contrasts between her male and female characters. The former often display nostalgia for the past and the mother country, while the latter look toward the present and the future, thereby breaking away from the domestic sphere. Rather than displacement, immigration is examined in terms of redistribution of power within the family and within the community, where gendered roles have been especially affected by the new space.

Since the mid-nineties, new voices have appeared and with them certain issues are being revisited. Some of the more traditional questions, like excision, polygamy, or parent-child relationships, have been approached from a new angle. For instance, Abibiatou Traoré's *Sidagamie* (1999) revisits the issue of polygamy in the light of AIDS and the risks that multiple relationships present for women and children. In *La petite Peule* (2000), Mariama Barry explores the mother-daughter relationship in terms of the mother's rejection and harshness toward her daughter. The narrator tries to understand her mother as a woman, her decision to divorce, and the consequences this decision may have on their family and their cultural environment.[8] Isabelle Boni-Claverie's *La grande dévoreuse* (1999)[9] and Célia Vieyra's *Une odeur aigre de lait rance* (2000)[10] address the issue of youth in the postcolonial African city. France does not or hardly appears in the scenery of these works and so they do not qualify as immigrant narratives.[11] Yet the author's space of writing is not incidental. For these works show a new quality of writing in their reflection of transnational and global issues, just as the authors are themselves more exposed to globalization and transnationalization.

New issues, directly related to France, have also been addressed; in particular, migration and youth in a postcolonial urban environment, for example in Nathalie Etoké's *Un amour sans papiers* (1999), Fatou Diome's *La préférence nationale* (2000), and Sandrine Bessora's *53 cm* (1999) and *Les taches d'encre* (2000).

Both the Cameroonian Nathalie Etoké and the Swiss-Gabonese Sandrine Bessora have been focusing on questions of legal papers regarding permanent residence and education. Etoké's *Un amour sans papiers* and Bessora's *53 cm* sharply contrast with their peers, male and female: while male writers of their generation continue to focus primarily on male characters, Etoké and Bessora on the contrary give their characters, male and female, the same complexity and depth.

These two young writers raise new questions. Etoké looks at immigration, raising the question: where are hope and opportunity located for African youth? While the previous generation has been denouncing the outdated image of France as a panacea, as the road to success, Etoké looks at it in terms of an impasse. To denounce is not enough: what else can African writers in general propose? What dream can they offer African youth? In the current context, young Africans know the limits and risks of going to France, and that it does not necessarily lead to success; yet they are left at an impasse, with very little or no other alternative, given the dire situation in their own countries. Furthermore, in juxtaposing the student life of Africans with that of clandestine African immigrants living in squats, and highlighting the lack of communication and solidarity between the two, Etoké raises both the question of class and the existence of an African community.

Like Manthia Diawara's film, *Rouch in Reverse* (1995), Bessora's *53 cm* subverts the traditionally Western practice of studying the Other and generates an ethnography of the French from an African perspective. With a ferocious sense of humor, Bessora becomes a *gaulologue*. In turn funny, caustic, or bitterly ironic, the narrator's gaze on French society unveils its many layers of complexities and aberrations, especially regarding the administrative procedures involved in obtaining residence permits or student ID cards.

By self-representing her experience, by subverting the stereotypical representation of the *sans-papiers* (illegal) immigrant, Bessora generates a new perspective on legal/illegal immigration.[12] Following in Beyala's footsteps, she brilliantly demonstrates that women, too, can use humor in their writing. Her second novel, *Les taches d'encre* (2000), likewise both witty and profound, further undertakes to expose the *petites manies* (small quirks) of the French, for instance, their consumerism. More specifically, it aims at exposing the many manifestations of hidden and overt racism, of the many ways in which the French reject racial mixing and multicultural influences. The author simultaneously looks at colonial history and at some of the most traumatic events in postcolonial Africa. Through her protagonist, Murielle, a young Rwandese who is trying to create a new life for herself, Bessora introduces the Rwandan genocide, the question of memory and amnesia. At the same time, Murielle, a replica of Zara in *53 cm,* is irritatingly funny, subversive, and iconoclastic. In juxtaposing colonial and postcolonial history, in fusing registers—the comic and the tragic—Bessora is systematically provocative. She raises, very subtly, questions of responsibility and of France's responsibility, past and present. By zeroing in on French society, she brings up the issue of defining Frenchness, forcing us to rethink the so-called universalist Republican ideals of equality in France.

La préférence nationale, a collection of short stories by Fatou Diome, in turn addresses issues of legitimacy, Frenchness, and the perception of ethnic difference in French society. A recurrent narrative emerges from the different stories, pointing out French racist prejudices and assumptions about a housemaid of color, and ultimately about women of color.[13] Most of the assumptions and verbal humiliations show a perpetuation of colonial imagery and stereotypical representations, where people of color are treated differently and are assumed to have an inferior education. Diome, too, by using a caustic, satirical tone, destabilizes the usual perceptions of alterity and third-world migration.

Compared with the previous generation of women writers, these young authors stand out in terms of age: most of them were barely in their twenties when they wrote their first novels. Together with Boni-Claverie, Diome, and Vieyra, they force us to redefine our notion of postcolonial literature and to no longer consider it a

monolithic entity. They demonstrate that age rather than gender becomes a key parameter in our analysis of these texts. Their context is different and they are confronted by a whole set of new issues. New parameters have been introduced—AIDS,
unemployment, the underground life, the conditions of women in prison, clandestine immigration, and the exploitation of women. To be born at the end of the seventies and the beginning of the eighties—to be twenty today—means something
different from what it did to the generation that turned twenty in the sixties or the
eighties. There is more uncertainty. They no longer have the enthusiasm of the first
generations of women who dreamt of participating in the building of newly independent nations. In the face of AIDS, of unemployment—in Europe as well as in
Africa—of civil wars, ethnic clashes, and the politics of exclusion, even genocide, the
initial dreams can only crumble, and the question of a viable future for African youth
becomes crucial.

As I pointed out in "Vingt ans après Mariama Bâ," gender becomes secondary to
age; we are beyond the gynocentric narratives of the eighties. These young women
are part of a new generation of African writers in Paris, who, like their male peers,
the Malagasy Jean-Luc Raharimanana, the Togolese Kossi Efoui, or the Djiboutian
Abdourahman Waberi, are *engagé* writers, who feel a moral responsibility and express
through their art their commitment to human rights.[14]

Ultimately, these new voices force us to look at multiculturalism and integration
in a manner that shatters prevailing paradigms of both French and African cultures.
Their use of humor and satire are part of their textual strategies of subversion. Their
concern over global issues reflects new developments in African literature.

MAGHREBI AND FRANCO-MAGHREBI WRITERS

Immigration has also been a very prominent issue in Franco-Maghrebi writing. As
early as in the eighties, in the economic and political climate of unemployment and
increasing xenophobia, France saw the young *Beur* (second-generation children of
Maghrebi immigrants) rise up and demand the right to be different: to be French
and Arab, to be neither French nor Arab.

A literature was born in the wake of a sociocultural movement, the *Beur* novel.[15]
Yet soon afterward this youth realized the dangers of their claimed difference, of
being defined by and confined to alterity and to a geographical space increasingly
laden with pejorative connotations: the *banlieues*. Likewise, the authors realized
that by creating this niche of difference, they were marginalizing themselves and
being sent back to the periphery of the central discourse. The mid-eighties saw an
explosion of first-person narratives by young men and women, denouncing the
stigmatizing gaze of the majority ethnic group in France. The Algerian Leïla Sebbar, although not a *Beur* herself,[16] focused on the young generation of children
born on the French territory, exploring the parent-child relationship.[17] She especially underlined the violence to which young girls were submitted.[18] In general,
Franco-Maghrebi women authors chose to highlight the difficult path for girls: the
way in which they were subjected to a certain kind of violence and to a much
stricter set of rules than their brothers.[19] In contrast to Beyala's works, for instance, here, immigration or biculturalism in France is not read as a positive, eye-
opening experience.

The nineties have witnessed a different tone and approach: immigration is currently being looked at in terms of memory and loss by Maghrebi woman writers. Revisiting the past, especially their family past and personal experience, a number of these writers are trying to come to terms with the difficult history shared by Algeria and France. The scars are still fresh and the wounds easily reopened.

In this regard, Leïla Sebbar's works are representative of the change of focus. In the nineties, her gaze shifted from the Maghrebi immigrants and the *Beur* youth to new directions: born of an Algerian father and a French mother, she has reflected on the issue of biculturalism paired with monolinguism and the silencing of the Arabic language—the fact that she could not speak the father tongue. Finally, she has explored questions of expatriation: what it means to be living here, and not there, to be away from the fatherland.[20] In collaboration with the Canadian writer Nancy Houston,[21] through an exchange of letters and conversations, she first addressed questions of exile.[22] Along the same line, throughout the nineties, she returned to publishing collaborative texts (and/or participated in collective anthologies and creative collections). These texts all revolve around the following issues: memory of Algeria and exile (*Une enfance algérienne*),[23] memory and childhood for the Francophones (*Une enfance d'ailleurs, 17 écrivains racontent*,[24] *Une enfance outremer*[25]). The recurring indirect question in these collections concerns the implications of being a Francophone person living in French space; about the discrepancies between the Francophone space of childhood and the French space of adulthood.

A younger and newer voice, Nina Bouraoui has also come to focus on questions of marginality, of being in an in-between space, culturally and linguistically. Born in France of a French mother and an Algerian father, Bouraoui, who moved to Algeria when she was five, also felt on the margins, both in Algeria and then upon her return to France.

Her most recent novel, *Garçon manqué* (2001), borrows from her life and experience of Algeria in the seventies. If the narration initially highlights the spatial segregation of sexes (women confined to the private space while men enjoy the public space), the protagonist, aware of the advantages of being a man, decides to cut her hair, call herself Ahmed, wear jeans, and take to the streets. The book soon sharpens its focus: through her friendship with Amin, a boy of similar mixed origins, and by way of her constant inner monologue, the narrator raises the issue of being born from/in two different cultures. Torn between two opposing directions, she tries to remain in control of a constantly surfacing violence.

The narrative flips back and forth between the two spaces, her two sets of life, always feeling *en porte-à-faux*, never quite belonging. There is no attempt on her part to try to reconcile the two sides of her heritage. Her acute consciousness and perception of alterity by the majority ethnic group (in both spaces) drives the narrative. Whether gazing at Algeria or at France, the violence of the tone and the urgency of Bouraoui's writing remain constant.[26] As such, they bring a sense of continuity to her exploration of anger, of the widespread malaise of the younger generation of Franco-Maghrebi writers.

In *Terre plurielle Maryam, une mémoire déracinée* (1995) Anne Tiddis expresses some of the same ambiguities and *déchirures* experienced by Bouraoui. *Terre plurielle*, at times a haunting song, at times a poem, at times a story, evokes the anxieties and the richness of being plural, of being an adolescent in Algeria between 1954 and 1964. *Les ravins de l'exil* (1996), a collection of six tales, further explores the multiple fissures the war caused in the land and its people. The setting shifts from Algeria to France. Both texts give a sense of loss and displacement, of longing for Algeria, especially among the parents' generation. As opposed to Franco-Maghrebi texts of the eighties, here the focus is more on the parents than on the second generation. The narrative alternates between gazes and spaces, Algeria/France, France/Algeria. It betrays a sense of loneliness, of isolation; this is not the atmosphere of the community, of the suburbs. Rather, it is the personal experience of exile, of being displaced and suspended in between two spaces, exiled from oneself. All Tiddis's works exude an incredibly raw intensity; in them, one feels the pain, the urge for purity.

In the process of understanding one's past through the eyes and experiences of the parents, the mother often appears as a recurrent feature in some of the recent texts. For instance, in Bouraoui's *Garçon manqué,* Nina, in Rennes (France) with her maternal grandparents, tries to trace her mother's itinerary as a child in France, then as a young law student at the university, and her decision to marry a young French Algerian in the sixties. *Fritna* (1999), by the Tunisian Gisèle Halimi, is another example of the autobiographical gaze on maternal conflicts.[27] Trying to recapture the past and, above all, to understand one's personal history become key in these narratives. Malika Mokeddem's *L'interdite* (1994), a virtual recapitulation of the author's own itinerary, raises the issue of constraints imposed on Maghrebi women and their anger and ambivalence toward these constraints.[28] Mokeddem's latest novel, *N'zid* (2001)—the first one to use Arabic in the title—demonstrates a vital need to examine the constructions of memory. Through her heroine N'zid/Nora, who suffers from amnesia after an accident at sea, Mokeddem explores what happens when a young woman has been deprived of her memory: what it may mean to be able to ignore the different elements that link the past to the present. Through her gradual recovery of memory, Nora can traumatize her character by forcing it to confront some of the humiliations she had to endure as a woman and as a foreigner.

Cérémonie (1999), Yasmine Chami-Kettani's first novel, in turn, examines history in its atemporality. Taking us from France to Morocco, Chami-Kettani looks at women's experiences when confronted by the old and by the new. The protagonist, newly divorced, has returned to her parents' home with her children. Her cousin, suffering from the pressure of being barren after several years of marriage, also returns from France to attend a marriage ceremony. Using the intertwined memories of the two characters' aunts and mothers, the author creates an echo effect. Being a young, divorced woman brings the protagonist to a similar position and status as her aunt Aïcha, who remained single and died from breast cancer. One memory generates another fragment of memory, passed from generation to generation.

As these women (mother, daughter, aunt, niece, and the memory of the absent ones) congregate, preparing for the wedding ceremony of the younger brother, they invite the reader to discover numerous examples of women's daily heroism and suffering.

Like Tiddis's work, Chami-Kettani's writing manages to convey a sense of both intimacy and diffused sadness. Wrapping the reader in this atmosphere, *Cérémonie* interweaves women's path, from yesterday to today, from their confrontation with a patriarchal society to their own suffering and fears of failure and death. Because all the memories are intertwined, they become atemporal and operate as collective tales and pieces of wisdom to transmit to the newer generations.

Assia Djebar's works are most representative of a change of tone and approach in Maghrebi women's writing, especially in terms of confronting history. In that respect, *L'amour, la fantasia* (1985) worked as a turning point. The author shifted her gaze from women in society to a more historically grounded time, that of colonial Algeria. Looking at the colonial construction of history and the general effacing of women's role in history, deconstructing colonial history, she was then able to confront the present situation.

The nineties have seen Djebar's most active commitment, a *prise de parole* vis-à-vis Algeria. *Le blanc de l'Algérie* is a testimony to the intellectuals, writers, journalists, and artists who, because of their positions or simply of what they represented, died by violent means in the past decade.

On the other hand, Djebar's writing has distanced itself, moving away geographically from the author's native country (*Les nuits de Strasbourg* is proof)—just as the author herself has distanced herself geographically and left France for a more neutral space. Since the mid-nineties, she has been living in the United States, first teaching at Louisiana State University and now at New York University. Twice an expatriate, from her own country and then from France, she has been interrogating the two spaces, France and Algeria (as shown in *Oran, langue morte,*1997), gradually embracing the Algerian culture in a more global process, looking at Islam in its historical context.[29]

The author has also been articulating more theoretically the complex issue of bilingualism/biculturalism. In *Ces voix qui m'assiègent* (1999), Djebar confronts the question of a Francophone space, of her own *Francophonie/francité* and the implications of the French language/space/culture on her writing and, eventually, on herself.

While fairly distinct, these very poetic and intense voices go essentially in three directions: a preoccupation with language and the question of bilingualism/biculturalism; a concern for the oppression of women, breaking away from their silencing; and a search for women's and mothers' recollection of history and the lost space. In all these texts, being a woman remains a key element and speaking out against patriarchy is still a priority.

In contrast to the women of sub-Saharan Africa, these authors directly address the issue of language, for it is directly related to their resolving of an often difficult bilingualism and biculturalism.[30] The markers of alterity vis à vis the majority ethnic group are still very visible. The recurrent violence of images and the textual intensity of the works add to a heightened sense of aesthetics. Along with the outstanding intellectual presence of Assia Djebar, Leïla Sebbar, who was already writing in the eighties, and long-time activist and writer Gisèle Halimi, new voices have emerged: Nina Bouraoui, Malika Mokeddem, Anne Tiddis, the filmmaker and writer, Yamina Benguigui, and more recently, the Moroccan Yasmine Chami-Kettani.

CARIBBEAN WOMEN WRITERS

Unlike African and Maghrebi women writers, who write for the most part within France, the majority of Caribbean women writers live outside the Hexagon. For instance, Gisèle Pineau lives in Guadeloupe; Suzanne Dracius-Pinalie lives in Martinique; and Maryse Condé lives in the United States.

Yet, as happens in some of the new African novels in Paris, the gaze in Caribbean female literature is no longer exclusively directed toward the Antilles. Most of these texts address the question of Antillans living in the *métropole* (mainland France) and, more recently, in the United States. This is true of the following texts: *L'autre qui danse* (1991) by Suzanne Dracius-Pinalie, *Un papillon dans la Cité* (1992) and *L'exil selon Julia* (1996) by Gisèle Pineau, *Malgré la pluie . . .* (1997) by Laure Moutoussami, and *Desirada* (1997) by Maryse Condé. While the creators live outside of the Hexagon, their protagonists wander, mentally and physically, between Paris and the Antilles.

L'autre qui danse is particularly representative of this physical and mental malaise. Rhevana, a young Martiniquan born in the *métropole,* searches for her roots. Thus, she floats between the illusory dream of the Africa of the "Fils d'Agar" and her sour, failed experience of the Antilles, which abruptly ends in her returning to Paris and her tragic death (letting her baby and herself die of hunger). Likewise, Laure Moutoussami's *A l'ombre de l'enfance* and *Malgré la pluie . . .* deal with some of the same fundamental questions of belonging and rootedness. In both novels, the protagonists return to the Antilles in an effort to break away from the past and reconnect with their origins. *Malgré la pluie . . .* shows the difficulties of readapting to the lifestyle and habits of family and friends there, especially because of the destructive effects of rumors and gossip. The tragic ending sanctions the impossibility of durable happiness for one who leaves the *métropole* in hope of finding his/her space on the island.[31]

Pineau's *Un papillon dans la cité* (1992) describes, in a more uplifting manner, the reverse itinerary: from Guadeloupe to the *métropole,* where an adolescent girl, reunited with her parents whom she has not seen for years, tries to find some anchor in the *cité,* away from Guadeloupe and the grandmother she misses. Her friendship with a young Maghrebi boy, who lives in the same housing project, helps her face her new environment and life.[32]

In *L'espérance-macadam* (1995), Pineau reconnects with the more traditional themes of Caribbean writing: the abuse of women, the psychological impotence of men—often manifested in alcoholism and domestic violence—incest and rape, and the precarious condition of life for both men and women in the Antilles.

In *L'exil selon Julia* (1996), through the narrator's gaze, Pineau describes the experience of a Caribbean family living in the *métropole* in the sixties. The novel differs from traditional childhood memories insofar as the grandmother's gaze is the one that carries memories. The narration thus goes backward: from France to the French Caribbean (first Martinique, then finally Guadeloupe). Once in the Caribbean, Man Ya's granddaughter, now an adolescent girl, sees things differently. Man Ya is finally perceived in her full dimension; the narrator not only discovers Man Ya's wisdom, but also the richness of the island as a geographical and cultural space. It is only then that she understands the difference between schooling and education, between cultural knowledge and instruction. Only then and there does she understand the extent of her grandmother's knowledge, and what being transplanted, displaced, means. Conversely, the book validates Caribbean culture and helps define the contour of one's *Antillanité* (Caribbeanness).

Pineau's more recent text, *L'âme prêtée aux oiseaux* (1998), continues in the same direction: the female protagonist ultimately finds an inner stability. A young, single, pregnant woman when she moved to Paris, Sybille detached herself from Guadeloupe. Yet she understands her young son's needs to look for his father and his roots on the island. Traveling to the United States with Lila, an old French woman and her long-time friend, Sybille is finally able to reconcile herself with the island. Unlike Condé's protagonist in *Desirada,* for whom, as we will see, traveling to the United States does not bring any peace of mind, going to the United States helps Pineau's narrator find love and peace with herself and the sense of being firmly anchored. In all of Pineau's texts, speaking and writing act as healers. Being able to speak out helps the protagonists resolve their inner trauma or anxieties. In her novels, unlike those of other Caribbean women, the narration brings a sense of relief and appeasement, bringing a hopeful note to the readers.

In *Desirada,* Maryse Condé explores the experience of migration. Her protagonists are confronted with what almost seems their normal destiny, leaving the island for a new space. To the usual route, from the island to Paris (or to the dream of returning to Africa), Condé adds the migration from one island to the other (from La Désir-ade to Guadeloupe), from Paris to the United States and Boston, and a constant back-and-forth between the United States and the Caribbean, between the United States and France. In *Desirada,* three generations of women illustrate the complex evolution of the dynamics of migration.[33] Through these three generations, Condé illustrates the phenomenon of globalization as it translates today for Guadeloupe and its inhabitants.

This novel attempts to identify the roots of a deeply engrained malaise that the characters carry within themselves. The crux of the matter is that moving away does not resolve any quest for identity or personal malaise: once she has left a carefree childhood, wherever Marie-Noëlle is, she carries around her "*mal-être,*" a pain that is intricately linked to her mother's indifference and lack of maternal love, and an ab-sence of bearings that is also reflected in her relationships with men. As she is sud-denly cut off from the innocence of her childhood, the protagonist wanders here and there, *blasée,* empty, sapped of energy.[34]

Condé draws a very somber portrayal both of Caribbean youth and of the island. Through Garvey, Marie-Noelle's half-brother, the author also explores the aspira-tions and fears of the adolescent and young Antilleans living in the *métropole.* For this young man, Guadeloupe, and Africa even less so, represents nothing meaningful or powerful.[35]

Migration in *Desirada* is examined in terms of inner malaise rather than as dis-placement. The main source of this sense of incompleteness, of deep dissatisfaction, goes back to unknown origins and questions of legitimacy. Female characters show the impossibility of becoming fully themselves because of a lack of retraceable mem-ory. Not until Marie-Noëlle is able to fill in the gap, the missing link of origins, can she truly inhabit the space she lives in. Until that moment, wandering about be-comes her definition, her second nature.[36]

These different Caribbean novels all converge toward the same idea: characters are often burdened by their past, unable to look freely toward the future. Through the personal stories of female protagonists, Caribbean women writers have been try-ing to recapture a collective past, to reconstruct the traumatic effects of slavery on its people, men and women, and to build a new Antillean his/her/story.[37] The ab-sence of cultural and historical roots, of an anchor, impels Caribbean expatriates to create a substitute identity. Contrary to what occurs in works by African writers in Paris, there is not much of a sense of solidarity and even less of a community among the Antilleans in the same situation. The emphasis, rather, is on isolation and the ab-sence of replenishment.[38]

   Compared with African women writers, another striking difference is the scarcity
of new, young Caribbean female voices. The already established writers like Condé
and Pineau have confirmed their visibility in terms of talent, creativity, and crafting
of their writing. Others, like Suzanne Dracius or Michèle Maillet,[39] have fallen
silent. Except for the Guadeloupean Dany Bebel-Ghisler, the production of new
voices takes place somewhere else: in Canada with Haïtian writers such as Marie-
Célie Agnant and J.-J. Dominique or in the United States with Edwige Danticat,
writing in English; or in Haïti with Yannick Laens.

CONCLUSIONS

Women Francophone authors writing in France have been redefining French space
and society by choosing to focus on their migratory heritage. All of them address
questions of cultural survival and expatriation from diverse points of view.
   The Caribbean voices are still haunted by a lack of official acknowledgment of
their traumatic past and history and try to find some anchor within themselves.
They point to the protagonists' wandering—whether to the African continent, to
the Hexagon, or more recently to the United States—and, conversely, their attempts
to return to the island, as strategies of cultural survival. Women authors have turned
toward their past, exploring the genealogical missing link (the absent father-geni-
tor) as a step toward defining their Caribbean selves. Their preoccupation with legitimacy reflects a broader scope, wherein they undertake to recapture their history
through the telling of women's stories. Displacement in that context is subsumed in
a general malaise, linked to an ontological feeling of displacement going all the way
back to the traumas of slavery and forced exile. Perhaps, by examining the roots of
this malaise, of this constant feeling of expatriation—exiled from the island and
from oneself—the authors will be able to define and valorize their Caribbeanness.
   Maghrebi and Franco-Maghrebi writers have also been looking at their past,
but from a different angle. Because of the enduring memory of the War of Algerian Independence, the questions of biculturalism and bilingualism have come to
the forefront. Biculturalism is expressed in terms of suffering and of ambivalence
toward the other culture and space. Literary production has shifted from predominantly second-generation narratives and direct testimonies about negotiations
with the French space and culture to narratives of expatriation and exile. Novels,
essays, and films have given us direct access to testimonies of Maghrebi immigrants, to their recalling of their early years in France,[40] while the most recent
texts choose instead to focus on a young generation trying to trace its history and
identity through its parents' itinerary. As the focus has shifted from the children
to an analysis of their parents' generation, their vision still reveals a stigmatizing
gaze: it has evolved from pointing out the stigma attached to Franco-Maghrebi
children living in the *banlieues* to memories of the stigmatizing gaze once directed
at their parents. The writing has gone through different stages: first, attempting to
reconcile the two sides of their heritage; then, exposing their perception of their
parents' immigration. The current phase is a confrontation of their claims to reconcile both their bicultural identities and their consciousness of their parents'
malaise. This exploration of the past, of memory in terms of both colonial history
and exile, is at a historic moment: a moment when France is beginning to confront

its own past and some of its problematic actions. Despite some still strong resistance, the silence surrounding France's responsibility during colonial times, regarding torture for example, is gradually being broken. By confronting an often painful heritage, Maghrebi and Franco-Maghrebi women authors help redefine history in a postmodern, postcolonial context. In doing so, they participate in the current reappearance of history within French literature and society.

African women writers, by contrast, look toward the present and the future, raising economically related, transnational issues of (im)migration, class, and the future of youth confronted with a postcolonial urban world. Rather than focusing exclusively on women, all of the new African voices express their moral commitment to human rights in general. Age, not gender, becomes a key parameter in the critical analysis of these postcolonial narratives. Unlike Maghrebi women (or their male peers for that matter), they do not question language. Bilingualism (or monolinguism) is not perceived as an issue. Rather, writers like Beyala or Bessora demonstrate that they have appropriated the French language; they have given it new tensions and twists, creating "*des mots baton manioqués*" (manioc-words, as Calixthe Beyala has coined it); they have invaded linguistic areas that until recently were seen as a male prerogative: from the vulgar to the obscene, from the violent to the funny and satirical. Their work on language, their textual strategies subverting the stereotypical representations of non-European immigrants, in particular through humor and satire, betray a defiant, provocative, self-confident writing.

Francophone women writers have been exploring in their works the *elsewhereness* of their voice. These explorations, although personal, reveal new developments regarding racial relations within French society. They also create new markers for Francophone literature, forcing us to redefine that *elsewhereness* of (other) French-speaking voices.

NOTES

1. For a detailed study of these changes in African women's writing, see Odile Cazenave, *Rebellious Women: A New Generation of Female African Novelists* (London: Lynne Rienner, 2000), translated by the author from *Femmes rebelles: naissance d'un nouveau roman africain au féminin* (Paris: L'Harmattan, 1996).

2. Odile Cazenave, "Vingt après Mariama Bâ: le roman africain au féminin," in *Africultures* 35, Masculin-Féminin, Paris: L'Harmattan (Février 2001): 7–14.

3. For a definition and an analysis of immigrant narratives, see Susan Ireland and Patrice Proulx, eds., *Immigrant Narratives in Contemporary France* (Westport, CT: Greenwood Press, 2001). See especially their introduction.

4. Some authors however, such as Véronique Tadjo, try to copublish with an African press, in particular Les Nouvelles Editions Ivoiriennes, located in Abidjan, Ivory Coast. It is especially true for youth literature, because the authors (Véronique Tadjo, Fatou Keïta, Kidi Bebey) aim at reaching out to children on the African continent.

5. Her involvement in the association Collectif Egalité, created together with the Antillean playwright Luc Saint-Eloy, and her protest against the lack of representation of people of color and minorities in the media have added to her mediatization. (At the 2000 "Remise des Césars," the French equivalent of the Oscar night in the United States, Beyala, together with Saint-Eloy, interrupted the show and read a written statement, asking for parity and more representation for minority people in the media.)

6. See *C'est le soleil qui m'a brûlée* (1987), *Tu t'appelleras Tanga* (1988), and *Seul le diable le savait* (1990).

7. See Cazenave, *Rebellious Women*.

8. Conversely, she also develops a more fleshed out portrayal of the father. He is tender and affectionate; he is the one who comes and consoles her after she has been excised. He is also the one who is financially unable to provide for them, who brings them along in his wanderings, from Senegal to Guinea, from the city to the village, from modest neighborhoods to slums.

9. *La grande dévoreuse*—the title refers to Abidjan, the capital of Ivory Coast—portrays the disillusionment and suffering of the young Amoin who left her village and her family in the illusory hope of improving her condition. The narration sanctions the tragic fate of the young couple, Amoin and Sax, who are confronted with poverty and the hardships of urban life, in which corruption and violence rule.

10. Célia Vieyra—the daughter of Myriam Warner-Vieyra, herself an established Guadeloupean writer living in Senegal, and of the Benin filmmaker (and writer) Paulin Vieyra—explores further how gender, youth, and the urban environment intersect. Vieyra combines some of the traditionally recurring themes—a young girl from a modest family raped by a classmate from a wealthy family, the young boy's denial of any responsibility, an unwanted pregnancy that leads her to infanticide, her family's rejection. What makes this new is that the author takes us to the less familiar scenes of a prison environment with female inmates. Also, although the first names (Kougnou) remind us of Senegal and the city, the descriptions are general enough so that it could be anywhere in Africa. Vieyra addresses the question of reintegration into social life for a young woman who has been deprived of her adolescence and who has become an adult in prison.

11. In Vieyra's novel, the last third of the narration takes place in Paris. Immigration is approached from a different angle: the protagonist goes to France to leave an inhospitable home—running away from a family that has erased her from its life—using her body as a commodity and her ticket to France. (She becomes a Frenchman's companion.) Combining the first person narrative with poems and letters, interspersed with stylized drawings of her own, Vieyra guides us to the unavoidable conclusion: Kougnou's inescapable feeling of loneliness, which has grown from her being unable to re-enter social life, her increasing isolation from the rest of the building in which she lives in Paris, her mounting anger, her fit, and finally, her drifting beyond life, all lead her to suicide by jumping from a window.

12. For a detailed study of Bessora's textual strategies of subversion, see Mireille Rosello's article, "New *Sans-papiers* Rhetoric in Contemporary France," in *Immigrant Narratives in Contemporary France*.

13. Some of her findings and context recall the Guadeloupean Françoise Ega's posthumous correspondence in the sixties in which she demonstrated the dire conditions Caribbean housemaids experienced and how they were treated as second-class citizens in the Hexagon.

14. The two above paragraphs borrow elements from my article "Vingt ans après Mariama Bâ: le roman africain au féminin."

15. For a detailed analysis of the Beur novel, see Alec G. Hargreaves, *Voices from the North African Immigrant Community in France; Immigration and Identity in Beur Fiction* (Oxford: Berg, 1991); and Michel Laronde, *Autour du roman Beur* (Paris: L'Harmattan, 1993).

16. Born of a French mother and an Algerian father in Algeria, she came to France as an adult.

17. See, for instance, *Shérazade* (1982), *Parle mon fils, parle à ta mère* (1984), and *Les carnets de Shérazade* (1985).

18. See in particular *Fatima ou les Algériennes du square* (1981).

19. Tassadit Imache's *Une fille sans histoire* (1989), Sebbar's *Shérazade* (1982), Farida Belghoul's *Georgette!* (1986), Djura's *Le voile du silence* (1990), Nini Soraya's *Ils disent que je suis une Beurette* (1993)—all illustrate the violence and difficulties encountered by the Beurettes.

20. See her collection of short stories, *Voies de pères, voix de filles* (Paris: Editions Maren Sell et Cie, 1988).

21. Nancy Houston, originally an Anglophone, has become one of the prominent Francophone writers on the literary scene in Paris. A number of her novels and short-stories deal with the issues of bilingualism and biculturalism, in particular, the consequences for an individual of carrying the burdens and ambiguities of collective history into one's personal life (see for instance, *L'empreinte de l'Ange* [1998]). Her essay, *Nord Perdu* (1999) addresses directly the question of being a Francophone within France, of living in a language and a cultural environment that are different from the ones in her childhood.

22. *Lettres parisiennes: autopsie de l'exil*. In collaboration with Nancy Huston (Paris: Barrault, 1986; Collection J'ai lu, 1999).

23. *Une enfance algérienne. Textes inédits recueillis par Leïla Sebbar* (Paris: Gallimard, 1997, Collection Folio, 1999).

24. *Une enfance d'ailleurs, 17 écrivains racontent*. With Nancy Huston (Paris: Belfond, 1993).

25. *Une enfance outremer* (Paris: Seuil, 2001).

26. When *La voyeuse interdite* (1991) was published, it created quite a stir, given both the writer's young age and the violence of the text, as well as the blending of atmosphere, where the frontiers between reality and the surreal become blurred. At the time, critics and readers thought that it was autobiographical because of the young age of both the protagonist and the narrator. Throughout her subsequent texts, Bouraoui made a point precisely of using protagonists that could be as remote as possible from her experience/herself. One common feature persisted, though: the violence of her voice and her images.

27. See *infra*. Mireille Rosello's chapter, "New Gendered Mosaics: Their Mothers, the Gauls," in which she addresses in depth the question of gender, memory, and the mother's narrative.

28. Born in Ksenadar in 1949 from a nomad family, Malika Mokeddem is today a doctor and a writer, living in Montpellier. All her books betray a sense of rebellion and a thirst for freedom. She herself had to struggle against the traditional upbringing for girls in a nomadic environment; to acquire, for example, an education, first in Oran, then in France. She has produced five books since 1990 and made a name for herself on the literary scene by raising a voice against all forms of women's oppression. At the same time, she has gradually asserted her Algerian heritage more forcefully. While a number of her texts choose the sea or the desert and the vast expanses of land as a setting, her characters contradict this apparent freedom of gaze.

29. See, for instance, her play *Les filles d'Ismaël*.

30. The question of monolinguism versus bilingualism is a recurrent issue, particularly in Franco-Maghrebi texts, in which the authors often do not speak the language of their parents (Arabic), and in texts of authors of mixed heritage.

31. Her first novel, too, showed the same hesitations between the island and the *métropole*.

32. In the portrayal of Caribbean family dynamics in the *métropole*, the novel recalls Myriam Warner-Vieyra's *Le Quimboiseur l'avait bien dit* (1979) or *The Family* (1992) by Buchi Emecheta. The novel contains all the usual themes of Caribbean female writing: a young girl left by her mother/parents, who start a new life in the *métropole* (Paris/London), a grandmother taking care of her, her disorientation and her cultural shock as an adolescent upon leaving the island to join her family in the city. The main difference is the absence of sexual abuse (which is central to *Le Quimboiseur* and *The Family*).

33. The generations are represented by: Marie-Noëlle, her mother Reynalda, Antonine (also called Nina), Reynalda's mother (who is the grand-mother of Marie-Noëlle), as well as Ranélise, Marie-Noëlle's substitute mother until her preadolescence. (Reynalda leaves for France soon after her daughter is born.)

34. Unlike La colonie du Nouveau Monde, for instance, there is no pole of attraction, nothing to keep her focused: neither religious faith, nor love, nor education, nor professional success. Rejected again and again by her mother and by men, she nevertheless succeeds in finding her own balance. She does so by unlocking the mystery surrounding her father's origins. She is the result of what she considers a monstrosity (that is, the forbidden union of her mother and a priest).

35. In that regard, her more recent novel Mélanire Cou-coupé (2000) revisits the question of (historical) roots and history and the relationship of the Caribbean to Africa. Unlike some of her earlier works, like Hérémakhonon, which evoked a powerful, ancient Africa and revealed an admiration for the continent, the relationship of a Caribbean protagonist to Africa, which is a metaphor of the relation between Guadeloupe and Africa, bears some undertones of vengeance and resentment. Like Djebar, Maryse Condé feels a need to reassess history and confront colonial constructions.

36. Interestingly, Maryse Condé, like Assia Djebar, has distanced herself both from home and from France, choosing the United States as her space of writing (and living). In "Finalement, on va arriver à simplement dire: Je suis ce que je suis," an interview with Catherine Dana, Maryse Condé stresses that for her France has never worked as a space for writing, that she always felt reduced to "une voix d'ailleurs," somehow objectified, if not "exotified." For that matter, Guadeloupe did not work either, as she shocked her Caribbean compatriots and did not fit the Guadeloupean definition. As the title of the interview suggests, it took her years to be able to write, say, and be as she wanted. This interview is part of the special issue Masculin/Féminin for Africultures 35 (February 2001): 19–25.

37. Children from the Antilles learn French history just as the rest of the métropole. In the French history program, very little appears on slavery and on colonization, colonialism, and decolonization. Children thus learn about their heritage essentially through folktales and storytelling.

38. See, for instance, Françoise Ega's Lettres à une noire (1978), published posthumously, in which she underlines the lack of solidarity—how the protagonist, a housemaid, is regarded as different by the French and looked down upon by her compatriots for being a housemaid. For a detailed analysis of the novel, see Patrice J. Proulx," Textualizing the Immigrant Community: Françoise Ega's Lettres à une Noire," in Immigrant Narratives in Contemporary France (2001): 141–49.

39. One should add Michèle Maillet, who has not been publishing since her two texts: Bonsoir, faites de beaux rêves! Antillaise, Speakrine . . . et remerciée (1982), based on her personal experience, and L'étoile noire (1990).

40. See in particular Yamina Benguigui's Mémoires d'immigrés (1998).

CHAPTER 14

Body as Subject

FOUR CONTEMPORARY WOMEN ARTISTS

WHITNEY CHADWICK

You do not realize how widely feminism is accepted in the States. But in France, if you declare: "I am a feminist" or if people think you are, well, your career as an artist might as well be over. People won't pay attention to you anymore.

—Orlan, 1998[1]

The terms "woman," "artist," "French," and "feminist" are less often combined in the history of contemporary art in France than in recent Anglo-American writing on the topic. The reasons for this, however, may be more usefully linked to specific cultural readings and representations of difference than to the dramatic conclusions suggested by performance artist Orlan. While it is true that the period of remarkable literary cultural production by French women initiated by the events of May 1968 has no clear parallel in the visual arts, the practices of internationally recognized women artists, when examined closely, reveal a strong engagement with theories of difference, intersubjectivity, and the body that have been widely circulated through the writings of Julia Kristeva, Hélène Cixous, Luce Irigaray, and others. Although engaged with issues of representation rather than critical theorizing, attention to the sexed, gendered, and socially coded body, to artifacts of the body, and to issues of female subjectivity in the work of artists from Niki de Saint Phalle and Orlan to Annette Messager and Sophie Calle recall Irigaray's observation that "Women's exploitation is based upon sexual difference; its solution will come only through sexual difference."[2] Irigaray's locating of difference *within* difference also calls attention to other kinds of difference: to the difference that may exist between the production of the work and its critical reception; to difference mapped across relationships between artist and viewer; to the problematics of reordering gender and sexual difference through the body.

Beginning in the early 1970s women artists' groups, from Spirale (founded in 1973 to study "smothered creativity" (*la création étouffée*) to Musidora (an association of feminist actresses and filmmakers founded in 1973), called attention to the lack of a female perspective in the visual arts while at the same time resisting the more extreme forms of ideological and sexual division advocated by some women's groups in the United Kingdom and the United States.[3] Events and publications from the 1970s that were specific to women visual artists included an issue of the feminist journal *Les Cahiers du GRIF* in June 1975 devoted to the broad topic of "creation" and including articles on and by women artists, and two publications of 1977: an issue of *Art Press International* titled "Femmes-Différence" that appeared in March and that featured writings on women painters and performance artists, and an issue of the French feminist journal *Sorcières* called "L'Art et les femmes."

Exhibitions that focused exclusively on the work of women artists were relatively limited during the 1970s and 1980s in comparison to feminist activities elsewhere. An exhibition called "Woman's Role in Contemporary Art" ("La Part des femmes dan l'art contemporain") was organized at the municipal Arts Center in Vitry-sur-Seine in 1984 and included work by 94 contemporary women artists, most of them painters and many of them living and working in Paris. The exhibition omitted video, as well as much installation and performance work (mainly for lack of funding and technical support). These limitations, taken in conjunction with Deputy Mayor of Vitry-sur-Seine Jean Collet's introduction, reinforce, as Kate Ince has suggested, a certain resistance to fully or radically exploring the boundaries of women's artistic practices.[4] Collet's insistence that the exhibition was not to be understood as "feminist," in order to avoid the tendency to create an "artistic ghetto" through too explicit an assertion of sexual difference, reiterated a long-standing cultural resistance to reformulating categories of difference as division, a resistance confronted by Orlan when she brandished a placard reading *JE SUIS UNE HOMME ET UN FEMME* at a feminist political meeting in Toulouse in 1971. Reversing the masculine and feminine pronouns that make up the only binary coding of nouns in French, Orlan's intervention called attention to both the ongoing ambivalence to feminism expressed by many French curators and writers, and to new ways of formulating difference in representation.

Interventions by French women artists into areas of female subjectivity, identity, and embodiment through practices that enact the body or subject in a performative fashion, however, predate both the contemporary women's movement and the events of May 1968 and originate in European post–World War II body art and actionism. Among these artists were Yves Klein, whose "actions" included a manipulated photograph of the artist throwing himself from a window, which was widely read as documenting an artistic suicide, and other members of the French group Nouveau Réalistes. Niki de Saint Phalle performed the first of more than twelve "shootings" in February 1961. These events involved sculptures and assemblages in which containers of paint had been embedded beneath the plaster surfaces. When "shot" with a pistol or rifle the containers spattered their contents over the surface. Organized as collaborative events with friends and other members of the Nouveau Réalistes—including Arman, Klein, Daniel Spoerri, Jean Tinguely, and others—which she had joined that year, these "actions" elicit multiple readings. One might view them as the final stage of a personal exorcism that began when she first collected knives, guns, meat cleavers, and so on, and used them in assemblages in the creation of which she imagined using the weapons to threaten men whom she felt inhibited her. She then progressed from throwing darts at pictorial representations of these same men to shooting at them with a rifle, and from there she progressed to the "shootings."[5]

Another reading of these works might rely on placing her "actions" in relationship both to her immediate artistic culture, which included the Nouveau Réalistes challenge to the overblown nationalistic and masculine rhetoric of Abstract Expressionism, and to a renegotiations of a history of European modernism that wrested notions of stylistic innovation from visual, if not literal, assaults on the female body, notably Picasso's *Demoiselles d'Avignon* and Matisse's *Blue Nude* (both 1907).[6] Throughout the 1950s, as Abstract Expressionist painting circulated widely in Europe, traveling exhibitions, catalogues, and critical texts emphasized the Abstract Expressionist painters' struggle to forge connections between individual subjective consciousness and image-making using metaphors of heroism, engagement, struggle, victory, and defeat. This critical rhetoric reinforced views of artistic creation as a totemic battle with elemental forces of silence, and asserted the painterly mark that resulted from the artist's action as an expression of a (male) human consciousness.[7] Against this rhetoric of physical and psychic engagement, the attitude of ironic distance embedded in Marcel Duchamp's view of the creative act as a matter of simple choice, and the influence of his politics of disengagement on the work of a younger generation of American artists of the 1950s like Jasper Johns and Robert Rauschenberg, as well as on the Nouveau Réalistes, can be seen in the tension between Saint Phalle's creating of a painterly mark through a physical action and the (now-mechanized and distanced) character of that action, as well as in a wresting of the creative act away from masculine action.

Although Saint Phalle's "shootings" challenged the construction of male subjectivity around notions of physical action and violence, critical responses to her performance/painting sometimes reconstituted her acts of violence as "feminine." François Pluchart suggested that, "Saint Phalle makes destruction her accomplice. In spite of appearances, this is an essentially feminine act. . . . It represents an attack on bourgeois morality, petty nationalism, war. It presents a specifically feminine morality culminating in the "Nanas" exhibited at Iolas Gallery."[8]

Setting aside the question of what might constitute a "feminine morality," one might argue that the radicalness of the "Nanas," and especially the monumental *Hon* (*She,* in Swedish) constructed at the Moderna Museet in Stockholm in 1966, lay precisely in their refusal of transcendent meaning in favor of an embodiment of the feminine that was at once playful and monstrous, and that embedded mythic Woman in the real. *Hon,* although created well before a contemporary feminist consciousness was asserted in the writings and practices of women artists in Britain and the United States in 1971, nevertheless anticipated subsequent attempts to rewrite femininity through the body.

Working in collaboration with Tinguely and Swedish artist Per Olof Ultvedt, Saint Phalle constructed a monumental reclining pregnant female 90 feet long, 27 feet wide, and 6 feet high. Visitors to the exhibition were invited to enter the figure (Saint Phalle referred to her as a "goddess") through the vagina and explore an interior that included a planetarium in her left breast and a milk bar in the right one:

> The reclining Nana was pregnant and by a series of stairs and steps you could get to the
> terrace from her tummy where you could have a panoramic view of the approaching

visitors and her gaily painted legs. There was nothing pornographic about the HON even though she was entered by her sex. . . . She was like a grand fertility goddess receiving comfortably in her immensity and generosity. She received, absorbed, and devoured thousands of visitors. It was an incredible experience creating her. This joyous, huge creature represented for many visitors and me the dream of the return to the Great Mother.[9]

Saint Phalle's *Hon* re-presented the maternal body as female sex demythologized and rewritten as entertainment (in one interior viewing area a Greta Garbo film screened). The sign of the woman's lack has been reconfigured and given new meanings, the abject pregnant and lactating body with its leakages and unboundedness is resealed, the terror of woman's interior space transmuted into a playground and viewing platforms. To view from within the female body—even if only through simulation—challenges psychoanalytic constructions of specularity, of an initiating of castration anxiety through a visual confrontation with woman's lack, by encouraging a literal and physical interaction with the body of the woman through her sex. Saint Phalle's *Hon* and the *Nanas* that were her near relatives, also reworked art historical notions of embodiment in ways both playful and far reaching.

While *Hon* was part sculpture, part performance, the work of a number of European women artists in the 1960s engaged in practices that produced meaning and exhibited the self through the body in performances that often had sources in Antonin Artaud's Theater of Cruelty and in the actionism of post–World War II European artists from Group Zero in Germany to Klein in France. Among the female practitioners of what came to be known as "body art" were Austrian artist Valie Export and French artist Gina Pane. In France, it is performance artist Orlan whose recent work has been most aggressively situated in relation to contemporary discourses of the female body. Coming of age in the 1960s, a decade of widespread protests and challenges to institutionalized authority, she has used her own body in performances and installations that began when she first exhibited the semen-stained sheets of her bridal trousseau in 1966 to comment on her own sexual activity and critique cultural expectations regarding bridal virginity. In the 1970s, she pasted a triangle of her pubic hair to a painting of a voluptuous reclining nude in the Louvre, inserting her own specific identity into the imagery of hairless, anonymous, and objectified femininity that dominates western art history. The following decade, she shocked audiences by displaying her magnified genitals, held open with pincers and with the pubic hair painted yellow, blue, and red (the last color supplied by menstrual blood). More recently, Orlan's manipulations of the body have become more invasive and more radical. In a series of works, called by the artist "*chirurgicales-performances,*" begun in 1990 in Newcastle, England, and continuing today in the ongoing project called "The Reincarnation of Saint Orlan," she has turned the operating theater into gallery and performance space, and used her own body to challenge western culture's objectification and aestheticization of female beauty, and to expose the fine line between the beautiful and the grotesque.[10]

Working collaboratively with a plastic surgeon, she has submitted her face and body to a series of plastic surgeries aimed at aligning her features with models of beauty computer-synthesized from details of famous works of art: the forehead of Leonardo da Vinci's Mona Lisa, the chin of Botticelli's Venus, the eyelids of a Raphael Madonna, the eyes of Gerard's Psyche, for example. As part of the performance, she has transformed the sterile operating theater into an elaborate stage set-ting complete with projections, sound, drapery, doctors, and technicians wearing de-signer ensembles, and so on.

The assembling of an image out of fragments creates not beauty (with its iden-tification with perfection), but a gory and grotesque pastiche, or parody, of artistic practices that seek perfection in the detail. As such, they recall Surrealism's disfig-uring of the human, often female, body as part of that movement's attack on West-ern rationalism and wholeness. And, as curator Sidra Stich demonstrated in the exhibition "Anxious Visions Surrealist Art," the deformed bodies of Surrealist art often relied as much in the literal disfigurements to be seen in the streets of Paris at the end of World War I as in the phantasms of the dream and the unconscious.[11] In a similar fashion, Orlan's surgeries also move between psychic images of ideal beauty and the grotesque reality of contemporary surgical interventions with their medicalization of femininity. Filmed in color, and often broadcast, the perfor-mances combine aspects of spectacle, horror movie, and real-life hospital drama. During them the artist, who is never fully anaesthetized, reads philosophical, liter-ary, or psychoanalytic texts.

Presented as artist performances, Orlan's surgeries raise issues crucial to under-standing the female body in contemporary Western culture. Drawing on discourses of art, medicine, and science/technology, she sites her body in relation to Fou-cauldian and feminist views of sex and the body as social, rather than material, pro-ductions and in relation to writings by Judith Butler and Luce Irigaray that call attention to the constructedness of nature itself. Emphasizing materialization rather than static matter, Butler projects: "A process of materialization that stabilizes over time to produce the effect of boundary, fixity and surface we call matter."[12] This focus on process and becoming, linked to postmodern views of identity as contin-gent, intersects with Orlan's use of performance to literally reshape the physical body and transform flesh and tissue (pieces of which she then preserves in resin and exhibits as if they were bits of sculpture). Linking the construction of identity to re-constructive technologies like cosmetic surgery, Orlan seems to embrace a vision of the cyborg body, a merging of biology and technology. Sociologist Kathy Davis has argued that cosmetic surgery is not about beauty, but about identity, and Orlan, by literally transforming herself, destabilizes both the notion of a natural, or unmedi-ated, body and the stability of identity.[13] She herself has argued that modern tech-nologies have made any idea of the natural body obsolete or, in Davis's words: "Her identity project is radical precisely because she is willing to alter her body surgically in order to experiment with different identities."[14]

In "Reincarnation," Orlan reads from three carefully chosen texts, one of which is a passage from Julia Kristeva's *Pouvoirs d'horreur* (*Powers of Horror*).[15] The reading of texts resituates the physicality of the performance in a theoretical and intellectual context. At the same time, the act of reading aloud while partially anaesthetized and undergoing surgery, prevents spectators from seeing her body as a passive and inert object, at the mercy of others. Instead she focuses attention on her body as active agent, controlling the activities of those who surround her in the operating room. Kristeva's description of the process of abjection—the formation of new bodily boundaries for subjectivity by means of the breaking of boundaries and the expul-sion of matter—becomes relevant to the new body formation that is taking place be-fore the spectator's eyes.

In an exhaustive analysis of the Reincarnation project, Ince argues that "the fe-
maleness towards which Orlan's surgical project shows her to be moving is subjec-
tively unfamiliar to the Western sociosymbolic order, a 'femininity' that is not
determined by phallocentric law or grounded in Western metaphysics."[16] Orlan's
move, then, is one that takes her into a performativity of sexualities and genders that
has drawn increasingly widespread critical attention at the end of the millennium.
Her choice of sources for her reconstituted flesh—the decision predicated not on
the alleged "beauty" of her artistic sources, but on the fact that she claims to admire
their qualities of character, among them androgyny, aggressiveness, vulnerability, on
so on—indicates the importance of nonmaterial traits in the physical construction
of her new identity as a woman.[17]

Locating subjectivity in shifting, contingent identities, and enacting it through
the body and its signs also characterizes the work of Annette Messager and Sophie
Calle. Like Orlan, Messager also came of age during the unrest of the 1960s. The
May 1968 student rebellion, begun at the University of Nanterre, quickly spilled
over into the streets of Paris. Many of its leaders had been involved with the Situa-
tionist International of 1957, a social movement with roots in Surrealism's revolt
against modernist rationality and utopianism that advocated poetic and violent resistance to social order. Messager and her artist friends—Jean LeGac, Paul Armand-
Gette, Sarkis, and Christian Boltanski—were influenced by the ideas of
philosophers and social critics including Guy Debord, Roland Barthes, and Michel
Foucault. Their writings, and the political and social upheaval of the later 1960s,
would exert a profound influence on Messager and her friends, all of whom have resisted hierarchy and easy categorization in their work. "In France," Messager wrote,
"there isn't conceptual art in the strictest sense of the term. The thinking behind
mélange and hybridization . . . comes to us from May 1968."[18]

In her early work, Messager satirized the compartmentalization of social space by
dividing her activities into those executed in her bedroom and those carried out in
her studio. At the same time, she distinguished between her activities as a collector
and as a creator by signing her works "Annette Messager Collectionneuse" or "Annette Messager Artiste." This division carried through into her obsession with dichotomies: nature/culture, male/female, intellectual/emotional, and so forth.
Within a large group of albums and collections that she assembled at this time (these
include 56 scrapbook-style albums made from about 1971 to 1974) is a subgroup of
collections in which women are presented as objects of violence. Les Tortures volontaires
(Voluntary Tortures, 1972) focuses on women's obsessions with physical beauty and the
body. Messager collected illustrations of women participating in beauty treatments
that range from mud baths and facial peels to more invasive and radical plastic surgeries. Images of forbidding mechanical apparatuses, manipulated physical positions,
and surgical reconstructions chillingly evoked the sacrifice of personal identity to socially defined expectations of female beauty in ways that anticipated Orlan's more
literal interventions into this territory.

In subsequent collections, including Les Effroyables Aventures d'Annette Messager truc-
queuse (The Horrifying Adventures of Annette Messager, Trickster, 1974–1975) and Mes Clichés
(My Clichés, 1976–1977), Messager made drawings on illustrations in pornographic
magazines that showed women as victims of sadomasochistic and sexual violence. In
these works, Messager in effect "rewrote" the images, drawing over the bodies of
other women in a Kafkaesque ritual that had the effect of making them her own. Re-

cuperating these images of women as objects, she inserted her own femininity into a process generally assumed to be carried out by men in response to formations of male sexuality and desire.

During this period, although Messager refused to identify herself as a "feminist," she was articulate about the privileges of masculinity and the social restrictions placed on women:

> If I didn't know what I wanted to do, I knew what I didn't want to do. In exhibitions, I saw strong and powerful painting, grandiose pictures, and I said to myself that perhaps there was something else. At the same time, I realized that the history of art was limited to a male history. . . . I was a woman who tried to make art. Therefore naturally, the problem of the feminine arose: I tried to see if there was something to show in this domain, a bit the way an ethnologist or a historian of primitive art shows the beautiful in the world of the Australian aboriginals.[19]

Messager continued to work with photographic representations of the body. In an extensive series of works titled *Mes Voeux* (*My Vows*) begun in 1988, she assembled small photographs of body parts into dense collections of images hung from walls in various arrangements. The photographs, stripped of context or individual identity and representing the body only through its parts, resembled the collections of ex-votos and devotional images found on altars in chapels and pilgrimage shrines. The words "ficelle" and "vouex" engage (French-speaking) spectators in a series of puns and word plays reminiscent of Duchamp's punning titles for his ready-mades earlier in the century, adding additional layers of linguistic signification to her dense and fractured visual imagery.

When assembled and displayed, the individual body parts presented in *Mes Voeux* signify not a single person, but an aggregate of bodies: old and young, male and female, active and resting. Her deliberate confusion of identities renders the identification of gender and sexual difference elusive and largely meaningless. Feminist views of gender as socially constructed rather than biologically defined underly these works, but they are equally indebted to Surrealism, a movement Messager has embraced because of its insistence on overthrowing dichotomies, synthesizing polarized states of being, rejecting the hierarchical classifications of western art, and exploring visual languages outside the mainstream (anthropological evidence and the art of the insane, for example). She was also aware, however, of the complicated and ambivalent attitudes toward women expressed by the (male) Surrealists.[20]

While her attitudes toward the fragmented body have multiple sources, she is insistent about rejecting notions of wholeness: "For me, it's a 'natural' gesture to rip bodies apart, cut them up. . . . It's also my desire to reveal scraps, fragments, instants of things; so that there are only a few precious traces, so that the viewer reconstitutes his or her own direction."[21] Fragmented imagery also carries gender implications for Messager; "I always feel that my identity as a woman and as an artist is divided, disintegrated, fragmented, and never linear, always multifaceted . . . always pictures of parts of bodies, fragments and close-ups. . . . I always perceive the body in fragments."[22]

Messager's *Pièce montée* (its literal meaning in French: an elaborately constructed and decorated cake, 1986) combines photographs of body parts with acrylic and oil paint. Carol Eliel has convincingly argued that its sources can be found in a photograph by the Surrealist photographer Jacques-Andre Boiffard. His *Untitled* (1930), a close-up of an open mouth displaying an engorged and dripping tongue, was included in an exhibition of Surrealist photography at the Musée National d'Art Moderne in Paris in 1985 and has been widely reproduced. In Messager's photograph, however, it is not the tongue that is the focus of attention, but rather the stream of photographic body parts that appear to have been vomited forth in a cascade of paint drips that suggest blood spraying from the distended mouth. A kind of existential horror clings to this thoroughly postmodern reworking of Edward Munch's famous *Cry.* The work also conveys powerful associations with Surrealism's poetic call for the breaking of boundaries and the dissolution and refiguring of the body through its parts, as seen in works from René Magritte's and Hans Bellmer's anagrammatic reworkings of the body to André Breton's call for a "convulsive beauty . . . fixed and explosive" in 1937.

In her influential essay "The Laugh of the Medusa" (1975), Cixous wrote, " If [woman] is a whole, it's a whole compound of parts that are wholes, not simple partial objects but a moving, limitlessly changing ensemble . . . an immense astral space not organized around any one sun that's more of a star than the others."[23]

Messager's body fragments call attention to what is missing, to what is unseen and perhaps unrepresentable. Introducing the question of absence, she draws attention to the ways that parts function as signs of the missing whole, of traces of that which remains invisible. This notion of the trace, and of the representation of artifacts of the body rather than the body itself, have figured prominently in the work of many contemporary women artists from Ana Mendieta to Kiki Smith to Messager and Sophie Calle.

In the series called *Histoire des Robes* (*The Story of Dresses,* 1988–1992), Messager displayed dresses as substitutes for the female body. Hermetically sealed in coffin-like *vitrines* as if they were sacred relics, they were accompanied by the memories and associations conjured up by the drawings and photographs attached to them with pins and pieces of string. Evocative of mortuary rituals of the laying out of bodies, they became fetishes, substituting for the absent body. While one piece in the series refers specifically to Messager's mother, others represent archetypal and idealized aspects of herself, reinforcing the fractured and multiple identities on which she has based her artistic practice from the beginning.

The work of Sophie Calle, although less invested in representing the body, also investigates the lack of a coherent or fixed identity, and the ways identity is produced through investigations of the traces left by the body, among them photographs, diaries and records of surveillance. She has used photography and text as tools to "provide evidence of [her] existence," as well as to expose the tension between the public and the private, indifference and desire, the observer and the observed. Through the assumption of shifting subject/object positions, she has explored issues of identity and the way that identities are often pieced together from a series of details. In *Les Dormeurs* (*The Sleepers,* 1979), she arranged for a different person to occupy her bed every eight hours for eight days. As her subjects slept in the bed imprinted with her body, she sat in a chair and observed them, photographed them, took notes, and occasionally exchanged a few words with them.

Calle's project, some 176 photographs and 33 texts, explores intimacy, vulnerability, and power. Invading other peoples' lives, even their sleep, she allowed them to invade her private space in ways that began to break down distinctions between self and other. Her work has been perhaps most effective in exploring the fine line between truth and fiction, and the ways that personal identity participates in both realms.

In 1983, Calle and Jean Baudrillard published the book *Suite Venitienne* (*Please Follow Me*), a collection of photographs and diarylike entries recording the artist's "shadowing" of a man she had met at a party in Paris while he was in Venice for two weeks on holiday.[24] Wearing a wig and disguise, and never making contact with the object of her attentions, she played out an elaborate transference of agency, appropriating the "male gaze," the conventionalized prerogative of public viewing, and producing the woman, traditionally the object of others' looks, as the embodied viewing subject. The pursuit of the unnamed "other" becomes, finally, a search for the self as the missing dialogue with an other that locates subjectivity in the world becomes instead a monologue with the self in the course of Calle's obsessive pursuit.

Calle's Venetian surveillance reversed an earlier work (*The Shadow*, 1981) in which she had her mother hire a detective-photographer to follow her without her knowledge to sites of personal significance where she could be photographed to "provide evidence of her existence." In *Fantômes* (*Ghosts*, 1991), Calle created deliberate ghosts by removing works from the permanent collection of the Museum of Modern Art in New York as part of a group exhibition titled "Dislocations."[25] She replaced Edward Hopper's *House by the Railroad* (1925), Amedeo Modigliani's *Reclining Nude* (1919), and Georges Seurat's *Evening Honfleur* (1886), among others, with texts describing what was originally there in the words of museum guards and others who had regular contacts with the works:

What I did was replace the paintings with people's memories of the paintings. Those of just anybody that used to pass it. I wasn't only interested in people who have to look at the painting, like curators, but also people who go by because they follow the same path, like when you take a road to go back to your house and you cross a street again and again because it's just there on your way. They can be somebody who cleans, the guards. . . . The interest lies in the traces people leave behind, in the details of life, when you don't know who they are, but you know what kind of toothbrushes they use, or how they leave their bed undone.[26]

For Calle, memories such as these represent a kind of truth. Robert Storr, the exhibition's curator, has likened her approach to that of Natalie Sarraute, Marguerite Duras, Alain Robbe-Grillet and other practitioners of the "new novel," in which the smallest of details are closely examined, since none is so ephemeral that it may be discounted as an essential clue to the identity of an elusive subject. When Calle turns the lens on herself, as she did in *Autobiographical Stories* (1988) the results were no less ambiguous. Here Calle combined photography and text in the elucidation of her own most intimate memories, including painful childhood experiences, infatuations, and odd moments. One panel of each work contained a written text, the other a large photograph showing an emblematic object or scene. In one, Calle describes a man whom she had admired since her childhood. At thirty, she decided to reveal her feelings to him and made an appointment to see him. She arrived carrying a white silk wedding dress in a suitcase. The last sentence of her text reads, "I wore it on our first night together." The dress, wrinkled and stained, appears in the adjoining image. Whether we accept Calle's "stories" as literal or fictional remains, the province of each viewer remains a matter of personal choice for Calle's intention is not to provide narrative closure. Rather, like the other artists discussed here, she has chosen ambiguity over certitude, fluidity over fixity.

Interest in rethinking the body in ways that renegotiate its materiality and its boundaries characterizes much contemporary art by women in France today. While the four artists discussed above continue to exhibit regularly in France and abroad, their influence on younger French women artists represents only one thread in a complicated cultural landscape. While there exists today a broad group of female visual artists, many of them recent graduates of the Ecole Nationale Supérieure des Beaux-Arts and other art schools, whose work reveals an interest in issues of gender and sexuality, their explorations have been as much shaped by the prominence of contemporary women filmmakers in France as they have by the traditions of the visual arts. National and international exhibitions—from the recent Bienale de Lyon to *Traversées*, a large survey of work by young contemporary artists mounted at the Musée d'Art Moderne de la Ville de Paris in Autumn 2001—suggest the growing centrality of time-based media in contemporary French art.

Chantal Ackerman's and Catérine Bréard's cinematic explorations of women's lives and female sexuality have proved to be a powerful influence on many younger women's decisions to forego the more static and material practices of painting and sculpture in favor of film and video. At the same time, the corporeal body as subject is often replaced with a new conception of the body defined neither by gender nor organs. Influenced by the theories of Gilles Deleuze, and no doubt also by writings on the cyborg or virtual body by the Americans Donna Haraway and Sandy Stone, many women are beginning to reinvent the body using film, computers, and video as media. Among them are Rébecca Bournigault, who has interviewed both men and women about how they perceive and feel about themselves and their bodies, Valérie Mrejen, whose practice includes the production of books, films, and videos, and the videos of Alice Anderson, who impersonated her mother's search for her daughter in the video film *Ma Mère* (1999–2001).

The current preoccupation with time-based media among French women artists suggests that the issues of fluidity, performativity, and transformation that preoccupied women artists from Niki de Saint Phalle to Orlan, Annette Messager, and Sophie Calle continue to shape women's artistic practices. As ways of thinking about the body, and about its representation, shift and change, women artists will continue to renegotiate this territory.

NOTES

1. Orlan, quoted in *Beauty Matters*, ed. Peg Zeglin Brand (Bloomington: Indiana University Press, 2000), 289–313; the quote is on 301.
2. Luce Irigaray, *je, tu, nous: Toward a Culture of Difference*, trans. Alison Martin (New York: Routledge, 1993), 12.
3. For a more extensive discussion of this phenomenon see Kate Ince, *Orlan: Millennial Female* (Oxford: Berg, 2000), 2–6.
4. Ibid., 5.
5. Pontus Hulten, *Niki de Saint Phalle*, exh. cat. (Bonn: Kunst- und Ausstellungshalle der Bundesrepublik Deutschland, 1992).
6. This issue has been extensively discussed in feminist criticism; see, for example, Carol Duncan.

7. For a discussion of this ideology in relation to the American artists Jasper Johns and Robert Rauschenberg, whose attitudes had much in common with those of the Nouveau Réalistes, see Jonathan Katz, "Jasper Johns and Robert Rauschenberg," in *Significant Others: Creativity and Intimate Partnership,* ed. Whitney Chadwick and Isabelle de Courtivron (London and New York: Thames and Hudson, 1993).

8. François Pluchart, "Fire Sermons," trans. Suzi Gablik, *Art and Artists,* 1.5 (August 1966): 26, attempted to differentiate Saint Phalle's violence, her cycle of destruction-creation, from Yves Klein's use of fire in a series of one-minute paintings in 1956, arguing that Klein's process transcended the initial destruction of the burning process, thereby transforming destruction into supreme and absolute, indeed transcendent, creative affirmation. Saint Phalle's destructive act, by contrast, was viewed as failing to become transcendent, remaining rooted in the mundane.

9. Hulten 1992, 168.

10. The most extensive discussion of this project is to be found in Kate Ince's *Orlan: Millennial Female,* op cit.

11. The exhibition was held at the University Art Museum, Berkeley, in 1992.

12. Judith Butler, *Bodies that Matter: The Discursive Limits of "Sex"* (London: Routledge, 1993).

13. Kathy Davis, *Reshaping the Female Body: The Dilemma of Cosmetic Surgery* (London: Routledge, 1995), 163.

14. Kathy Davis, "'My Body Is My Art': Cosmetic Surgery as Feminist Utopia?," in *Embodied Practices: Feminist Perspectives on the Body,* ed. Kathy Davis (London, Thousand Oaks, New Delhi: Sage Publications, 1997), 168–81.

15. Julia Kristeva, *Powers of Horror: An Essay in Abjection,* trans. Leon S. Roudiez (New York: Columbia University Press, 1982).

16. Ince 2000, 124.

17. Ibid.

18. Messager, cited in Sherry Conkelton, "Annette Messager's Carnival of Death and Desire," *Annette Messager,* exh. cat. (Los Angeles and New York: The Los Angeles County Museum of Art and the Museum of Modern Art, New York, 1995), 11.

19. Jean-Michel Foray, "Annette Messager, collectionneuses d'histoires," *Art Press* 147 (May 1990): 17; cited in Carol S. Eliel, "'Nourishment You Take:' Annette Messager, Influence and the Subversion of Images," in *Annette Messager* 55.

20. See my *Women Artists and the Surrealist Movement* (Boston: New York Graphic Society Books, 1985).

21. Cited in Eliel, "Nourishment You Take," 67.

22. Ibid.

23. Hélène Cixous, "The Laugh of the Medusa," trans. Keith Cohen and Paula Cohen, *Signs: A Journal of Women and Culture* (Summer 1976): 889.

24. *Suite Venitienne* (Paris: Editions de l'Etoile, 1983); English edition *Suite Venitienne/Please Follow Me.* Trans. Dany Barash (Seattle: Bay Press, 1988).

25. Robert Storr, "Dislocations" (New York: The Museum of Modern Art, 1991).

26. Ibid.

CHAPTER 15

Unmasked!

HÉLÈNE CIXOUS

The eagle, the vulture, the black vulture, the red kite, any kind of black kite, any kind of raven, the horned owl, the screech owl, the gull, any kind of hawk, the little owl, the cormorant, the great owl, the white owl, the desert owl, the osprey, the stork, any kind of heron, the hoopoe, and the bat.

—Leviticus, 11:13–19

These are the birds that you shall revile, those that shall not be eaten, as they are unclean for you. These are impure, do not defile yourselves by eating them.

And the woman who becomes pregnant and gives birth to a son will be ceremonially unclean for seven days, and she must wait thirty-three days to be purified from her bleeding. She must not touch anything sacred. But if it is a child of female sex that she gives birth to, even worse, for two weeks she will be unclean, and she must wait sixty-six days before being unsoiled from her bleeding.

"Birds, women, writing," as I read the chapter from Leviticus, form a series of equivalencies. A very poetic chapter from Leviticus presents me with a long, strange list of what is prohibited and what is allowed, you are sacred, you are defiled—oh, the interminable inventory of abominations. In the anguish-producing dictionary of species of the air the verdict is returned. Here are species that I never watched out for which are called *unclean.*

For a long time I've been dreaming of the *uncleanliness* of the stork, am I really going to have to stay away from it?

I'm not associating birds, women, and writing because it's a game. I see clearly that there is a no-man's-land and (*imundus*), a park of the cursed, a Reservation hated by man-made decrees where these species of birds are found that I for one honor and cherish. Birds, women, and that literature I call "writing," the noblest in my view, a free traveler along edges and abysms, the one that confers upon the language it traverses all its primordial strangeness.

The one I love goes off willingly to travel down into what Genêt called "the lower depths," others say "the grottoes," down into the most hidden, most elusive regions, the most difficult to work, the most sensitive to the touch, down into the unconscious, and the bodily passions. They can be reached by borrowing the ladder of writing that goes down to the roots.

That writing suffers in fact the fate of birds, women, the unclean. Because it runs the risks of its truths, because it makes its way into places where danger grows—there are few people there—it is joyfully received only by "people whose souls are already shaped," as Clarice Lispector says: people who know that one's approach to each thing is made gradually and painstakingly—including the passage across the opposite of what one is approaching. Those people who, alone, will understand very slowly that this book takes nothing away from anyone. The character of G. H., for example, gave to me little by little a difficult joy; but it was a joy.

Why is there such a great conflict between these birds and the others? The others have the feeling in fact that something is being taken away from them. While actually nothing is being taken away from them, rather one wishes to give them something. But how is that?

Let's switch continents: let's follow Gandhi. How he is *hated* in India today, as yesterday. He died as a result. It's true, he had a portion of the Indians with him, mostly those *on the bottom.* He didn't demand, he didn't request. But he did, and he showed what he did. So, many experienced this action as an offense to their nonaction. Love the supposed "lower depths" and you'll see that the words that make the law are deceiving.

But what disgust we feel upon pronouncing the word *unclean,* we who are taught disgust. And yet "unclean" means simply (in no-man's-land) not clean. And that the world is defined as being clean. One stroke of a word, and a whole Economy has established its rigorous measures over the universe.

But what does not-clean mean?—none of these mixed dishes, undisguised, unprepared, not transformed in appearance so as to become edible. Certain things, creatures, actions have remained raw, alive, ever since the moment of creation. "They have continued to be the root," divines Clarice Lispector. The root is twisted, doubled up, entangled, it digs with all its force into the ground, evil and good happily mingled, before the tree with two separate halves, it is humble (*humílis*) for it knows that nothing is simple, that it is itself not simple, thought is a struggle with itself, one cannot reach, but one can stretch, from the two forces together springs forth *the moment.* And this energy is joy.

Now, it is joy that is prohibited—the thing that escapes all economies. It is with joy that I am beside myself. In the non-self ether of the earth, down in the depths.

I do not understand people's disgust for roots, or their fear of joy. I do not understand that insidious joyless thing called misogyny. I have tried hundreds of times, for hundreds of years, to understand why the eagle, woman, the stork, the poetry of upper and lower depths are things they can't swallow. In vain.

And why when the World started to recount its history there was already in the voice of narration the harsh stress on misogyny, and why there is no memory without this poison.

Who then could have invented "justified" hatred, the right to hate? And all these churches and religions that are built on the rock of hatred, bastions of the World against everything that they (the editors of Bibles) call "*unclean.*" First there were the

Bibles, fathers, sons and grandsons, those magnificent apocalyptic monsters, who do not hide, no, they pride themselves on the triumphs of unjust, criminal kings. On the one hand, they love David, the handsome king, killer, for the sake of adultery, of Uriah, the loyal soldier, and on the other hand, they stone adulterous women.

But who, then, could have written their Bibles and their Korans? The book with everything mixed together, Moses and Job with David, the just and the unjust alike?

And amidst the assemblage of just heroes and criminal heroes, all male, who, then, which man—which woman—could have slipped in amidst this clash of arms, angers, incests, crimes, and punishments, the minuscule and sublime garden of the *Song of Songs?* One thousandth part of the whole is reserved for indigenous love. From this garden where he and she give of each other totally, one as great as the other is beautiful, one as powerful as the other is tender, is descended the line of equally loving couples.

A thin, fragile genealogy doomed from one end to the other to a tragically realistic fate: those two are intolerable. The rest of you, strangers whom love brings into harmony, you are abominable to a world in which discord and divisiveness reign. Return then to obscurity, you Tristans and Isoldes, you Romeos and Juliets, get out, Paolo and Francesca, trespassers without visas, anomalies, mistakes, deviations of the imagination, outlaws, Bible-outcasts, return to obscurity Jan and Jennifer, there is no place on our continents for this irreducible twosome.

The Bibles never died thereafter, and they engendered most of the books we read. And today fierce hatred is still authorized and naturalized as human. "Me, me, me, me me me," says hatred. Or rather: memememe . . . so how could it ever get in a "you"?

Most humans but not all, most books, except for a few. For there are "the happy few," a small number, the miracles, a handful of charming grains of sand in the desert of millennia. The secret guardians of the inestimable richness in being two different yet equal beings in terms of strengths and differences. Both as much one as the other, equally mysterious. All those who love and who think, who think and who think about loving, know that there exist during every period a few clandestine beings, born to watch over the little double flame, that it doesn't go out. Sparks in the darkness. Why do you keep watch, while the human tribe sleeps across the earth, indifferent to misfortunes, to wars, to joys, to massacres? Asks the watcher. There has to be someone, Kafka answers. Watchers, prophets of the present, agents for the most arduous, most dangerous cause there is: to love the other, even before being loved. Without waiting, without counting. The cause of "you";

No, poets—real poets—do not hate the other, its impossible, how could they give up half their language, why would they want to cut their tongue in two and spit out one half? Those philosophic lovers who live in the forest of languages cannot be in favor of closing the borders and ejecting one word out of every two. But what about misogynist poets, are there some such just the same? Ah yes, poor guys, they are half-poets. They write Portraits of Mistresses with a suicidal ink. For one kills oneself to kill.

Stay away from us, you women, say most of those Males.

Let's stick with men, with smokers, with brothers. What clubs, boudoirs, swimming parties, pubs, reserved temples! There are even countries where the sea water is cut off to avoid contact. "Women not admitted. Gentlemen only." But is it love among men—or rather friendship—that weaves the bonds of these fraternities? No, of course not, it's war. Yes, but war is still an agreement among brothers to kill one another. History, as it has been proudly recounted, is the sum of all the fratricides. Women are not even counted among the dead. They were sent off every which way with the children and the sick in the genocides that History sweeps behind its door. Even death is not shared equally. Duet for men, tanks against tanks, planes against planes. For the women, the stake, just ashes in the Seine.

But that's all Helen's fault, say the Bibles.

That's what the wicked old men in the chorus of the *Agamemnon* cackle. Everything is her fault, and the fault of her name. Such is the stress of the Ancients. It is She-to-be-hated [*Elle-haíne*] who sinks the ships, dooms the men, takes the towns.

Ho! Mad Helen, who single-handedly destroys so many lives in Troy.

Then we hear the immortal voice of Aeschylus (author of the *Agamemnon*) responding to the blind old men he has created:

> Direct not your curses against Helen
> As if she alone, killer of men,
> As if she all alone
> Had destroyed the lives of all those Greeks.

Thus when Theater was in its infancy, a man who was at once woman, daughter, father, old man, God, or sister, had already given voice to the clash between Lying and Truth, between giving one's opinion and speaking what is right. And Aeschylus knew then that in the end the blood of the father would win out, with unjust glory, over the blood of the mother. He was already lifting his voice in endless mourning.

Here I am at the Theater. It's not by accident. If I were asked: is there a social space in this country where the disease (misogyny) is not at home? What would I say? Wherever I go it's there, in every public place. Schools, universities, parliaments, places where the words of democracy whirl about—they are all stricken with the countless symptoms, stiffness, blindness, treachery, uneasiness, hypocrisy, death and rape drives, denial.

Except the theater. It is there, in what was once a Temple and which doesn't forget it, in the enclosure where the mysteries take place that are called: rehearsals, acting . . . mise-en-scéne, incarnation—it is there that the incidence of misogyny will be the lowest, or else nonexistent.

Because no one can set foot on the sacred planks of the stage, in the hopes of approaching the living heart of the mystery, without having first stripped from head to foot down to one's self: for the aim and the mission of these agents (actors as well as director and author) is to increase the odds of the birth of the You: I shall speak about the actors. They have arrived.

Undecided, detached, undressed, without any rank, unarmed, without any particularity. Joyously prepared for fate. There are no brothers, there are no wars. He might have been born she. She will perhaps be taken for him tonight. They have come to become unknown.

This sort of abnegation can't be accomplished painlessly, He touches on She. Rubbing of shoulders. He or she is someone who for a certain time (hours, days) no longer is. Is no longer self. Let us follow the formidable rite: first He/she is laid bare, stripped, dis-figured, practically to the point of becoming nobody. Now before the mirror He/she puts on a mask. This is not a metaphor: "Persona" puts on one of those masks, magic figures that come from Bali or Italy, always the same ones. Perhaps there's only one mask produced by all these masks. The mask is very striking, with big enormous features, a long nose, protruding teeth, bushy eyebrows. This is because the mask must muster all its force to combat the actor's face, chase it away, rapidly impose a totally alien image.

When the person turns his/her mask toward the mirror, he/she no longer recognizes him/herself. He/she doesn't recognize him/herself in the mask either. The mask is there to keep the self from getting its face back. It is apotropaic: it chases the self away. Later the mask might be replaced by serenely beautiful make-up. There is no one endowed with consciousness there in the mirror. The separation is complete. First phase of the child-birth. Next to take place: the magnificent and painful coming-into-the-world. The labor is long. Behind the mask, for the moment, there's a panting absence. The interior space is free for the other. For the coming into being of Henry V, Desdemona, or King Lear. Yes: one woman one man or the other, the space is ready to receive them without distinction as to sex, age, race. There is no particularity.

That's the way it is for the outer shell left of Him/her, a copious skin subject to the processes of incarnation. What is happening inside this sensitive shell, all ears, still uninhabited? Tense, attentive, it waits. For the character to come. Queen or assassin, anything is possible. Or a combination.

If there were a remnant of self, of identity, of worry, of memory in the actor, if there were any preoccupation, the coming-into-the-world couldn't take place. (Sometimes, uptight, gripped with anguish, inspired by the demon of impatience and mistrust, the mask cannot bear the wait and rushes to heave on to the stage a fabricated character that exudes immediately shame and deception. But a simulacrum cannot last.)

The wait is done neither sluggishly nor purposely. It is attentive, open, set. Painful because it is passion, but also a promise of what is to come. Mute invocation: Come! Come! Then into the fertile night that stretches out between the text of the play and the still uninhabited bodies, the souls of the characters step forth. They speak. I don't know exactly what happens next. The souls of the characters speak into the ear of the bodies. And then there is contact between one another, an internal contact, which is not simply touch, but which imprints, permeates the support—the subjectile—that affects the Truth-Incarnate of Cordelia or Macbeth in the living cloth of this somebody who is not a woman, who is not a king, who is an adolescent-mother, who has no historical experience and no academic knowledge, he/she is neither savant nor discriminator, nor analyst, but rather a yes, he/she is absolute assent. Internally. His/her inside is assent. Hear, o hear, the Theater is all virgin ear.

Now: the immense personage enters his/her innermost self-less heart. And now an unknown countenance covers the actor's face, under the influence of the character's violent passions. That's the way it works: a transfiguration comes into the bare shell. And it astonishes us all. For here's Hamlet, and it's the first time I'm seeing him, and I hadn't imagined him this way. I remember my surprise when I saw

Orestes. He had just made his appearance (or was just resurrected), and it was then that I first met him. (If I unfortunately "recognize" a character, it's because the actor has resorted to a vulgar copy of reproductions.)

And there's nothing to stop a woman shell from receiving the transfiguration of a male character. For here, in this kingdom that stretches beyond oppositions and exclusions, it is well known, from having had the experience so often, that it's the soul, that is, the heart—and its moods—that makes the face, the voice, the inexplicable and complicated truth of a human creature. *May I* thus be another woman, another man, who I am not myself? In this human crucible of ours, who would call into doubt "the equality of the sexes"? Who even thinks it? The creature is. All creatures contain infinite possibilities of being an other. One possibility is just as good as another. If our internal world were reduced to a single self and a single sex, what a boring scene it would be, what sterility. It's up to us to be peoples and be placed under the spell. But to accomplish this one must have the utmost courage to let go of the ballast of the self, to leave oneself unweighted on the celestial platform. Let go of the weight of the self, but not the memory, or the trace. For he/she becomes not simply quite-other. The most delicate and most precious aspect of the transfiguration, without which there would be neither joy nor learning, is that I-can-be-another (creature)-whom-I-am-not-myself: it is perhaps the most wonderful of experiences to be able to pluck the chance and pleasure of being another person all the while knowing that I am not the other, only the place with the scent of the other, and that me-my-other is taking place. For a little while, at least.

For this extreme boundary state can last only so long as it is performed, acted, created. And only so long as the actors remain within the sacred enclosure. But during this time I am both, I am another person who retains at the same time my not-being that other. This is why the actor is always trembling a bit for fear of not being enough, being too much, not being quite exactly too clumsily the other. He's continually touching up the creature. It involves, in secret a marriage, love. Between the actor and the character. Sublime respect. "Am I sufficiently you and not too much you? Am I loving you right?" the actor asks the character. It is in this incessant effort to be exact, neither more nor less, that there appears the point of absolute inexchangeability, where sexual difference can be sensed. At the point of contact is located the tiny yet unbridgeable gap that separates and keeps us two, together, both together, two together. As when, making love, we get a taste of the unknown.

All of us have once wished in a dark recess of childhood to "be in the Theater": to die and be reborn Phèdre or a boy. To experience the frightening thrill of being taken over. And the only reason we didn't do it is that we were afraid of passing over into the other and never coming back. But we've remained on the borders of this dangerous and prophetic curiosity. We remember having had the desire to be You, for a whole lifetime.

That's why we go to the Theater with the emotion of someone getting ready to be transfigured. Who knows who I shall be, a moment from now, in the fertile night?

Translated by Keith Cohen

CHAPTER 16

The Nieces of Marguerite

Novels by Women at the Turn of the Twenty-First Century

Catherine Cusset

"O's granddaughters are making strides out in the open," we read in an article entitled "Quand les femmes disent tout" ("When Women Tell All"), which appeared in the May 24–30, 2001, issue of the *Nouvel Observateur,* after the phenomenal commercial success of Catherine Millet's book *La Vie sexuelle de Catherine M.* Indeed, while *Histoire d'O* appeared in 1954 under the pseudonym Pauline Réage, and while its audacious treatment of sex made everyone think that it had been written by a man, today's women no longer hesitate to deliver to the public the story of their own sexual adventures using their own name. In fact, they sometimes even give their own name to the narrator or to the main character, thus allowing for easy identification of author with narrator. We could take these "strides out in the open" as marks of progress, and the filiation of these women novelists with O would be nothing but honorable were it not for the appearance, here and there in the text of the *Nouvel Observateur* article, of a few terms connoting an otherwise absent disapproval: the author speaks of the "dropping of a gynecological bomb on the French publishing world"; later, we read: "Enough of hedonism, make way for hyperrealism and genital miserabilism"; and again (concerning my own book, *Jouir*): "It seems a little as if light porn were becoming the new floral art of the no-longer-so-uptight female bobo."

If today all agree that novels written by women are devoting more and more space to the body as well as to the realistic description of the sexual act, another credo likewise predominates: the "dropping" of this "gynecological bomb" apparently signifies the death of imagination and metaphor, and, by consequence, of literature itself. Women, it would appear, have appropriated for themselves the erotic bastion in order to more easily assassinate the dying novel—and, in passing, to fill the pockets of their editors thanks to the commercial viability of this literary prostitution.

In 1997 I published *Jouir.*[1] I had only one ambition, which was to speak about myself in the most accurate way possible. To speak about me: my sex life, my desire, my love affairs—that is, to speak about what most mattered in my life. What mattered to me above all else was to be able to put into words the contradiction that exists between the devouring desire for one-night stands, on the one hand, and love—the fear of falling out of love, the fear of making a lover suffer—on the other. I decided to write this text not as a linear narrative, because this linearity would not have allowed for the representation of the multiplicity of desire, but rather as a mosaic of small scenes, without commentary, the raw narration of facts and the juxtaposition of stories that contain within themselves their own commentary.

The reaction to my novel really surprised me. Jérôme Garcin set the tone by publishing in the *Nouvel Observateur* (August 25, 1997) a long article entitled "La rentrée sera chaude" ("The New Literary Season Promises to Be Hot"), in which he devoted the first page to my book in order to wax indignant, *O tempora! o mores!*, that the Gallimard publishing house, which 80 years earlier had published Gide's *Symphonie pastorale*, today brings shame upon itself by publishing such a book as mine.

I came to the realization that the old taboos were still in place and that an unease exists as concerns the representation of female sexuality. In fact, one can even speak of contempt for the female sex, as does Camille Laurens in *Dans ces bras-là*, in which she provides us with a remarkable analysis: "You see in his eyes that he saw in yours, oh, so that's what you want, that's what interests you—a sort of petty glow that stabs you like a dagger and puts a mask of stone on your face, you can no longer smile, you no longer have a face. I have seen this bolt of lightning, often, even coming from serious lovers—this contempt for my sexual being, the horror of the wound, this contempt for who I am" (249). I learned that my book belonged to a category, "the erotic novel," which includes many of my fellow sisters whom I have read, for the most part, without it ever occurring to me to place them in such a category that forces them to enter the world of literature by the back door.

And it is this very categorization that I question here today. I have never thought about a book in terms of its theme. The only thing that I find important is the writing. Nathalie Sarraute writes in *L'Ère du soupçon*:

> The sense of life to which, in the long run, all art harks back (the "intensity of life" that undoubtedly, as Gide said, "is what gives things their value"), has deserted these erstwhile promising forms and betaken itself elsewhere. By virtue of the ceaseless movement which tends to bring it ever nearer to the mobile point where, at a given moment, experiment and the peak of effort meet, it has broken through the earlier novel form and forsaken, one by one, all the old, useless accessories.[2]

These lines, in which Sarraute defends the author's right to abandon realist descriptions, characters, and the traditional form of the novel, have lost nothing of their timeliness. An ever more present sexuality in novels written by women as well as an ever increasing degree of rawness of style are without doubt the new forms that today's writing has found in order to express a reality that is no longer that of 50 years ago and to "[incite] the reader to attain to a truth whose conquest denotes hard-won struggle."[3]

We are the granddaughters of O, so be it. But there is another filiation that seems more important to me. Between the ages of 18 and 22 I read a lot of Marguerite Duras. I read *Hiroshima mon amour* after an unhappy love affair and I cried all the tears out of my body. During the two years of cramming in *hypokhâgne* and in *khâgne*, little pockets of freedom reserved for the reading of *Le ravissement de Lol. V. Stein, Un barrage contre le Pacifique,* and *La vie tranquille* gave me a chance to breathe. I read *La douleur* just after my last *agrégation* exam and I felt like I had come back to life. With a friend who also loved the book, we spoke of "the writing of silence."

Later, I'd had more than my fill of Marguerite Duras and I threw her out.

Is she or isn't she a great writer? Many still ask themselves this very question today. What is certain is that several generations of women writers have been greatly influenced by her. She found a new way to speak about desire, and to make desire the subject, the only subject, by getting rid of all that was not essential. She transformed language. She had no fear of repetitions, of spoken language, of ugly phrases, of choppy sentences, of the word "*ça*"; it liberated language from the burden of literature.

These days, I read more women authors than men. This is not a choice decided upon in advance. It happens by pure chance. It is because I have the impression that in books written by women, something more is happening. And I believe that this is so because of Duras. Because all of us are, in a more or less direct way, the nieces of Marguerite.

And so I come to the body. It is very much present, there is no doubt about that. And it is the very books in which the body figures prominently that have brought their greatest success to contemporary women writers: there was Duras's *L'amant* (Minuit), which won the Prix Goncourt in 1984; followed by the international success of Alina Reyes's *Le boucher* (Seuil) in 1988; Annie Ernaux's *Passion simple* (Gallimard), a 1991 bestseller that made impassioned waves; Virginie Despentes's controversial *Baise-moi* (Editions Florent Massot) in 1994, which was picked up by the more mainstream publisher Grasset in 1999 and which we no longer hesitate, today, to recognize as a classic; Marie Darrieussecq's *Truismes* (POL) in 1996, whose huge popularity can only be compared to Françoise Sagan's *Bonjour tristesse;* Christine Angot's *L'inceste* (Stock) in 1999; Camille Laurens's *Dans ces bras-là* (POL) in 2000, whose commercial success was assured even before the book was awarded the Prix Femina; and most recently, *La vie sexuelle de Catherine M.,* by Catherine Millet (Seuil, 2001). All the publishing houses are busy publishing these books—not just the famous Franck Spengler publishers, where today the majority of writers published are women. For every single one of these writers, her most erotic book is also the one that has met with the greatest success.

In all of these books, the language is blunt, precise, or suggestive. Millet, for example, examines masculine anatomy with such precision that it has been labeled "surgical"[4]: "He was not circumcised. A prick that immediately slides out of its foreskin to greet your gaze gives rise to excitement by its resemblance to a smooth monolith, while a foreskin that can be made to go back and forth, uncovering the member like a huge bubble that forms on the surface of soapy water invites a finer sort of sensuality, its litheness spreading itself in waves all the way to the orifice of the partner's body" (16). Ernaux starts the narration of her *Passion simple* with the description of a porn flick: "The cock reappeared in the hand of the man and the semen spilled out onto the belly of the woman. I am sure that one ends up getting used to such an image, but the first time is nothing short of overwhelming" (11). *Baise-moi* also opens with the description of a porn flick: "The girl is on all fours and carefully spreads the two white globes of her big ass. A guy . . . rams his dick into her in silence . . . by dint of moving her ass as convincingly as she can, she even ends up making you forget her belly, her stretch marks and her ugly face. An amazing feat. Nadine lights up a smoke without taking her eyes off the screen. She's impressed"

(6). While Ernaux finds watching the sexual act on television overwhelming, for Despentes, watching becomes a simple act of everyday life, an act every bit as banal as lighting a cigarette. But for both, the vocabulary remains the same: it provides a precise and neutral description in which the gaze focuses on the naked body.

The sexuality about which these women write in their novels is more often than not of the transgressive type. It is, in fact, this transgressive character, this awakening of desire despite norms and taboos, and this taste for the abject that justifies this textual rendering of sex. In Reyes's novel, *Le boucher,* the butcher is a somewhat repugnant character: he is fat; he is vulgar; his hands are full of blood and guts. This does not keep the young woman narrator from being sexually attracted to him: "I looked at the butcher and I wanted him. And yet he was ugly, with his blood-stained apron clinging tightly around his big fat belly. But his flesh was lovable" (42). The check-out girl's intense sexual encounter with the butcher ends with a sadistic scene of sodomy: "He came up to me, pressed his hard prick on my ass. I wanted to turn around, but he grabbed me by my hair, yanked my head back, and started to ram his prick up my anus. I was in pain, stuck on my chair, condemned to stare up at the sky" (69). In *Truismes,* disguised within the narrative voice of a naive woman narrator who accepts her bestiality without much anguish, Darrieussecq describes a violent masculine sexuality, thus playing upon her readers' sadistic fantasies: "By taking me away for a three-day weekend with the treasurer and his dobermans, my boss thought he would forever make me lose my taste for debauchery. He thought that the old clients would now once again be able to make the well-behaved, docile *little girl* do her work . . ." (39). Without a single crude word, without any direct description of sexuality, the woman narrator suggests rather obviously a scene of sodomy: "While the clients couldn't get enough of my derrière, I, personally, would have preferred that they take a different sort of interest in me" (36). In her novel *L'inceste,* Angot also discusses sodomy, but in a much more shocking manner, since she's speaking about her own father. In a paragraph entitled "Sodomy," we read: "I was moaning. He was giving me my chance, few men would do this, this would perhaps be one of my only chances, or maybe even my one and only chance to experience in my life this sensation that certain women, many women, adore, and in fact complain that neither their husbands nor even their lovers most of the time are willing to give them" (205). The father's discourse here replaces the description of the act. This discourse, with its pragmatic realism beyond any and all morality, is even more suggestive than would be a description of the act itself. The word "sodomy" also figures in the writing of Ernaux, in her journal *Se perdre,* which retraces the day-by-day story of the passion whose concentrated narration she had penned ten years earlier. Isolated between two periods at the end of a journal entry and closing the description of a brief encounter, the word "sodomy" suddenly makes the body jump out from between the lines, giving a sexual reality to this narration of absence, of waiting, and of passion, a reality that cannot fail to expose the author and to provoke in reaction a verbal violence on the part of the critics and of the readers, who know that the woman writing these lines, the one who lives this passion and this "sodomy," is not a young woman.[5]

The subject, then, of most of these novels or narratives by women is a limit-testing experience. In the case of Ernaux, the extreme experience is an emotional one: of waiting, of exclusive passion; in the case of Despentes, it is that of the absence of emotion: dehumanization, the unsentimentality of sex in a pragmatic world; for

Reyes, it is the vertiginous sexual attraction for a man whose body and words are repugnant; for Angot, it is incest; in the case of Darrieussecq, the metamorphosis into
a pig, although experienced without anguish and accepted, leads the narrator into a
situation where she is exploited and hounded by men. The wonderful book by Florence Dugas, *L'Evangíle d'Eros*, published by Blanche in 1997, is, like Millet's, about a
sexual limit testing experience: Dugas describes a three-way sadomasochistic experience that almost left her dead. Millet's limit experience is one of numbers: it is an
experience that turned out well and was enjoyed by the author, but it is one that
most of the readers will no doubt find to be monstrous, even unbelievable. Laurens's
book seems to be the only one that does not address a limit experience, but rather
tells a "normal" story with which all women can identify. But even Laurens manages
to turn her narration into one that recounts a limit experience when, as she describes
her project at the beginning of her book, she announces its exclusive object of interest: "It aims to be a book about men, about the love of men: as both objects of love
as well as loving subjects, they are the object and the subject of this book. . . . It will
be a book about all the men of one woman, from the first to the last. . . . I will give
to the character this precise character trait (I got it from my mother . . .): not having, for all these years, been interested in anything but men" (14).

Laurens's statement also helps us to understand that it is neither the crudeness
nor the obscenity and the transgression of taboos that justifies the success of these
feminine "erotic" books at the end of the twentieth century. It is rather the coherence of their project and the commitment of their narrative voice. Why the body?
Here again, it is Laurens who provides us with an answer: "You'll tell me, maybe
you'll say (but no, you say nothing): 'And why the body? Why desire, why sex?' Because it's a means of knowledge, and surely the best when it comes to sexual difference, and the difference is, after all, sexual above all else! The Bible says 'to know' for
'to make love'; therein all is said, and here it is: I love men who want to know me'
(132). The body is the subject, that is true, but the point is not to satisfy the reader's
voyeuristic desires and to enrich the editor: the body is the subject because it is the
site of the most intimate, of the most profound, of the most unique exploration, the
only such exploration that can take place outside of social and moral norms. It comes
as no surprise, then, that here, eroticism goes hand in hand with reflection about
writing itself and about the limits of representation.[6]

So, is Millet's book a work of literature or not? Yes, insofar as it is "written," insofar as the slangy brutality of certain words offers a spicy contrast, just as is the
case with Sade, when they are inserted in rigorously classic sentences whose numerous subordinate clauses, be they circumstantial or relative, chisel their object
with precision. Yes, again, insofar as the female narrator, whom the author makes
little attempt to disguise, announces with the same precise consciousness the exact
limits of her project: "But how well I'd been screwed that night, the back end
gripped tightly, worked over, stuffed, and the top of my body sent flying forward . . . ! I remember quite clearly thinking to myself, during these minutes, in a
moment of consciousness that brings crystal clarity to pleasure, that one day, I'd
have to find the means to express in written form this extreme joy we feel when
our bodies, attached one to the other, experience this sensation of coming un-
folded" (106). The object of the book, what justifies its writing, is there, in the
heart of that sensation, and the writing's goal is to deploy, to extract the sayable
from the unsayable like a pearl from the oyster. Even if hers is a case of a sexuality

lived differently, Ernaux's project in *Passion Simple* is similar. After having described the porno film that she found by accident when she turned on the television, she writes: "It seemed to me that writing should strive for that—this impression that the scene of the sex act provokes, this anguish and this astonishment, a suspension of moral judgment" (12). We could thus say that what is at stake is to tear writing away from words in order to project it on the side of the body, of the unsaid, of the unsayable: a Duras-like project if ever there was one.[7] In *L'inceste*, Angot's feat consists of representing incest as the very metaphor of her own writing or, vice versa, her writing as the visible sign of the incest of which she was the consenting victim in her adolescent years. The body and the writing fuse here into one single mark, and Angot denounces, almost violently, the illusion of power that we hold over words, over our own words: "I would have liked to have something else to tell. Other than that. To write is not to choose your own narration. Rather, you can take it in your hands and calmly put it down on the page. . . . I would have liked to take another project in my arms, but I wasn't consulted" (174).[8] Angot takes the criticism with which her writing has met and turns it around (just as her father turned her around in order to sodomize her) to make its "shortcomings" the very mark of her writing, its structure, and, as a consequence, its very strength: "I reach the limit, with the mental structure that I have, my incestuous mental structure, I mix it all up, it has its advantages, its connections, ones that others don't make, but too much is too much, as they say, it's the limit. I mix it all up, I go too far, I destroy it all (103)." The strength of the book is therefore not the narration of the incest (even if these pages are, in all their simplicity, almost unbearable), which could be taken, as Angot says, for "a shitty testimony," but rather the relationship that she establishes between the body, the mental structure, and the writing, punctuation included: "I need to get rid of my punctuation, I have to adopt a more ordinary, more natural one, so that people need make less effort, it's ridiculous, it was ridiculous. And especially since the French word for comma, *virgule*, etymologically speaking means a little penis [*verge*]" (106).

This bodily struggle with writing, this "fortification against madness," which allows Angot to go forth into the unrepresentable, goes hand-in-hand with an assumed rejection of the well-formed sentence and the novelistic form: a rejection of "literature." But nowhere is the break with "literature" more evident than in the case of Despentes. What the two heroines of *Baise-moi* put to death is not only men, assholes, bastards, cops, the bourgeois, but also is humanism itself. In the longest murder scene of the book, Nadine and Manu turn up at an architect's place in order to steal his diamonds before they kill him. The man, who shows no signs of fear, says to Nadine, who is the better educated of the two girls: "You are quite a character. We have barely crossed paths, but it feels like a real meeting. I can't help being . . . incredibly fascinated. I sure wouldn't mind making other pacts with you" (221). Nadine is floored to hear him dialogue with her and to try to put the moves on her as if they were at a reception: "He continues, taking his time, absorbed by his own thoughts. Nadine hasn't batted an eyelid. He's flirting. She can't believe her eyes. Is he going to end up proposing to her a quick lick of the tongue in her crack for the road?" (222). Nadine responds to the seduction with vulgarity, with crass realism, even though she has the hots for the architect. This scene is one of the cruelest in the book, because it points at the naiveté of those who still believe in the power of words and are unable to conceive of violence: "He is not afraid. He can't imagine even for a second that they could do him harm. He puts out his wrists, finds the day exciting" (224). Manu puts an end to the seduction by issuing a brief order: "Hey fat ass, kill that creep for me, will you" (225). Nadine doesn't hesitate, not even a second. She kills him with even more conviction because she'd almost let herself be trapped by the sweetness of his words. The conclusion is anything but sentimental: "Wow, you shoot with real class, nice how you do that with just one hand and so straight. It's so Angel-of-vengeance, I love it. You're making progress, fat ass, congratulations" (226). It is this rejection of mildness, of humanist gentleness that characterizes *Baise-moi*. What gives strength to this book, perhaps the most American of French books with its "Bonnie and Clyde" or its "Thelma and Louise" side, is not the violence of the acts or the coarseness of the language, but the poetic coherence of the world vision that it proposes, a vision that is pragmatic and unsentimental.

I would like to suggest here that it is not simply their "eroticism" that explains the success with which these books by women have met in recent years, but rather the coherence of their project, the justified union of a subject and of a writing. Whether we take a hyperrealist novel like *Baise-moi*, a fable like *Truismes*, or autobiographical novels like those of Reyes and Laurens, or even autofictional narrations like those of Angot and Millet, the work on form, on language, stretches the limits of what can be said and finds new ways to represent what might be referred to as modern sensibility.

This formal exploration does not necessarily happen by way of an exposure of the body. Many women novelists write books about subjects that are not erotic, even when they are inspired by their own life or by their childhood, such as Régine Detambel, Geneviève Brisac, Agnès Desarthes or the uncategorizable Amélie Nothomb, who made a sensational entry onto the literary scene with *Hygiène de l'assassin* in 1993 and who has since published a book every year. Her short, energetic novels, often written in the form of a dialogue, are constructed around one idea, and the narrative voice leaves nothing unsaid. Her jubilant provocation is particularly well suited to the two books she devotes to her childhood, *Le Sabot amoureux*, in which she talks about her childhood in China, and *Métaphysique des tubes*, which reinvents her first two years in Japan. She writes in *Le Sabot amoureux*: "I've always known that adulthood didn't count: from puberty on, our existence is no more than an epilogue. In Beijing, my life was of the utmost importance. Humanity needed me" (37). This contemptuous and humorous rejection of adulthood characterizes her writing, in which the short sentence and the peremptory formulation reflect a vision of the world that does not let itself be invaded by doubt.

Even authors of the so-called erotic books have written other books that have nothing to do with eroticism: such is the case of Reyes, Ernaux, Laurens, and Darrieussecq. The three books that follow *Truismes* explore absence, "phantoms" that inhabit the head of the female narrator, especially the last and most poetic novel, entitled *Bref séjour chez les vivants*, which intertwines the interior voices of a mother and her three daughters. Angot's other books are not particularly erotic, either: in them, she wrestles with the limits of representation in order to attempt to stage this "Angot subject," this "I" that escapes us. But when eroticism is no longer available as a convenient category into which we can put those works that disturb, it becomes more difficult to establish a classification. What do we do with women novelists who do not bare their bodies? How do we categorize them? These writers could be called "modest" authors. They deliberately avoid the kind of autofictional writing that certain malicious critics label exhibitionist, and they often even choose male narrators in order to avoid all possibility of identification by the reader. I would now like to conclude by discussing some of these authors.

In the book that brought her public recognition, a book entitled *La Puissance des mouches,* Lydie Salvayre describes in an almost autistic manner the road that leads a man to murder. The narrator, who is in prison, takes turns speaking to the judge, to the psychoanalyst, to the prison's male nurse, but we do not hear their responses. He talks about his life as a guide at the Abbey of Port Royal, his discovery of Pascal's works, the only passion of his life, and above all, his childhood, spent between his mother, the victim, and the father whom he detested, "her killer, that's what I've called him for as long as I can talk, her killer whom my mother still forces me, from her grave, to call Dad" (11). The motivating force of the book is hate: "Do you know, *monsieur* Jean, that when hate has you in its grip it takes over your entire being? It infests it. And devours it whole. Hate, *monsieur* Jean, has the power of flies" (85). Salvayre's book is devoid of tenderness, of affection. The hero is a wicked man. From beginning to end, his discourse is a cry of hate. The following book, entitled *La Compagnie des spectres,* also takes the form of a cry. It is a seventeen-year-old girl's monologue in which she is speaking to a bailiff who has orders to evict the girl and her mother. She pleads with him to excuse her mother's irrational behavior, saying the mother believes that they are back in 1942 and thinks that the bailiff is a collaborator. By way of these austere, violent, sometimes hysterical monologues written from the perspective of the victim, Salvayre devotes her writing to the denunciation of evil and cruelty as well as of indifference.

In the case of Sylvie Germain, we find ourselves somewhere in between history and the fairy tale. Her first book, entitled *Le Livre des nuits,* a novelistic as well as a poetic masterpiece, received no less than six literary prizes when it came out in 1985. In this book, which situates itself somewhere in-between a fantasy and an epic, she tells the story of three generations of a peasant family, the Peniels, following their lives from the Franco-Prussian War in 1870 until the end of the Second World War. Her following books, *Nuit d'ambre* and *Jours de colère,* follow the form of an epic and describe the fate of men caught up in the flow of history, as if they were caught in a spider web, and torn apart by their passions. After *L'enfant méduse,* a devastating novel about the rape of a child, began what we have become accustomed to calling the Prague cycle: *La Pleurante des rues de Prague, Immensités, Eclats de sel.* We find the biblical inspiration of this last book in a number of her other books and also in the book that follows, entitled *Tobie des Marais* (*The Book of Tobias*). In *Eclats de sel,* the narrator, Ludwik, keeps on running into people who all end up talking to him, curiously enough, about salt: a young man at a tram stop, the man at the newsstand, a child, a cleaning woman at a hospital, and so on. "You've forgotten it all; you've let the taste of everything fade, the salt of your memory has turned yellow and that of the vows of friendship with the world, with people, has gone bad. Pff!" (102). Ludwik is struck with full force, as if slapped in the face, by this contempt on the part of the child. As he goes from one encounter to the next, a feeling slowly awakens inside of him, at first a certain uneasiness, then something akin to a realization when he finds a postcard he'd written stuck in a book that had been left to him by an old professor who had just died: "All alone and face to face with himself, he was gripped by a sharp, icy shame. . . . The old man had kept his memory alive and his thinking intact, while he, Ludwik, had forgotten" (159). This shame that grips Ludwik when he finds himself face to face with himself is the very subject of the book, as well as the object of Ludwik's quest. Germain tracks down a subtle feeling that belongs to the domain of the unsayable and that is a matter of individual moral conscience: the shame of forgetting. The tension in Germain's books comes from the spiritual quest that animates her characters, from their search for meaning "in a blood-, sweat-, and tear-stained fog that covers our time" (146).

Marie Ndiaye's books, just like those written by Salvayre and Germain, are characterized by a tension that is, in her case, too, that of an inner quest. Ndiaye's language, made up of long sentences and classical construction with ample adjectives that describe exactly and with utmost precision the feelings or the appearance of the characters, reflects this quest whose object is never reached. *En famille,* one of her longest novels, recounts the wanderings of a character called Fanny (one of her aunts gave her the name, which is not her own) in search of her family; *Un temps de saison* deals with the Kafkaesque journey of a man who lives in a small town and whose wife has disappeared; *La sorcière* is about the desperate attempt of a woman abandoned by her husband as well as her teenaged daughters to reunite her divorced parents; *Rosie Carpe* tells the story of a woman, the mother of a sick boy, who has nothing and decides to search for happiness in Guadeloupe, where her brother lives. Ndiaye's novels are not realist novels. They are entirely constructed around the anguish that inhabits these characters who are endowed with the kind of imagination that mainly allows them to foresee misfortune, the misfortune of others, for which they feel guilty since they are unable to prevent it. "Lagrand was feeling the same distress, the same feeling of abandonment. What could he do for this man? 'Oh, how I ache all over,' he murmured" (*Rosie Carpe,* 262). When Lagrand takes Rosie's dying child to the hospital and learns that he is suffering from leptospirosis, an illness transmitted in the urine of rats, he exclaims: "I said nothing to his mother even though I knew I should tell her—I almost knew it, not quite clearly enough to keep me from pretending that I didn't, but enough to be constantly reminded of the fact that there was something important that I should say!" (271). "Almost," "not quite . . . enough," "enough": Ndiaye's mark is there, in these three adverbs that give the exact measure of the narrator's guilt, reflecting his madness, which is one form of identification with the misfortune of the world. What characterizes the protagonists of Marie Ndiaye's novels is their ability to see, which endows them with a Kafkaesque sort of lucidity and paranoia:

> An inexpressible rage seized Lagrand. He had understood perfectly well that Lazarus, even if he felt technically responsible for the death of this man, did not have a clear understanding (the kind of understanding that is bare and without pity) of the fact that he had forever removed from life a soul that had belonged to it and who knew it and who saw himself disappear and over whom Lazarus did not lean for so much as a single second. (265)

Whether the novels written by women around the turn of this new century expose their author's body or hide it under the veils of fiction, they have two points in common: on the one hand, we witness in them a liberation of language, which translates into an inventive alloy of spoken language and slang (especially in the dialogues) with a classically rigorous, Proustian or poetic syntactical construction; on the other hand, we find no omniscient narrator. They present their vision of the world through a precise and limited angle: a narrator's subjective gaze, often distorted by strong emotion (anguish caused by the threat of exclusion, desire, pain). These are not realist novels in which the narrator is separated by a certain distance from the characters.[9] The vision of the world in these works is a fragmentary one, a vision whose characters, who are in search of meaning, reveal incoherence and absurdity above all else. On this foundation of nonsense float little islands of consciousness, of obsessional searching, and of anguish. In Ndiaye's fine novel La sorcière, we can see a metaphor of contemporary writing. The narrator teaches her own adolescent daughters the "powers" that she herself inherited from her mother and that the women in her family pass down from generation to generation. This power is the "ability to see into the future and into the past" (12). In order to acquire it, a difficult apprenticeship, one that calls for a serious work of concentration, is necessary. And the results are far from certain, because all depends on the gift with which one was born. The girls, Maud and Lise, are gifted: "After eleven months, the first teardrops of blood ran down their cheeks on the same day" (12). The tears of blood are released each time the woman who has been initiated succeeds in "seeing." But the two adolescent girls, true protagonists of a modern novel who care little for any type of values, only use their gift for pragmatic purposes in order to obtain material information useful in their everyday lives: "A small scarlet drop was flowing slowly down Lise's left cheek. . . . 'No basketball tomorrow, it's gonna rain, damn it'" (50). The mother's ambition is more spiritual, but her gift is more limited: "In fact, the gift I had been given was ridiculous since it only allowed me to see those things that lacked significance. With much pain, I'd set into motion my divinatory technique, or my retrospective vision, but, no matter how serious the subject, I could only ever see the unimportant details, details that revealed nothing at all: the color of an outfit, the appearance of the sky, a cup of coffee steaming delicately and held by the person on whom I was concentrating my extra-lucid gaze. . . ." (13). This gift, this ability to show "unimportant details" that "revealed nothing at all," may be the very thing to which the ambition of novels written by women today limits itself: to be able to say, with accuracy, that which lacks significance.

We also find the suggestive and powerful image of the tears of blood in Germain's Le Livre des nuits. One of her characters, Violette-Honorine, has, on her temple, a spot that bleeds in certain circumstances: "For the second time, Violette-Honorine felt the blood come to the surface of her left temple and start flowing slowly down her cheek. This time, she said nothing. She now knew that this blood was not hers, that it was flowing from the wound of another body, from the pain of another heart. And this time again Jean-François Tige-de-Fer was the only one to notice the child's distraught pity, the madness of her gaze" (189).

In Germain's case, just as in Ndiaye's, this blood that flows from the body of the woman is the sign of identification with the misfortune of the world and of a vision too painful to bear.

Not all the novels written by women present us with a vision of the world as painful and as anguished as that of Germain and Ndiaye. What these women novelists do have in common, however, is the image of the novelist as a "seer," a seer of details: what the novels of women deliver to us today is a vision of the world that is fragmented and focused on the body, or on absence, or on pain.

Translated by Eva Valenta

1. The point of departure of the book is a formal question. I had just read several books by Hervé Guibert, and Renaud Camus's book, *Tricks*, in which the author relates three months of homosexual encounters in bars in Paris, New York, San Francisco, Berlin, etc., in a style of writing that Roland Barthes, who wrote the book's preface, called "neutral." I wondered whether I could write in this neutral manner and I decided that the answer to that question was no. "I am jealous of homosexuals, jealous of my gay friends, jealous of Renaud Camus and of Hervé Guibert, even if Hervé is dead. I read them and I reread them. Whether it is in Paris or New York, or London, or Berlin, or Sydney, or in San Francisco, they desire a body and they take it. They write about it with the same simplicity: without emotion, without anguish, without guilt" (*Jouir*, 23).

2. Nathalie Sarraute, *The Age of Suspicion*, trans. Maria Jolas (New York: George Braziller, 1963), 60.

3. Ibid.

4. See Jean-Paul Guichard, "La mariée mise à nu par. . . ." (Women's Bodies, Women's Gazes in Turn-of-the-Century Literature), *Sites. The Journal of 20th-Century/Contemporary French Studies* 6.1 (Spring 2002).

5. In Ernaux's case, the taboo that is broken is not only that of sexual representation, but also that of sexuality associated with a certain age. This is so for men as it is for women, as we know from the outraged reaction of the critics to Serge Doubrovsky's book, *L'après-vivre* (Grasset, 1994), in which he describes the injections he had to give to his own penis just before sex in order to get an erection. The critics were almost unanimous in finding the work to be in extremely bad taste.

6. Jean-Paul Guichard also brings this to our attention in his article "La mariée mise à nu par. . . ."

7. In *Quitter la ville*, Angot recognizes Duras's influence on her own writing when she compares herself to Anne Garréta: "She is so Sarraute and I so Duras with a Vellemin tendency, 'I love you, I cry, you kill me, what an event' (you are killing me, tendency Angot)," 81.

8. Notice the words chosen here by Angot ("take [the narration] in your arms [*bras*]," which are the same as those chosen by Laurens for the title of her novel *Dans ces bras-là* (*In These Arms*), as if writing were quite literally "embraced" by women writers.

9. Nancy Huston, a Canadian Anglophone who writes in French, is doubtless the only woman writer today who resorts to using this distance and this divine omniscience for which Jean-Paul Sartre virulently reproached François Mauriac.

Christine Angot

Vu du ciel. L'Arpenteur-Gallimard,1990.
Not To Be. L'Arpenteur-Gallimard, 1992.
Léonore, toujours. Fayard, 1994.
Interview. Fayard, 1995.
Les autres. Fayard, 1996.
L'usage de la vie (Théâtre). Fayard, 1997.
Sujet Angot. Fayard, 1998.
L'inceste. Stock, 1999.
Quitter la ville. Stock, 2000.

Normalement suivi de *La peur du lendemain*. Stock, 2001.

Geneviève Brisac

Petite. De l'Olivier, 1994.
Week-end de chasse à la mère. De l'Olivier, 1996.
Les filles. Gallimard, 1997.

Catherine Cusset

La blouse romaine. Gallimard, 1990.
En toute innocence. Gallimard, 1995.
A vous. Gallimard, 1996.
Jouir. Gallimard, 1997.
Le problème avec Jane. Gallimard, 1999.
La haine de la famille. Gallimard, 2001.

Marie Darrieussecq

Truismes. POL, 1996.
Naissance des fantômes. POL, 1998.
Le mal de mer. POL, 1999.
Bref séjour chez les vivants. POL, 2001.

Agnès Desarthes

Quelques minutes de bonheur. De l'Olivier, 1993.
Un secret sans importance. De l'Olivier, 1996.
Cinq photos de ma femme. De l'Olivier, 1998.
Les bonnes intentions. De l'Olivier, 2000.

Virginie Despentes

Baise-moi. Florent-Massot, 1994.
Les chiennes savantes. J'ai lu, 1999.
Les jolies choses. J'ai lu, 2000.
Mordre au travers. J'ai lu, 2001.

Régine Detambel

L'amputation. Julliard, 1990.
L'orchestre et la semeuse. Julliard, 1990.
La modéliste. Julliard, 1990.
Le long séjour. Julliard, 1991.
La quatrième orange. Julliard, 1992.
Le vélin. Julliard, 1993.
Le jardin clos. Gallimard, 1993.
La lune dans le rectangle du patio. Gallimard, 1994.
Le ventilateur. Gallimard, 1995.
La verrière. Gallimard, 1996.
Elle ferait battre les montagnes. Gallimard, 1998.
Icônes, poésie. Champ Vallon, 1999.
La patience sauvage. Gallimard, 1999.
La chambre d'écho. Seuil, 2001.

Florence Dugas

L'Evangile d'Eros. Blanche, 1997.
Post-Scriptum. Blanche, 1999.

Dolorosa Soror. Le cercle, 2001.

Marguerite Duras since 1984

L'amant. Editions de Minuit, 1984.
La douleur. P.O.L., 1985.
La musica deuxième. Gallimard, 1985.
La mouette de Tchekov. Gallimard, 1985.
Les enfants, avec Jean Mascolo et Jean-Marc Turine. Film, 1985.
Les yeux bleus, cheveux noirs. Editions de Minuit, 1986.
La pute de la côte normande. Editions de Minuit, 1986.
Emily L. Editions de Minuit, 1987.
La vie matérielle. POL, 1987.
La pluie d'été. POL, 1990.
L'amant de la Chine du Nord. Gallimard, 1991.
Le théâtre de l'amante anglaise. Gallimard, 1991.
Yann Andrea Steiner. POL, 1992.
Ecrire. Gallimard, 1993.
Le monde extérieur. POL, 1993.
C'est tout. POL, 1995.

Annie Ernaux

Les armoires vides. Gallimard, 1974.
Ce qu'ils disent ou rien. Gallimard, 1977.
La femme gelée. Gallimard, 1981.
La place. Gallimard, 1984.
Une femme. Gallimard, 1988.
Passion simple. Gallimard, 1992.
Journal du dehors. Gallimard, 1993.
Je ne suis pas sortie de ma nuit. Gallimard, 1997.
La honte. Gallimard, 1997.
L'événement. Gallimard, 2000.
La vie extérieure. Gallimard, 2000.
Se perdre. Gallimard, 2001.

Sylvie Germain

Le livre des nuits. Gallimard, 1985.
Nuit d'ambre. Gallimard, 1987.
Jour de colère. Gallimard, 1989.
L'enfant Méduse. Gallimard, 1991.
La pleurante des rues de Prague. Gallimard, 1992.
Immensités. Gallimard, 1994.
Eclats de sel. Gallimard, 1996.
Tobie des marais. Gallimard, 1998.
Cracovie à vol d'oiseau. Editions du Rocher, 2000.

Camille Laurens

Index. POL, 1991.
Romance. POL, 1992.
Les travaux d'Hercule. POL, 1994.
Philippe. POL, 1995.
L'avenir. POL, 1998.
Quelques-uns. POL, 1999.

Dans ces bras-là. POL, 2000.

Catherine Millet

La vie sexuelle de Catherine M. Seuil, 2001.

Marie Ndiaye

Quant au riche avenir. Editions de Minuit, 1985.
La femme changée en bûche. Editions de Minuit, 1989.
En famille. Editions de Minuit, 1991.
Un temps de saison. Editions de Minuit, 1994.
La sorcière. Editions de Minuit, 1996.
Hilda. Editions de Minuit, 1999.
Rosie Carpe. Editions de Minuit, 2001.

Marie Nimier

Sirène. Gallimard, 1985.
La girafe. Gallimard, 1987.
Anatomie d'un choeur. Gallimard, 1990.
L'hypnotisme à la portée de tous. Gallimard, 1992.
La caresse. Gallimard, 1994.
Celui qui court derrière les oiseaux. Gallimard, 1996.
Domino. Gallimard, 1998.
La nouvelle pornographie. Gallimard, 2000.

Lorette Nobécourt

La démangeaison. Sortilèges, 1997.
La conversation. Grasset et Fasquelle, 1998.
Horsita. Grasset et Fasquelle, 1999.
Substance. Pauvert, 2001.

Amélie Nothomb

Hygiène de l'assassin. Albin Michel, 1992.
Le sabot amoureux. Albin Michel, 1993.
Les combustibles. Albin Michel, 1994.
Les catilinaires. Albin Michel, 1995.
Péplum. Albin Michel, 1996.
Attentat. Albin Michel, 1997 et Mercure, 1998.
Stupeur et tremblements. Albin Michel, 1999.
Métaphysique des tubes. Albin Michel, 2000.
Cosmétique de l'ennemi. Albin Michel, 2001.

Françoise Rey

La rencontre. Pocket, 1994.
Nuits d'encre. Pocket, 1995.
Blue movie. Blanche, 1997.
Marcel facteur. Pocket, 1997.
Loubards magnifiques. Mille et une nuits, 1999.
La brûlure de la neige. Albin Michel, 2000.
Peur du noir, Le cercle, 2001.
Mazarine. Le cercle, 2001.
Fantasmes de femmes (collectif). Blanche, 2001.

Alina Reyes

Le boucher. Seuil, 1988.
Lucie au long cours. Seuil, 1990.
Au corset qui tue. Broché, 1992.
Derrière la porte. Robert Laffont, 1994.
Quand tu aimes, il faut partir. Gallimard, 1996.
Le chien qui voulait me manger. Gallimard, 1996.
Moha m'aime. Gallimard, 1999.
Poupée, annale nationale. Pocket, 1999.
Corps de femme. Zulma, 1999.
Lilith. Robert Laffont, 1999.
L'exclue (inédit). Mille et une Nuits, 2000.
Ma vie douce. Zulma, 2001.

Lydie Salvayre

La déclaration. Julliard, 1990.
La vie commune. Julliard, 1991.
La médaille. Seuil, 1993.
La puissance des mouches. Seuil, 1995.
La compagnie des spectres. Seuil, 1997.
Quelques conseils aus élèves huissiers. Verticales, 1997.
La conférence de Cintegabelle. Seuil, 1999.
Les belles âmes. Seuil, 2000.
Le vif du vivant. Cercle d'art, 2001.

Annie Saumont

Quelquefois dans les cérémonies. Gallimard, 1981.
La terre est à nous. Ramsay, 1987.
Les voilà, quel bonheur. Julliard, 1993.
Si on les tuait. Julliard, 1994.
Le lait est un liquide blanc. Julliard, 1995.
Je ne suis pas un camion. Julliard, 1996.
Après. Julliard, 1996.
Embrassons-nous. Julliard, 1998.
Noir comme d'habitude. Julliard, 1999.
Hollywood. Eden, 2000.
C'est rien ça va passer. Julliard, 2001.

CHAPTER 17

The Doorway of the World
WOMEN IN CONTEMPORARY FRENCH-LANGUAGE POETRY

MARIE ETIENNE

I. THE HOME

Some Basics

In the outline of her short story "The Scholarship,"[1] Katherine Mansfield places these words in the mouth of her hero Kenneth, her masculine double, "I've no desire to rush into this affair they call Life. No, my job is to hide in a doorway or to squeeze under a porch till it's all over." The doorway or the porch. Is this the position of the artist observing the world from within his residence? Or the position of the woman who does not stray from the family perimeter?

More recently than Mansfield, the Indian filmmaker Satyajit Ray composed a film that has always stayed with me, although it is now very old, called *The Home and the World.* He describes the passage from *inside* to *outside,* from the protected and restrained universe of the house to the outside's dangerous chaos.

For me everything is here, everything is in this oscillation, this essential coming and going, between interiority, tranquility, even physical immobility, and travel in the vast unknown. That's what everything comes down to for everyone, I mean for women and men, for artists and others, but we know that culture has stressed teaching men to hurry, to take risks in far-off adventures, while women learned to wait, to look after the house.

From childhood, girls become accustomed to moving about very little. Author Yvonne Verdier[2] discusses the shepherdesses of Minot (Burgundy, 1930) who are busy in the cow pastures with mending work—we know that the games of peasant boys and peasant girls involve hands, but sometimes these girls' hands don't play, they are useful, they repair what is damaged, while the little boys who watch the sheep are able to run about. Some of them, much later on, leave the circle of houses and occasionally go as far as Paris to be seamstresses. Verdier[3] explains that this is the beginning of a movement toward art, given that seamstresses and embroiderers are intellectuals (they know the alphabet, since they have young girls embroider it on trousseaux) and artists. As for the embroiderers, are they not also painters? Let us quickly remember Louise Labé's adorable expression: embroidering is painting "with a needle."

One day, on the radio (which I listen to often—it is my way of being outside-inside, of being at home thinking and listening to others, their murmuring), a woman spoke to me, a musician, a double bass player, Joelle Léandre. She said that being alone was the condition of being oneself. And that being oneself is being alone.

To leave oneself, one's house, without losing oneself or ceasing to be open, permeable, is an unending voyage that is the source of desire; desire to live, desire to become.

When one has an object, as the Freudians say, or, in other words, a task that one absolutely loves, one must devote oneself to it unconditionally. Without this, there is no duration. No work. Is it possible for women who were educated, until recent times (1950 in France and still today though in a more deceitful manner), to take care of their children, their husbands, and their homes, to pursue an object that concerns only them, without finding themselves selfish?

Nancy Huston[4] asks, is it possible to decide to be selfish? This is necessary in order to write, to turn in on oneself, in one's own room, ceasing to be passed through, constantly passed through. "Women are taught to find their identity in . . . marriage and motherhood. And thus, they are unlikely to claim a talent that requires their entire being." They are taught to give themselves within the home, within the domestic sphere. Giving oneself to the outside, to a party, a work is of another order.

Therefore, some basics. Give primacy to work; it has priority. Have a place of one's own. Go out, create bonds with the world. Do not pretend to be yourself, to be recognized as such, through a great man. On this subject, as well as others, remain vigilant. Even Beauvoir, the virtuosa of feminism, always considered herself inferior to Poulou (Jean-Paul Sartre): "I will not get married unless I meet someone more accomplished than myself, my double" (quoted by Nancy Huston). Finally, endure; in other words, continue to work (to write), to publish.

A few years ago, I was asked, along with other writers, to gather together some poets I liked in a brief twentieth-century anthology[5] for teens. I limited myself, with some regret, due to lack of time, to the first half of the twentieth century, believing it would be easier, time having already accomplished the job of sorting. Of course, I wished to include women. At the home of a friend who has an immense library, I leafed through a shelf of anthologies to see how they were put together. The oldest dated from after World War II.

In each of the volumes, the author, always a man, took care to include women. They were there, and yet, I discovered with astonishment, different each time. While from one volume to the next, the same men could be found, the women did not endure. They didn't last; gave in; gave up their place. Why? It was heartrending. At the time, I could find no reply. I was simply alarmed, almost frightened, by the unstated idea of a fatality, an unbreachable law, an unfightable combat.

For the present article, I have retained three women from the previous exploration, Anna de Noailles, Catherine Pozzi, and Marie Noël, each of whom represents for me the behavior of a woman for whom writing is essential.

Of these three, the most worldly is Anna de Noailles, the most intensely intellectual and in love is Catherine Pozzi, the most intensely mystical and in love is Marie Noël.

These three female stances are exemplary in both their diversity and their similarity, because, despite their great talent (although I am less certain of Noailles's)
they did not succeed in working elsewhere than from their own homes, with the help
of love, through love. The subordination is there. The subordination remains.

Three Women[6]

Anna de Noailles. *Le coeur innombrable,* 1901. *Derniers vers et poèmes d'enfance,* 1934
(posthumous). New editions of her works by Fasquelle.

Marie Noël. *Poésies et chansons de la guerre,* 1918. *Chants des quatre temps,* 1972 (posthumous). New editions of her works by Stock.

Catherine Pozzi. *Poèmes,* the journal *Mesures,* 1935. New editions of her *Diaries* by
Editions Claire Paulhan and of her poetic works by La différence, 1988.

Before 1914, in France, art still had some patrons, aristocrats.

Countess de Noailles frequented the salons and held her own. An enlightened
woman of letters, seductive, she was worldly. But does this necessarily mean that she
was in the world? Having the world come to her was a particular way to be in it, and
to influence it, a female way. She was the good hostess.

In her *Journal[7]* Catherine Pozzi paints a rather unflattering portrait of Anna de
Noailles, which I find accurate, nonetheless. With the publication of her *Coeur innombrable,* the countess became famous; she was the Great Poet, the Queen of the Salons. In 1927, "Enter Anna, in a little mandarin or pink woolen coat—there was some
discussion of the hue—with a gold beret, a straightened feather behind her ear. . . ."
And in 1930: "While Costes and Bellonte[8] are flying over the Atlantic, Anne de
Noailles stamps and bustles about, writes to the heroes' wives, introduces them, bap-
tizes them, invents them, describes them, greets them, annexes them, hugs them,
knows them, she believes that glory can be caught like a head cold."

Like Anna de Noailles, Catherine Pozzi lived in early-twentieth-century Paris—
worldly, bourgeois, aristocratic. She first became a part of this world at the side of
her celebrated writer husband, Edouard Bourdet, then with Paul Valéry, her "highly
elevated love," during the course of their nearly secret, eight-year relationship. But
after their break-up, which distanced her from the Parisian salons, from journalism
and politics, she held on to only a few friends: Julien Benda, Jacques Maritain,
Pierre-Jean Jouve, Jean Paulhan. . . . As it was for Marie Noël, her broken and passionate love marked a turning point for her, isolated her from the world, and emptied an already fragile body. "Must the body be killed in order to become spirit?
There appeared a host and the fall began."[9]

Like Colette Peignot, Bataille's Laura, Unica Zürn, Bellmer's companion,
Catherine Pozzi felt ripped to pieces, broken.

> Quand je serai pour moi-même perdue
> Et divisée à l'abîme infini,
> Infiniment quand je serai rompue
> Quand le présent dont je suis revêtue
>
> Aura trahi
> Par l'univers en mille corps brisée
> De mille instants non rassemblée encor,

De cendre aux cieux jusqu'au néant vannée
Vous referez pour une étrange année
Un seul trésor

(When I will be lost for myself
And divided in the infinite abyss
Infinitely when I will be broken
When the present that I am wearing

Will have betrayed
By the universe into one thousand bodies broken
From a thousand instants not yet gathered,
From ashes to the heavens to the exhausted nothingness
You will remake for one strange year
Just one treasure)

("Ave")[10]

What grips me most is not so much her leaving Paris, her suffering in love, her physical illness, but rather her refusal to publish; in other words, her desire to disappear. Self-effacement. Although her friend, Jean Paulhan, tried to convince her to publish, she refused up to the very end.

It is true that her works (poems, essays, journal, correspondence) were not destined for publication, but rather to the chosen one (Paul Valéry, who read her journal and an essay, *De libertate*, which she claims he borrowed from her) and to herself. It is through her journal that she reflects (on) herself as before a mirror, reconstituting an image of herself "in a thousand broken bodies." Yet she has so much talent that her journal is not secondary writing, providing information on a period and a work accomplished elsewhere. It is the work " . . . we would continue to write each other these letters that resembled combat beyond death between the 'disembodied, untamable women.'"

Her refusal to appear and even to publish can be partially understood in what she said about the countess, her foil, "Here, coveting and playacting. For the Bal des Petits Lits Blancs, Madame de Noailles invented a golden glove . . . we run where it shines and place ourselves in the spotlight."

Marie Noël was born in Auxerre, a small city known for its handicrafts; she lived in the family home until her death. Her poetry sometimes seems like the familiar popular refrain, but she gets carried away by a spirituality that takes on the appearance of courtly or Christian myths. Religious passion and an unlived human passion gave a fervent austerity to her life and her work. "I never got over songs," she stated simply.

For Aragon, Colette, Mauriac, Montherlant, she was the greatest French poet of her time. Personally, I can see some connections between her and the American poetess Emily Dickinson.

Il la prit par la main un soir
—C'était la plus humble des reines—
Il posa la couronne d'or
Sur sa tête comme un trésor.

(He took her by the hand one night
—She was the humblest of queens—
He placed the golden crown
On her head like a treasure)

"Chant du chevalier"[11]

Her life in the world was limited, not to say nonexistent, but her life in thought had an intensity that approached that of mystics. Relinquished passion in love was transformed into passion in religion.

II. THE OUTSIDE

The War, for Starters

Men have a talent for coming together in groups, for creating journals, publishing houses, writing in newspapers. For producing war machines. "You go out into the street," said André Breton, "and you shoot at random."

Groups stand at odds with other groups. It's a war. They make war. And thus the transfer, in France, from politics to aesthetics, including vocabulary (*avant-garde* for example), resulting in bad faith and scorn. One group proclaims itself better and above all *avant-garde*. The *avant-garde* is self-proclaimed. We are ahead; we precede the others on modernity's path; we proclaim it and come to believe in it, establishing a kind of terrorism.

The battle, which is purported to be of an aesthetic order, is often very cynical, a combat between generations. *Avant-garde* is that which is young. Early on, the Romantics said "modern" to mean "new."

Women do what they can and in so doing forget their own battle. They are with the men, but in places whose origins and power are not their own. Therefore they are often just one element among others, tiny soldiers lost in the clamor of the battle. In an unwinnable situation, because age matters for them: it matters more than for men. Is she pretty? How old is she? And, beginning at age 50, when she is not sufficiently well known, she is old; she is only old. In her case it is not a question of talent, but of age and appearance.

Modernity. "Mud-dernity?" [*"Merdonité"*][12]

Asking if one knows how to write with and within one's times is a legitimate and necessary question. And even, asking how to write *before* one's times, in advance, yes, how to pull the times along behind, showing them a path they will come to recognize, "without chasing after the fantasy of a continuously budding youth and an avant-garde that is over the hill as soon as it has been identified."[13]

But above all the goal is to be careful not to be duped by this repetitive atmosphere, where the avant-garde is a tradition, because "always newer, always for a shorter time, and always overwhelmed . . ."[14]

As for me, the question I would like to ask of you, and of myself, is "how, in wanting to be modern, can one not forget oneself, but rather make oneself coincide with the world's becoming?"

There are answers. Among men. Women (I'm speaking of artists, writers) are modern without saying so. They are inscribed in their times. They are timeless: Woolf, Yourcenar, Sarraute. I put Duras to one side, too emotional, too sentimental. They don't say "Be Hugo or nothing," rather, they say "be yourself, different."

For Virginia, what was important was exploring that thing that was in her and that she sought to bring to light through writing. As for Sarraute, who liked Woolf very much, she stated that she had searched for the voice that "did not resemble," her own unique voice.

It would seem that, when they are great, women have neither strategies nor theories. Or at least not the same ones that men have. In any case, when they express ideas, they do it differently.

On Certain Strategies

"For women power appears to be forbidden. Wanting to exercise it comes down to breaking a taboo," wrote Michelle Coquillat in 1983 in a text published by Editions Mazarine.[15]

I complain, we—we women—complain (at least when we are lucid, when we examine the world around us, which isn't always the case) about not having enough presence in so-called powerful places, places where we could act: publishing houses, journals, literary intrigues. Whose fault is this? Perhaps our own to a certain extent.

A friend (he is an important journalist) recently said to me, "You women, what makes you different from men is that you don't like the battle." He's right. One must enjoy the battle and accept exposing oneself in order to direct—or at least codirect—the debates, readings, demonstrations, in a way other than as an adored mistress, a woman behind a great man, or an icon.

You could reply that battles are sterile, that debates—on the world's stage, when one is an artist, when one is a writer—don't count at all. It is better to remain, if not in the clouds, than at least in one's papers and in one's room, writing, writing, devoting oneself only to one's writing, listening only to its murmuring, shutting oneself off from that of the world.

Indeed. Is it possible? Is it desirable? Is it sustainable? In any case, one is taken to task, reviled, held in contempt, and criticized, one cannot come out of it unscathed, one is struck before opening one's mouth. But let's open it! We are not pure, purity does not exist, saintliness does not exist, "I mind my own business, I am a poet or a novelist, only art interests me." What a beautiful, insidious line! *Doucement avec l'ange* ("Go easy with the angel"), a poet recently wrote—Ludovic Janvier who gave this title to his latest collection (published by Gallimard in the Arbalète collection)—indeed, I applaud the expression, above all in matters of poetry and poets, go easy with the angel, certain of the being pure, of being the guarantors, but guarantors of what?

So we gather ourselves together, build families, which allows exclusion, excommunication, and the confusion of aesthetics and politics, for example. Go easy with the angel; in other words, let us not misjudge ourselves, let us look thoughtfully at what is happening around us, and try to understand. And, if possible, to act a bit.

And so, women, yes, we women, where are we in the struggle? Are we even present? Once again, I'm talking about poetry (I wouldn't dare venture into other areas). Once again, I'm speaking of combat, of places where action can take place, at least a bit, in France.

They are in journals, let me list a few of them, from 1970 on. Jacqueline Risset (*Tel Quel*), myself (*Action poétique, la Quinzaine littéraire, Aujourd'hui poème*), Christiane Veschambre, Catherine Weinzaepflen (*Land*), Vénus Khoury-Gatha, Marie-Claire Bancquart, Françoise Han (*Europe*), Claire Malroux (*Poe&sie*), Fabienne Courtade (*Ralentir travaux*), Vannina Maestri (*Java*), Corinne Bayle (*Le Nouveau Recueil*), Florence Pazzotu (*Petite*), Christiane Chevigny (*Aires*), Béatrice Bonhomme (*Nu(e)*). They rarely lead (poetry) publishing houses. I can only think of Martine Mélinette at Le Cheyne in Chambon-sur-Lignon. Occasionally, they do lead readings, meetings, or even festivals, alone or in groups: Liliane Giraudon (Le festival de Cogolin, the new BS, at the Marseille CIPM), myself at the Théâtre National de Chaillot.

Do they participate in literary groups? In so far as these have become nearly invisible or have disappeared, let me only mention Michèle Grangaud, at l'OuLiPo. In all, with few exceptions, don't they remain in the background? Why? Why don't even the youngest appear in the first row of the "class picture" that, in my opinion, constitutes the issue of the *Magazine littéraire* on "New Poetry"? The photo has been touched up, manipulated, it goes without saying. Only two women, Michèle Grangaud and Nathalie Quintane, appear in this photo, but there is no accompanying article for them.

Whose fault is this? Not necessarily men's. Not necessarily that of those who are around us and who often really love us. So, let's get out of our houses, but be careful—the street is dangerous: there, the pen won't do, or else we need a sharpened pen. A stiletto?

III. A BRIEF GLOSSARY

The meaning of the word glossary: a dictionary explaining the meaning of little known words. Poetesses are not known well enough. This explains the choice of the word.

The organization. The poetesses have been grouped within the decades of their first publications (with the exception of the first three: Marie Noël, Catherine Pozzi, and Anna de Noailles). Actually, if a woman's life concludes at the age when she is no longer loved (as Saint Beuve wrote about Madame Des Houlières in his *Portraits de femmes*), a poetess's begins at the age when she is published! It should be noted that I have placed some of them elsewhere in order to accentuate an aspect of their presence that I find important.

The bibliography. I have only included, in order to be brief and, I hope, efficient, the first and last of their works, which gives an idea of the length of their presence on the poetic scene.

The contents. The notes on the authors are brief, partial, partisan. What else could I do when I wanted them to be numerous? The authors who appear before the 1950s are noted without comment. A limit had to be imposed.

Francophones poetesses. There are many, there are no works in France that list them, that present them all, consequently my knowledge of them is incomplete.

The 1950s

Andrée Chédid (Lebanon). *Jonathan,* Paris: Seuil, 1955. *Territoire du souffle,* Paris: Flammarion, 1999. Lebanese, born in Cairo, poet and novelist, she has lived in France since 1946.

I have made the following statement about Chédid, as well as Khoury-Ghata, de Baron-Supervielle (see below), and other Francophones: they are from here and still from elsewhere. This is why they move me. They carry two countries, two cultures. They carry their bags. They think they have settled in the country of France, but their bags in the hallway affirm the opposite. They have sought acceptance and recognition. They have found them. At what price? Paris is welcoming. Paris is difficult. In the cases of Chédid and Khoury-Ghata, the war is subjacent, on the verge of breaking the surface of language. But for Andrée Chédid, there is something calm, something thoughtful, seeking to make the link and hold this devouring, destructive thing at a distance. Austerity is *de rigueur*.

> Devant la faillite des croyances, la pénurie de l'espoir, il est urgent que *soit* la
>   poésie.
> Elle ne console de rien, elle ne possède rien, sa loi n'est pas de marbre.
> Mais prenant et délivrant parole, elle multiplie nos vies.
> (Faced with the failing of beliefs, the shortage of hope, it is urgent that there *be*
>   poetry.
> It consoles nothing, it possesses nothing, its law is not made of marble.
> But taking and freeing words, it multiplies our lives.)
>
> (Andrée Chédid, *Territoire du souffle*)

Joyce Mansour (Egypt).   *Cris,* Paris: Seghers, 1953. *Trous noirs,* Brussels: La Pierre d'alun, 1986.

The following is from an article I wrote for *La Quinzaine littéraire* (no. 584) concerning the publication of her complete works by Actes sud, in 1991.

> It was publicly rumored that she was beautiful, Egyptian, a champion runner; that her running brought her into the surrealist fold where all the members were at her feet. She is exalted as the woman behind the great man, suspected of having asked Breton to rewrite her texts (woe to women who practice their talent near famous men!). So reading her, discovering her as she is in herself is so much more difficult because she contributed to her image of a sensual woman having a wild time: "J'ai ouvert ta tête / Pour lire tes pensées / J'ai croqué tes yeux / Pour goûter ta vue / J'ai bu ton sang / Pour connaître ton désir / Et de ton corps frissonnant / J'ai fait mon aliment." ("I opened your head / To read your thoughts / I bit into your eyes / To taste your sight / I drank your blood / To know your desire / And of your shivering body / I made my food.") (*Cris*). When looked at carefully, Joyce Mansour reflects an image of herself that brings her out of the beaten paths of eroticism as a genre, bringing her to inhabit the figure of a woman for whom the sexual act condenses all figures of loss of self and enslavement: "Je suis le cerf à genoux, je suis le chasseur debout . . ." ("I am the kneeling stag, I am the standing hunter . . .") (*Iles flottantes*). No sublimation of the partner, but rather indifference, harshness because eroticism is the body, and the body is doomed to sickness and to eroticism. . . .

Marianne Van Hirtum (Belgium).

Les Insolites, Paris: Gallimard, 1956. *Le Trépied des algèbres,* Limoges: Rougerie, 1999.

She is a poet and a painter. Her poetry bears the mark of her familiarity with the surrealists.

J'ai vu le coq ajouré
Il a laissé la chaleur de son souffle rare
Les indépendances en caleçon de bataille
s'amplifiant de bains ébouillantés . . .
C'est un enfant d'acier:
la nouvelle cohorte. Ils sont cinq.
Ils ne sont pas six.
Ils sont généralement pieux.

(I saw the hemstitched rooster
He left the warmth of his rare breath
The independences in battle trunks
worsening in scalding baths . . .
This is a child of steel:
the new troops. There are five of them.
There are not six.
They are generally pious.)

(Quoted by Christian Descamps, *Poésie du monde francophone,* Bourdeaux: Le
Castor astral, 1986).

The 1960s

Marie-Claire Banquart. *Le Temps immobile,* Paris: Denoël, 1960. *La Paix saignée,* preceded
by *Contrée du corps natal,* Obsidiane, 1999.

She juggles two sorts of writing, one poetic, the other theoretical. *Contrées du corps
natal,* through her regions of origin (Aveyron through her mother and through her
father Pas-de-Calais), and the archives where she finds her inspiration, the lives of
the anonymous "so ephemeral and so precious" (16), alternatively results in prose
texts and poems, where Picardy's old dialect, peasant songs, the crimes of lords, and
the author's "I" intermingle.

Marguerite se tua de travail—jusqu'à ce que vînt le Roi—Que de blé, que de
farine—elle porta sur son échine. . . .

(Marguerite killed herself with work—until the coming of the king—So much
wheat, so much flour—she carried on her spine! . . .)
And the author adds, compassionately: "L'échine de la femme de peine, le bébé
qu'on endort. Pas plus." ("The spine of the laboring woman, the baby put to sleep.
Nothing more.")

The 1970s

Anne-Marie Albiach. *Figure vocative,* Paris: Fourbis, 1991. *Etat,* Paris: Mercure de France, 1971.

The issue of the journal *Action poétique* that was devoted to her in the spring of 1978
admittedly caused a scandal in the restricted but explosive world of poetry, above all
due to a (non)text by Jean Daive, who presented what remained of an excerpt of *Etat,*
once the text was removed: the punctuation. Among contributors to the journal were
Edmond Jabès, Louis Zukofsky, Alain Veinstein, Keith Waldrop, Mitsou Ronat,
Jacques Roubaud, Jean Daive, and Claude Royet-Journoud. . . . In her interview with
the journal, the poetess, whose detractors reproached the conceptual character of her

work, declared, "I do not think it is possible to say that my texts are abstract. In fact, they reveal the physical side of breath, of the Voice (in relation to an obsessive memorial music, a continuous overshadowed Opera) and of syntax. . . . In *Etat* this aspect is not noticeable at first glance, but it is the one that assures that all writing bears within it a physical engagement."

Silvia Baron Supervielle. (Argentina) .   *Espace de la mer,* Thierry Bouchard, 1973. *Essai pour un espace,* Paris: Arfuyen, 2001.

The author shares her writing activity between prose, poetry, and translation from Spanish into French (Borges, Wilcock) or the inverse, from French into Spanish (Yourcenar). She claims a particularly fertile double cultural and linguistic community in her tight, dense prose texts that, in my opinion, constitute a genre of their own, neither *récit* (story), nor poem, nor even meditation, such as: *L'Or de l'incertitude* (Paris: Corti, 1990), *Le Livre du retour* (Paris: Corti, 1993). Her poetry, in contrast with her prose, is somehow silent, nearly oriental, but both are somehow in search of a lost clarity or an absolute book that brings opposites together:

> Un silence
> dont la goutte
> ne tombe pas
> au sol
> ne monte pas
> au ciel
>
> (Silence
> whose drop
> does not fall
> to the ground
> does not rise
> to the sky)
>
> (quoted in the journal *Duelle* 3, Paris).

Nicole Brossard (Quebec).   *Suite logique,* Montreal: Hexagone, 1970. *Musée de l'os et de l'eau,* Montreal: Ed. Du Noroît, 1999.

Her prose poetry has a drive that blends in a kind of *allegro* the sentimental facts of a love life with those of the world in which it bathes.

> Au bout de la lucidité ça cogne le cœur et la civilisation là-bas quand tu regardes *jadis* comme un grand carré de sable éclairé de larmes halogènes, ça surprend toujours encore plus lorsque vient le temps de nous enlacer, de laisser passer le corps librement *slick* entre nos peaux douces et les générations de filles qui, sans jamais se douter de ce qui les attendait au bout de la lucidité et parfois de l'été, voulaient tellement.
>
> (At the edge of lucidity the heart and civilization over there are beaten when you look at *days of old* like a big square of sand lit up by halogen tears, it is always more surprising when comes the time for us to embrace, to let the freely *slick* body pass between our soft skins and the generations of girls who, without ever thinking about what awaited them at the edge of lucidity and sometimes of summer, wanted so much.)
>
> (*Vertiges de l'avant-scène,* Quebec: Ecrits des Forges, 1997).

Danielle Collobert.   *Meurtre,* Paris: Gallimard, 1964. *Survie,* United Kingdom: Orange Export, Ltd., 1978.

She has published two books in Jean-Pierre Faye's *Change* collection. Along with Mitsou Renat, she is one of the forces behind the journal of the same name. She wrote little and died young. Nonetheless, for those who knew her, and for others, too, her texts mark, permeate, through their form chiseled with dashes, through the singular voice that lives there.

> . . . des heures à préparer le moment de la parole—le corps présent / dans l'imaginaire—parole projetée / ce soir impossible / toujours le mur d'anti-vision. . . .

> (. . . hours spent preparing the moment of the word—the body present / in the imaginary—projected word / that impossible night / always the wall of anti-vision. . . .)

> (Quoted in *Poésie du monde francophone* by Christian Descamps, Bourdeaux: Le Castor astral, 1986).

Claire Malroux.   *A l'arbre blanc,* Limoges: Rougerie, 1968. *Suspens,* Bourdeaux: Le Castor astral, 1986.

Translator of Emily Dickinson. Her poetry is intimist, discreet and more scholarly than appears. It is also more tragic, when she evokes the Occupation, although without pathos.

> Le trou de la serrure découpe une allée
> de branches en fleurs sous lesquelles
> des vêtements gonflent indolemment sur une corde à linge
> et une enfant nue se balance
> rescapée du temps

> (The keyhole carves out a path
> of flowering branches under which
> clothes indolently puff up on a wash line
> and a naked girl swings
> a survivor of time)

> (*Soleil de jadis,* Bourdeaux: Le Castor astral, 1998, and New York: Sheep Meadow Press, translated by Marilyn Hacker, 2000).

Vénus Khoury-Ghata (Lebanon).   *Au sud du silence,* Paris: Saint Germain des Prés, 1975. *Elle dit,* Paris: Balland, 2000.

"Conquering a new identity while conserving the old one at the same time is like walking on a tightrope. . . . Basically, I had my eye on two identities and two ways of writing. I was suffering from a cultural squint," she states.

> Les hommes et les cigognes sont de passages
> seul le cerisier est sédentaire
> répétait ma mere

> (Men and storks are passing by
> only the cherry tree is sedentary

my mother would repeat)
(*Anthologie personnelle,* Arles: Actes sud, 1997).

Jacqueline Risset   *Jeu,* Paris: Seuil, 1971. *Les Instants,* Farrago, 2000.
   A member of *Tel Quel* in the sixties and seventies, a professor of French literature
at the University of Rome, she is a poet, a translator of Dante, and a literary critic.

   —ah approche-toi explique
   Elle, distraite,
   ne bouge pas
   entends, peut-être.

   (—oh come closer explain
   Distracted,
   she does not move
   Listen, maybe.)

   (*Les Instants*)

Annie Zadek   *Le Cuisinier de Warburton,* Paris: Editions de Minuit, 1979. *Roi de la valse,*
Paris: L. Mauguin, 1998.
   I discovered Annie Zadek 20 years ago, when she was published by Lindon (Editions de minuit) and, for me, she pioneered a kind of writing that was truly apart; it
has elements of both theater and poetry, that later made me think of some of Bern-
hard's plays, where sometimes the linguistic unit—presented like a line of verse—
corresponds to my sense of musical phrasing, to the respiratory unit, as well as to the
movement of thought. Thus:

   mais qui pourrait le supporter
   qui pourrait accepter de vivre dans de telles conditions
   ces portes qui claquent
   ces courants d'air continuels
   ce froid
   cette humidité
   les vêtements
   les draps
   on se couche dans l'humidité
   on se couvre d'humidité
   on s'y enroule
   et pour finir
   on se vêt d'humidité
   mais tout cela ne serait rien s'il n'y avait pas
   cette impression
   cette sensation
   cette certitude qu'il est encore là . . .

   (but who could stand it
   who could stand to accept living in such conditions
   these slamming doors
   these constant drafts
   this cold

this dampness
clothes
sheets
we lie down in dampness
we cover ourselves with dampness
we wrap ourselves in it
and finally
we clothe ourselves in dampness
but all this would be nothing if there wasn't
this impression
this feeling
this certainty that he is still there . . .)

(*La Condition des soies,* Paris: Editions de Minuit).

The 1980s

Martine Broda.   *Tout ange est terrible,* Clivages, 1983. *Poèmes d'été,* Paris: Flammarion, 2000.

She wrote her thesis on Pierre Jean Jouve, has translated Celan, is a theorist of love in lyricism (*Dans la main de personne,* Paris: Editions du cerf, 1986, *L'amour du nom,* Paris: Corti, 1997) and is, of course, a poet.

au bord des larmes, au bord des larmes tremble
ce qui n'en finit pas d'attendre
le bonheur.

(on the verge of tears, on the verge of tears trembles
what never stops waiting
for happiness.)

(*Poèmes d'été,* Paris: Flammarion).

Sylviane Dupuis.   (Switzerland). *D'un lieu l'autre,* Lausanne: Empreintes, 1985. *Géométrie de l'illimité,* Geneva: Dogana, 2000.

She writes essays, plays, and poetry with a good deal of white space and demanding words.

Telle est sa soif
que rien
pour la désaltérer
que pas même
Dieu.

(Such is the thirst
that nothing
to satisfy it
that not even
God.)

(*Figures d'égarés,* Lausanne: Empreintes)

Liliane Giraudon. *Some postcards about C. R. J.,* Le-Revest-Les-Eaux: Spectres familiers, 1983. *Homobiographie,* Tours: Farrago, 2000.

She leads meetings, readings, and journals, she writes short stories, poems—or at least something along the lines of fragments: sharpened, and open, open onto what is hidden, improbable, supposedly difficult. In her *Je marche ou je m'endors* (Paris: POL, 1982), "Chroniques" and "Morceaux de cahiers" are notations of instants of life that seem to fly, stealing away toward secrecy, toward intimacy, an essence, a fervor and an audacity that allows the border to be crossed, as it allows ban on appearance and writing to be broken, the lot of women of the past. Like her short stories, her poems are violent and cruel.

> Le plus étrange c'est la tête
> quand l'esclave a le droit
> au baiser.

> (The strangest is the head
> when the slave has a right
> to a kiss.)

Michelle Grangaud. *Mémento-fragments,* Paris: POL, 1987. *Le calendrier des poètes,* Paris: POL, 2001.

She belongs to L'Ouvroir de littérature potentielle (OuLiPo), in other words, she only works within constraints. In her case, as in the case of another "Oulipien," Jacques Jouet, the invention of constraints is often astonishing, in any case, delightful. It is the constraint that lends coherence to the text, that holds it, comprised as it is of nonsubjective considerations, without any link between them.

> L'autorité est un caractère spécifiquement humain.
> La nuit, la silhouette élancée des gratte-ciel fait penser à des minarets.
>   L'autorité est l'attribut du père.
> Les toits rougeâtres des pavillons banlieusards sont dominés par les tours
>   énormes et vitrées où sont installés les bureaux.
> Le père est prince est prince le père est principalement interdicteur.

> (Authority is a specifically human characteristic.
> At night, the sky-scrapers' soaring silhouettes brings to mind minarets.
>   Authority is an attribute of the father.
> The reddish roofs of the suburban houses are dwarfed by the enormous glass
>   towers where the offices are set up.
> The father is a prince a prince is the father is principally a prohibitor.)

> (*Etat civil,* POL, 1998).

Geneviève Huttin. *Seigneur,* Paris: Seghers, 1981. *Litanie des cafés,* Paris: Seghers, 1991.

She has published little; she also writes radio scripts. Her first book, *Seigneur,* noted by Mathieu Bénézet, was noticed at the time for its burning nobility.

> Dans le trouble, l'attente de, tu es éternellement avec ses mots. Comme une toile tu as tendu au second plan de son supplice un grand fond muet, irresponsable, mais quel esprit se lève en toi quand ses blessures le font crier. . . .

(In the turmoil, in waiting for, you are eternally with his words. Like a web, you stretched in the background of your torture a great silent depth, irresponsible, but what spirit rises in you when his wounds make him cry out. . . .)

Josée Lapeyrère. *La Quinze-chevaux,* Paris: Flammarion, 1987. *1 sur o,* Ulysse fin de siècle, 2000.

Noticed by Mandiargue in the seventies (she published *Là est ici* in 1976 with Gallimard), she collaborates on books with visual artists, and is a visual artist, as well as a psychoanalyst, herself. Her style of writing is both familiar and scholarly, light and serious, alive.

> je cherche à lâcher prise je cherche
> à m'alléger c'est le bon côté de la chose
> une promesse si stupide ne doit pas être tenue
> vous le savez bien il a changé le jour
> où vous avez accepté d'être surprise
> racontez-nous qu'avez-vous appris
> pendant toutes ces années avec cet homme?

> (I'm trying to let go I'm trying
> to become lighter that's the good side of things
> such a stupid promise must not be kept
> you know full well he changed the day
> when you accepted to be surprised
> tell us what have you learned
> during all these years with this man?)

> (*1 sur o,* Ulysse fin de siècle, 2000).

Anne Portugal. *Les Commodités d'une banquette, Paris: POL, 1985. Dans la reproduction en deux parties égales des plantes et des animaux,* photos by Suzanne Doppelt, Paris: POL, 1999.

What I find most striking and convincing in this author's work is her humor and use of daily life (themes and language).

> voyez comme elle passera Noël
> accompagnée de télégramme d'encouragement
> avec un dais tendu sur des tringles de cuivre
> et des anneaux
> Apollinaire disait d'elle
> et trotte et trotte et trotte
> trotte la petite souris

> (see how she gets through Christmas
> accompanied by an encouraging telegram
> with a dais stretched on copper hangers
> and rings
> concerning her Apollinaire used to say
> and trot and trot and trot
> trot little mouse)

> or even:

Ah l'amour mitoyen
l'amour mitoyen ah

(Oh adjoining love
adjoining love oh)

(quoted in *Banana Split*, number 27, a Marseille-based journal, run by Liliane
Giraudon and Jean-Jacques Viton; it has since stopped publication).

Esther Tellermann. *Première apparition avec épaisseur*, Paris: Flammarion, 1986. *Guerre extrême*, Paris: Flammarion, 1999.

She is a teacher and a psychoanalyst. All her works are published by Flammarion.
The present director of Flammarion's poetry collection, Yves di Manno, wrote the
following about one of her books, *Pangéia*: "Truly, each one of her *récits* is only one lap,
an isolated chapter of this enigmatic récit alternatively sketched out, subdued, confident of its source and returned to its own ashes, after setting fire to places and expressions."

Après avoir dépassé les frontières des sables and des glaciers, ils s'entourèrent
d'apparence.

(After having gone beyond the borders of sands and glaciers, they surrounded
themselves with appearance.)

(*Pangéia*)

The 1990s

Ariane Dreyfus. *Les Miettes de décembre*, Le Dé bleu, 1997. *Les Compagnies silencieuses*, Paris:
Flammarion, 2001.

This author's poetry feeds on her life. And as her life is lively, advancing with
giant steps, with wide strokes of enthusiasm (dance, cinema, literature, finally—especially—love), her poetry is simultaneously dense and fragile, luminous and shadowy; it develops "from the most banal turns of phrase that are also slightly distorted,"
and it "twists itself in all directions," to use Ariane Dreyfus's expressions regarding
Supervielle and Rimbaud.

Décoiffée par le vent à moitié, au lieu de parler ou de caresser ou de tousser ou de chantonner ou d'être immobile, elle souriait. Quand elle sourit elle se montre au soleil et ses
cheveux tièdes se soulèvent.

(Her hair half undone by the wind, instead of talking or caressing or coughing or humming or being still, she was smiling. When she smiles she shows herself to the sun and
her warm hair rises up.)

(*Une hisoire passera ici*, Paris: Flammarion, 1999).

Pascalle Monnier. *Bayart*, 1995.

Author of just one book, *Bayart*, Pascalle Monnier has been silent since its publication. Unfortunately. *Bayart* seduces by intertwining myth and biography: "né un dimanche, parmi les herbes hautes, dans l'odeur du fleuve, dans l'odeur des fraisiers chauffant au soleil, des allées de catalpas et de marronniers, et les ormes le long des chemins, se souvient de l'époque où il montait les escaliers un pied rejoignant l'autre, de cette époque de bébé où la maison était toujours sombre . . ." ("born one Sunday, among the tall grasses, in the odor of the river, in the odor of the strawberry plants warming in the sun, lanes of catalpa and chestnut trees, and the elms along the paths, remembers the time when he climbed the stairs one at a time, that childish time when the house was always dark . . .")

With audacious simplicity, this writing uses subtly modified clichés of language, "Et cette maison, Tim, est-ce que tu la trouves jolie? / Ces volets verts, c'est beau, non?" ("And this house, Tim, do you think it's pretty? / Those green shutters are pretty, no?") (17). Or in *Bayart*, "donc prenez garde je vous aime prenez garde il fait froid la nuit tombe comment vivre comprenez-vous? ("so watch out I love you watch out its cold at night is falling how can you live do you understand?")

Nathalie Quintane. *Remarques,* Le Chambon-sur-Lignon: Cheyne, 1997. *Saint-Tropez—Une Américaine,* Paris: POL, 2001.

A prolix young author, she has fun, has fun with us, giving us an image of the world through her footsteps (*Chaussure,* Paris: POL, 1997), the myth of Saint-Tropez or Joan of Arc, in language that irony causes to stutter.

> D'un côté, des filles toutes refaites, de l'autre, des femmes en tailleur-escarpins.
> D'un côté, des filles excentriques, toutes belles, toutes refaites. D'un autre, des
>   femmes portant tailleur et escarpins . . .
>
> (On the one hand completely redone girls, on the other women in suits-and-
>   pumps.
> On the one hand, eccentric girls, all beautiful, all redone. On another, women
>   wearing suits and pumps.)
>
> (*Saint-Tropez,* Paris: POL, 2001).

"I do not define myself as a poet, even if it is my official profession. I like to work in intersections, between literature and contemporary art."

Valérie Rouzeau. *Les ailes et les fruits,* Multiples, 1992. *Neige, rien,* Unes, 2000.

What most enchants me, in this last work, is language that is handled just roughly enough to surprise, but not enough to topple over, to destroy itself.

> A ce qu'elle voit chance n'y est pas
> Toutes les étoiles mauvaises en boule
> Solitude et poissons d'hiver
> Et mercure descendre et fièvre monter
> tout considéré pas bon signe
> Va froidir chasser le beau fixe.
>
> (From what she sees luck not there
> All the stars bad in a ball
> Solitude and winter fish
> And mercury go down and fever go up

all things considered not a good sign
Going to get cold chasing good weather.)

Anne Talvaz. *Le Rouge-gorge américain.* La main courante.
She has published little. Yet her poems have a solid grace:

Elle mettait des plumes de paons si cela lui plaisait et tant pis pour la
malchance,
matelassée de robes cousue de bijoux
incrustée d'or. Elle soupesait sa propre valeur,
de son regard aigu d'idole. Pour elle-même elle était hors de prix . . .

(She wore peacock feathers if she felt like it and too bad for the bad luck,
padded by dresses sewn with jewels
inlaid with gold. She felt the weight of her own value,
with her sharp idol's gaze. For herself, she was priceless . . .)

(To my knowledge, this poem is unpublished.)

2000 and Beyond

Marie-Laure Dugoit. Erotic, ironic, hallucinatory, this is what I will say about her, or
rather, about her texts.

Attachées à une corde tendue par des piquets,
les filles d'inégale hauteur, rousses et laiteuses,
trépignaient côte à côte,
le sein lourd, les yeux brillants.

(Attached by a rope stretched to pickets,
the girls of unequal height, red-headed and milky,
would stomp along side by side,
heavy breasted, shiny eyed.)

(Published in the journal *Incidences* 7, out of Marseille).

Frédérique Ghétat-Liviani. In certain texts, like this one, I like the resemblance to a
children's story, that finally sinking into the juice of language blended to an extreme:

. . . La guerre n'a de cesse.
Et les noms des enfants autrefois si doux à prononcer deviennent étrangers à
leurs propres mères.
. . . Le seigneur demande qu'on les lui amène afin qu'il les dévore. Qu'il n'en
reste plus rien.
Aux enfants ils demandent leurs noms.
Le 1er répond: Je m'appelle brgbrgbrgbrgbrgbrgbrgbrgbrgbrgbrgbrgbrgbrg.
Le 2e répond: je m'appelle qbgqbgqbgqbgqbgqbgqbgqbgqbgqbgqbgqbgqbgqbg.
Le seigneur au comble de la haine tente de les avaler mais lorsqu'il les porte à
sa bouche
toutes les lettres imprononçables s'agglutinent et l'étouffent.

(The war is unending.
And the names of the children once so sweet to pronounce become foreign to
their own mothers.
The lord asks that they be brought to him so he can devour them. So that
nothing will be left of them.
He asks the children their names.
The first answers: My name is brgbrgbrgbrgbrgbrgbrgbrgbrgbrgbrgbrgbrgbrg.
The second answers: My name is
qbgqbgqbgqbgqbgqbgbgqbgqbgqbgbgqbgbgqbgqbgqbg.
The lord at the peak of hatred tries to swallow them but when he lifts them to
his mouth
all the unpronounceable letters clump together and choke him.)

(*Action poétique* 162)

IV. FOLLOW THE WOMAN *["SUIVEZ LA FEMME"]*.

Despite our societies' lack of interest in literature and especially in poetry, the latter
is doing fine in France, thanks for asking. It is doing so to such an extent that I close
this article with sadness. I have not spoken as I should have, as I would have liked
to, about all of them. About all who, in my eyes, deserve it. Especially since French
women from France are not alone. Since there are French women born elsewhere,
foreigners living in France, foreigners living elsewhere writing in French. How can I
take all of them into account, without letting, for this time at least, any of the precious voices be lost? One day they must all be brought together, the women from
Quebec, Belgium, Switzerland, Africa, the women from the Antilles, Madagascar,
Asia, perhaps also. . . .

Also it is necessary to reflect, truly reflect, on the reasons that women have been
so few on the poetic scene for so long. Especially in France, according to some. This
fascinates me. Is it true? And if so, why? I have a hard time believing it, I try to explain it with waves of vague or isolated reasons because I have no others, like the role
played by Molière's satire *Les Femmes savantes* for generations of girls—still required
reading, required study in France, in middle schools and high schools. Perhaps it put
a halt to the movement spurred on by aristocratic women who held their salons,
from the sixteenth century until the end of the eighteenth, in 1789, at which time
they left for foreign courts.

The fact is that in poetry, in France, there are few women, or else they are not well
known and must be rediscovered even in the last 40 years of the twentieth century.
I have lingered over these since it is my topic.

As far as attempting to distinguish particular aspects of women's writing, I do not
feel capable of it. First of all because I fear, like others, ghettoization or separation;
secondly because I do not feel that this study is urgent. There are better things to do.
Or it must be examined from different angles, which, instead of widening the gaps,
would enrich reflections on literature. For example, how do women conceive of poetry? Like a *Great Genre*, in which to drape themselves, and which makes them incapable of or indifferent to other genres? How do they see themselves in the present
world? Are they unaware of it? Do they integrate it? Do they even think about it? If
not, why? And so on. It merits further inquiry.

Let me just point out, in conclusion, that women's liberation (contraception, abortion, the right to vote) occurred only yesterday. Women are young, very young. We still don't know what they are capable of doing with their freedom.

V. INDEX

The 1940s and Before

Edith Boissonnas (Switzerland).
Paysage cruel, Paris: Gallimard, 1946. *Etude,* Paris: Gallimard, 1980.
Anna de Noailles.
Marie Noël.
Catherine Pozzi (see Part I for Noailles, Noël and Pozzi).
Gisèle Prassinos. *La Sauterelle arthritique,* Paris: GLM, 1935 (reprinted in *Trouver sans chercher,* texts from 34 to 39, Paris: Flammarion, 1976). *La Fièvre du labour,* Urville-Nacqueville: Motus, 1989.
Angèle Vannier. *Poèmes choisis: 1947–1978,* Limoges: Rougerie, 1990.
Louise de Vilmorin. *Fiançailles pour rire,* 1939. *L'Alphabet des aveux,* 1954. See *Poèmes,* Paris: Poésie/Gallimard, 1970.
Marguerite Yourcenar. *Le Jardin des chimères,* Paris: Perrin, 1921. *Les Charités d'Alcippe, La Flûte enchantée,* Belgium: Liège, 1956; Paris: Gallimard, 1984.

The 1950s

Andrée Chédid (Lebanon).
Joyce Mansour (Egypt).
Marianne Van Hirtum (Belgium).

The 1960s

Marie-Claire Bancquart.
Lucienne Desnoues (Belgium). *Toute la pomme de terre,* Paris: Mercure de France, 1978 (her first publication in France). *Anthologie personnelle,* Arles: Actes sud, 1998.
Anna Greki (Algeria). *Temps forts,* Paris: Présence africaine, 1966.
Anne Hébert (Quebec). *Poèmes,* Paris: Seuil, 1960. *Poèmes pour la main gauche,* Quebec: Boréal, 1997.
Claire Lejeune (Belgium). *La Geste,* Paris: Corti, 1966. *Le Livre de la soeur,* Brussels: Labor, 1993.
Nadia Tueni (Lebanon). *Les Textes blonds,* Beirut, 1963. *Archives sentimentales d'une guerre au Liban,* Beirut, 1982. *La Terre arrêtée* (posthumous), Beirut, 1984.
Liliane Wouters (Belgium). She has been publishing since 1966. *Panorama de la poésie française de Belgique,* Belgium: Les Eperonniers, 1976. *Anthologie poétique,* Tournai: La Renaissance du livre, 2001.

The 1970s

Anne-Marie Albiach.

Sylvia Baron Supervielle.

Claude Ber. *Lieu des éparts,* Paris: Gallimard, 1979. *Sinon la transparence,* Marseille: Ed. Via Valeriano, 1996.

Nicole Brossard (Quebec).

Claude de Burine. *Hanches,* Paris: Saint-Germain-des-Prés, 1971. *Le Pilleur d'étoiles,* Paris: Gallimard, 1997.

Lydie Dattas. *Noone,* Paris: Mercure de France, 1970. *L'Expérience de bonté,* Paris: Arfuyen, 1999.

Danielle Collobert.

Sophie El Goulli (Tunisia). *Signes: poèmes,* Tunis: Ed. STD, 1971.

Luce Guilbaud. *La Mutation des racines,* Paris: Saint-Germain-des-Prés, 1975. *La petite feuille aux yeux bleus,* Le Dé bleu, 1998.

Françoise Han. *L'espace ouvert,* Paris: Saint-Germain-des-Prés, 1971. *L'Evolution des paysages,* Paris: Cadex, 2000.

Vénus Khoury-Ghata.

Rina Lasnier (Quebec). *La Part du feu,* Ed. du songe, 1970. *Mémoires sans jours,* Saint-Laurent: Bibliothèque québécoise, 1995.

Madeleine Gagnon (Quebec). *Les morts-vivants,* Quebec: HMH, 1975. *Le Deuil du soleil,* Quebec: VLB, 1998.

Claire Gebeyli (Lebanon). *Mémorial d'exil,* Paris: Saint-Germain-des-Prés, 1975. *Cantate pour l'oiseau mort,* Paris: L'Harmattan, 1996.

Claire Malroux.

Clémentine Nzuji (Zaire). *Le Temps des amants,* Kinshasa: Mont Noir, 1969. *Arts africains: signes et symboles,* Belgium: De Boeck université, 1999.

Jacqueline Risset.

Annie Zadek.

The 1980s

Gabrielle Althen. *Présomption de l'éclat,* Limoges: Rougerie, 1981. *Sans preuves,* Editions Dune, 2000.

Tanella S. Boni. *Labyrinthe,* Akpagnon, 1984. *Il n'y a pas de parole heureuse,* Le Bruit des autres, 1997.

Martine Broda.

Fabienne Courtade. *Nous infiniment risqués,* Verdier, 1987. *Ciel inversé,* Paris: Cadex, 2001.

Hélène Dorion (Quebec). *L'Intervalle prolongé. Chars et voiles,* éd. du Noroît, 1984. *Sans bord sans bout du monde,* Paris: La Différence, 1995.

Sylviane Dupuis (Switzerland).

Marie Etienne. *La Longe,* Temps actuels, 1981. *Anatolie,* Paris: Flammarion, 1997.

Liliane Giraudon.

Michelle Grangaud.

Françoise Houdart (Belgium). *Meeting people,* Paris: Hatier, 1982. *Belle-montre,* Belgium: L. Wilquin (Belgium), 2000.

Geneviève Huttin.

Leslie Kaplan (United States) *Le Livre des ciels,* POL, 1983. Only her first books can be considered poetry.

Josée Lapeyrère.

Anne Portugal.

Anne Rothschild (Switzerland). *L'errance du nom,* Geneva: E. Vernay, 1982. *Draperies de l'oubli,* Belgium: Les Eperonniers, 1990.

Agnès Rouzier. *Le fait même d'écrire,* Paris: Seghers, 1985.

Amina Saïd (Tunisia). She published tales, short stories and seven collections of poetry.

Métamorphose de l'île et de la vague, with a preface by Abdellatif Laâbi, Paris: Arcantère, 1985. *De décembre à la mer,* Paris: La Différence, 2001.

Véronique Tadjo (Ivory Coast). *Latérite,* Paris: Hatier, 1984. *A mi-chemin,* Paris: L'Harmattan, 2000.

Esther Tellermann.

Céline Zins. *Par l'alphabet du noir,* Paris: Christian Bourgois Editeurs, 1979. *L'arbre et la glycine,* Paris: Gallimard, 1991.

The 1990s

Nadine Agostini. *Berceuse à deux voix: paroles de lui pour écrits d'elle,* Chambery: Comp'act, 1996.

Oscarine Bosquet. *Chromo,* Paris: Fourbis, 1997.

Huguette Champroux. *Le Cavalier King Charles,* Paris: Fourbis, 1996. *Dirigeable,* Main courante, 1999.

Judith Chavanne. *Entre le silence et l'arbre,* Paris: Gallimard, 1997.

Carole Darricarrère. *La tentation du bleu,* Tours: Farrago, 1999. *Tectonique des plaques,* Chambery: Comp'act, 2001.

Ariane Dreyfus.

Caroline Dubois. *Summer is ready when you are: Françoise Quardon* (with Jean-Pierre Rehm), Nantes: Joca seria,1995. *Je veux être physique,* Tours: Farrago, 2001.

Vannina Maestri. *Débris d'endroits,* Saint-Quentin de Caplong: Atelier de l'agneau, 1999.

Sabine Macher. *Rien ne manque au manque,* Paris: Denoël, 1999. *Carnet d'a,* Théâtre typographique, 1999.

Cécile Mainardi. *Grièvement,* Toulon: Telo Martius, 1991. *La Forêt de porphyre,* Ulysse fin de siècle, 1999.

Michèle Métail. *La carte de la sphère armillaire de Su Hui : un poème chinois à lecture retournée du IVe siècle,* Théâtre typographique, 1998. *64 poèmes du ciel et de la terre: les métriques paysagères 1,* Saint-Benoît du Sault: Tarabuste, 2000.

Katalin Molnar (Hungary). *Konférans pour lé zilétré,* Marseille: Al Dante, 1999. *Quant à je (Kantaje),* Paris: POL, 1996.

Pascalle Monnier.

Sandra Moussempès. *Exercices d'incendie,* Paris: Fourbis, 1994. *Vestiges de fillette,* Paris: Flammarion, 1997.

Isabelle Pinçon. *Je vous remercie, merci,* Le Bruit des autres, 1999. *Emmanuelle vit dans les plans,* Le Chambon-sur-Lignon: Cheyne, 1994.

Nathalie Quintane.

Liliane Ramarosoa (Madagascar). *Anthologie de la littérature malgache d'expression française des années 80.* Paris: L'Harmattan, 1994.

Tita Reut. *Résister colère.* Paris: Atelier F. Bordas, 2001. *Persiennes d'Héctates.* Paris: La Différence, 1990.

Valérie Rouzeau.
Hélène Sanguinetti. *De la main gauche exploratrice.* Paris: Flammarion, 1999.
Anne Talvaz.

2000 and Beyond

Marie-Laure Dugoit, Frédérique Ghétat-Liviani, Sophie Loizeau, Anne Parian, Florence Pazzottu: poems published in journals since the 1990s.
Véronique Vassiliou. *Seuils,* illustrations by Claude Chaussard, Harpo &, 2000.

Translated by Dawn Cornelio

NOTES

1. Katherine Mansfield, *Cahier de notes* (Paris: Stock, 1995).
2. Yvonne Verdier, *Façons de dire, façons de faire* (Paris: Gallimard, 1980).
3. I cannot bring myself to use the feminine-tagged terms "auteure" and "écrivaine." On the other hand, "poetess," though ugly, is an old term.
4. Nancy Huston, *Journal de creation* (Arles: Actes sud, 1990).
5. Marie Etienne, *Poésies des Lointains* (Arles: Actes sud, 1995).
6. An allusion and homage to the collection of Robert Musil's short stories of the same title.
7. Catherine Pozzi, *Journal* (Paris: Claire Paulhan, 1999).
8. Two aviators who linked Paris and New York.
9. Catherine Pozzi, *Journal.*
10. Catherine Pozzi, *Poèmes* (Paris: Gallimard, 1987).
11. Marie Noël, *Chants d'arrière-saison* (Paris: Stock, 1961).
12. The original French, *merdonité,* is Michel Leiris's expression.
13. Patrick Léchichian, *Le Monde,* March 2001.
14. Marcelin Pleynet, *Tel quel,* 1966, quoted by Paul Louis Rossi in *Les Gémissements du siècle* (Paris: Flammarion, 2001).
15. And used again in *Les Femmes au pouvoir: mythes et fantasmes* (Paris: L'Harmattan, Bibliothèque du féminisme, 2001).

CHAPTER 18

Profile of a Filmmaker
CATHERINE BREILLAT

ANNE GILLAIN

*Women are supposed to be the
view and when the view talks
back, it is uncomfortable.*

—Jane Campion

*We are led to believe that
talking about sex and sexuality
is a sign of lust. By no means.
Sex is a territory of identity.*

—Catherine Breillat

Catherine Breillat long ago sailed safely around the treacherous cape of the second film, upon whose shoals numerous female directors in France have foundered in recent years. With an impressive bibliography of films to her credit (besides being a novelist, she has authored eight films and is the coscriptwriter of nine others), Catherine Breillat is a highly gifted filmmaker whose work is a milestone in the expression of the feminine in film. In this respect, she personifies the Francophone exception: it is well known that female cinematographic creation has flourished in the last ten years in France, Quebec, and Belgium. Let us recall some statistics. Of the some 20,000 filmmakers worldwide, only 600 are women, a figure that translates to 3 percent of the international film industry. In spite of these statistics, there are currently in France as many first films made by women as by men. Several box-office hits like Colline Serreau's *Trois hommes et un couffin*, Sandrine Veysset's *Y aura t'il de la neige à Noël?*, Tonie Marshall's *Vénus Beauté (Institut)*, and Agnès Jaoui's *Le goût des autres* have encouraged producers to support films made by female directors. In fact, it can now be considered a well-established tradition. In the past year, however, feminine expression in film has taken a new direction, and Catherine Breillat has played a significant role in this evolution.

When a woman director was asked to define the difference between her work and the work of a male director, she would most often reply, "There is none." That was deceiving and, of course, erroneous. Are we to believe that women—finally permitted self-expression after centuries of artistic silence—have nothing new to say when their experience has so little in common with that of men? Yet it was taboo to identify what was specifically feminine in the creative process. In retrospect this prudence seems wise; it was no doubt necessary not to be so provocative as to risk losing hard-fought gains. In 2000 the situation radically changed. In the words of Paule Baillargeon, a Quebec director: "Men have done what they had to do; they continue to do it; they do it well. So why do the same thing? So that we can become men, too? Maybe we'll all become young white American males. And yet it is so important for us to tell our story to our daughters and sons, to everyone. It's our viewpoint—a different viewpoint—of the world." Agnès Varda echoed those words that same year: "It's certain, now in the 1990s, or I should say in 2000 since we're changing centuries, that the women I see in France as well as America are making films that affirm their sexuality, and sometimes in a radical way. It's as if there were another step to reach, a step that consists of different approaches to sexuality—different from those proposed and accepted in films made by men" (*Mandy,* 2000).

In France, this step has already been taken, and it is indeed sexuality that affirmed the difference and provoked a scandal. The pretext for the polemic was a film entitled *Baise-moi,* based on the novel of the same name by Virginie Despentes, and directed by Despentes and Coralie Trihn Thi. After its release in June 2000 in movie theaters with a rating that prohibited admission to anyone under 16, the film provoked outraged reactions from extreme-right family organizations. The Council of State decided to give it an "X" rating, as a pornographic film. (The rating prohibiting admission of anyone under 18 does not exist in France.) When the directors refused the rating, which essentially spells a film's box-office—not to mention artistic—demise, it was simply banned and removed from circulation. This situation provoked an outcry in film circles, and Catherine Breillat was one of the first to take up the banner. Her film *Romance* had received a lot of praise—and criticism—the previous year because of her use of a porn-film actor and a scene showing a nonsimulated sexual act, including a shot of an erection in the foreground. In *Baise-moi,* the two protagonists are porn-film actresses and the film opens with an extremely brutal rape that sets the scene of the story that follows. The young woman who was raped in the opening scene forms a vigilante duo with a companion in misery: they have sex with men and kill them immediately following intercourse. Noël Burch, in his unpublished article entitled "Anger of Women/Lethargy of Men," offered the following savory plot synopsis: "[It's about] two very ordinary women using men like disposable dildos, buggering them with magnum bullets after they're done." We have it figured out: *Baise-moi* is the hard-core *Thelma and Louise.* The hue and cry the film raised in France, a country of sexual tolerance, was stupefying. In his analysis of the phenomenon, Noël Burch first zeroed in on the hypocrisy of newspapers—for example, the usually subdued *Télérama*—that attacked the film from a stylistic perspective as being "formless, chaotic, uncontrolled, a primal film of flashes, no doubt inspired by a certain hopeless drive, but signaling a total incapacity to frame, to align two shots, to project anything besides a declaration of intent." Aesthetics here is merely an excuse; for the film, while not a masterpiece, is a serious and effective work. As Burch notes, *Baise-moi* unmasks a reality carefully hidden in most instances: female anger toward the French male establishment, which is unacceptable in the radical form proposed by its makers: "Anger toward those men who far too frequently still harass, beat, and rape women, who abandon them when they're pregnant . . . or who, more typically, force them into the double work day, from laziness or a male sense of entitlement." The sexuality then is not what shocked the public. The film neither titillates nor resembles an X-rated film, as its directors stressed. When asked by a journalist where she would "place" herself on a scale between pornographic and author-based (art) films, Coralie Thrin Thi answered: "In my view, author-based films are one of those pain-in-the-ass French films where nothing happens, and porno is like masturbation. Our film is neither one nor the other" (Burch 2000). Burch was entirely right when he wrote that the film was banned not "because there is an association between sex and violence a little more 'raw' than in other films, but because this sexual violence is perpetrated by women against men and it stirs up unspeakable fantasies and fears!" The crime that caused it to be banned in France, a country of freedom of expression, is the crime of "*lèse-phallus*" (outrage against the phallus). The film's directors gave voice to something as new as it was revolting to the established order. In this respect, *Baise-moi* is as symbolic a film as *Et Dieu créa la femme* was at the dawn of New Wave cinema. An aesthetically mediocre film, *Et Dieu créa la femme* is an important turning point in the perception of the feminine and of sexuality. Bardot, with her hair cascading down her back and dancing a wild mambo in bare feet, replaced the "dolls" in minks, high heels, and permanents of the 1950s. Just like *Et Dieu créa la femme* in its day and time, *Baise-moi* violates a taboo in the perception of the feminine. Like Bardot nude in the sun under her sheet, the murderous rage acted out by the two porn actresses is the female body speaking, saying it is no longer willing to submit. Catherine Breillat had reason to protest against the banning of *Baise-moi* as vehemently as she did. At the height of the scandal, she had been called into question by an extreme-right organization for "contesting the court's decision," to which she retorted: "The trial is inept. The horrible association *Promouvoir* (Promote) and its president André Bonnet were trying to turn me into an anti-establishment symbol. This man is hoping to use me to make a name for himself and has attacked me as a confederate—of course, in his mind, as a woman I can *only* be a confederate" (Breillat 2000). These polemics made Catherine Breillat all the more visible and confirmed the notoriety she had acquired at the time the film *Romance* was released. Since her use of words is as effective as her use of images, Catherine Breillat has become the darling of the media. She is seen and heard everywhere. In lead stories of magazines and newspapers, as a guest of television and radio, she has discussed a phenomenon vastly more far-reaching than the *Baise-moi* scandal, a phenomenon which has, in fact, taken on the proportions of a veritable filmic and literary tidal wave: what is at stake is an expression of sexuality whereby the body expresses itself, without masks or pretenses. Several works have recently celebrated physical beauty and physical pleasure in a variety of modes: Brigitte Roüan described in *Post Coïtum Animal Triste* the passionate and adulterous pleasures of a 40-year-old woman and a young man; *Beau travail* by Claire Denis, a choreographed film about the French Foreign Legion, follows the homoerotic tropisms of masculine bodies; Chéreau's *Intimité*, which won the Golden Bear award in

Berlin, shows a couple who live only for their fevered and clandestine caresses. Annie Ernaux, in her book *Se perdre,* describes her passionate liaison with a crude Russian diplomat. As the novelist very rightly retorts to charges of immodesty: "What you are allowed to experience, you're allowed to write about" (Ernaux 2000). Catherine Millet, the literary sensation of spring 2001, lost no time in applying Ernaux's dictum. Married and an art editor, she recounts an entire existence of anonymous sexual encounters at Parisian orgies in her book *La vie sexuelle de Catherine M.* The book sold some 120,000 copies and focused the attention of the media and the public by casting a new light on female sexuality. This somewhat disparate collection of films and books has a common theme: the female body evolves freely in torrents of sweat, viscous bodily fluids, and sperm while the heart and the brain are not necessarily invited to the party. In adopting a life independent of the panoply of feelings and intellectual justifications, the female body has become in artistic representation what it has always been for men: a space of freedom and knowledge.

We should add that all this is clearly a change from classic feminism. When Breillat declares: "Women are in the human body, not in the social body" (Breillat and Denis 1999), she places herself at the center of a new controversy and far removed from Beauvoir and her radical antinaturalism. This does not mean regression to the biological. Breillat clarified her position when a journalist asked her "where she stood" after *Romance:* "Basically, normal film focuses on the soul and pornography on the body. My goal is to go beyond this dichotomy" (Breillat 2000). In effect, what Breillat advocates is a symbolic reappropriation of a feminine realm that for centuries has been dissected by the imaginary of men. This can only be achieved by first making a clean sweep of the codes of representation imposed by tradition. That is exactly what Breillat does in her films. The two extremes of the deformation of the feminine in film are pornography, on the one hand, and Hollywood, on the other—ass and romance. Each in its own way caricatures, fetishizes, and exploits women. Myths of Hollywood-style, soulful love relationships, wherein the woman either loses out or is submissive, are no less pernicious than the obscene close-up shots of X-rated films. Reaching a universal public and molding the collective imaginary, these myths actually become an ideological shackle that advertising and social mores adopt in an endless game of mirrors. In her films Breillat is reexamining both pornography and Hollywood myths. If sexuality is at the heart of her work, it is because she believes it essential to redefine it in relation to the duality ass/romance of male portrayals.

In her most recent film, *A ma soeur,* which can also be considered her best film to date, the heroine watches a television interview of an artist, played by the Italian actress Laura Betti, who clarifies Breillat's position: "It is a research on the sexual problem, not on sexuality. . . . The sexual problem is the most obvious, the one that everyone is familiar with." Sexuality is in effect not only a universal space for women—a no man's land, one might say—that transcends national and social boundaries, but also a space that has been undergoing profound mutations within the last century. Furthermore, in spite of some progress, it remains what it has always been through the ages: the space of the greatest restriction for women. Paule Baillargeon sums it up very well: "How does the body behave when you are free, and how do you film women in all their singularity? Women want to understand their own sexuality, their sensuality. What is it they desire? In fact, women have never had the luxury to really desire. They were told what to desire. They were forced for so many hundreds and thousands of years. All these things are inside of us. It's a heritage" (Mandy

2000). Catherine Breillat's work assumes the weight of this heritage with an obstinacy, a lucidity, and an artistic mastery that lends unusual power to her discourse. The
voice that speaks in the films refuses all pretence. In the words of Claire Denis,
"There is one constant: women approach things more brutally . . . never by disguising
themselves" (Breillat and Denis 1999). Something takes place in Breillat's films that
is rare: the unveiling of a truth that always has been known but has been kept secret
through an acknowledged complicity between men and women. This truth is brutal.
In fact Breillat describes herself as "a kamikaze scriptwriter": kamikaze because she
plunges into the unknown to explode the dominant codes. She takes drastic measures
to reveal new forms and is uncomfortably uncompromising. Her method of working
is ascetic: "There are deeply obscure forces within me that I don't even explain to myself. The explanation is the film. Suddenly, the film is very frontal. I can't escape this
frontalism. I cannot be indirect because I don't know beforehand what I am about to
unearth" (Breillat and Denis 1999). Making a film is a bringing into the light of day;
it is giving birth. The imaginary of Breillat was fertilized by this ancestral female heritage that Paule Baillargeon described and, film after film, she defines and clarifies the
contours of an identical figure of the feminine, purified of men's beautiful, false fantasies: "I think men have made some admirable films representing the dreams of
women, their fantasies about women. But when they tried to portray women's reality, they got it all wrong" (Nizan 2000). This reality is the stuff of her films.

Catherine Breillat is an author in all the New Wave splendor of the word. The
sharpness of her polemical gift brings to mind the young Turks confronting the old
order in the 1960s. Like them, Catherine Breillat bases her work on a personal, autobiographical vision; like them, she writes her own scripts and dialogues. This explains the coherence and remarkable continuity of her work. If she is currently the
fashion of the day, it is because her concerns contain an underlying logic that she
knew how to convey before anyone else and that have finally burst forth. All of her
films of the past 15 years deal with the same issue. In film after film, we see the same
concerns, each time formulated in a hauntingly insistent, but slightly different, perspective. Like all authors, Catherine Breillat's personal spin or take deforms the real.
We need only extricate the reality, buried so long, that her obsessions allow her to
expose. For her, it is a bitterness involving the reconciliation of feeling and sex with
an overvaluation of maternity as the last refuge of female fulfillment. "I believe that
a woman is not complete unless she has had a child," she says in *Romance*. We have always known what Breillat is saying to us, but to finally see it take the form of a coherent, masterful, and artistic discourse is an important development.

The reality of women in her films first arises from a specific sort of gaze, that
same gaze Agnès Varda hoped and prayed for when she said:

> A woman must not be defined by the man who looks at her, by the gaze of men, by
> those men who have oppressed her: her father, her husband, her lover, her brother all
> looking at her, and she herself, who has become accustomed to existing by this gaze.
> The first feminist gesture is to say, well, okay, they may be looking at me, but I'm look-
> ing too. The act of deciding to look and deciding that the world is not defined by how
> they look at me but how I look at them. (Mandy 2000)

Razor-sharp, this gaze, new in cinema, analyzes sexual relations with painful lucidity. Different narrative devices are used to present this gaze in films. In *A ma soeur,* the

entire plot evolves under the watchful and critical eye of an adolescent girl who reluctantly witnesses the deflowering of her older sister by an Italian Don Juan. Reluctantly, because acting as an alibi for her sister, she accompanies her everywhere. She is forced into this role of chaperone by parents who cannot imagine the extent of their daughters' complicity. So she is on a twin bed in their bedroom during her sister's painful deflowering. In *Romance,* the voice-over serves as the instrument of this distancing. In love with a husband who refuses to have sex with her, the heroine engages in numerous sexual encounters out of spite and frustration. Her raw and bitter interior monologue accompanies the screen images of her adventures. The Quebec filmmaker Lea Pool remarked: "It is interesting to see how difficult it is to show what never is actually revealed, that is, what lies beneath feelings of love. It is very difficult to show what is happening inside someone who is experiencing that kind of desire" (Mandy 2000). Thanks to these *mises en abyme* (frame stories), which forbid a portrayal of sexuality without distance, Breillat exposes the inner workings of desire. She also highlights what constitutes in her mind the greatest danger for the woman: her alienation through the desire of the man. "When a woman gives in to this imperious desire in which she becomes nothing, there is a sullying," she affirms categorically (Breillat and Denis 1999). The specter of this "nothing" is what motivates Breillat's characters. In film after film, they refuse in various ways to yield to this male desire. In Breillat's films the woman does not give herself, does not abandon herself; she is not captive of, let alone honored by, the male's sex. The traditional terminology is tantamount to admitting to vassalage in the sexual act. This type of sexuality can only be, in Breillat's view, a fool's deal. Monique Wittig's provocative phrase may come to mind here: "A lesbian is not a woman," which means that the lesbian breaks all traditional codes of sexual behavior as defined by heterosexuality. Breillat achieves the same thing within the heterosexual framework, a considerable *tour de force.* The radical nature of her action is glaringly evident if we compare her with other first-rate women filmmakers, who are more reticent than she to dive into unfamiliar waters. Let us take, for example, Laetitia Masson's extremely successful film *A Vendre.* Like those of Breillat, Sandrine Kimberlain's character is angry. Betrayed at the beginning of the film by the man she loves, she decides to run away from home and to engage solely in sexual relations with men for a fee. She refuses any kind of emotional attachment. First of all, it should be noted that sexuality is not represented in this film, which incessantly repeats the same scene: the young woman, whenever asked for love, asks for money. Furthermore, the story's conclusion reverts to traditional, sentimental romance. The other, main character of the film is a detective looking for the fugitive woman. He has been hurt by a woman in the past and, when he catches up with the heroine at the end of the film, the two characters find their match in each other and form a couple. This mimetic rescue operation is not possible for Breillat.

As creatures of desire who refuse to submit to male desire in accordance with society's rules, Breillat's heroines are destined to remain frustrated. This is the catch—22 in her work. All her stories are based on this premise, and frustration is portrayed in the form of two basic scripts. In the one script, the heroine is an adolescent virgin who experiences this state as a flaw she must get rid of. Such is the case in *Fillette* and *A ma soeur.* "It's horrible to be a virgin," says the heroine of *Fillette,* a rebellious little pest of fourteen who drives any man who approaches her crazy. Her own brother says: "She's got fire up her ass, but watch out, because she's got a computer in her head." This pithy remark brilliantly emphasizes the distancing of desire, which is characteristic of all Breillat's characters. In *A ma soeur,* the female persona is, we have noted, divided between two adolescents: a tall beauty who will surrender in a fool's game to a handsome Italian and a short, fat girl who observes everything and as a result is scathingly knowledgeable. The other script of frustration involves the adult woman, prisoner in a couple where the man is either semi-impotent (*Romance*) or a suppressed homosexual (*Parfait amour*). The distorted perspective these films present may have originally been an ethical vision, but it is not lacking in didactic value: frustration sets in slow motion what cannot be dwelled on during physical pleasure. Opaque and dazzling, physical pleasure, especially in films, does not speak of desire. Only the slow frustration of physical pleasure allows for its depiction and analysis. Moreover, it should be stressed, a considerate lover, he who conceivably would enable the reconciliation of brain and ass, is not what Breillat's women want. In *Romance,* the heroine finds a gentle and virile partner in Paolo, a role played by the porn star Rocco Siffredi. Still, she leaves him. Danger hovers over all sexual relations, as this obscene remark of a rapist sums up: "I fucked you, you whore." The fat little girl in *A ma soeur* witnesses in a tearful rage the defeat of her older sister, a victim of the usual pressure tactics, this time applied by the Italian stud in order to have his way with her—he even gives her a phony engagement ring he has stolen from his mother—and decides she will lose her virginity to a man she does not love. In *Romance,* the heroine, remarkably played by Caroline Ducey, attains the height of physical pleasure at the hands of a professional sado-masochist (the excellent François Berléand). In these sexual games, to which she has freely consented, the heroine escapes male desire as she affirms her own, resulting in an ecstasy that pushes her body beyond its corporeal limits.

The high priestess of "films tendance cul" (erotic films), Catherine Breillat does not like the tangled mess of the sexual act: four legs, four eyes, two sexual organs are too much. In a beautiful close-up shot of a sado-masochistic scene in *Romance,* she isolates the subject of her work like a surgeon in the operating room: the female sexual organ. We see only the raised skirt of the heroine, her closed thighs, and the slit probed for its wet readiness by male fingers. It is easy to believe here that the woman is reduced to what she has always been in the worst macho tradition: a hole in which the rapist vents his rage and fear. "I don't want to see who's fucking me. I want to be a hole, a chasm. The more gaping, the more obscene it becomes, the more it must be me, the intimacy of me, the more I become absent. It's metaphysical: The more a prick thinks it possesses me, the more I disappear. I am emptied," says the heroine of *Romance.* Through the literal use of this cliché, Breillat gives it its vertiginous infinity: "We have to believe that this sexual organ is symbolically much larger than its actual size; it is this symbolic size that is feared, a real black hole of ghostly dimensions, from which the world is born and returns to die" (Breillat and Denis 1999). This hole for Breillat is first and foremost the hole of birth, as she calmly affirms: "It is possible to view the act of giving birth as the biggest sexual act of all" (Breillat and Denis 1999). This implacable logic in the end eliminates the male subject altogether. It is not by chance that the heroine of *Romance* finally conceives a child by her husband in an almost imperceptible embrace or that her name is—like the virgin of the immaculate conception—Marie. Peace is achieved at the end of the film in a large close-up shot of the head of a foetus emerging from a distended vagina. These two large close-ups of the female sex, unusual for Breillat, mark the only two moments of inner peace achieved in the film.

"You stick your dick three times in a row in the same chick, and you're done for. You'd be better off fucking a she-goat—at least she'll remember you later." These disenchanted remarks are those of a provincial Don Juan, not a bad guy really, who is going to fail miserably with the heroine of *Fillette*. Men have a rough time in Breillat's films. Not only are they subject to chronic impotence; but they also suffer the piercing retorts of their rebellious prey. The heroine of *Fillette* abandons the aging Don Juan with a savory speech: "I despise you. Next time you want to ejaculate, I'm not your washbasin. . . . You must realize your life is behind you. Don't you ever want to kill yourself at 40?" When she finally loses her virginity, she does it with an anonymous boy her own age and of her own choice. She addresses him brutally when he starts to give her a few preliminary kisses: "So, are you going to make up your mind? Stop drooling on me." The dialogue in Breillat's films alone is worth the trip to the movies. Lively, believable, and spicy, it allows women to be as crude and frank in their speech as men are normally expected to be. With no trace of commonness, they elegantly appropriate the sexual vocabulary that men usually consider their private domain. Physically and linguistically castrated, there's not much left for them. Catherine Breillat's work offers, needless to say, an image of men that breaks with all the standard portrayals. Mysterious and opaque just as women are in male-directed films, they remain existentially impenetrable. We will never know why Paul, the man Marie loves, rejects her. Nor will we ever know why the young man in love with the 30-year-old woman in *Parfait Amour* is cold when she shows her desire for him. In Breillat's films, the male characters surprise us inasmuch as the filmmaker enjoys reversing clichés. Paul, the husband in *Romance,* is a male model; the role of Paolo, the gentle and sensitive lover, is played by a porn star; the expert in sado-masochism assists at the birth of Marie's child: we leave him in a scene where he is in the process of tying up his female partner and find him again later on in a scene in which he is dressed in a white coat and green head cover next to Marie in labor. This hilarious ellipsis is typical of Breillat's provocative style.

The sexual imagery matches the realism of the dialogues. As Agnès Varda noted, women do not film bodies the way men do.

> What seems most obvious to me, whether in my own films or in others', is that men seem to cut up women's bodies more frequently and show more often what we might technically call the erogenous zones. They show women's thighs, women's breasts, women's behinds. It seems to me that when women film women, they show their entire bodies, the parts are not as small, there is a tendency to show the entire woman, the entire body of a woman. (Mandy 2000)

Not only do Breillat's films characteristically present bodies in their entirety, but they also present sex scenes in sequential shots and in real time. The two lengthy scenes in bed with the older sister and the Italian in *A ma soeur* together take up more than half of the film. Catherine Breillat is also as attentive to the exactness of gestures as that of words. Whether she requires her actors to engage in nonsimulated sexual acts, as in *Romance,* or is content with an enactment, the position of the bodies is never improvised but rather the result of careful staging: "I am almost always the one who finds positions of the body that are often more unusual than people think and extremely important, because the positions of bodies in love scenes is not natural at all. The framing of love scenes is very precise because each body has its own set of movements. I then have to put the actors in those positions" (Mandy 2000). Thanks to this careful staging, there is nothing false or equivocal in the portrayal of sexuality in Breillat's films. The body speaks its language, and the image faithfully reproduces it. Nor does Breillat hesitate (in *Romance* and *A ma soeur*) to show male sexual organs. The erect penis is glaringly absent in the films of male filmmakers, as we know. On the subject of the erection in film, it would be impossible not to quote at length Jeanne Labrunie's remarks on the subject:

> Most films made about men and women hide the male sexual organ. Why is this issue of the male sex so scandalous? Why does the public want to hide that? Why are they so scandalized at the sight of the male sex, erect or not? I don't know but from a historical perspective, it might be said. . . . Just look at passages from Sartre, very moving ones, I might add, in which he describes the male sex. He finds it rather ugly and pathetic. Men often have a double view of their sex: they think this dangling thing is sort of pitiful, but they also think that this object that gives them fantasies of power—especially during an erection—is magical. So how should it be portrayed in films? This is a question that male filmmakers have always asked themselves, I believe. If they don't film it during erection, this dangling thing looks pretty pitiful. But if they film it during erection . . . there's already a problem here since an erection lasts a limited amount of time, not very long. From a cinematic viewpoint, this is a problem because numerous takes are often involved, and it's complicated for a man to film his sex during an erection because at a certain point there won't be an erection any longer. . . . It's a sort of a humiliation. This is a speculation on my part. I am trying to imagine and to understand. So, they don't film it. The character is cut off at the waist and filmed from the mid-thigh downward: the sex is more or less hidden.
>
> Cutting a body robs it of its integrality, thus of its integrity, because a body signifies something and says something in and by its entirety. Furthermore, the moment [a body part] is not revealed, a crazy desire to fantasize immediately takes over. Thus, we start to imagine that there's a lot more of it than there really is. Most importantly, it seems to me that a correlation exists in the tradition of cinema between, on the one hand, the non-filming of this part of the male body and, on the other hand, the excessiveness of things that are substituted for this male sex. What I mean is that in classical genre films such as detective stories or war films, all these categories of works which tend to repress male sexuality even more than other films, this sexuality is shown in the form of revolvers, pistols, weapons, knives, mortar shells, and so on—things that represent, in a certain way, male power on the offence and that, obviously, never lose an erection. (Mandy 2000)

In her film *Sale comme un ange*, Breillat revisits precisely this type of genre film and its clichés only to undermine them. The principal male character is a cop in the purest macho tradition. Played by Claude Brasseur, he gives great displays of his virility with a revolver, especially in one scene in which he shoots a pyramid of glasses during a stag party. The plot is about his passion for the young wife of a rookie policeman who works with him. She ends up sleeping with him but remains strangely untouched emotionally. He tries in vain to convince her to get a divorce. At the end of the film, he learns from the husband (who suspects nothing) that she is pregnant. The husband expresses surprise because, he tells the detective, he always took precautions: "You know women. As soon as they've made themselves a kid, they want nothing to do with you. You're just a money machine. That's what they're thinking of; they rip off your sperm." The macho then realizes that the young woman used him to become pregnant. At this very moment, the police premises are attacked, and the husband is killed instantly. The final scene is at the cemetery. Brasseur shouts at the widow and slaps her. The film ends with a close-up of the young woman's face. Stupefied at first, a smile of victory slowly spreads over her face. This triumphal expression can be found in many of Breillat's films and it gives her endings their brio and imagination. *Fillette* also ends with the complicitous and radiant smile of a girl who while she may have lost her virginity has not lost her soul. These smiles radiate so much happiness that they amply compensate for all the frustration portrayed in the films. In *Parfait amour,* the film takes the form of a flashback based on a true incident: a young man kills a 30-year-old woman in a fit of murderous rage after she has a hearty laugh at his display of sexual inadequacy. The echo of her laughter continues to be heard throughout the film. *Romance,* like *Sale comme un ange,* ends with the husband's funeral. Before leaving for the hospital to deliver her baby, Marie turns on the gas in the room where her husband is sleeping. In the final scene of the film, a scene reminiscent of Buñuel, we see her in the funeral procession, walking behind a horse-drawn hearse. "What Marie needs is to be born unto herself, through herself, without the intermediary of romance. Birth is an ordeal, and ordeals are always ugly" (Breillat and Denis 1999). Breillat is not stifled by the politically correct; nor is she shackled by upright feelings or morals. The truth she is tracking down pays no attention to trends and is not afraid of misunderstandings. The image that dominates her work is that of birth, which cannot be separated from disorder, chaos, and the unexpected. The explosive ending of *A ma soeur* is a good example of the ambiguity that is a trademark of all of her work.

At the end of the story, the mother is driving her two daughters back to Paris. The tension mounts in the long car-ride scene. The mother smokes a cigarette; the older daughter, betrayed by her Italian, is sobbing; the younger sister is eating. Huge trucks pass by menacingly close to the car. The spectator feels that death lurks not far away. During the night the mother pulls into a rest-stop to take a nap. A truck driver kills her and the older sister and rapes the younger sister. The silent rape scene reveals her sexual pleasure. In the last take, she tells the police, gazing all the while at the audience: "I was not raped. If you don't want to believe me, don't believe me." This ending, like the one in *Romance,* borders on fantasy. However, it undeniably reflects in metaphoric terms a sort of fulfillment for the female character. The rapist has transformed her into a woman in the sort of anonymity she has wished for previously. He has also eliminated the two crushing figures of femininity, her mother and her sister, that had trapped her in a space of overeating and obesity. Births are ugly. She is born amidst the ugliness of rape. Breillat's women get what they want at the end of her films and emerge victorious in her stories. They find their sexual identity without having to admit defeat in the usual way.

From the beginning of film, we have been forced to immerse ourselves in the fantasies of the male imaginary. In the words of the Italian filmmaker Francesca Comencini, "It's terrible, a terrible violence to force female movie-goers to conform to convention, which belongs to men and to which women must, in a certain sense, also adhere" (Mandy 2000). Catherine Breillat's work, which provides women an image stripped clean of the male varnish accumulated through the ages, shields us from this type of violence.

Two important accounts have been written of the status of women in the twentieth century, both of them autobiographies: one by a sex symbol, Brigitte Bardot; the other by a great intellectual, Simone de Beauvoir. Both these women, in radically different ways, represent two leading symbols of the feminine in the twentieth century. Brigitte Bardot, the female sexual object, tells us in her biography about her rebellious nature and her horror of her status as a screen star. Her suffering caused her to identify with helpless animals, victims of a power from which they cannot hide. Like them, she perceived herself as having no choice but to submit to the dictates of her lovers, her directors, and her public. Simone de Beauvoir—a thinking, autonomous subject—seems just the opposite. Yet her memoirs reveal a kind of bitterness. At the end of *La femme rompue,* she writes the famous words: "I was had." The rebellious sex object and the "had" subject have something in common: both admit defeat. While this lucidity represents progress and deserves our praise, we might still hope as we see the films of Catherine Breillat and other women filmmakers that women artists of the twenty-first century will succeed through their work in changing, in a deeper and more lasting way than any laws could, the image of women and in transforming the courageous recognition of failure into an affirmation of victory.

Translated by Margaret Colvin

WORKS CITED

Breillat, Catherine. "Le cinéma grand et cru." *Elle,* February 2000.
Breillat, Catherine, and Claire Denis, *Cahiers du cinéma* 534, April 1999.
Burch, Noël. "Colère des femmes/Flegme des hommes," *Tausend Augen* 21, January-March 2001.
Ernaux, Annie, "Entretien avec Michèle Manceaux," *Marie-Claire,* May 2000.
Mandy, Marie. *Filmer le désir,* documentary film, Arte 2000.
Nizan, Jean-Marie. *Femme et cinéaste,* documentary film, Arte 2000.

CHAPTER 19

French Women Making Films in the 1990s

GENEVIÈVE SELLIER

The important place held by women filmmakers in France was confirmed in the 1990s. This took place within the very unique context of a heavily subsidized film industry restricted by a government policy that obliges all television networks, both private and public, to invest in the film industry. Such investments must be made in proportion to their profit margins, against the backdrop of a strict institutional separation of these two audiovisual media. This system has enabled the production of anywhere between 150 and 180 films, depending on the year, some making only a brief appearance in movie theaters before being recycled for television networks and the commercial video circuit.

This is the context in which, beginning in the 1970s, women filmmakers emerged in France in ever-increasing numbers (although still far from achieving parity). Relegated for many years to the category of "art films"—that is, small-budget cinema—and deprived of the kind of longevity needed for their films to be noticed, many of them today seem to have broken through these two barriers;[1] critics increasingly apply criteria that confirm how widespread women's films have become, even if the term "auteure," which was recommended by the ministerial decree feminizing professional titles, is one that film critics never use.

A few statistics help us appreciate the new place these women filmmakers have achieved within the French film industry: in 1997, out of 125 government-sponsored films (of the 163 films produced or coproduced), 16 were by women (and 20 out of the 163 films produced were by women). The proportion of films benefiting from advances against sales is higher: 12 out of 52 films. But there were only 5 films by women among the 46 government-sponsored "debut films."

In 1998, 10 debut films out of a total of 58 were made by women; 12 films by women benefited from cash advances (out of a total of 55); and of 148 government-sponsored films (out of 183 produced or coproduced), 22 films were made by women (and 25 films out of 183 produced or coproduced).

To put these figures into words, the trend of the late 1990s confirmed the growing place of women in filmmaking, but at a still modest level of about 15 percent. The role of the governmental authorities as an incentive remained limited, since the percentage of women filmmakers assisted by cash advances was barely more than 20 percent.

Finally, from a budgetary standpoint, in 1997 1 film made by a woman exceeded the 50-million franc barrier (out of 22 films that achieved this); 13 films by women had a budget of less than 20 million francs; of this last group, 4 had a budget of less than 5 million francs.

In 1998, 2 films (out of 22) had a budget of more than 50 million francs; 17 films had a budget of less than 20 million francs, but only 2 films had a budget of less than 5 million francs.

Hence, even though films by women proportionally are much more often low-budget films, this trend is growing weaker.

The triumph of *Trois hommes et un couffin,* by Coline Serreau, was considered exceptional in all respects when it was released in 1985; by the late 1980s and the 1990s, however, the number of commercial successes among women's films had grown, an indication that they were emerging from the "ghetto" of the "art film." Between 1990 and 2000, 24 films made by 17 women filmmakers exceeded 400,000 moviegoers throughout France.[2] (Coline Serreau, Josiane Balasko, Diane Kurys, and Nicole Garcia each had 2 or 3 films to their credit in that decade.[3]) And the phenomenon continued to grow: 10 of these films were released between 1990 and 1995; 14 films were released between 1996 and 2000 (most of these in the last 2 years of that period). While cash advances against sales and their privileged target, "art films," remain an efficient means in France for women to gain access to filmmaking, these filmmakers no longer hesitate to take on more "popular" films: as Brigitte Rollet has shown, they are often innovative in ways that in part explain their success.[4]

In my attempt to delimit this phenomenon, I will analyze a selection of 24 films, taking into account their critical reception. In terms of genre, psychological dramas and dramatic comedies (the form of choice of "intimist" authors) represent the largest number within my sampling: about ten films. It will quickly become apparent, however, that many of them are in fact a result of hybridization with popular genres, especially boulevard comedy either in its classic form or as it has been reinvigorated by the café-theater, as, for example, *La Crise, Vénus Beauté Institut, La Bûche, Le Goût des autres,* or *Ça ira mieux demain. La Nouvelle Eve, Nettoyage à sec, Le Fils préféré, Le Petit prince a dit,* and *Y aura-t-il de la neige à Noël?* can be explicitly considered "intimist" art cinema, and even then they possess a very structured scenario that often falls short of the criteria. *Place Vendôme,* which could be considered a psychological thriller, is a part of this same group.

By contrast, *Gazon maudit* or *Le Derrière* unabashedly claim to be boulevard comedy; *Marquise, Les Enfants du siècle,* and *Saint-Cyr* are historical films; and finally, *La Belle verte* is an isolated incursion into the realm of science fiction. These "genre" films, quite noticeably, are not necessarily the biggest commercial successes: *Marquise* and *Les Enfants du siècle,* if we consider their budgets, could even be deemed failures. *Saint-Cyr,* by contrast, whose budget was very modest for a historical film, fared well, even though Patricia Mazuy's stylistic choices made it much more decidedly an "auteure" art film than the two other films just mentioned.

Women filmmakers seem, then, to be successful in hybridizing "art" and "genre" films, and this at a time when art films (especially by male filmmakers) are in the throes of a creative crisis, in spite (or because?) of a system of financing completely independent of their success with moviegoers.

There is an even more accurate indicator than the mere box office to measure the popularity of women filmmakers' movies: the relationship between the number of moviegoers in Paris as opposed to France as a whole is a good indicator of the type of public attracted by a film. In fact, surveys on the cultural practices of the French, undertaken on a regular basis by the Ministry of Culture, have shown that movie-theater attendance in France is greatest among white-collar employees and those employed in higher-level intellectual professions, Parisians, and people in the field of higher education. These three categories overlap quite a bit.[5] They also have the highest rate of attendance at other cultural events. The "auteur" or art film is favored by 15 percent of white-collar employees and those in intellectual professions; by 16 percent of Parisians (within the city limits); and by 16 percent of those in higher ed-ucation. As far as taste in movies is concerned, then, the biggest difference between Paris and the rest of France is to be noticed in comedies, the genre most preferred by the French (an average of 30 percent), except for Parisians (15 percent); the art film, on the other hand, is the genre preferred by Parisians (16 percent), compared with the average of 4 percent among French people in general. The comparative popularity of a film in Paris and the provinces is thus a good gauge of its sociocul-tural level.

Le fils préféré, for example, Nicole Garcia's second film, was viewed in 1994 by about 259,000 Parisian moviegoers and 284,000 provincial moviegoers (a ratio of 1:1.1), whereas in the following year, Balasko's Gazon maudit was viewed by around 785,000 Parisians and 3,200,000 provincial moviegoers (a ratio of 1:3). Bearing in mind the sociocultural composition of French film audiences, it can be inferred, in-dependent of the total figure of audience members (seven times greater for the sec-ond film as for the first) that the public of Gazon maudit was much more working-class than that of Le Fils préféré. Yet this phenomenon, which only confirms the typically French sociocultural difference between boulevard comedy and/or "art" film, tended to disappear as the decade progressed, as the boundaries between genres in women's films became increasingly mixed. The great success in France in 2000 of Le Goût des autres, the first film of the actress and director Agnès Jaoui, had a ratio of 1:2.7 be-tween Parisian and provincial moviegoers, whereas the "harder" of the women's art films that same year, Saint-Cyr, resulted in a ratio of 1:1.7, probably because it was la-beled a historical film. The sociocultural gap among the films made by women thus seemed to be diminishing, as if the sacrosanct opposition in France between elite culture and mass culture—a division which has structured French cinema since the emergence of the New Wave—was gradually challenged by women filmmakers. (This theme is, in fact, the subject of Le Goût des autres . . .).[6]

It is also apparent that most of these films highlighted actors of extremely varied backgrounds, exploding here as well the divisions between elite culture and mass culture, between art cinema and commercial cinema. These frequently polyphonic movies united and often even resuscitated—by using them in ways counter to their images—actors long considered action/adventure types, such as Gérard Lanvin (Le Fils préféré, Le Goût des autres) or Jean-Marc Barr (Le Fils préféré). They conferred re-newed youth upon almost forgotten actors of the big screen, such as Claude Rich (La Bûche, Le Derrière), arranged surprising encounters between actors of different and sometimes opposing genres, generations, and backgrounds (Gazon maudit, Marquise, La Bûche, Vénus Beauté Institut, Le Goût des autres, Ça ira mieux demain), thereby demonstrating in the casting an inventiveness that is a key to the popular success of these films. Far from the often rarefied atmosphere of art films—Chabrol, Téchiné, Assayas—due as much to the small number of characters as to the directors' continual reliance on the same actors, film after film, our women filmmakers practiced diversity not only in terms of inspiration, but also in terms of casting.

Women's films also broadened the variety of female roles in a cinema that, whether commercial or elitist, traditionally favored very young actresses, reserving for the male roles greater diversity in terms of age and physical type. The palette of female roles, both lead and supporting, was extended in the 1990s, thanks largely to films by women. (It seems in the meantime that they have gained widespread acceptance.) The most striking example is Balasko, who successfully imposed her unruly type, inventing a female transgressive comic figure in the traditions of farce, in a register that never made her the object, but rather the generator, of laughter. In her wake (and following the legacy of the café-theater), several actresses with atypical physical features were able to access lead dramatic roles: from Anémone (*Le Petit prince a dit,* Pascal, 1992) to Anna Alvaro (*Le Goût des autres*) and Karine Viard (*La Nouvelle Ève*). Actresses well beyond 50 were offered strong, seductive roles, such as Maria Pacôme (*La Crise*) or Françoise Fabian (*La Bûche*); and women filmmakers also gave roles of considerable complexity to great French actresses in or near their forties and fifties, such as Catherine Deneuve (*Place Vendôme*), Miou-Miou (*Nettoyage à sec*), Sabine Azéma and Emmanuelle Béart (*La Bûche*), Juliette Binoche (*Les Enfants du siècle*), Isabelle Huppert (*Saint-Cyr*), Nathalie Baye (*Vénus Beauté Institut, Ça ira mieux demain*). This multiple diversification of female roles and characters is undoubtedly one of the most visible effects of women's seizure of power behind the camera, but its impact is still hard to measure when one considers the importance that the collective imaginary—constructed by film over the last 100 years—has had on social relationships. Might it be possible to detect the beginning of a radical break in the gendered double standard that rules the norms of seduction in our society?

Even if the critical reception of a film cannot be completely isolated from its success with the movie-going public, the former operates fairly autonomously in France. This is because the critics who serve as a "benchmark" (those referred to as the Elite Five, that is, *Le Monde, Libération, Les Inrockuptibles, Télérama,* and *Les Cahiers du Cinéma*), and who frequently make it possible to obtain advances against sales for the next film, do not judge films according to their greater or lesser capacity to attract a public, but rather according to cinephilic criteria consisting of a combination of formalism and *auteurisme* that forms the creed of elite circles in France.

While the traditional, popular press varies the size of its articles according to "commercial" criteria, the high-brow press, whether specialized or not, makes it a point of honor to ignore this rule. The result is that films rating only a paragraph are often big-budget ones, like *Marquise, Les Enfants du siècle, La Crise, La belle verte, Le Derrière,* and *La Bûche,* considered genre films for commercial purposes. What matters most here is the sociocultural gap. The only woman filmmaker to succeed in making the critics respond in a different way was Josiane Balasko, with her film *Gazon maudit* (1995). The disdain usually reserved for boulevard comedy was sidetracked by the magnificent performance of the actress-director-producer: the audacity of the subject matter—female homosexuality—as well as its treatment, conquered the habitual reserve shown by the cultivated critics for a genre that usually evokes consensus. Agnès Jaoui would repeat this exception in 2000, when *Le Goût des autres* confronted a major taboo in French society: that of sociocultural divisions of which critics are both a driving force and a consequence![7] This was undoubtedly the beginning of a new attitude on the part of women regarding the opposition between elite culture and mass culture. This division is particularly evident in France, where the figure of the "artiste maudit" (whose value is recognized only by his peers) is still the nec plus ultra for film critics—since any commercial success that reaches beyond the normal public of art and experimental movie houses is automatically suspect in terms of its artistic value.

A close examination of the critical reception of films made by women suggests that the decision of many of these filmmakers to combine categories and genres has met with strong resistance: the relative flop of two recent historical films is a case in point. *Marquise* and *Les Enfants du siècle* each proposed a rereading of canonical literary history by enlisting the codes of popular film: for Véra Belmont, it was a rereading of the relationship between the creators of the *Grand Siècle* and royal absolutism by way of an anecdote about rival lovers. A creative compromise between a popular theme (the loves of an actress) and a subject of high culture (the rivalry between Molière and Racine), the film was very poorly received by critics and even denigrated by its leading actress, Sophie Marceau, who apparently had taken a cue from her husband, the filmmaker Zulawski. Only *Studio,* the monthly magazine of popular cinephilia (if this is not a contradiction in terms!), praised the film, while more high-brow critics treated this illegitimate mixture of popular cinema and monuments of literary heritage with disdain.

Diane Kurys did not fare much better with *Les enfants du siècle,* in spite of the radiant presence of Juliette Binoche, duly labeled an "art film" actress, unlike Sophie Marceau. The filmmaker attempted a rereading of the liaison between Musset and Sand that tarnished the image of the romantic poet in order to highlight the portrait of a "woman of letters" whom our literary history considers minor. Kurys, like Agnieska Holland some years earlier for her *Rimbaud Verlaine,* was treated with disdain, in keeping with her crime of cultural *lèse-majesté.* Yet her description of the difficulties faced by a woman breaking into the literary world of the nineteenth century, and of the isolation she encountered because of her love for a poet as gifted as he was frivolous, highlighted in an original manner the difference in creative attitudes between a man and a woman in a literary milieu marked by undisputed male domination. But this type of approach remains taboo in France, where the cult of great (male) authors has been elevated to the rank of national specialty.

By contrast, the critical and commercial success of two "dramatic comedies," *Vénus Beauté Institut*[8] and *Le Goût des autres,*[9] showed a creative way around the barriers of art film. Both these films examined contemporary malaise in French society: one, the solitude of independent women; the other, cultural divides. These typify the malaise of a postindustrial society in which middle classes dominate and symbolic capital (as Bourdieu uses the term) has often replaced economic capital as the mechanism of social domination. A second point these films have in common is the polyphonic approach: although Nathalie Baye is the central character of *Vénus Beauté Institut,* the two films weave their story around a song sung by several clearly distinguishable voices. In *Vénus Beauté Institut,* the activity in a beauty salon is a pretext for presenting female figures as diverse as possible in terms of their age, appearance, style, and temperament. These films challenge the narrative mode inherited from the New Wave, with a narcissistic, solitary (male) figure, an alter ego of the author, at the center of the story, a formula still used by Assayas or Desplechin (see *Ma vie sexuelle* or *Fin août début septembre*). The films of Marshall and Jaoui also challenge the "sociological" gaze fixed on alienated female characters, which Chabrol has been imposing successfully since

Les Bonnes femmes (1960) to *La Cérémonie* (1995). The New Wave constructed a gendered division of narrative structure that reserved for male heroes the privilege of constructing the viewpoint with which the spectator would identify; however, films that focused on one or several female characters reduced the protagonist(s) to being the object of the gaze (of the filmmaker/of the spectator).[10]

Breaking with this dichotomy, the films of Marshall and Jaoui are constructed in such a way that the spectator (whether male or female) can take turns occupying all the roles, as in the "soap operas" analyzed by Tania Modleski.[11] Directors Jaoui and Bacri have been using a polyphonic system for a long time, but in Jaoui's film the satirical, scathing verve is toned down a little in order to give each of the characters a chance.[12] The two films couple an incisive observation of contemporary social behavior with an empathetic gaze upon each of the protagonists, leaving the ending open to the spectators' choice. Perhaps this is the beginning of a new position on the part of the *"auteure,"* who no longer defines herself as an exclusive subjectivity, but rather as an empathetic gaze focused on others. The different way of constructing the male subject and the female subject in our culture, the former in a "for me" mode, the latter in a "for others" mode, is undoubtedly related to this alternative perspective by a film director.

Paradoxically, in Jaoui's film it is a woman who represents elitist culture (in the film, Anne Alvaro is a respected avant-garde theater actress, just as she is in real life), while the other pole—that of economic capital devoid of cultural capital—is embodied by a man (Bacri), a business executive. This humorous reversal of a recurrent schema in New Wave film (the male protagonist, an intellectual or an artist, is often in love with a woman whose beauty is her sole capital and the cause of his downfall), results in the overturning of the story's stakes: eminence, distinction, values associated with the possession of cultural capital, coupled with the disdain felt for the person who lacks these values, are challenged by other, affective values. The film could be criticized for its reinforcement of elitist culture, since Bacri is "saved," first by the revelation of Racine, then by abstract art. But the play with which the movie comes to a close, Ibsen's *Hedda Gabler*—whose title role is played by Anne Alvaro—is a part of the humanistic culture that denounces male domination and has nothing to do with abstruse formalism or dusty academics. Furthermore, the passion that the actress imparts to her role makes the "revelation" experienced by Bacri credible. It is possible to interpret these *mises en abyme* of a play within a play as a sort of dream the filmmaker had of her own film as an emotional meeting-place with her audience, beyond cultural divisions. To a certain extent, the success of her film achieved and legitimized that dream.

In dealing with the solitude of "independent" women, *Vénus Beauté Institut* addresses a subject that, while less taboo in French society, still contains many formidable pitfalls, especially the one that constitutes *the* mortal sin for film critics: "cheap sociologizing." By adopting the viewpoint of the leading protagonist Angèle, played by Nathalie Baye, Tonie Marshall avoids these real or supposed stumbling blocks. The gaze of Angèle alternates between the gaze of desire (directed on the men with whom she flirts), the gaze of an observer carrying out her professional duties, the sweetly detached gaze as she listens to her clients, and the empathetic yet critical gaze directed toward her female friends and colleagues. The film gives us access to other characters by means of her gaze and questions the contradictions that confront women who try to be both economically and emotionally autonomous. Marshall takes seriously the milieu she is describing and its characters, in spite of its low sociocultural status—in contrast to Chabrol's *Les bonnes femmes,* which, with a typically male, elitist gaze upon a socially dominated female milieu, derided the work and lives of his female characters, employees in a household appliances store.

The first part of *Vénus Beauté Institut* explores with great acuity the importance of a (relatively) qualified job in the life of a woman, as well as her desire to have male partners accept the type of sexual relationship they usually experience as a threat to their ability to master and dominate. The film's second part brings to light the film-maker's own contradictions: male desire is portrayed, in the end, as the determining factor. First we see Robert Hossein, the pathetic old playboy who lures the beauty salon's youngest employee into his lair, and who turns out to be an ideal lover in the end. As a result of having been coincidentally present during the couple's lovemak-ing, Angèle stops resisting the advances of the star-struck lover who has been pur-suing her since the film's opening. Thus, the force of male desire imposes its law on the female (desire), after all. The film's ending, with its humorous evocation of fairytales, cannot make us forget that, despite its attempt to explain the complexity of female desire, it ultimately results in women's "defeat" when confronted with male desire. But, as the film's popularity showed, this contradiction was certainly presented in a more effective manner than would have been the case in an openly "feminist" film.

We could conclude, then, that the growing success of women's films—extremely varied in terms both of genres and budgets—not only points to their becoming com-mon currency (a victory in itself), but also offers in many instances a way of over-coming the perverse dichotomy—of which French film has made itself the champion—between art film and commercial cinema. By achieving the status of cre-ator, women filmmakers are challenging the repressive power structure that long confined them to the status of alienated female consumers of a subculture from which men emphatically distanced themselves in an affirmation of both their cul-tural and their social dominance.

We will conclude with the confrontation between these 24 hugely successful women's films and the art films whose fame has spread beyond France.

The list of women's films that made a cultural impact in the 1990s is certainly not complete. Films not analyzed in this essay include, for example: *Personne ne m'aime* (Marion Vernoux, 1994), *Minna Tannenbaum* (Martine Dugowson, 1994), *Petits arrange-ments avec les morts* (Catherine Ferran, 1994), *Pas très catholique* (Tonie Marshall, 1994), *En avoir ou pas* and *A vendre* (Laetitia Masson, 1995 and 1998), *J'ai horreur de l'amour* (Lau-rence Ferreira-Barbosa, 1997), *Post coïtum animal triste* (Brigitte Roüan, 1997), *Si je t'aime . . . prends garde à toi* (Jeanne Labrune, 1998), Catherine Breillat's films *Parfait amour* (1996) and *Romance* (1999), the films of Claire Denis *J'ai pas sommeil* (1994) and *Beau travail* (2000), the films of Agnès Merlet *Le fils du requin* (1993) and *Artémisia* (1997), and finally *Baise-moi* (2000) by Virginie Despentes and Coralie Trihn Thi, whose careers were brutally interrupted by censorship.

It is possible to evaluate this apparent separation between an artistic success and a commercial success in a variety of ways: many of these films came close to reach-ing the 400,000-spectator mark, which was my rather arbitrary cutoff. Hence, one may think that beyond the 24 (relatively) successful films I have examined, a more widespread phenomenon characterized the 1990s: the new visibility of films by women, regardless of their category.

Finally, it seems that many of the same characteristics can be found in the films that are not in my sampling; that is, polyphony, putting the subjectivity of the "auteure" on the backburner in deference to an empathy for the characters, a rather specific sociocultural setting, and a preference for heavily structured scenarios.

Yet this selection of films also exposes a divided gaze—between the women filmmakers driven by a kind of radicalism and those who instead aim toward consensus. Behind this dichotomy there undoubtedly lies a fundamental difference in their positions as women in society. On one end are those whose gaze is (consciously or otherwise) oriented by traditional "female" values of compassion, generosity, altruism, and the desire to be loved; on the other are those who use cinema as a tool for rebellion against the patriarchal, macho order. Between these two poles we can find all the possible variations, including the most contradictory ones imaginable. Contrary to what we expect, challenging the patriarchal order is not the exclusive territory of art films: the two attitudes are present at both ends of the sociocultural spectrum. *Le Goût des autres* is a good example of a consensual film, whereas *Gazon maudit* uses comedy as a tool to denounce male domination. At the other end of the spectrum, *Romance* and *A vendre* share an undeniable radicalism in their vision of sexual relationships. But is this reason enough to speak of a criticism of patriarchy in the case of Breillat's films?

We will conclude, then, by citing the diversity of women's cinema in France in the 1990s and its relative autonomy vis-à-vis the rather heavy-handed aspects of French cinema, whether they be economic, aesthetic, or sociocultural.

Translated by Margaret Colvin

NOTES

1. Among the women filmmakers active in the 1980s and 1990s, about twenty of them made at least three films; about ten of them made five films.

2. See the well-documented book by Carrie Tarr with Brigitte Rollet, *Cinema and the Second Sex: Women's Filmmaking in France in the 1980s and 1990s* (New York: Continuum, 2001).

3. In chronological order: 1990: *La Fête des pères* (Fleury), *La Baule les Pins* (Kurys), *Un weekend sur deux* (Garcia); 1991: *Ma vie est un enfer* (Balasko); 1992: *Après l'amour* (Kurys), *La Crise* (Serreau), *Max et Jérémie* (Devers), *Le Petit prince a dit* (Pascal); 1994: *Le Fils préféré* (Garcia); 1995: *Gazon maudit* (Balasko); 1996: *La Belle verte* (Serreau), *Y aura-t-il de la neige à Noël* (Veysset); 1997: *Marquise* (Belmont), *Nettoyage à sec* (Fontaine); 1998: *Place Vendôme* (Garcia), *Un grand cri d'amour* (Balasko); 1999: *La Bûche* (Thompson), *Le Derrière* (Lemercier), *Les Enfants du siècle* (Kurys), *Mon père, ma mère, mes frères et mes sœurs* (Turkheim), *La Nouvelle Eve* (Corsini); 2000: *Ça ira mieux demain* (Labrune), *Le Goût des autres* (Jaoui), *Saint-Cyr* (Mazuy).

4. Brigitte Rollet, "Women and Popular Genres in France (1980s–1990s)," *Sites, the Journal of 20th-Century and Contemporary French Literature* 4.1 (Spring 2000): 87–96.

5. See Olivier Donnat, *Les Pratiques culturelles des Français,* a 1997 survey, La Documentation française, 1998.

6. By way of comparison, a movie by a male director such as *Comment je me suis disputé (ma vie sexuelle)* (Despleschin, 1996) garnered a Parisian audience of 117,000 and a provincial audience of 136,000 (1:1.15), whereas a boulevard comedy like *Le Dîner de cons* by Francis Weber (1997) had 1,500,000 Parisian spectators and 7 million provincial spectators (1:4.7).

7. I refer readers to the argument that at the end of 1999 divided the cultivated critics and the makers of "French quality," such as Leconte and Tavernier.

8. Tonie Marshall's film received the César award for best film, which gave her flagging career a boost and enabled her to exceed one million spectators with the film.

9. It was hot on the heels of *Gazon maudit*, with 3.7 million tickets sold compared with almost 4 million for Balasko's film.

10. See Geneviève Sellier, "Masculinity and Politics in New Wave Cinema," *Sites, the Journal of 20th-Century and Contemporary French Literature* 4.2 (Fall 2000): 471–88; and by the same author, "La Nouvelle Vague, un cinéma à la première personne du masculin singulier," *Iris* 24 (1997).

11. Tania Modleski, "The Search of Tomorrow in Today's Soap Operas," *Film Quarterly* 33.1 (1979): 12–21.

12. As the ethnologist noted in her interview with *Télérama* (March 15, 2000), "The only extreme character is Angélique"; this homemaker, the wife of a business executive, is "the only woman who finds no grace in the eyes of the filmmaker, who makes her a grotesque character" (*Positif* 469, March 2000).

One can see in this residual misogyny a blind spot in the French vision, which refused to question the relationship between the sexes in social terms, so that the harsh or abusive wife is the bad subject par excellence, especially to an independent woman like Jaoui (see also the character of the mother in *Un Air de famille*). The visible shift in their inspiration toward less satire and more "humanity," confirmed in *Le Goût des autres*, dates from their collaboration with Alain Resnais.

SELECTED FILMOGRAPHY OF FRENCH WOMEN FILMMAKERS IN THE 1990S

Akerman, Chantal. *Nuit et jour* (1991), *Un divan à New York* (1996), *La Captive* (2000)

Angel, Hélène. *Peau d'homme, cœur de bête* (1999)

Anspach, Solveig. *Haut les cœurs!* (1999)

Balasko, Josiane. *Gazon maudit* (1995)

Belmont, Vera. *Milena* (1991), *Marquise* (1997)

Breillat, Catherine. *Parfait amour!* (1996), *Romance* (1999)

Cabrera, Dominique. *De l'autre côté de la mer* (1997), *Demain et encore demain* (1998), *Nadia et les hippopotames* (2000)

Cahen, Judith. *La révolution sexuelle n'a pas eu lieu* (1999)

Calle, Sophie. *No Sex Last Night* (1996)

Carrière, Christine. *Rosine* (1995), *Qui plume la lune?* (1999)

Corsini, Catherine. *Les Amoureux* (1994), *La Nouvelle Eve* (1999)

Cuau, Emmanuelle. *Circuit Carole* (1995)

Deleuze, Emilie. *Peau neuve* (1999)

Denis, Claire. *S'en fout la mort* (1990), *J'ai pas sommeil* (1994), *Nénette et Boni* (1997), *Beau travail* (2000)

Despentes, Virginie and Coralie Trinh Thi. *Baise-moi* (2000)

Devers, Claire. *Max et Jérémie* (1992)

Dubroux, Danièle. *Border Line* (1992), *Le Journal d'un séducteur* (1996), *L'Examen de minuit* (1998)

Dugowson, Martine. *Mina Tannenbaum* (1994)

Ferran, Pascale. *Petits arrangements avec les morts* (1994), *L'Age des possibles* (1996)

Ferreira-Barbosa, Laurence. *Les gens normaux n'ont rien d'exceptionnel* (1993), *J'ai horreur de l'amour* (1997)

Fillières, Sophie. *Grande petite* (1994), *Aïe* (2000)

Fontaine, Anne. *Nettoyage à sec* (1997)

Garcia, Nicole. *Un week-end sur deux* (1990), *Le Fils préféré* (1994), *Place Vendôme* (1998)

Holland, Agnieszka. *Europa, Europa* (1990), *Rimbaud Verlaine* (1997)

Jaoui, Agnès. *Le Goût des autres* (2000)

Krim, Rachida. *Sous les pieds des femmes* (1997)

Kurys, Diane. *La Baule les Pins* (1990), *Les Enfants du siècle* (1999)

Labrune, Jeanne. *Si je t'aime . . . prends garde à toi* (1998), *Ça ira mieux demain* (2000)

Lemercier, Valérie. *Le Derrière* (1999)

Lvosky, Noémie. *Oublie-moi* (1995), *La Vie ne me fait pas peur* (1999)

Marshall, Tonie. *Pas très catholique* (1994), *Enfants de salaud* (1996)
Vénus Beauté Institut (1999)

Masson, Laetitia. *En avoir (ou pas)* (1995), *A vendre* (1998)

Mazuy, Patricia. *Saint-Cyr* (2000)

Merlet, Agnès. *Le Fils du requin* (1993), *Artemisia* (1997)

Miéville, Anne-Marie. *Lou n'a pas dit non* (1994), *Après la réconciliation* (2000)

Obadia, Agnès. *Romaine* (1997), *Du poil sous les roses* (2000)

Pascal, Christine. *Le petit prince a dit* (1992), *Adultère (mode d'emploi)* (1995)

Pisier, Marie-France. *Le Bal du gouverneur* (1990)

Roüan, Brigitte. *Outremer* (1990), *Post coïtum animal triste* (1997)

Serreau, Coline. *La Crise* (1992), *La belle verte* (1996)

Simon, Claire. *Coûte que coûte* (1996), *Sinon, oui* (1997)

Thompson, Danièle. *La Bûche* (1999)

Treilhou, Marie-Claude. *Le Jour des rois* (1991)

Varda, Agnès. *Jacquot de Nantes* (1991), *Les Glaneurs et la glaneuse* (2000)

Verheyde, Sophie. *Un frère* (1997)

Vermillard, Marie. *Lila Lili* (1999)

Vernoux, Marion. *Personne ne m'aime* (1994), *Rien à faire* (1999)

Veysset, Sandrine. *Y aura-t-il de la neige à Noël?* (1996)

Zauberman, Yolande. *Moi Ivan, toi Abraham* (1993)

PART III

France-USA

CHAPTER 20

Debate.

WOMEN: A FRENCH SINGULARITY

INTRODUCTION

The three articles composing this debate are among a half dozen that discussed historian Mona Ozouf's book *Les mots des femmes* and appeared in *Le Débat* of November/December 1995. In her book Ozouf posits that, historically, women's liberation in France had enjoyed a unique cultural specificity that had been more beneficial to women than what she characterized as the aggressive *"différencialisme à l'américaine."* This thesis divided feminists and historians alike. Included in this issue of *Le Débat* were essays by Bronislaw Baczko, Elisabeth Badinter, Lynn Hunt, Michèle Perrot, and Joan Wallach Scott, as well as a response by Mona Ozouf.

Part I. The French Exception

BY ELISABETH BADINTER

I. A preliminary observation: Mona Ozouf's book in fact has a double agenda. Part one proposes a series of portraits of women, through which Mona Ozouf tries to reach their individual personalities as well as their relationship to men. In part two there is a shift to a comparison of two types of feminism, French feminism and American feminism. These are different topics. What might be criticized here is her attempt to answer the question of the difference in the relationships between the sexes in the United States and in France in terms of the difference between French and American feminism. I totally agree that there is a difference. I even think I was the first to point it out, in *XY,* in which I talked about French *exception,* and not only French *singularity*—I take this up again in the preface to the American edition of *XY.* As far as my own position is concerned, I simply prefer to situate that difference in the relationship between the sexes, rather than between the two feminisms, whose difference is a secondary, derivative phenomenon, a consequence.

There is no doubt that when one observes the last three centuries in England (prior to considering the United States), Germany, or France, there exists in France

a *privileged* relationship between the sexes. I take full responsibility for the value judgment implied here. It is this relationship, as I understand it, which explains why
feminism is different in each country.

II. The relationship between the sexes is a complicated question and it resists sim-
plification. It nevertheless seems to me, since I have studied the question as it traverses the history of three centuries, that between men and women in France there
is more gentleness, a greater solidarity, and more seduction than in other European
countries. Nothing horrifies the French more, be they men or women, than the war
between the sexes or their segregation. Just compare the mixed character of our salons, in the past and today, with the careful segregation of the sexes that has long
been the norm elsewhere.

Consider the reaction provoked in France by the protests of the *précieuses*. It is a
fact that in their milieu the men certainly heard that demand for liberty formulated
by the women. They clearly represented a social microcosm, but a microcosm that is
not as small as has been claimed. Compare English reactions to the same type of
protests in the same period 1650 to 1690. The men's response was extraordinarily
violent, and insulting. Not only were women's demands for freedom challenged,
they were not even taken seriously: rather they were rejected as the threat of social
decadence and dissolution. In France Molière is always quoted as being the *précieuses's*
greatest enemy, the one who sends them packing. But Molière's irony in *Les Précieuses
ridicules* is the very symptom of the attention and of the importance he accords the
question. Then if you consider that Molière is their most virulent critic on this side
of the Channel, you can gauge how different is the violence of the English pam-
phlets. The companions of the *précieuses,* their literary and social counterparts, acted
upon their questioning of marriage and of motherhood, their demand that the intellectual life of women be taken seriously and respected. They sneered, but they
took these demands into consideration, and they changed. Salon culture, of which
Mona Ozouf gives some elegant eighteenth-century examples, illustrates the
spreading of this phenomenon. Yet it would be an error once again to reduce its influence to a few circles within the capital. It is a cultural phenomenon—with its center in a very privileged circle; but it has a much larger social effect, if only through its
provincial ramifications. The crucial factor for me is that the men, in that privileged
human group, gave in to women's claims as a step forward for civilization.

The same difficult consent is found with each new upsurge in feminist protest, in
the eighteenth, nineteenth, and twentieth centuries. Each occasion brought a challenge to and a redefinition of male identity. In France, as opposed to England, Germany, or the United States, particular circumstances meant that men finally
accepted these changes in the name of *civility*—despite their initial reticence, despite
the pain of change, since any shift in identity is painful. French men heard women's
demands with more ease, I am tempted to say more affection. There is one significant exception: the men of the French Revolution, and in particular the *Montagnards*.

I could repeat today what I have just rapidly described at its beginnings. If one
were to conduct a general analysis of feminist demands and of women's demands—
since I consider that it is the whole of French female society that has changed and
not just that part permeated by feminist willpower—one would find that on the
whole they have had more success than elsewhere. Men have listened to them more

attentively, even if they fret more articulately than in Germany, America, or, for example, Holland. And even if there is still a lot to be achieved . . .

III. Why is that? I've been asking this question for years. All I can do for the time being is to hazard a guess at an answer. I have the feeling that French men are less frightened of women than Anglo-Saxon men. The difficult relations between men and women in the United States as well as in Germany stems ostensibly from a terrible fear: each sex is frightened of the other. I am not saying that that fear does not exist in France, but it is less pronounced. The root cause of this must be the mother/son relationship. Small French boys have not been "possessed" by their mothers to the same extent; they have not been their exclusive love-object. Let us not forget that throughout the history of this country women have as often as possible abandoned their children to wet-nurses: that too is a French exception. A consequence of this milder maternal investment is that boys are less castrated by the omnipotence and omnipresence of their mothers. The inverse has happened in German society in which the role of the mother has been overvalued to such an extent that women have been allowed to be little else. This explains the violence of German feminism today and the significant fall in the birthrate. The break can only be brutal.

I insist, in passing, on the need not to restrict the comparison to powerful American culture only, but to extend it to other European countries. Only against these two backgrounds does the French exception stand out with sufficient clarity. The term exception can evidently be contested for its positive connotations even if the differences are admitted. I know it makes American feminists angry. I defend it nonetheless.

IV. I thoroughly agree with Mona Ozouf on the importance of universalism in French feminism. Today's feminisms can be structured around a dividing line between the *universalists* and the *differentialists*. The two tendencies exist everywhere. In France differentialism is represented by thinkers like Hélène Cixous or Luce Irigaray. They have had an enormous influence in the United States, a significantly smaller one here. The majority of French feminists are universalists, even if they don't know it. On this point, Mona Ozouf is right. Where she might be criticized is in her abusive generalizations about American feminism, reducing it to a vulgar caricature of the type engendered by radicalism. American feminism cannot be reduced to an exclusively differentialist position. A large part of the movement is universalist. There is a whole liberal sphere of influence inherited from Simone de Beauvoir; it exists mainly on the Left and is a universalist form of feminism, careful not to provoke the war between the sexes and remaining distant from the militant tendency. Militant radicalism, mainly embodied in the lesbian movement, stems from the belief that the relationship between the sexes is intrinsically violent and that women will only be saved by absolute segregation. It corresponds to Andrea Dworkin's famous formula: any penetration of a woman by a man is rape. However significant, this extreme position is far from being unanimous. American feminism speaks in other voices to which we owe it to ourselves to pay attention.

Translated by Anne-Marie Smith

Part II. "Vive la différence!"

BY JOAN WALLACH SCOTT

Mona Ozouf's book is beset by contradictions. Its first part consists of historically grounded, elegant sketches of learned and cultured women; its second part is an ahistorical polemic. The individual differences among women, Ozouf insists, defy any notion of collective (female) identity; yet these individuals are used as evidence for another kind of collective identity: a French national character (*"une essence commune," "un génie national"*). As she admonishes her readers to attend to nuance and complexity, her own arguments throughout the book are reductive and simplistic. In the name of admiration for French women's irony, good humor, and lack of aggression, she launches a furious, humorless attack on feminism in general, and on American feminism in particular. In striking contrast to the benign, genial countenances presented in her gallery of notable women looms the scowling, contorted visage of Mona Ozouf.

The intensity of Ozouf's anger seems to me to exceed the reasons she offers for it, and it defies the explanatory capabilities of this historian. Perhaps those who know her better can account for her strident intervention in fields she has not addressed before (the history of women, the history of feminism—both French and American—and feminist theory) and for which she lacks the kind of expertise she brings so artfully to bear on her studies of the French Revolution. The anger, whatever its origins, is the source of many of the book's problems—its manicheanism and its ahistoricity in particular.

The entire book is conceived as an attempt to protect the integrity of an imaginary "French feminism" against "perversion" by an imaginary American feminism. Ozouf's "French feminism" does not correspond to any historical period or movement; instead it seems to consist of an attitude about sexual difference embraced by some generality of French women, who are typified by the ten she sketches. (That the ten are in no way typical seems to bother Ozouf not at all, the variety of their characters—one is generous, another stubborn, one anxious, another avid—substitutes for any attention to social diversity.) The attitude she ascribes to French feminists accepts sexual difference as a natural boundary, although it often refuses social stereotypes of femininity; it understands that to recognize feminine specificity "n'est nullement consentir à une inégalité" (is by no means to consent to an inequality) (77). Not only do Ozouf's feminist heroines believe in the idea of universal human equality (some well before the idea's time), but also they realize its possibilities in their individual lives. Indeed, it is their ability to live as individuals, but also as women—to accept their difference but not to be limited by it—that establishes the "originality" and the "singularity" of Ozouf's version of French feminism. Those who offer critiques of prevailing gender inequalities by attacking the ideologies or structures that implement them, those who suggest that sexual difference has been systematically constructed and that its effects produce imbalances of power between the sexes are excluded from her definition of French feminism. Simone de Beauvoir's *Second Sex* is written off as an aberration (in contrast to Beauvoir's life, which, with its love affairs and extraordinary literary accomplishments, makes her exemplary), as are the works of Luce Irigaray and Hélène Cixous. These two are deemed to be unrepresentative of French opinion (how are the educated aristocrats portrayed in the first section of the book any more typical? one wonders), since they are members of an intelligentsia "campé aux marges de la société" (camped out in society's margin) (387). In fact, they are decidedly un-French, having been appropriated by the enemy: American feminism.

American feminism is portrayed by Ozouf as a monstrous, man-hating lesbian, who dares to dignify "le rapport homosexuel entre femmes comme le modèle d'une jouissance sans domination" (the homosexual rapport between women as the model of a bliss without domination) (387). This harpy sees all men as rapists and harassers; she is the enemy of women's progress because it leads to "backlash" and she is impatient with the slow pace of reform; she is both a prude and a zealot; she wears her victimhood like a holy robe.[1] Worst of all, perhaps, this lesbian separatist, this consciousness-raising evangelist of "la nouvelle religion féminine américaine" (the new American feminine religion) (388), deals in theories of collective identity and social determination that, but for their substitution of gender for class, pose the same threat to individualism that Marxism once did. In fact, it would only be a small exaggeration to say that Ozouf's American feminist is a postcommunist transsexual: a male worker turned lesbian whose oppressor is now men instead of the bourgeoisie.

The source for Ozouf's scathing caricature of American feminism is Christina Hoff Sommer's book, *Who Stole Feminism?*, hardly a neutral text in the American "culture wars." Sommers is a conservative philosopher who (like Camille Paglia) has made a career of attacking feminism in the name of feminism. Her epithet, "gender feminism," which refers to all those who think that sexual difference must be understood as a culturally, historically specific set of relationships, has been taken up by the religious and political Right. On the eve of the Beijing conference, the Pope condemned those "gender feminists" who taught that sexual difference was a variable, not a fixed or eternal concept. And Republican presidential hopeful Bob Dole, playing to the fundamentalist Christian Right, warned that Hillary Clinton ought not to be associated with events in Beijing, where "gender feminists," who insist there are five genders(!) not the God-given two, were trying to foist a subversive agenda on the world. The specter of sexual deviance is regularly used in the United States to discredit those who want fundamental change in the situation of women, whatever the strategy or analysis they employ.

It is usually pointless, because it mixes genres, to respond to caricature with serious evidence (in this case about the sheer variety, past and present, of American and French feminisms). Yet when one is responding to a historian, one is moved nonetheless to offer some corrections: Women in the United States got the vote in 1920, not 1914 (12). Hubertine Auclert addressed the Congress of Marseille in 1879, not 1878 (222), and she was hardly the first French feminist to argue for the primacy of political rights for women (211). Although Auclert may have been the most outspoken suffragist during the Third Republic, she rightly acknowledged many predecessors, among them Olympe de Gouges in 1791 and Jeanne Deroin in 1848. Arguments about the social construction of gender are neither new nor rigidly deterministic and they have long counted French women among their proponents. Nor are analyses of male interest and male domination peculiar to contemporary American feminism. For example, Jeanne Deroin refused to take her husband's name, calling it "le fer brûlant qui imprime au front de l'esclave des lettres initiales du maître, afin qu'il soit reconnu de tous comme sa propriété" (the burning iron that imprints on a slave's forehead the initials of her master, so that she may be recognized as his property).[2] And Hubertine Auclert (whose militance Ozouf seriously underplays) denounced the male "*intérêt du sexe*" that led to the hypocritical practice of preventing women from voting because they were supposedly under the influence of priests, while allowing those very priests to exercise the rights of citizens.[3] The psychiatrist Madeleine Pelletier, who held to the kind of universalist notion of individualism Ozouf extols, nonetheless counseled women to refuse all signs of femininity; difference, she thought, would always be treated as inferiority, and since the universal individual was equated with the masculine, women had no choice but to present themselves "*en homme*" (as a man). In the history of French feminism, and in the history of French democracy more generally, the relationship between universal equality and female particularity has been far more troublesome than Ozouf is willing to admit.[4]

But instead of pondering the difficulties, Ozouf repeats without question the justifications politicians and others gave from 1789 to 1945 for the exclusion of women from citizenship. Women (as a whole category, she suggests) supported the Church during the Revolution and continued to do so during the nineteenth century; they were thus threats to the stability of successive republics. In a book with very few notes, one wonders what Ozouf's evidence is for this "fact." And anyway, she says, as if aware of the fragility of the religious argument, women were quite happy with improvements in education and civil status; they didn't really want or need to vote. Indeed, since French women were equal where it really mattered, the vote was not relevant for questions of independence and autonomy—as individuals (so her ten sketches demonstrate) women could exercise autonomy in their intimate (that is, in their sexual and domestic) lives. Still, the vote creates problems for her insistence on the fact that equality and difference maintain a comfortable hierarchy in modern French political thought (395).

Ozouf claims that women didn't get the vote until 1945 because they were associated with particular interests and thus could not be considered as independent individuals—the prerequisite for citizenship (376). The distinctively "radical" French tendency to refuse particularity when thinking about universals led inevitably to women's political exclusion. This means, although Ozouf won't acknowledge it, that universality and masculinity were synonymous. Otherwise, universal thinking would have the same problem with male particularity as with female. It does not occur to Ozouf to ask what generations of feminists did ask: why is it that women's interests are "particular" while men's are not? The failure to ask that question allows Ozouf, unwittingly perhaps, to reproduce as somehow natural or inevitable the thinking that, I would argue, created an impossible situation for French feminists who wanted to claim rights as universal individuals but were prevented from doing so by the equation of universality and individuality with masculinity. They were in the oxymoronic situation of women claiming the rights of men. (And they were regularly attacked as monstrous, as "homme/femme" or "femme/homme" or hermaphrodites, for that reason.)

Ozouf seems to believe, with the early opponents of women's suffrage, that sexual difference is a more primary difference than others. She speculates that differentiation according to sex was a way of protecting France against the radical "indif-ferentiation" implied by democratic principles of equality (351). Women somehow provided a guarantee against the leveling sameness (whatever that actually means) of equality. But why women? Why didn't differences among men or among social groups or races provide a guarantee against sameness? And if, as she maintains later, France was uniquely original in its ability to balance equality and difference, why was anyone worried that equality would eliminate difference? Why did sexual difference become a primary way of signifying difference in the age of democracy? These are the kinds of *historical* questions that are entirely absent from *Les mots des femmes*.

This inattention to history structures the entire book. Ozouf writes as if there is rarely any change at all in concepts and categories. As far as sexual difference is con-cerned, she maintains (gleefully in the case of Simone de Beauvoir) that "the body" is a determining force independent of its social construction. Relations between the sexes don't seem to be fundamentally affected by social and political developments. The effect of the Revolution is seen as additive rather than transformative: "le com-merce heureux entre les sexes" (the happy commerce between the sexes) initiated by Old Regime aristocrats combines with egalitarian democracy to produce an original amalgam in which seduction and ambiguity happily characterize amorous (hetero-sexual) relationships (395). It is ironic that in this book the author of an article on "*l'homme nouveau*" (the new man) of the Revolution does not entertain the possibility that in new contexts the meanings of terms like woman and man might be funda-mentally altered.

But terms do change and some of the key concepts on which Ozouf relies changed radically in the course of the three centuries she covers. "Individual" did not mean the same thing in the eighteenth century as in the twentieth, and its meaning changed several times in the course of the nineteenth century. "Citizen" lost its heroic association with independent individualism by the time of the twentieth cen-tury—the age of mass democracy. The vote, too, had acquired different significance when, at last, it was extended to women. No longer the assertion of the will of the sovereign people, it was seen simply as an occasional exercise of political choice within limited parameters. Once the equation of individuality, citizenship, and man-hood came undone, it became possible to enfranchise women. So it ought not to be surprising that as de Gaulle recreated the French Republic in the wake of Vichy, women served as a symbol of the power and willingness of the nation to accommo-date and unify its many different constituencies.

The commitment to a unity of differences that Ozouf takes to be a mark of an original and transhistorical French national character may in fact date from this postwar period. Whether or not that is case, these notions of unity and national character are prescriptive and polemical, they do not describe the varied and con-tested beliefs and practices of French people or even of successive French govern-ments. Evocations of national character create "imagined communities" that do not preexist their enunciation. These evocations draw their strength from comparisons with "others" deemed to be their opposites, their negations, or their enemies. The comparisons serve to consolidate otherwise disparate points of view, to replace de-bate and conflict with consensus and commonality, to create a unity that overrides differences. Thus Ozouf's use of American feminism as the subversive threat to France creates an illusion of a united French womanhood when, in fact, there are conflicts and differences among French women and among French feminists.

When subjected to close and careful analysis, the rhetoric of "national character" yields great insight for historians—as the work of Rogers Brubaker on France and Germany clearly demonstrates.[5] But when the historian offers "national character" as an explanation for a problem (in this case, the "timidity" of French feminists as compared with American feminists, and the late date at which the vote was granted to French women), then readers ought to beware. They ought to ask what Mona Ozouf's stakes are in writing a nationalist polemic that domesticates feminism and offers French gender relations as exemplary. They ought to ask how this book's anti-Americanism is related to other attacks in France on American cultural hegemony. They ought to ask why gender has, at this time, become a national issue and whether this book is an isolated phenomenon, or an example of a more general international development. In short, they ought to treat Ozouf's book not as the history of a country in which the battle of the sexes has never been engaged, but as a partisan document in the gendered political struggles of the late twentieth century.

Part III. Counting the Days

BY MONA OZOUF

My first reaction—apart from gratitude for Le Débat, for those women and the one man who have read my book with such critical vigilance—is one of incredulity. I feel like the young innocent who finds himself fighting in a battle for which he is assured he signed up voluntarily (or even that he himself declared it) and who rubs his eyes, at once fascinated by a spectacle of unexpected violence, and yet with a paradoxical feeling of unreality and invulnerability, strangely convinced that he will remain untouched by the crossfire. For many of the projectiles flying across those texts—and especially one of them—seem to be aiming at an imaginary book, one that is not mine, in any case. In order to spend more time addressing those critiques that really hit the mark, I would first like to field the erratic cannon fire.

If I had wished to write a book on French feminism (as Joan Scott suggests), it would have indeed been little more than a brief sketch, to put it mildly. If I had wanted in a handful of pages to write a history of American feminism, it would have pushed the caricature even further. This was obviously never my intention. Can we even call Les Mots des femmes a history book? It is more like an article of contraband smuggled back and forth across the frontiers of literary criticism, of the history of ideas, of the philosophical essay. And this is perhaps what accounts for feeling secure when confronted with the accusation of sketchiness, which, I agree, would hit me face on had I ever harbored the great ambitions and bad intentions attributed to me.

So what precisely was my intention? It would not be superfluous to begin with that—since the object of the exercise might have appeared incongruous: an escapade into unknown territory in which the author advances heedlessly without the required specialization kit, a monstrous composition in the light of academic requirements, with its epilogue ill-fitting the preceding portraits of ten women themselves arbitrarily selected; an airy demonstration of which both the ends and the means remain unclear. Why this style? Why this approach? asks Michelle Perrot.

I've nothing to say about the style: the style is the woman—and I don't believe I adopted a particular style for this book. There remains the approach: I did not want to produce a scholarly work—is that compulsory?—and I confess outright the influence of my own literary tastes upon my choices, my admiration for the work of my ten chosen writers, and also the satisfaction I derived from showing the inventiveness, courage, intelligence, and wit employed by these women who have been mystified all too often. I enjoyed my promenade through the destinies of these ten women and I am fully aware of the frivolity of this justification. Treading the paths of these ten women was nonetheless guaranteed to bring me back to the long fight women have waged for their rights and the importance of that movement in our century. That provided me with the opportunity to renew former reflections on the fate that the French Revolution and then the Republic have reserved for women in France, to reflect therefore on the question of French identity. But it also gave me the opportunity to pursue new thinking since at the same time I was reading the bestsellers of American feminism and they raised certain questions: why does the feminist movement here not enjoy the same visibility and energy as it does over there?

Why, with the odd exception, has feminist protest in France not reached the same level of aggression? Why do French studies of women's history, in constant expansion in the universities, not lend themselves to rewriting universal history in the light of this new history? Why do the French resist thinking about people of the same sex as a community? I am infinitely grateful to Lynn Hunt for understanding that my intention was not at all to reduce thriving American feminism to its most extremist characterization—of which, unfortunately, Joan Scott here gives an illustration—and I wonder why this extremist version of American feminism, which has its theoretical foundation in French thought, has nonetheless made so little impact in France, where it seems offensive, unintelligible, and sometimes even untranslatable.

Since I'm addressing the problematic comparison with America, I want to make it clear that the accusations of anti-Americanism leveled against me are once again like those projectiles that stray a long way from my book and from my feelings. If I selected the American comparison—even if I wholly agree with Elisabeth Badinter that it should be extended to other European countries—it is because it seems legitimate, fertile ground for comparison: two countries that in the course of their history have shared the founding event of a revolution; two countries that in their "declarations" have affirmed the universal values of liberty and equality. The fact that feminist protest in each has followed such a different course awakens our curiosity and calls for an explanation. I am astonished, moreover, that in my book the observation of this asymmetry seems scandalous when it is peaceably acceptable when it comes from other pens. In an authoritative study Claire Duchen[6] has just made the same observation, and she wonders whether the conclusion to be drawn is not "the little impact feminism has made in France." That relative and so frequently evoked "weakness" of French feminism is, according to Michelle Perrot, a commonplace, well documented in recent studies—she knows them well, has often initiated them—studies dedicated to bringing to light the dense, ingenious, and varied life of little-known feminist movements. I too have read those books; they have taught me a lot, but the revelation of hidden treasures[7] does not change the global verdict on the relative timidity of the French feminist movement: "Group life is weak," says Michelle Perrot. Did I ever write anything else? And so my sense of unreality increases.

This sense is never so intense as when I reread my book through the eyes of Joan Scott. According to her, I have allegedly minimized the importance of the French Revolution; I say precisely the contrary, "as far as it concerns equality between the sexes, the Revolution changed everything" because it brings into effect, as Bronislaw Baczko emphasizes more strongly than I, a movement that turns against the very precautions and restrictions it instigated. Once again from the pen of Joan Scott, I am alleged to think of Beauvoir's *The Second Sex* as an aberration in contrast to her exemplary life, and once again the opposite is true. *The Second Sex* was one of my fetish books and I still admire it, but my discovery of Beauvoir's life when I read her correspondence threw a bucket of cold water on that. Still according to Joan Scott, I have "severely minimized the militant ardor of Hubertine Auclert," and yet I describe the passionate pathos of a life exclusively devoted to the cause of women. I could give many examples of such misprision and I wonder whether it is the cause or, on the contrary, the consequence, of such foul play.

It is now time to tackle the real objections, the ones that hit the bull's eye. The reading that perturbs me the most is the one that uncovers in *Les mots des femmes* an attitude typical of French complacency, an inane ethnocentrism. Suggesting that relations between the sexes are more enjoyable in France than elsewhere is an easy target of derision! And then to evoke the "exquisite courtesy" that reigns in France,[8] land of rolling hills, of gentle ladies and charming refrains, land nurtured by the twin breasts of gallantry and Gallicism; and suggest that the book owes its success to the way in which it pleasantly flatters national vanity: *Les mots des femmes* would have one believe that France is that happy country in which we can still talk of love. I am not insensitive to the ridicule—"*niaiseux*," as they say in Quebec—attached to my book when it is presented thus, and I admire Elisabeth Badinter for braving this ridicule along with me, and with even more audacity than myself, since her knowledge of comparative history, considerably more extensive than my own, leads her not only to talk about the singularity of France, but of the "*French exception.*"

I don't know about exception but I think those women whose itineraries I have related—a far cry from tales of innocence, free from worry and conflict, since for one of them the wheel of destiny will bring blindness, for another the guillotine, another exile, others a disastrous marriage—all share something essential that protects them from suspicious acrimony toward the opposite sex; that is, confidence in the civilized quality of relationships, born of the mixing of the sexes, which is characteristic of aristocratic society and which has been transmitted to democratic society. It is this quality that softens the asperity of life and helps bear the burden of the days. Once again, I am grateful to Lynn Hunt for understanding that the subject of my book is also what Necker called "the legislation of outlook and manners." When I was writing it, I had in mind that trend in French literature that is a plea for "social gentleness," which social mores generally guarantee for women and for the weaker members of society whom they protect. The ten women I chose show how that unwritten legislation helped them, if not to circumvent constraints, at least to displace and tame them, by inscribing them into what Lynn Hunt calls the "texture" of life. They also claim to share a belief in love and furthermore in friendship, which they have often cultivated with more felicity than they have cultivated love. Is this derisory? That belief in love prevents the relationship between men and women from being interpreted as a war between the sexes. Furthermore, an awareness of the precariousness surrounding both birth and human development leads to the belief that it is unrealistic to want to negotiate all the conditions of exchange in love or in friendship. An invisible chain links that natural French confidence in social mores and the French resistance to the legislation of human relations.

I persist in thinking that the long history of shared activities and sentiments between men and women that so struck Vallès when he returned to Paris from the streets of London has endowed the relationship between the sexes in France with a pleasant hue. It is for that reason, moreover, that the separatist protests of the Mouvement de libération des femmes (MLF) in its heyday were unacceptable here. I therefore run the risk of naiveté. But naiveté is not the only accusation against which I must defend myself; against ignorance also, since, and here's a second, heavy objection, I do not use the concept of *gender* in my argument, a concept that has become the hallmark of studies in women's history, even history in general for those who claim that gender, like class in the past, is henceforth the major variable against which everything else is measured. That very abstention puts me in bad odor and ranks me a bad case in the camp of the bad, where Joan Scott lines me up with American fundamentalists and with the Pope in person, who she claims has just condemned those guilty of using this notorious concept. She even posits *in fine* the hypothesis of a wider conspiracy in which my book allegedly participates, and this in the *Jdanovian* mode: "It is certainly not fortuitous that. . . ." I feel that I am about to make my case even more condemnable here.

The word "gender," which is almost untranslatable into French, has two definitions. One is minimal: gender is a cultural construct built upon biological determination. I willingly subscribe to that definition without believing in all the virtues ascribed to it. The attention lent to the aspect of sexual identity that is a product of history and of human activity is quite simply an isolated case of that powerful research movement, which for 20 or 30 years has snatched the following away from nature in order to restitute them to historicity—tears, fear, laughter, childhood, the sense of smell, of the obsolete, death. Thomas Laqueur's book, which is constantly cited as emblematic of the productiveness of the notion of "gender," can be filed away in that vast library that devotes itself to revealing human artificiality everywhere and enumerates "inventions" and ready-made, mass-produced concepts; however interesting this may be, it does not amount to a revolution in interpretation.

The second definition of gender is maximal: gender is a relationship of power in which everything is historically and socially constructed. Nature has nothing more to say about femininity, and politics has everything to learn. That definition, which does away with biological determination, postulates an absolute separation of sex and gender (*genre*). In my view, there are two disadvantages to this idea: on the one hand it leads to the denial of the link between identity and consciousness of one's sex; on the other hand it allows one (the differentialists for example) to hold onto biological determination and to preach to women about the exploration of that incomparable feminine nature. With one we are stuck in the concrete, with the other in abstraction; with one imprisonment, with the other illusion. Joan Scott is in the latter camp, maintaining that it is reactionary to suggest that a specific aspect of feminine existence is anchored in nature and escapes our will. We are bordering here on those horrific constraints that Lynn Hunt sees as dominating American society. Her very interesting paper makes of that refusal the hidden link between extreme Left and extreme Right, pro-life and pro-choice, linked in the unlimited self-affirmation of the individual. That belief in the individual's absolute right to be himself, which passes paradoxically under cover of attachment to subcultures and communities, is for her the determining factor in the dissolution of social cohesion.

Reading Lynn Hunt we can delve a little further into what remains an enigma. American feminism has indeed, as Michelle Perrot recalls, made much use of Foucault's "tool-box," whereas French feminism has neglected to exploit this source. Is it because a French ear captures more easily the accents of Foucault's ferocious nihilism, the explosive mix of despair and sarcasm? Is it because French feminism senses to what extent the inclusion of this devastating philosophy in any movement of progress is, to say the least, problematic? Is it furthermore because the French now know that the critique of democracy can be heard equally on the Right and on the Left? Here are, once again, examples of French singularity, which it would be interesting to study. One can understand what the feminism of gender asked of Foucault: first the interpretation of human relations as relations of power, hidden everywhere, having infiltrated everywhere, microscopic and without limits; second, the affirmation of the self as an unalienable value, the absolute right to authentic individuality, to heterogeneity, the seeking-out, in direct line from Nietzsche, of modes of existence as different as possible, the denial of all shared morality. This is no doubt a very simplified reading of Foucault, little concerned with linking the Foucault of the destitution of the subject to the Foucault of concern for oneself ("le souci de soi"), cutting through the rich meandering of his thought to get straight to what seems essential: the deconstruction of sexual difference, the triumphant affirmation of individual singularities, hatred of the common norm, the refusal of the universal.

According to Lynn Hunt, America's problem—and it is not an ill from which France can claim immunity—lies there. No one accepts constraint any longer, and when it is forced upon one, it is interpreted in strictly anthropological terms: there are only victims, faced only with executioners, which is a way of denying the forces over which human nature has no control. But precisely. What Les mots des femmes tries to show is that women's existence is in itself a protest against absolute artificiality. I see Joan Scott lurking in the wings: Why should women offer a particular counterpoint to the artificiality of democratic society? And if one insists on jeopardizing the egalitarian leveling out it promises, why not bet on racial or even character difference just as well as sexual difference? In her view these questions are entirely absent from my book. But I suspect that she didn't notice them because the answers they suggest were not acceptable to her. They do not subscribe to that ideology for which everything is cultural, or everything political. The book reserves a particular fate for Tocqueville's idea, according to which, since "not only does democracy make every man forget his ancestors but also hides his descendants from him," the family, reigned over by woman, is and will be the last pocket of resistance to the sad forgetting of the chain of being. So women's existence is a counterforce to social atomization and the family a fixture among the vertiginous excesses of democratic society.

I am amply persuaded of this by the reception women gave the French Revolution. Men's central belief in the Revolution is that the world begins with them, but women are most uncomfortable with that belief. They are on the side of transmission and belong to that chain of being that Tocqueville said is shattered and whose links are kept apart by democracy. And that is why women's resistance to the Revolution, more than being a religious resistance, is a resistance to that revolutionary time that denies filiation. Joan Scott challenges me to answer from where I derive the conviction that women, as a category, opposed the Revolution with a collective bad grace. Where? In hundreds of boxes of archives—I do open them—in which the missionaries of the Revolution, be they representatives or officials commissioned to observe public opinion, lament, decade after decade, month after month, the obstinacy with which women, attached to ancestors, to tombs, to tradition, to the sound of bells ringing at six o' clock, to the immemorial scansion of village life, ridicule the revolutionary calendar, its pomp, its dictates, and its extravagant Year I. A man can believe that he is constructing a new society upon a tabula rasa and can see himself as a "new man." A new woman? Women's consciousness of time, one that is spontaneously Burkian, inscribes itself as a foil to that particular utopia.

That for me is the core of my book, and this was so well grasped by Lynn Hunt and Bronislaw Baczko who made it even clearer to me. Lynn Hunt even goes so far as to suggest that the substance of the book is a meditation on our common subjection to decrepitude and death. In her view, what is unmasterable in our lives is only secondarily sexual determination, and is essentially the fact that all of us, both men and women, are transient. Is it possible to disagree with her? Yet the purpose of *Les mots des femmes* was not as wholly metaphysical as this. It was to make apparent women's particular relation to time. Governed by the biological clock that decides their tempo, women count the days differently from men, more attentively than men, who can afford not to count them; they count them in terms of the events and breaks in the fabric of their lives, such as puberty and menopause. As Madame de Staël said, theirs is a more brutal link with destiny; because of the slowness of pregnancy, they know better about patience and length of time. All this arms women against the utopia of the tabula rasa, against willful arrogance and the illusion of being their own origin.

That is not tantamount to returning, in pure essentialist tradition, to the naturalness of woman. It is simply a manner of postulating, as Bronislaw Baczko's text suggests, a female "register" of time, a way of living it in a less discontinuous, disengaged way—with more constancy and more linking. Literature shows us this, and sociological observation makes a plea for this. Nor does this amount to a denial of freedom, for freedom and constraint can only be evaluated in relation to one another. Such is the lesson of Rousseau's *La nouvelle Héloïse,* a decisive lesson for those women whose accounts I solicited. The character of Julie in *La nouvelle Héloïse* illustrates the double nature of existence as analyzed by Hannah Arendt: the experience of life binds woman to a situation she has not chosen; but moral and intellectual experience offers her the possibility of transmuting that arbitrary attachment into a personal endeavor. The instrument of that recreation is education; for, as Bronislaw Baczko recalls, paying well-deserved homage to Condorcet, it is the faith in education that opens a decisive breach in the wall of women's exclusion from citizenship. To the men of the Revolution, this seemed fully justified by nature herself. But these same men also professed that through education, nature can be transformed in an almost unlimited way. The women in my book have gambled upon that revolutionary promise as the very opportunity for their release from subjection.

Can we fail to insist that the educational gains through which women have conquered their autonomy are in fundamental harmony with women's way of linking the future to the past? The aim of education is to transmit an age-old heritage of language, customs, culture, and knowledge. It is also a heritage of constraint, which education converts into the capacity to snatch life from the jaws of fate. Of that play in education between freedom and constraint, past and future, there is no nobler example than that proffered by Simone Weil. She wants to help the workers of Puy emancipate themselves from managerial oppression and create a freer, nobler life for themselves. To whom does she subscribe for her new project? To none other than old Sophocles, whom in her opinion the working class, but we may add women too, can ask for the secret of their freedom.

Translated by Anne-Marie Smith

NOTES

1. I cannot refrain from comment here on the complete misreading Ozouf offers of Susan Faludi's *Backlash.* Faludi does not argue against reforms for women, she just describes the forms of resistance to them. And she hardly blames men as individuals, but links male resistance to questions of the symbolic and material construction of masculinity. Ozouf inverts the arguments of a number of authors, presenting them as saying exactly the opposite of what they have written.
2. Jeanne Deroin, "Profession de foi" (Paris: Bibliothèque de l'Arsenal, Fonds Enfantin 7608, 39), 40.
3. Hubertine Auclert, "Les hypocrites," *La Citoyenne,* March 27, 1881.
4. It goes without saying that the counterexamples for Ozouf's arguments about American feminism are as numerous as are those for French feminism. There are, of course, important differences between the histories of feminism in both countries, but not of the kind she discusses.
5. Rogers Brubaker, *Citizenship and Nationhood in France and Germany* (Cambridge, MA: Harvard University Press, 1992).
6. Claire Duchen, "Féminisme français et feminismes anglo-américains: spécificités et débats actuels," *La place des femmes* (Paris: La Découverte, 1995).
7. On feminist sociabilities, see, for example, Christine Bard, *Les filles de Marianne, Histoire des féminismes 1914–1940* (Paris: Fayard, 1995).
8. Françoise Gaspard used this expression in her article, "Parity: Why Not?" in *Differences* 9.2 (1997).

CHAPTER 21

Lacan and American Feminism
WHO IS THE ANALYST?

JUDITH FEHER-GUREWICH

Lacan describes the psychoanalytic process as a dialectic between what he calls "*l'instant du regard*" (the moment of the look) "*le temps de comprendre*" (the time to understand) and "*le moment de conclure*" (the moment to conclude). In other words there is that decisive moment when for the first time the analyst and the analysand look at each other. Then comes the time to understand what this encounter is about. Last, the moment to conclude occurs when the analyst and analysand change places. The analysand can sit in the analyst's chair because he or she has discovered that the analyst's knowledge has become irrelevant. The analysand has figured out what his or her desire is, so that the function of the analyst is now exhausted.

If I can risk an analogy here I would say that the moment of encounter between Lacan and feminist theory happened in the late seventies when feminist theory brought Lacan to the academic scene. This moment was, as it is the case in analysis, fraught with misunderstandings. In the ten years that followed, the relationship unraveled, oscillating between love and hate. The moment to conclude, I would suggest, seems to be right on schedule as feminist theory has shifted its position, discovering in the process the true nature of its desire.

This analogy is of course a ploy of my own making, because as far as they are concerned, the parties involved have never been more at odds. In fact they are no longer talking. However I would like to argue that the tumultuous relationship between Lacan and American feminist theory has not ended up in a failure, as many people have suggested, but has brought to life, mainly through the work of Judith Butler, the most radical insights of Lacanian theory. I must immediately point out, however, that Butler herself may be surprised by this rapprochement, since her work has systematically debunked the hypocrisy that plagues Lacan's writing in general, and his theoretical articulation of sexual difference in particular. Such a demonstration, of course, requires not only a brief review of the relation between Lacanian theory and feminism but also an explanation of how Lacan is usually perceived (by himself and others) and how his theory can be rearticulated if the objections of his feminists detractors are taken into account.

IF THE TRUTH BE TOLD: A HISTORICAL REVIEW

While it took over ten years for both feminist theory and myself to sort out our love-hate relationship with Lacan, Lacanian psychoanalysis itself has spent little time examining its own ties with feminist theory, either in America or in France, for that matter. On the contrary, Lacanian psychoanalysis has become increasingly reactionary when it comes to bringing its critical acumen to issues that specifically refer to the rights of women and homosexuals. Recently, Eric Fassin, Michel Feher, Michel Tort, and others pointed out how Lacanian analysts have condemned "parity" for its lack of respect for "the Name of the Father" and sexual difference. It is important to note, however, that in France the political weight of psychoanalytic feminist theory had already waned by the end of the seventies. Lacan's vision of the "feminine" as radically Other was felt by French women as less problematic than the challenge posed by the American slogan "the personal is the political."

The Lacanian revolution of the sixties and seventies had a very complex agenda. It played on two grounds: the psychoanalytical and the erotic. On the one hand, it transformed the praxis of psychoanalysis by offering a rigorous grid to interpret the formation of the unconscious, which in turn provided the analyst with the freedom to negotiate transference without being encumbered by rules of technique or by the injunction to keep a neutral stand. On the other hand, Lacan himself also had the ambition to affect and transform the cultural and social ideals of his time. There is no doubt that Lacan wanted to be the French Freud on more than one count. To free Freud from the repressive Victorian era that informed his conviction that sexual fulfillment was necessarily impossible because the bedrock of castration would always stand in its way, Lacan lifted the rock and exposed the dialectic of desire between the sexes. He emphasized over and over again that if there is "no sexual relation" (one of his favorite slogans), this is certainly not an impediment to sex as long as the asymmetry between man and woman can be acknowledged. Therefore, it is not entirely surprising that in the late nineties certain Lacanian analysts reverted to their "victory" of the seventies to deplore the antierotic effects of "parity."

In the United States, the end of the seventies marks the moment when Lacan was ushered into women's studies by his most vehement French critics: Luce Irigaray, Hélène Cixous, and Julia Kristeva. The golden age of academic feminism was then confronted with new theoretical challenges. It had to digest at once not only Lacan's obtuse and not welcoming *Ecrits* but also the poststructuralist denunciation of the phallocratic intent of his theory—a theory that had apparently debunked Freud's biological determinism only to reclaim on a different basis the universality of the Law of the Father.

Of course, when theories are imported, interesting things happen: in this case the social and historical context of the seventies that led Lacan's French detractors to propose feminist revisions of his reading of Freud was lost in translation. In France, Irigaray, Cixous, and Kristeva had different axes to grind. Yet, on the whole, they continued to work within the Lacanian theoretical framework, and their intent was to find alternative discourses that would allow women to define their identity without being part and parcel of the phallocratic order. Yet this phallocratic order was not only in the text; it was also all around them. Simply to speak up in a different voice was unheard of. From there to challenging the theory itself in order to reveal some inner paradoxes that could in turn be used to prove that Lacan was sometimes at odds with himself was impossible in the climate of the Lacanian circle. Lacanian theory could not be closely examined in order to prove that Lacan's phallocratic intent was not necessarily confirmed by his clinical and theoretical insights. This approach, which would have required an atmosphere in which scholarship could rise above political allegiance and ideology, was not in the spirit of those times.

The fact that this context did not travel across the Atlantic was no mere accident. The era of deconstruction favored a more critical approach in the sense that the intent of the author is by definition already contradicted by the intent of the text itself. This situation was in part responsible not only for the downfall of Lacanian theory in feminist circles, but also for the demise of the alternative approaches proposed by Lacan's French feminist critics.

Thus, when American feminists were confronted both with Lacan and his detractors, they had to figure out on their own what both camps were actually saying. Unlike their French colleagues, they did not respect "the inner logic" of the Lacanian system and they struggled long and hard to discover a way to use the signifier and the symbolic order as flexible systems that would allow different social and sexual configurations no longer dependent on the binary system of sexual difference. Since Lacan himself demonstrated that femininity is nothing but a masquerade meant to produce desire in men, they were quick to advocate the implosion of gender altogether, thus allowing the signifier to reconfigure the body, displacing the locus of erotic pleasure and in the process breaking the artificial divide between homosexuality and heterosexuality. In the same spirit, these feminists used Lacan's analysis of Freud's clinical cases (Dora, in particular) to show how psychic pathologies were nothing more than strategies of social resistance. In this approach, hysteria's politics of defiance are by far preferable to degrading submission to the ideals of patriarchy. Thus feminist theory turned Lacan against himself. The discourse of the hysteric became the spokeswoman of feminist resistance and Lacan was attacked, along with Freud, for seeming to require that women accept their castrated lot.

Yet this path of fomenting resistance against phallocracy implies that the only identity available to women is a negative one: one could not say what a woman is, only what she is not. The objective became a woman constituted in and for herself. This is where Lacan's French feminist critics came in handy because of the perception that they offered "content" to the category of the feminine. This is how Irigaray, Kristeva, and Cixous became the sophisticated essentialists of the postmodern era (a fate they certainly did not expect or wish).

A feminist debate was therefore set up on the academic stage of poststructuralism. This debate led to a split between the proponents of gender deconstruction and the defenders of essentialism. The first camp devised strategies to expose the phallocentrism of Lacan by means of denunciation, derision, or caricature. For the proponents of this camp, resistance to the phallic order was the only path for a feminist theory in which desire and subjectivity were considered to be constituted through language. Therefore, any attempt to search for a gender identity outside its boundaries would only further alienate women by depriving them of the possibility of dislocating the "phallic" valence of meaning.

The essentialist camp, by contrast, insisted that "the feminine" as body, as writing, as fluids, as rhythms, can escape the net of language, and in that sense can "speak" an alternative language of its own making even if it is only in the margins of patriarchy.

Such a debate was of course far from pleasing to those feminists who opted for a more traditional criticism of psychoanalysis to forge their own definition of the feminine. They too ended up with an essentialist model—although it was more humanistic in the sense that, here, it is through the affective intersubjective relation to the mother that the typically feminine can emerge. This new model of the self, fed by relational qualities, was meant to counter the masculine ideal of autonomy and assertion; in that sense, it stood in direct opposition to Freud's notion that the resolution of the Oedipal complex consists in an identification with the attributes of the father, the boy receiving the right to use phallic power, the girl benefiting from it. However, by opposing Freud these feminists also lost the possibility of differentiating the category of gender from its biological underpinnings. The difficulty of negotiating sexual difference through castration anxiety and penis envy was replaced by a sexual difference that is a given from the start. What becomes the content of the repressed is precisely those feminine qualities that must be given a chance to reemerge for the benefit of both men and women.

It is not surprising, therefore, that such an approach appeared simplistic to those feminists who had gone through the rites of passage of structuralism and deconstruction. By the time the nineties came around, everyone was exhausted and ready to throw in the psychoanalytic towel, in both France and America.

Psychoanalysis slowly left the academic scene; in the process women's studies lost some of its appeal. The essentialists found some sympathy among those American feminists who still believed in "identity politics." Meanwhile, Irigaray and Cixous were exonerated from their essentialist bent when Gayatri Spivak gave them a new place in postcolonial studies (1992, 69–71 and 74–81).

The champions of gender deconstruction, led mainly by Judith Butler, joined ranks with the new interdisciplinary world of queer theory, where Lacanian psychoanalysis received its ultimate slap in the face. Since it had become clear that the symbolic could not be turned against itself to open up the possibility of new strategies to redefine the scope of desire and subjectivity, Lacanian psychoanalysis became labeled "hetero-normative." This meant that when all was said and done, there was no major difference between Lacan and his nemesis: the American ego psychology. "The time to understand" had finally hit home as the patriarchal intent of Lacanian psychoanalysis was at long last exposed from within rather than from without. For the first time, Judith Butler did ten years down the line what the French Feminists had failed to achieve. In her approach, the symbolic order does not afford, as it was first believed, a measure of flexibility, which had allowed feminism to tinker with the divide between the sexes. Beyond Lacan's category of gender as an imaginary construct or masquerade, heterosexuality remains the only logical outcome that is coherent with the ethics of psychoanalysis. In the words of Butler: "My view is that the distinction between symbolic and social law cannot finally hold, that not only is the symbolic itself the sedimentation of social practices but that radical alterations in kinship demand a re-articulation of the structuralist presuppositions of psychoanalysis and hence of contemporary gender and sexual theory" (2000, 19).

The Lacanians themselves (an active minority in academic circles) could no longer argue that feminists or queers had misread Lacan by confusing the position of the father in the social sphere with his universal function at the level of the symbolic. According to them, therefore, the sexes are not divided along biological lines but along their fantasmatic relation to the phallic signifier. No longer fooled by the complexities of Lacanian jargon, queer theory came back on the offensive: does the phallic signifier not ultimately realign the sexes along their biological destiny? If sexual difference is not a given but is achieved only through the process of the Oedipal dynamics, as Freud had shown, did Lacan really transform this universal principle when he subsumed the manifest injunction of a real father figure to a law that relied on the structure of language and kinship? And more to the point, what did Lacanian psychoanalysis really want? Can it tolerate another definition of desire other than an heterosexual one, since the submission to the symbolic is the condition of culture?

From this angle, there is little doubt that queer theory and Judith Butler in particular have exposed the tautological defense of Lacanian theory (2000, 21). Yet in my view, unbeknownst to herself, Judith Butler has shown the way that would allow Lacanian psychoanalysis to undo its own collusion with its patriarchal and heterosexist intent. Here, however, I have to introduce a new player, absent during this ten-year debate: the practice of psychoanalysis itself. It is interesting to note that none of the protagonists in this academic arena has ever wondered if "heteronormativity" would take on the same form in a society that has already undermined patriarchal ideals, thus forcing its members to revise the contents of their fantasy life. In hindsight, it has become rather evident that psychoanalysis affects but also reflects the culture in which it is practiced. So on the rare occasion when Lacanian psychoanalysis is actually practiced in the United States—where social ideals have undergone important transformations in the last twenty years—it becomes possible to pick up where Judith Butler left off and reexamine Lacanian principles without "the pressure" of the context out of which they had emerged.

WHO IS THE ANALYST?

In her recent book, *Antigone's Claim,* Judith Butler presents us with a penetrating critique of Lacan in which she articulates specifically what is wrong with his concept of the symbolic order: "The symbolic place of the father does not cede the demands for social reorganization of paternity. The symbolic is precisely what sets limits to any and all utopian efforts to reconfigure and relive kinship relations at some distance from the Oedipal scene" (2000, 20). While it is difficult to take issue with her argument from the perspective of the Lacanian ethos, if this question is tactical from the reality of the clinical situation, I would argue that the symbolic does not set limits to utopian efforts; rather, these utopian efforts are the effect of the symbolic order. And the symbolic order in question has already assimilated the demise of the father both as the authority figure in the family and as an ideal in society. These utopian efforts or fantasies endeavor to discover, as Judith Butler suggests, new configurations—social, emotional, or professional—that no longer take into account the gender divide: the object of desire has now revealed itself as a montage of traits—neither typically masculine nor typically feminine—which in turn holds a promise of happiness and erotic fulfillment.

Yet postmodern analysands are not radically different from their predecessors of the patriarchal era, even though they are themselves part of the structure of these new families, in which "the stability of the maternal cannot be secured, and neither can the stability of the paternal" (2000, 22). They will also be led to discover that the fantasy they strive to achieve and that remains painfully out of reach is only a contingent effect of those repressed signifiers that have marked their history as desiring subjects. In that sense, the analytic process that Lacan has described remains the same, as long as the symbolic is understood as that which constitutes the subject through a net of signifiers, whose function is to define a limit, or lack, from where desire for what is radically other than oneself can emerge. In other words, the symbolic, as a landmark of history (any history), by definition contains experiences of loss and separation, which in turn produce a fantasy that we could continue to call Oedipal if we understand the concept as what "appears" to soothe the difficulty of existence. It is only through the deconstruction of this fantasy that the risk of entering the terrain of such radical otherness can be taken.

So when Butler asks, "What will the legacy of Oedipus be for those . . . where the place of the father is dispersed, where the place of the mother is variously occupied or displaced, where the symbolic in its *status* no longer holds?" (2000, 22). I feel that I can answer that the legacy of Oedipus must again stand on its feet; and if Lacan has made any contribution, it is to have given us the tools to separate the symbolic from the paternal injunction. The interdiction does not emerge from the symbolic but rather as a device that prevents access to the fantasy, and in that sense, maintains its status of impossibility. If the patriarchal family structure provided the illusion that the father had the keys to the realization of the fantasy but refused the child access to it, today the situation has reversed itself.

Our postmodern neurosis no longer deplores the arbitrary violence of the father; instead, it is bent on denying the debilitation of those on whom we depend. The deficient parent must be protected so that the "burden of proof" remains with the child, who can blame him- or herself for having been inadequate in pleasing the other. The old paternal injunction, instead of being produced by social imperatives, becomes an interdiction that the subject creates in order to keep the illusion that he or she is the sole architect of his or her misery. In other words, if love is refused, there is no one else to blame than oneself. The function of psychoanalysis is therefore to bring about the lifting of this interdiction in order to allow the patient to venture into the landscape of these utopian efforts to which Butler refers. Taking that chance seems to me precisely what Butler is advocating.

"Le moment de conclure," therefore, opens up uncharted lands in which Lacanian psychoanalysis, feminism, and queer theory may yet discover new possibilities of exchange. There is no question any longer that gender, as Butler puts it, "is a fabrication inscribed on the surface of the body" (1998, 347). The analytic situation confirms daily that both men and women have no ambition to incarnate or resist specific gender roles. Yet sex goes on, and the enigma with which the dialectic of desire is imbued continues to haunt the human psyche despite social change and scientific breakthroughs.

Isn't it therefore the case that the notion of sexual difference, so central to psychoanalytic thinking, is simply what refers to that which cannot be captured, because while it surges from what is within us, it also implies an otherness that always remains beyond our grasp? Sexual difference therefore is not what it appears to be, even if, for both the Freud of Victorian Vienna or even for the Lacan of the French sixties, the scene where this enigma was played out was still the classic patriarchal structure of the conjugal family. It may have taken the paradigmatic shift of new family structures to expose the fundamental asymmetry between the concept of sexual difference in the social sphere and its counterpart in psychoanalytic theory.

To illustrate how sexual difference should be understood through this new Lacanian grid, I will refer again to the words of Judith Butler: "Is it [sexual difference] not a thing, not a fact, not a presupposition, but rather a demand for rearticulation that never quite vanishes . . . but also never quite appears?" (2001, 427). In other words, when it comes to the realm of erotic strivings, social discourse and gender roles fail to provide an adequate answer, causing the unconscious chain of desire to seek new signifiers that in turn only reveal that the question must remain open-ended.

Even more to the point: "The human, it seems, must become strange to itself . . . to reachieve the human on another plane." Isn't this precisely what the analytic process entails? To discover in oneself that that which escapes the solace of words is precisely the place where desire originates? "This human . . . will be one that is constantly renegotiating sexual difference in a way that has no natural or necessary consequences for the social organization of sexuality" (Butler 2001, 432). The process of deconstructing the Oedipal fantasy is just what leads the analysand to shift position in relation to his or her desire to allow him- or herself to be surprised by its unexpected path. "By insisting that this will be a persistent and open question, I mean only to suggest that we make no decision on what sexual difference is, but leave that question open, troubling, unresolved, propitious" (2001, 432). I would simply add here that the analytic process transforms this "troubling" question into the realization that difference is precisely what makes sex possible, therefore permitting the subject to become liberated from "the social organization of sexuality"; that is, desire becomes free from the constraints imposed by gender roles.

It may be a bit far-fetched to say that the analysand (feminist or queer theory) has come full circle to sit firmly in the chair of the analyst (Lacan). Indeed, this is a curious analysis, since neither of the parties was directly aware of its occurrence; nor would either one necessarily accept the roles in which I have cast them. But again, as Freud as shown, we are all prisoners of transference. It may not be an accident that my own historical circumstances have brought me to a point where I could not let go either of feminist theory or of Lacanian psychoanalysis. Other feminists and other analysts may have the same experience or will come to it in the future. The renowned feminist theorist Drucilla Cornell, in her recent books *Freedom, Identity and Rights* (New York: Rowman and Little Field, 2000) and *Feminism and Pornography* (New York: Oxford University Press, 2000) has already proposed new theoretical formulations that reinterpret the concept of the feminine through a revised version of the symbolic order. According to Cornell, women must be wary of the pernicious enjoyment they derive from their systematic resistance to the phallic order. Precisely because the phallic order is not the symbolic, they should on the contrary acknowledge their responsibility as desiring subjects (accepting the past as productively flawed), which in turn will open up for them those possibilities—social, political, or legal—in which women can finally turn the oppression of the past (their history) into the guide for the future. Only then can a new fantasy emerge, a fantasy—Cornell calls it the imaginary domain—that is no longer devoted to exposing oppression but rather to moving beyond it. Only then can the "enjoyment of resisting" be dissipated in order to define more clearly the task that lies ahead.

This new reading of Lacan proves once again the fruitful dialectic between feminism and Lacanian psychoanalysis. They have loved each other in the seventies, hated each other in the eighties, and demystified the roots of their strife in the nineties. Hopefully the new century may help them foster their recent insights, so that ten years from now the question treated in this essay can be asked again.

WORKS CITED

Buhle, Mari Jo. *Feminism and Its Discontents: A Century of Struggle with Psychoanalysis.* Cambridge, MA: Harvard University Press, 1998.

Butler, Judith. *Antigone's Claim.* New York: Columbia University Press, 2000.

———. "The End of Sexual Difference." *Feminist Consequences, Theories for the New Century.* Ed. Elisabeth Bronfen and Misha Kavka. New York: Columbia University Press, 2001.

Cornell, Drucilla. *The Imaginary Domain.* New York: Routledge, 1995.

———. *At the Heart of Freedom.* Princeton: Princeton University Press, 1998.

———. *Between Women and Generation: Legacies of Dignity.* New York: St. Martin's Press, 2002.

Feher, Michel. "Parité et Pacs. Anatomie politique d'un rapport." *Au delà du Pacs: l'expertise familiale à l'usage de l'homosexualité.* Ed. Daniel Borillo, Eric Fassin, and Marcela Iacub. Paris: PUF, 1999. 13–43.

Spivak, Gayatri Chakravorty. "French Feminism Revisited: Ethics and Politics." *Feminists Theorize the Political.* Ed. Judith Butler and Joan Scott. New York: Columbia University Press, 2001; first published in 1992 by Routledge (New York).

Tort, Michel. "Homophobie psychanalytique." *Le Monde,* October 15, 2000.

CHAPTER 22

The Symptom of "American-Style Feminism"

JEAN-PHILIPPE MATHY

This essay is about what French critics of the United States call "American-style feminism" (*le féminisme à l'américaine*) and the way it has been used in public debate, essays, and media accounts throughout the 1990s. The end of the Vietnam War, the progressive decomposition of the Soviet Bloc, and the liberalization of French political and cultural life in the 1980s had led many to believe that the traditional anti-Americanism of the cultivated elite, especially in its Cold War version, was on its way out. In fact, new sources of hostility toward the United States emerged in the following decade, forcing observers of the French intellectual scene to revise this somewhat hasty diagnosis.

There is a long list of recent issues in which America appears again both as a (counter)model and a threat, a forerunner of what France might become if the proper lessons are not drawn from the American example. These issues range from the retrospective evaluation of the French Revolution to the agreements of the General Agreement on Tariffs and Trade (GATT), from Euro-Disney to *la malbouffe* (a neologism: eating bad, processed food, including fast food in general) and from *l'affaire du foulard* (the headscarf affair) to the debate on political correctness. Of all the American objects that have focused the attention of public opinion in France, none perhaps has unleashed more passion in the media and in political and intellectual circles as *le féminisme à l'américaine*. Issues of gender and sexuality have infused old discussions of American cultural imperialism with a renewed affective intensity, revealing the extent to which sexuality and national identity are intertwined in collective imaginings.

I will examine the rhetoric of the Other in recent discussions of American feminism in France by drawing on two sets of public debates, one on sexual harassment and political correctness and the other on *parité*. The two sets of controversies somewhat overlap in terms of chronology. The first one extends from the aftermath of the Thomas-Hill Affair (1991) to the polemics against "the new Stalinism" of sexual codes of conduct on American campuses (1993–1994), while the French movement for parity, born in the 1980s, gained momentum in the middle of the following decade, leading to the passage of a law mandating equal representation of men and women on electoral lists and in elected bodies in June 2000.

The first debate revolves around a cultural phenomenon born in the United States and making its way into France, while the second one, more political and philosophical in nature, was about an instance of gender inequality specific to France among advanced industrial countries.[1] Despite these differences, the criticism of American society in both cases is strikingly similar. The monotony of the arguments put forward is only matched by the extreme plasticity of these arguments, their ability to fit the mold of a variety of apparently unrelated issues, from the future of the Republican school system and the crisis of French cinema to the globalization of agro-business.

The same words crop up from one editorial to the next, from *Le Point* to *Le Nouvel Observateur,* from *Le Monde* to *Le Débat,* from Elizabeth Badinter's articles to Pascal Bruckner's essays: *modèle anglo-saxon, guerre des sexes, dérive puritaine, tribalisme, chasse aux sorcières, néo-stalinisme, contagion américaine* (Anglo-Saxon model, war of the sexes, excessive Puritanism, tribalism, witch hunt, neo-Stalinism, American contamination). French intellectuals, regardless of their ideological stance, seem to agree on one thing, the need to protect the Republican legacy from American excesses. The argument is based on three key notions whose function is both to account for the American difference and to underscore the threat it poses to French society: *puritanisme, différentialisme* and *communautarisme* are the three cardinal sins of the contemporary United States.

The use of the term "puritanism," which refers to a specific moment in the development of Anglo-American Protestantism, is improper when applied to the contemporary United States. In fact, the land of televangelists, dry counties, and sodomy laws is more Victorian than Puritan. But semantic accuracy set aside, the nature of the crime is patently clear to critics of American gender relations: at the root of the dictatorship of political correctness and the all-out war of the sexes in the New World lies a deep-seated hatred of sexuality.

An editorial in *Le Nouvel Observateur* entitled "Uncle Sam and Love" goes to the heart of the matter, so to speak: "The nightmare par excellence on the other side of the Atlantic . . . today, as yesterday, is love. To eliminate it, they have tried everything. First, repression, that is to say Puritanism. Then, trivialization, that is to say liberalized practices with their parade of scientific surveys and sexual gossip. Lastly, the final solution, that is to say American feminism (*le féminisme à l'américaine*)" (quoted in Scott 1997, 71). The puritanical interpretation often enables critics to account for apparently contradictory aspects of American culture, such as extreme prudishness on the one hand, and widespread vulgarity and pornography on the other. The polemics proceeds by dehistoricizing cultural processes (eternal America, "today as yesterday") or by referring to American feminism in the singular, as if it were a monolithic movement. Françoise Giroud et Bernard-Henry Lévy, for example, contend that "*le féminisme américain a dérapé dans une sorte de délire haineux*" ("American feminism has turned into a kind of hateful delirium") (my emphasis). Puritanism as the transhistorical explanation for the sorry state of gender relations in America is coupled with an equally totalizing construct, which works as its positively valued opposite: that is, the "culture of seduction" that the French (and other Europeans) are said to have inherited from *l'érotique des troubadours.* This national *art d'aimer,* a mixture of playful eroticism and seductive witticism, is set in sharp contrast to what Pascal Bruckner describes as "the incapacity of men and women on the other side of the Atlantic to communicate outside of coercive regulations" (1995, 188). Americans hate sex, while the French love to love. On the one hand, we have the resentful delirium of American feminism, and on the other, the harmonious *commerce* between the sexes that has prevailed for centuries in French society. The systematic exploration of this pair of opposites can be found in Mona Ozouf's *Women's Words: An Essay on French Singularity,* in which she combines the emblematic figures of the patrician *salonnière* and the plebeian *institutrice* to argue that "if we grant French women the force of this primary conviction—they see themselves first as free and equal individuals—we understand that, sheltered by such a conviction they can experience sexual difference without resentment, can cultivate it with joy and irony, and can refuse to essentialize it. That may explain the original course taken by feminism in France and its distance from the Anglo-Saxon model" (274). For Ozouf, "the nation, unique in the world, where a familiarity of exchange between the sexes triumphed, was *bonvivant* France" (235). Salon women, according to Madame de Rémusat, "fabricated unity with diversity" (235), thereby actualizing even before the days of the Republic what would become the ideal of the Republic. The refined manners of the courtly aristocracy are one of the finest products of French civilization. "The salon," Ozouf argues, "gave the civilized French monarchy intellectual and moral harmony, which was the work of women. . . . Feminine arts civilized men, and from one end of the social ladder to the other. . . . According to the lesson of Montesquieu then, being a woman in France is a civilizing art" (1997, 230, 231, 234).[2]

This kind of generalization, based on an abusive transfer to the totality of a national culture of behaviors and practices limited to specific segments of the elite, however influential they may have been historically, easily lends itself to criticism, as when Françoise Gaspard derides "the exquisite courtliness that supposedly prevails in male-female relations in France." "Illustrating this 'exquisite courtliness,'" she goes on, "is the behavior of the Socialist representative who responded to his colleague Suzanne Sauvaigo's remarks to the minister of the interior regarding the rape of a policewoman in the urban rail system by saying: 'You are the last person this would have happened to.' Another example: the senator from the *Rassemblement pour la République* (RPR) who was heard to say as Representative Nicole Catala approached the rostrum, 'Here comes the vaginal symphony'" (1997, 102).

The national-republican image of France's past as a historically coherent civilizational legacy lends its support to a second group of arguments that can be summed up under the rubric of "differentialism/communitarianism." As the parity issue comes to the fore in the mid-nineties, eclipsing political correctness as the preferred vector of Americaniphobia, one moves from the passions unleashed by sexual politics to more philosophical discussions of the best way to foster democratic *vivre ensemble* in a national space challenged by immigration, ethnic politics, and identitarian quests of all kinds.

American culture appears to its critics as guilty of two related crimes in this regard. First, the peculiar conception of pluralism prevalent in the United States naturalizes social differences between men and women, blacks and whites, gays and heterosexuals, and so on by foregrounding "biological" or "physiological" characteristics ("differentialism"). Second, via the notion of multiculturalism, American society further institutionalizes these differences by granting specific political rights to the groups so constituted. To the advocates of the French Republican model, this second phase in the naturalization of social differences ("communitarianism") leads to factionalism, tribalism, ethnic warfare, the "Balkanization" or "Lebanonization" of the nation-state.

Just as the courtly tradition is opposed as a whole to puritanism, Republican universalism, as a key component of French singularity, is viewed as totally incompatible with the American version of representative democracy. In the words of Oliver Duhamel, the French Republican form of democracy, "when fundamental principles of constitutional law are concerned, knows neither Blacks nor Whites, neither tall nor short, smart nor stupid, rich nor poor people, neither women nor men" (quoted in Mossuz-Lavau 1998, 66). The citizen as abstract individual may well be a philosophical fiction borrowed from Enlightenment metaphysical conceptions of the rational subject, it nevertheless must remain, its supporters argue, a necessary fiction that protects the democratic compact from all forms of discrimination and oppression based on differences associated with essentialized group membership.

This *intégriste*, dogmatic version of citizenship often relies on what Françoise Gaspard has called "an ossified interpretation of the values of the Republic" that conveniently ignores the tensions and contradictions in the history of the Republican project itself and leaves no room for any adaptation of the political culture to new expectations created by social change. The proponents of *parité* were accused by Elizabeth Badinter, among others, of undermining the Republican consensus regarding the management of social, racial, and sexual relations by introducing disruptive foreign elements *made in America*.

In an article entitled "No to Quotas for Women," Badinter blamed *les paritaires* for advocating nothing short of the overhaul of the entire political system and trying to impose on their compatriots "a communitarian democracy of quotas imported from the United States." In Badinter's view, the profoundly divisive nature of America-style identitarian democracy would pose a direct threat to the unity of the Republic, pitting particular categories of citizens against others, turning France into the Gaza Strip. "The ideology of quotas creates sordid and humiliating calculations. For example, there would not be enough Muslim representatives and senators compared to the number of Jews in the Assemblies. And what about gays, 18–30 year-olds or handicapped people, and so on? In the United States, this kind of war has already begun in all spheres of society. Quotas are politically correct."

Two important elements of Badinter's argument need to be underscored. First, the assertion that "quotas are politically correct" enabled her to link the two debates I have kept separate for the sake of analytical exposition, thereby adding to her critique of communitarianism the emotional charge previously associated with the attacks on "puritanism." Second, the implication that parity supporters are somewhat guilty of antipatriotism by substituting the American model to the time-tested native tradition of *courtoisie cum* Jacobinism would end up forcing her opponents to reassert their commitment to universalism in an effort to eschew accusations of Americanism.

Reacting to the combined criticism of radical feminists and *anti-paritaire* universalists, the proponents of parity readily acknowledged that Republican universalism was not the genuine article, but a male-centered distortion that has served to deny women their full participation in social and political life. Their point, however, was not that there was too much universalism in French democracy, but rather that there was not enough: parity would extend (universal) rights to the entirety of the human race, men *and* women. In fact, the *paritaires'* central claim is that "le genre humain est double" (the human race is double): consequently, universalism itself is two-fold.[3] As Gisèle Halimi puts it, "Parity replaces republican universalism by a double universalism, which is neither man nor woman, but man and woman at the same time" (2001, 226).

Françoise Collin, by no means an enthusiastic supporter of parity, has remarked that, paradoxically, it is universalism itself that has promoted the sexualization of power and that "parity thus attempts to desexualize power by extending it to both sexes." Therefore, Collin goes on, "the true universalism (not a monoversalist universalism but a pluriversalist universalism) is parity. Parity would be an attempt to rediscover what has been concealed, the women who have been eclipsed behind a concept of the individual that is tailored to the image and the likeness of the male human being. Parity would demonstrate that there are several (and at least two) ways of being an individual, of embodying the universal, or, more concretely, the common world" (1997, 118–19).

The leading advocates of *parité* took pains to deny any accusation of differentialism, conceived as advocating quotas or any other form of the recognition of difference beyond the gendering of the citizen. Granting parity to women in the National Assembly, they claimed, would not open the door to similar claims of numerically equal representations by "communities" based on race, ethnicity, or religion.

"Could parity," Françoise Gaspard asked, "be one of the signs of the much-feared 'communitarization' of French society, and could its legitimization, in the French public (and juridical) space, break from Enlightenment universalism? Could French exceptionalism be under attack? . . . To formulate the question in such a way . . . leads to the assimilation of women to an ethnic community or a minority defining itself through adherence to a particular religion, physical characteristics (the handicapped) or else the choice of a life as a couple outside of the norm (gays and lesbians). Relations between men and women cannot, as is well known, be put on the same level as other social relations inasmuch as women cut across all categories, whether socioprofessional, ethnic or based on age" ("De la parité" 1994, 41). In another publication, Gaspard made the additional argument that, far from paving the way for group identity politics, the demand for *parité* was more likely "to undermine ethnic or religious communities, which remain founded on patriarchal power structures" (Gaspard and Gage, "Parity: Why Not?" 1997, 100).

Gaspard's reference to "French exceptionalism" and "Enlightenment universalism" in the same sentence suggests that philosophical discussions of abstract individualism are rooted in more pressing, and more volatile, issues of nationhood and collective identity. Universalism, which strikes many observers of the French scene as an obsolete notion mobilizing outdated, fossilized eighteenth-century conceptions of the metaphysical subject, is such a burning question because it dovetails with emotionally charged issues regarding the future of the imagined community. One of the many ironies of the parity debate is that those who reject the inscription of social, ethnic, and religious differences in the law of the land do so in the name of the *République*'s political and philosophical "exceptionalism." The quasi consensus, among intellectuals, journalists, and politicians of both genders and all ideological persuasions, against the threat of *communautarisme à l'américaine* lends some truth to the cliché that universalism is the French form of cultural specificity.[4]

The transatlantic nature of the discussion of Republican universalism and the remarkable consensus regarding its desirability among *paritaires* and *antiparitaires* alike (they disagree on the historical content of the notion, not on its value as a basis for the social contract) points the interpretation away from universalism as a philosophical concept toward considerations of nationhood and cultural particularism. The *paritaires'* forceful denial that they were advocating group identity politics through the introduction of quotas in the electoral process has a lot to do with the fact that their opponents successfully redescribed *parité* as a foreign concept, deeply corrosive of the French national character. For them, to support parity was tantamount to being unpatriotic.[5]

Badinter's reference to political correctness inserts the *parité* debate within a whole series of related controversies over the deleterious influence of American culture: not only political correctness and sexual harassment, but also Euro-Disney, the Affair of the Veil, the GATT's negative impact on French cinema, José Bové versus McDonald's, the fate of French *belles-lettres* on American campuses, and so on. As mentioned earlier, Badinter's linkage of *parité* with political correctness transfers to the first issue the negative charge attached to the second, and further delegitimizes her opponents by lumping them together with American feminist and multiculturalist radicals.

This mobility of the American reference across widely different areas of contemporary social, cultural, and economic life raises a number of interesting points regarding ideological processes. What do Muslim students from a suburb of Paris insisting on wearing a veil in public schools have in common with José Bové, a *Cévenol* farmer/activist opposed to the agricultural policies of the World Trade Organization, one might ask? And what does that have to do with the future of French cinema? The signifier "America" is what links all these events together along a metonymic chain of equivalencies. In fact, "America" works here as an empty signifier, a pure marker of negativity that can assume a variety of contents depending on what issue is at stake (whether it is sexual harassment in the workplace, antismoking campaigns, transgenic corn, or reality shows on TV).

The same individual may activate the American marker (as a negatively valued sign) in a variety of contexts and at different moments in time. The assumption is that the reference will always be decoded in the same way: to adopt American ways of doing things would mean the end of the French difference. The underlying connectivity of all the contexts in which this is true means that all the other, past references are mobilized when one instance is singled out: everyone knows what is at stake when the word "American" is mentioned.[6]

Take, for example, socialist leader Lionel Jospin's use of the American reference in two different occasions. In the immediate aftermath of the Affair of the Veil, in 1990, raising the specter of American-style multiculturalism, the then minister of education celebrated what he called the French model of interethnic relations: "I am not in favor of substituting the Anglo-Saxon model of the communities for the integrationist, individualistic French model. In a word, I am opposed to differentialism, but I am also against assimilation" (*Le Débat* 1990, 16–17). Six years later, in the seemingly quite different context of the *parité* issue, when asked whether sexism should be assimilated to racism, Jospin made a strikingly similar statement, transferring the American reference from multiculturalism to feminism: "It all depends on what the target is: real acts of segregation, or words. I don't really want people to import in France the American 'political correctness'" (*L'Express* 1996).

The main point here is that the equation between racism and sexism had been attributed by the journalist who asked the question to Yvette Roudy, former Minister of Women's Rights, a member of Jospin's own party. Jospin's retort is both an indirect rebuff to Roudy and a clear indication of where her position had gone wrong: it would end up turning France into another America. As in Badinter's statement previously quoted, the reference to political correctness serves to discredit unacceptable views held in France by French people by pointing to their American origin, as if questioning the "republican tradition" from within in fact meant assaulting it from without.

The signifier America carries connotations that are operative in various contexts because the American way of life *as a whole* is said to pose a threat to (what is construed as) its opposite, that is, the French way of life *as a whole* (its own empty signifier being *la République*). The Republic has come to stand for French exceptionalism itself, for everything that is worth protecting from the consequences of American-led global developments in a variety of areas, from international trade to the internet, from NATO air strikes against the sovereign state of Serbia to the crisis of *laïcité* (secularism), and from religious separatism to the worldwide dissemination of Hollywood products.

Recent developments in the theory of ideology help us delineate the symbolic processes at work in this type of cultural nationalism. In *The Sublime Object of Ideology*, Slavoj Zizek draws from the work of Ernesto Laclau and Chantal Mouffe to elucidate the way the identity of a given ideological field is created and sustained. Laclau and Mouffe have underscored the fundamental ambiguity of the signifier in social discourse. The ambivalent nature of signifiers stems from the proliferation of signifieds that can be associated with any one of them. Meaning is thus free-floating among signs, and the function of ideological formations is to get rid of ambiguity by stabilizing meaning within a given symbolic structure. Laclau and Mouffe call this process of semantic stabilization articulation: "The practice of articulation, therefore, consists in the construction of nodal points which partially fix meaning; and the partial character of this fixation proceeds from the openness of the social, a result, in its turn, of the constant overflowing of every discourse by the infinitude of the field of discursivity" (1985, 113).

In Zizek's own reformulation of Laclau and Mouffe's theory, the multitude of "floating signifiers, of proto-ideological elements" that are available to ideological articulation within a given cultural or symbolic configuration "is structured into a unified field through the intervention of a 'nodal point' (the Lacanian *point de capiton*), which 'quilts' them, stops their sliding and fixes their meaning" (1989, 87). Each one of the non-tied elements or floating signifiers have an open identity which receives a specific content when they are associated with other elements within a particular chain of signification. "The 'quilting' performs the totalization by means of which the free floating of ideological elements is halted, fixed—that is to say, by means of which they become parts of the structured network of meaning" (1989, 87).

Zizek goes on to give a few examples of how the same element can retroactively receive different identities depending on the symbolic chain within which it is inserted. In a field structured by the master-signifier "Communism," the privileged signifier "class struggle" will confer a precise and fixed meaning to a variety of other elements, such as democracy, feminism, ecologism, the peace movement, and so on. The same signifiers, however, are invested with different, even opposite, meanings when articulated within another field, say that of neoliberalism. In communist discourse, "real," socialist democracy is opposed to "bourgeois formal democracy"; for liberals, by contrast, Soviet-style democracy, far from being "real," was a lie, a simulacrum of democracy. Zizek argues:

What is at stake in the ideological struggle, is which of the "nodal points," *points de capiton,* will totalize, include in its series of equivalencies, these free-floating elements. Today, for example, the stake of the struggle between neo-conservatism and social democracy is "freedom": neo-conservatives try to demonstrate how egalitarian democracy, embodied in the welfare state, necessarily leads to new forms of serfdom, to the dependency of the individual on the totalitarian state, while social democrats stress how individual freedom, to have any meaning at all, must be based upon democratic social life, equality of economic opportunity, and so forth. (1989, 88)

"America" and "American" can be said to perform a similar quilting function in current debates over French cultural identity. The process of articulation explains why a wide range of social, political, cultural, and economic developments find their meanings under the umbrella of "Americanization." As we saw, the same indictment of the American way of life crops up now and again in discussions of feminism, public education, current philosophical trends, race relations, mass media, trade agreements, information technology, linguistic policies, or belletristic curricula. I have noted elsewhere that the ever-present theme of American cultural relativism, for example, "dovetails nicely with the preservation of republican rationalism: to defend the canons of classicism and high modernism against postmodern relativism is at the same time to safeguard the French model of cultural identity" (2000, 15).

A few years ago, in an essay entitled "Are you Democrat or Republican?," Régis Debray transferred the opposition between "republican" (i.e., French) and "democratic" (i.e., American or "Anglo-Saxon") worldviews to a plurality of domains, thereby generating two parallel (and incompatible) chains of equivalencies corresponding to one another term by term: universalism-nation-idea-professor-written culture-people-equity-memory-civism, and so on, on the one hand, and particularism-community-image-lawyer-orality-masses-equality-amnesia-moralism, and so on, on the other.

The totalization implied in the process of ideological formation accounts for another well-known feature of nationalist discourse, that is, its propensity to generalize in a reductive way. It is banal to remark that nationalism treats the opposite cultures or societies it constructs ("them" and "us") as ahistorical, homogeneous entities. Ideology derives its power from what Laclau and Mouffe call "the desire for a structure that is always finally absent" (1985, 113). Society as a "sutured, well-defined totality" is impossible because the movement of (political, social, cultural, etc.) differences undermine all attempts to establish coherent, unchanging institutional forms of social and political order devoid of internal tensions. As a consequence, "any discourse is constituted as an attempt to dominate the field of discursivity, to arrest the flow of differences, to construct a center" (1985, 112). But the desire for structure always find its limit in the fundamental "openness" or "contingency" of the social, what Laclau and Mouffe call "antagonism," the constitutive principle of social dynamics.

Neorepublican discourse in France today is such an ill-fated attempt to construct a center for collective identity and prevent social and ethnic antagonisms from tearing apart the fabric of national life. Since *la République* as an ideological construct can only be conceived as a closed system of interrelated elements, any attempt to modify any one of these components (by introducing *parité* in the electoral process or by allowing public school students to wear Islamic veils, for example) is bound to threaten the whole edifice. The internal solidarity of all the elements of the system also implies that disassociating pressures cannot be the products of internal tensions: they can only come from outside, the result of the inoculation of the natives with subversive foreign ideas.

That is where the signifier "American feminism," as a deadly combination of puritanism and differentialism, comes into play: it is the missing piece in the puzzle of the crisis of the Jacobin and courtly legacy, the external element preventing the desired closure of the social, in this case the harmony of gender relations. As such, it is both a symptom and a fetish, embodying the function of the Other in ideological discourse. Ideology works like a dream, according to the logic of metaphoric-metonymic displacement evidenced by Freud in *Die Traumdeutung*. In the case of anti-Semitism, Zizek writes, "the basic trick is to displace social antagonism into antagonism between the sound social texture, social body, and the Jew as the force corroding it, the force of corruption" (1989, 125).

A similar process of displacement is at work in the French-American culture wars. As Joan Wallach Scott puts it, the United States once again has become "the whipping-boy, the location of the enemy in another place" (1997, 87). For the national-republicans, it is unthinkable that the questioning of France's cultural wholeness could be home-grown, for if it were, that would mean there is no agreement on what "home" is all about, which is precisely what must be denied. The French do not hold a monopoly in the practice of ideological displacement, however. The same is true of American complaints about French cultural arrogance and disregard for minorities. Claire Moses sees a "kind of ultra-nationalism" at work in transatlantic controversies: "We blame the French for presenting aspects of ourselves we do not like but that we refuse to acknowledge (such as our elitism, our racism, our class prejudices). France (or Europe) would be impure, the United States would be pure" (1996, 13). Commenting on Moses's remarks, Christine Delphy argues that the French were guilty of a similar kind of projection/transference during the sexual harassment debate, "their caricatural version of the Hill-Thomas Affair enabling them to attribute racism and puritanism to the United States alone, thereby feeling unburdened, absolved" (1996, 45).

Displacement is complemented by a second operation also found in dream work, that of condensation: "The figure of the Jew," Zizek writes, "condenses opposing features, features associated with lower and upper classes: Jews are supposed to be dirty *and* intellectual, voluptuous *and* impotent, and so on. What gives energy, so to speak, to the displacement is therefore the way the figure of the Jew condenses a series of heterogeneous antagonisms: economic (Jew as profiteer), political (Jew as schemer, retainer of a secret power), moral-religious (Jew as corrupt anti-Christian), sexual (Jew as seducer of our innocent girls). . . . In short, it can easily be shown how the figure of the Jew is a symptom in the sense of a coded message, a cipher, a disfigured representation of social antagonism; by undoing this work of displacement/condensation, we can determine its meaning" (1989, 126).

In xenophobic discourse, immigrants are reputed to be lazy, and yet, they work hard enough to steal jobs from native people. As for American culture, it is faulted for being collectivistic (it advocates group rights, the standardization of taste and behavior performed by the American Way of Life is out to homogenize the planet, etc.) and individualistic (the obsession for individual rights undermines the national compact). Americans are both puritanical and crass, legislating sexual behavior in the bedroom and the classroom while polluting the world with their porn industry and their vulgar, voyeuristic reality TV shows. Similarly, condensation leads to contradictory statements on the part of critics of American feminism. "What's going on," Joan Wallach Scott asks, "when America and American feminism are under attack *both* for daring to ask for the representation of sexual difference in politics and for seeking to eliminate it in personal relationships? Why are the French critics of feminism so eager to defend sexual difference as a social practice and so quick to denounce it as a political demand?" (1997, 88).

Moving from Freud to Lacan, Zizek adds another feature to the way the figure of the Other captures our desire: it enters "the framework of fantasy structuring our enjoyment." Laclau and Mouffe's assertion that "'society' does not exist" echoes Lacan's famous statement that "there is no sexual relationship." In both cases, the scenario of fantasy acts as a screen masking these fundamental impossibilities, filling out the void of the Real. In Zizek's words, "the stake of social-ideological fantasy is to construct a vision of society which *does* exist, a society which is not split by an antagonistic division, a society in which the relation between its parts is organic, complementary" (1989, 126). This is why most nationalist writings espouse a corporatist vision of the imagined Community as an organic Whole that would be forever viable if only contamination from foreign insiders (*l'ennemi de l'intérieur*) could be cordoned off and pressures from outside eliminated. How then, Zizek asks, do we take account of the distance between the organic vision of a sutured, well-defined totality and the actuality of a social body racked with antagonistic struggles? In the paradigmatic case of anti-Semitism, "the answer is, of course, the Jew: an external element, a foreign body introducing corruption into the sound social fabric. In short, 'Jew' is a fetish that simultaneously denies and embodies the structural impossibility of 'Society'" (126).

The fetish of American feminism (or puritanism or differentialism or communitarianism or multiculturalism) simultaneously denies and embodies the structural impossibility of a reconciled (neo)republican order. The anger directed at American culture derives its energy from the threat it poses to what Etienne Balibar has called the "affective community," France as a political/cultural entity with which its denizens can identify and develop a libidinal attachment. Hence the sexual charge invested in issues of national character: either the other is out to steal or ruin our enjoyment (as when American repressive puritanism threatens the French *art d'aimer*) or she or he is in possession of a superior *jouissance* that lures our own away from us (the fateful attraction of American popular culture).[7] French Americanophobia often moves back and forth between two opposite poles: the conviction that "French singularity" has, throughout the ages, built institutions that are strong enough to withstand the American threat and the fear that this might no longer be true.

One of the ironies of the French-American culture wars is that most of the arguments used by the French are borrowed from American critics of political correctness and the narcissistic "culture of victimization," from Christopher Lasch and Naomi Wolf to Katie Roiphe and Christina Hoff Sommers. The French debate on the consequences of modernity is often framed in terms of a *reaction* to American cultural processes and American social commentary, as if the United States were indeed showing the way. Not only is American culture privileged as the main purveyor of both factual information and interpretive framework, but it is unwittingly acknowledged to provide both the disease and the cure, thereby disproving the view that *le sexuellement correct,* as Pascal Bruckner puts it, is reaching hegemonic proportions in the United States. The dissenting American authors the French are so fond of quoting seem to have been able to find within their own intellectual and political traditions enough resources to formulate a critique of what they dislike about cultural change in their own country.

Symptom as displacement means, however, that French attacks on social trends made in America, although informed by American texts, are less about the United States as they are about the challenges facing contemporary France. "America" has always been a metaphor for modernity and its discontents in French writings and the latest forms of this metaphorization point to the lack of consensus among intellectuals, journalists, and politicians on how to face the new developments commonly labeled "postmodernity" and "globalization." The most perceptive French analysts of these developments tend to replace the simplistic explanation by direct, unmediated American influence with a more complex model that takes into account the transnational character of societal changes in (post)industrial democracies.

In this particular instance, the Tocquevillean model, which has unseated Marxism as the preferred interpretative paradigm of modernity in dominant French intellectual circles since the mid-eighties, suggests that the crisis of Enlightenment republicanism is rooted in changes in the practice of democracy and in the definition of citizenship in France (and concurrently in the United States) rather than in the direct, unmediated influence of American culture. The United States, rather than being the source of the Great Transformation, is simply its most accomplished manifestation.[8]

Although the issue of sexual harassment first arose in the American context, its quick insertion in the political debate in France shows that many sectors of French society were ready to take up the issue. Similarly, the speed with which the principle of *parité* became law belies the widespread notion (in the United States) that the hegemony of universalist categories prevents any move toward greater gender equality in the Republic. Only eight years went by between the publication of Françoise Gaspard, Claude Servan-Schreiber, and Anne Le Gall's book, *Au pouvoir citoyennes! Liberté, égalité, parité,* which brought the issue to the attention of the media and of a large audience and the vote of the parity law on June 6, 2000.

The acceptance of the principle of the equal representation of men and women in elected bodies by public opinion and the (largely male) political class, whatever the latter's motivations might have been, surprised even the most ardent supporters of parity, who thought it would take decades to achieve.[9] So much for the entrenched resistance of Jacobin abstract universalism in contemporary France! In truth, the decomposition of the old republican model is in a rather advanced stage, both in theory and in practice. The generation currently at the top of the political and cultural power structure grew up during the Fourth Republic, in many ways the swan's song of the Third, and came of age during the Algerian War and the "events of May 68," reenacting on the barricades, one last time, the epic struggle of the interwar Left. Once the "children of May" give up their power to the next generation, raised in the postimperial, Europe-oriented France of the Gaullist and Mitterandian years that saw the parallel decline of the two pillars of the Third Republic, the School and the Parliament, what will be left of the Jacobin legacy? The most interesting developments in the near future may well have to do with the extent to which the French will succeed in safeguarding essential components of their own political and cultural specificity in the face of the new challenges posed by the triumph of individualism and the extension of the claims of egalitarian democracy to an ever-widening array of social groups.

1. In 1993, almost 50 years after conquering the right to vote, French women still made up only 6 percent of the National Assembly, barely more than in 1946 (5.7 percent), as compared to 40 percent of female representatives in Sweden. The situation was not different at the local level: a mere 7.6 percent of French mayors were women in 1995.

2. In addition to old regime court culture, the Republican legacy is also described as a civilization threatened by powerful economic and cultural forces in current debates on globalization under American leadership. Pierre Bourdieu, for example, denounces the neoliberal destruction of what he calls "a *civilization* linked to the existence of public service, the republican equality of rights, rights to education, health, culture, research, art, and above all, right to work" (1998, 30).

3. For an extensive description of the philosophical underpinnings of the parity movement, see Sylviane Agacinski, *Politique des sexes* (Paris: Seuil, 1998).

4. Ernst Robert Curtius, one of the most perceptive foreign students of French culture, put it famously when he wrote that in France "all the claims made by the universal idea are imported into the national idea. It is precisely because France fulfills her national ideal that she believes that she can realize a universal value" (1932, 19). Paul Valéry underscored the paradoxical character of this nationalization of the universal when he wrote of his compatriots that "our special quality (sometimes our ridicule, but often our finest claim) is to believe and to feel we are universal—by which I mean, men of universality. . . . Notice the paradox: to specialize in the sense of the universal" (quoted in Derrida, *The Other Heading: Reflections on Today's Europe.* Bloomington: Indiana University Press, 1992). On the universalist character of French feminism, see Naomi Schor, "French Feminism is a Universalism," *Bad Objects: Essays Popular and Unpopular* (Durham: Duke University Press, 1995).

5. That the debate of *parité* is largely about the future of national sovereignty in the context of globalization is evidenced by the fact that the idea gained increasing currency during the 1990s in transnational organizations such as the United Nations and the European Community. In the French context, what had started as a demand from militant women in radical leftist groups and in the Green Party in the 1980s, became the *cause célèbre* of "establishment" politicians and intellectuals who met in international conferences and on expert panels within the EEC (see Mossuz-Lavau 1998, chap. 2). The proportion of French women in the European Parliament has always been much higher than in national Assemblies (30 percent versus 6 per cent in 1994). *Parité* is in many ways a European idea, even though the French are the only ones so far to have made it into a law for national elections.

6. This explains why the same intellectuals are mobilized along the plurality of fronts opened up by the (U.S.-led or U.S.-inspired) neoliberal attacks on the Republican legacy. Badinter and Debray, for example, fought side by side against another threat to the Republic, that of multiculturalism, represented by Islamic students in public schools. In an open letter to Lionel Jospin, they rose to the defense of "the French version of democracy" which, they wrote, "is not a mosaic of ghettoes where the rule of the strongest can be dressed up as freedom for all. Dedicated to free inquiry, committed to the growth of knowledge, and confident in the sole natural light of men, the

Republic has its foundation in the schools. That is why the destruction of the schools would hasten that of the Republic" (*Le Nouvel Observateur,* November 2–8, 1989).

While neo-Republicans and members of the post-68 *deuxième gauche* disagree on some issues (such as the veil or *parité*), they usually come together when the U.S. "culture of narcissism and victimization" is concerned. Jacques Juillard, for example, who has been at times quite critical of Debray's version of Republican orthodoxy, lent his support to the widely shared critique of "American radical feminism" (1997).

Generally speaking, the virulence of Americanophobia in recent years can be attributed to the dismay, among representatives of both the Old (neorepublican) and New Left (*deuxième gauche*), at seeing 68-style *gauchisme* come back to France via the United States. As Pascal Bruckner, another critic of political correctness, put it, "we've already had sixties radicalism [*le gauchisme*], which is another version of these movements [PC and multiculturalism], and we know what it's all about" (quoted in Granjon 1994, 23).

Those who, a decade earlier, had praised the American Revolution as a counterexample to the murderous excesses of the French one, and used the American liberal tradition to discredit the Marxism, Nietzscheism, and structuralism of the French philosophical sixties, were now appalled at what they saw as the return of academic Stalinism on American campuses.

7. See for example the following passage in Jacques Juillard's already quoted editorial on the war of the sexes in America. At one point, the author asserts his solidarity with the American male, "caught between the feminist party that wants to castrate him and the matrimonial party that dreams of caging him." Faced with such a predicament, his chances of survival are limited, and so he has to compensate, Rambo-style: "He makes war, and dreams of dominating the planet. For those of you preoccupied by American imperialism, it's useless to say so to their diplomats; better to whisper sweet nothings to their women" (cited in Scott 1997, 71). In other words, the cure for American sexual frustration (or, at the opposite end of the spectrum, repressive desublimation) is the ancient French art of courtly love.

8. Pascal Bruckner's analysis of contemporary cultural trends, for example, wavers between an explanatory model based on the existence of similar developments in all advanced industrial democracies and the idea that the United States is contaminating the rest of the world. "America," he writes, "because of its magnetism, is endowed with a gift for propagation, a capacity to export its worst shortcomings while keeping for itself its virtues, which are great" (1995, 164). On the other hand, in a passage devoted to the shift in legal culture from fault-based responsibility to the politics of victimization, Bruckner concedes that "for the past thirty years or so, an outstanding mutation, very close to the American evolution, is affecting our country" (129), thereby implying that the changes were the product of an indigenous process. "In this respect," he concludes, "mentalities are very similar on both sides of the Atlantic" (130). Which is it, unilateral contagion or parallel evolution?

9. One could read on the back cover of Janine Mossuz-Lavau's brief history of the parity movement (published in March 1998) that "Lionel Jospin's promise to inscribe parity in the Constitution may lead us to expect fierce battles ahead." Two years later, *la parité* had become law.

WORKS CITED

Agacinski, Sylviane. *Politique des sexes.* Paris: Seuil, 1998.
Badinter, Elizabeth. "Non aux quotas pour les femmes." *Le Monde* (June 12, 1996).

Bourdieu, Pierre. *Contre-feux. Propos pour servir à la résistance contre l'invasion néo-libérale.* Paris: Liber-Raisons d'agir, 1998.

Bruckner, Pascal. *La tentation de l'innocence.* Paris: Grasset, 1995.

Collin, Françoise. "Parity and Universalism." *Differences, a Journal of Feminist Cultural Studies* 9.2 (1997): 118–19.

Curtius, Ernst Robert. *The Civilization of France. An Introduction.* Trans. Olive Wyon. New York: Macmillan, 1932.

Debray, Régis. "Etes-vous démocrate ou républicain?" *Contretemps. Eloge des idéaux perdus.* Paris: Gallimard, 1992.

Delphy, Christine. "L'invention du 'French Feminism': une démarche essentielle." *Nouvelles questions féministes* 17.1 (1996): 45.

Fassin, Eric. "Dans des genres différents: le féminisme au miroir transatlantique." *Esprit* 196 (1993): 99–112.

Gaspard, Françoise. "De la parité: genèse d'un concept, naissance d'un mouvement." *Nouvelles questions féministes* 15.4 (1994): 33–44.

Gaspard, Françoise, and Jennifer Curtiss Gage. "Parity: Why Not?" *Differences, a Journal of Feminist Cultural Studies* 9.2 (1997): 93–104.

Granjon, Marie-Christine. "Le regard en biais. Attitudes françaises en face du multiculturalisme américain (1990–1993)." *Vingtième siècle, revue d'histoire* 43 (1994): 18–29.

Halimi, Gisèle. "Parité, la nouvelle cause des femmes: un entretien avec Gisèle Halimi, propos recueillis par Jocelyne Praud." *Contemporary French Civilization* 24.2 (2001): 221–34.

Jospin, Lionel. "Le moment ou jamais." *Le Débat* 58 (1990): 3–19.

Juillard, Jacques. L'Oncle Sam et l'amour." *Le Nouvel Observateur* January 2–8, 1997.

Laclau, Ernesto, and Chantal Mouffe. *Hegemony and Socialist Strategy. Towards a Radical Democratic Politics.* Trans. Winston Moore and Paul Cammack. London: Verso, 1985.

Mathy, Jean-Philippe. *French Resistance. The French-American Culture Wars.* Minneapolis: The University of Minnesota Press, 2000.

Moses, Claire Goldberg. "La construction du 'French Feminism' dans le discours universitaire américain." *Nouvelles questions féministes* 17.1 (1996): 13.

Mossuz-Lavau, Janine. *Femmes/Hommes: pour la parité.* Paris: Presses de Sciences Po, 1998.

Ozouf, Mona. *Women's Words. Essay on French Singularity.* Trans. Jane Marie Todd. Chicago: The University of Chicago Press, 1997.

Scott, Joan Wallach. "'La Querelle des femmes' in the Late Twentieth-Century." *Differences, a Journal of Feminist Cultural Studies* 9.2 (1997): 70–92.

Zizek, Slavoj. *The Sublime Object of Ideology.* London: Verso, 1989.

CHAPTER 23

Made in America:
"FRENCH FEMINISM" IN ACADEMIA

CLAIRE GOLDBERG MOSES

This article originated in puzzlement and frustration. Much has been written in the United States about a "French feminism" influenced by Lacanian psychoanalysis and by other poststructuralist explanations for women's condition, of which Hélène Cixous, Julia Kristeva, and Luce Irigaray are the most significant exemplars along with the group Psych et po. This "French feminism," however, is strikingly different from the feminism I encounter in France where, as a historian, my work affords me frequent opportunities to meet and talk with feminists. Although I would be hesitant to assume a disjuncture between an American version of "French feminism" and an "actually existing feminism" in France merely on the basis of personal impressions, I have become emboldened to problematize this issue now that French women themselves have begun to produce histories of their movement that provide insights beyond my observations. I begin exploring this question by summarizing from recent French histories, asking how French historians describe France's feminist movement and where they locate the French feminists we in the United States most typically read about. I turn next to what U.S. scholars have come to know as French feminism, looking for its genesis in the English-language works that first used the term. My intention is neither to explicate nor to evaluate the French theorists who figure in the "made-in-America" version but to interrogate the process by which naming occurs and a historical record is constructed. How and why did Americans come to define their own "French feminism"? What does this tell us about the meanings Americans assign to "French" and even to "feminism"? Does it matter to French women if Americans misunderstand or misrepresent their movement? Does the seeming disjuncture between "made-in-America French feminism" and the made-in-France histories mask a disjuncture between theorists and movement activists or perhaps even between "theory" and "history"? And to what extent does the question of "French feminism" reflect unresolved struggles at play within the U.S. women's studies community: our difficulties in representing feminism as at once theorized and activist and in writing theorized histories and historicized theory, as well as the limitations of interdisciplinarity in academic feminism and transnationalism in feminism more broadly?

"FRENCH FEMINISM" I: FRENCH WOMEN WRITE THEIR HISTORY

During the past two decades, French scholars and movement activists have produced several histories and personal retrospectives that focus on the 1970s and early 1980s, the years during which "French feminism" as a category first appeared in U.S. publications. The earliest of these French works is Anne Tristan and Annie de Pisan's 1977 *Histoires du M.L.F.*[1] More recent studies include two histories of the women's liberation movement in Paris: Francoise Picq's *Libération des femmes: Les Années-mouvement* (1993) and Monique Rémy's *De L'Utopie à l'intégration: Histoire des mouvements de femmes* (1990); a 1981 volume introduced by Simone de Beauvoir, *Chroniques d'une imposture: Du Mouvement de libération des femmes à une marque commerciale* (1981), which focuses on one important split in the French movement and includes articles by Christine Delphy, Geneviève Fraisse, and Marie-Jo Dhaverhas; and a history of the movement in Lyon (*Chronique d'une passion: Le Mouvement de libération des femmes à Lyon*), published in 1989. Articles by engaged intellectuals have appeared in feminist periodicals and in a 1991 collection, *Crises de la société: Féminisme et changement,* edited by the Groupe d'Etudes Féministes de l'Université Paris VII.[2]

In all these histories, the central protagonist is the Mouvement de libération des femmes (MLF)—the women's liberation movement—which, like the U.S. movement at the same moment,[3] staked out its positions in opposition not only to the traditional, conservative Right but also to the "Old" Marxist and Marxist-Leninist Left and to liberals, including those feminists who played by the rules of the established liberal state. Again like the U.S. women's liberation movement, it was leaderless and structureless—a collection of groups, most of which formed in the early 1970s and which came together for demonstrations and for biweekly meetings of the "assemblées généraux" held at the Beaux Arts, the French School of Fine Arts. All the histories stress the multiplicity of these early groups. Psychanalyse et politique, familiarly called Psych et po, which figures prominently in the U.S. construction of French feminism, was just one of many. Some groups were named (Féminine, Masculin, Avenir; Féministes révolutionnaires; Femmes en lutte; Les Pétroleuses; le Cercle Elisabeth Dimitriev; le Cercle Flora Tristan), but most went unnamed at the time and remain so in these histories. Some were short-term ad hoc action groups; others were interested in developing theory. Some were organized at universities, *lycées,* or workplaces; some in neighborhoods (these seem to have included more working-class women); some around marital status or sexual identity; some around specific themes. According to Nadja Ringart, the idea that there could be a group capable of discussion and production with no organization and no hierarchy seemed totally unintelligible and unbelievable to the men around us, and even to some of the women. The first issues of the *Torchon brûlé* (an MLF publication), in 1971, brought us a lot of mail. How many times did we happily explain the nature of the movement to women who wrote to us: "Dear Madame" (or even "Dear Sir"), "How may I join your organization?"[4]

For their constitutive discourses, these French women turned to the intellectual paradigms of 1968, especially to postcolonial, Maoist, and Trotskyist (anti-Stalinist) Leftists; but according to these histories they were also influenced by earlier French feminists and by feminists elsewhere, as well as by Marxism, existentialism, and Freudianism.[5] Simone de Beauvoir's support of the MLF seemed to matter deeply

to the authors of these histories and, I assume, to their co-activists.[6] A few key professors—the sociologist Andrée Michel and the historian Michelle Perrot are
named—also played a role in introducing youthful activists to a feminist legacy.[7] The
influence of U.S. Second Wave feminism is recognized in these histories, confirming
a conversation I recall with Liliane Kandel about the importance of French translations of Betty Friedan's *Feminine Mystique* and Kate Millet's *Sexual Politics*. One of the
first French demonstrations designed to capture the attention of the media—the
laying of a wreath on the tomb of the unknown soldier in honor of the unknown soldier's unknown wife—was planned in solidarity with the first nationwide feminist
demonstration in the United States, the August 26, 1970, "strike" on the fiftieth anniversary of women's suffrage. Picq identifies the importance of early texts by the
Redstockings and other U.S. radical feminists published in *Notes from the Second Year;*
and works by Carol Hanisch, Anne Koedt, Naomi Weisstein, and Margaret Bentsen
were translated and republished in a summer 1970 special issue of *Partisans*. The
British women's liberation conference at Ruskin College, Oxford, is also frequently
mentioned and was clearly important to French MLF activists.[8]

At first, French feminist theoretical work was published in already existing Left
periodicals like *Les Temps modernes, Partisans,* or *L'Arc*. In 1971, the MLF's own *Torchon
brûlé* was first published. In 1973, the group Psych et po founded a publishing house,
des femmes, which brought out *Quotidien des femmes,* and next, *Des femmes en mouvements*—journals that reached an audience numbering in the tens of thousands.[9] In
1977, came *Histoires d'Elles,* followed in 1978 by *Cahiers du féminisme*. Liliane Kandel
counts 35 feminist periodicals circulating nationally in 1979, among which were several important scholarly publications: the women's history journal *Pénélope; La Revue
d'en face;* and *Questions féministes,* now published as *Nouvelles questions féministes* under the
editorship of Christine Delphy.[10] The theory that one reads in these publications focuses primarily on patriarchy and its institutions of social control. Although the
struggle for abortion was the central organizing crucible throughout the 1970s and
early 1980s, abortion politics were embedded in a broader theoretical discourse
challenging patriarchal constructions of the family, housework, heterosexuality, and
especially motherhood. Rape, woman battering, and pornography were frequent
topics in the late 1970s and into the 1980s. Much of the theory was published
anonymously, signed simply by "a woman," "the women," "some women," or "a group
of women."

However, I can identify from the histories and from their later signed publica-
tions several women who played leading roles in organizing and strategizing: Chris-
tiane Rochefort, Monique Wittig, Gille Wittig, Antoinette Fouque, Françoise
Ducrocq, Christine Delphy, Emmanuele de Lesseps, Anne Zelensky, Annie Sugier,
Jacqueline Feldman, Nadja Ringart, Cathy Bernheim, Michèle Le Doeuff,
Geneviève Fraisse, Odile Dhavernas, Marie-Jo Dhavernas, Françoise Picq, Liliane
Kandel, and Judith Ezekiel. As editors and frequent authors for *Questions féministes,* Simone de Beauvoir (the journal's titular head), Monique Wittig, Delphy, Lesseps,
Colette Guillaumin, Nicole-Claude Mathieu, and Monique Plaza helped to develop
what Delphy termed "materialist" feminism; editors and authors of *La Revue d'en face,*
including Marie-Jo Dhavernas, Ezekiel, Kandel, and Picq, held a similar politics.
Hélène Cixous figures in these histories as the best known of the authors closely associated with Psych et po. Luce Irigaray's work in the 1970s is likened to Cixous's:
both were grounded in psychoanalytic theory and stressed the specificity of woman,

but following a "violent rupture" between Irigaray and Psych et po in late 1974, the two theorists kept their distance.[11] Julia Kristeva never associated herself with the MLF or with feminism—indeed, she often railed against both in the popular press— and these histories make no mention whatsoever of her or her work.

Theoretical differences were usually most heated when related to questions of immediate strategy and especially to concerns that the MLF might be co-opted by working through the liberal state. For example, French feminists worried over the dangers of relying on a class- and race-biased judicial and incarceration system in the struggle against rape. Similarly, they disagreed on an appropriate stance toward the campaign to legalize contraception and abortion through legislative action or ministerial fiat.[12] Simone de Beauvoir and Anne Zelensky's call to form a structured organization (the Ligue des droits des femmes) from an amorphous, structureless movement brought this dissension to a head. Differences about the nature of women—the equivalent of U.S. conflicts about "essentialism" versus "social constructionism" or "equality" versus "difference"—caused contentious disagreement as well; but it was only after 1980, when the theoretical debate over sexual difference became enmeshed with a power struggle for control of the MLF, that this one issue came to define the split within the French women's movement.

In the late 1970s, the movement that was diverse but cohesive in its early years began to fragment. The French mass media, in highlighting this dissent, categorized feminism into three tendencies: "class struggle," "Féministes révolutionnaires," and "Psych et po." The taxonomy seems to have stuck in general consciousness, although these histories claim it is too simplified to capture the multiplicity of the movement. Françoise Picq, for example, both uses and challenges the taxonomy, noting regretfully that the reductionism turns a diversity of "groups, projects, forms of struggle, [and] themes of reflection" into three neat "tendencies," dividing "that which was melded together."[13] But she does recognize that serious splits among feminists were sapping the movement's strength; indeed, she entitles this section of her book "The Tendencies against the Movement."

On a more positive note, however, these were also the years when feminist activism reached out most broadly. A 1977 Lou Harris poll found that 64 percent of both French women and French men declared their agreement with "the movements that struggle for women's liberation."[14] This was also a time when feminist enterprises were established: bookstores, cafes, restaurants, a press agency, and most of the periodicals named above. Lyon's Women's Center opened in 1976, Paris's first battered women's shelter in 1978.

In reading these French histories, what strikes me is how like the U.S. movement it all seems. Picq makes this very point: "From one side to the other of the Atlantic, our preoccupations converged; our debates were the same."[15] The language of 1968 parallels the language of the U.S. New Left; the protests and demonstrations resemble our zap actions and marches; and the U.S. and French movements were similarly structureless and leaderless, sometimes cohesive, at other times strained by disagreements around issues of autonomy (non-mixité) versus solidarity with the male Left, reformism versus revolution, pressure on the state versus cultural politics, a gay/straight split, and a split among lesbians over lesbian separatism. Also familiar is the political context—governments with little sympathy for radical feminism that nonetheless caved in to some quite significant demands, especially for contraception and abortion rights and for equal pay and opportunity—and the sense of a movement whose energies were spent by the early 1980s. It may seem ironic to those of us who blame conservative Republicans for the troubles U.S. feminism faced in the 1980s that in the French accounts it is the socialists, who came to power at the same moment, who are blamed—for co-opting radical feminism but then dashing feminists' hopes that the alliance would be fruitful. Yet despite striking similarities, there were important differences between the two movements. First, the tripartite French taxonomy does not match the taxonomy of liberal/radical/socialist that emerged at the same time in the United States. French "class struggle" feminists, for example, do not parallel U.S. socialist feminists but rather worked much more closely with the male-dominated Left (especially communists and Trotskyists), often subordinating feminist-defined priorities to (male) worker-defined ones. Féministes revolutionnaires and many other small groups resembled in various ways both socialist and radical feminists in the United States but were more resolutely social constructivist than either. Nor does Psych et po parallel U.S. cultural/radical feminism: although both expressed essentialist views, Psych et po's theorizing on female subjectivity, grounded in Lacanian psychoanalysis, is quite unlike American cultural radicalism. Finally, U.S. liberal feminism finds no counterpart within the French MLF.

Furthermore, French feminists' relationship with the Left is quite different from that of U.S. feminism. In France, which has a significant, organized, and powerful Old Left, the established discourses, politics, and theories of class analysis have influenced feminists in ways that contrast with the United States, where the discourses, politics, and theories of Black resistance were the more crucial influence. French "class struggle" groups worked more closely with male-dominated Left parties and unions than did U.S. women's liberation groups; although in symbiotic contrast, groups like the Féministes revolutionnaires seemed fiercer in their anti - Old Left sentiments than similar groups in the United States.[16] It seems, too, that consciousness-raising groups never played a significant role in France. Picq seeks to explain this by noting the French disdain for rigidly organized discussion, a characterization of our "CR" groups that most U.S. feminists would vehemently deny. Finally, as narrow as the U.S. women's liberation movement may have been in terms of class, age, and race, the French movement as represented in these histories seems even narrower, limited to France's major cities and to well-educated women,[17] and energized mostly by young women who felt comfortable with a certain kind of boisterously radical, antistate cultural politics.

The French histories end with the early 1980s and the coming to power of the socialists. By then, the energy spent in movement infighting—like the split among the editors of *Questions féministes* that culminated in a court battle over the name of the successor publication (*Nouvelles questions féministes*)—had taken a serious toll. But according to the French histories, it was the struggle between Psych et po and all the other feminist groupings (who found a certain unity in their opposition to Psych et po) that dealt the movement its most devastating blow. As Christine Delphy has written: "it is not a question of attributing to [Psych et po] the responsibility for everything that has gone wrong in the Movement . . . its troubles are shared by all women's movements in all of the industrialized countries. But it is in France and in France alone that the movement has also been attacked internally."[18] Although it would be difficult to reconstruct the "real" story or to determine whether Psych et po fully deserves the blame heaped on it by other French feminists, I believe it is crucial that U.S. feminists not only know about this struggle but also understand how we ourselves, in our ignorance of the politics that give meaning to theory, figured within it.

As I already noted, disagreements among French feminists (as among U.S. feminists) were ongoing throughout the 1970s. All the histories of French feminism describe a contentious atmosphere at the "assemblées généraux" gatherings; these assemblies, says Picq, were "explosion[s] of ideas, immediately contested and often abandoned. There was insolence and derision. The floor was open to everyone, but it had to be seized with authority. The law of the jungle ruled."[19] But for the most part, such disagreements are viewed with equanimity; indeed, the histories suggest that the movement flourished by encouraging differing views and strategies. Psych et po alone is presented as a threat to the movement by seeking to dominate and thereby obliterate this diversity.

In the pages of these histories, Psych et po emerges not so much as just another group among many with differing agendas and strategies but as a kind of "religious cult."[20] We read of Psych et po's tightly controlled and rather secretive internal structure, the meetings "day and night" that meant, as former member Nadja Ringart put it, "a complete break with the rest of our social lives." The psychoanalyst Antoinette Fouque was the group's leading personality and reportedly also the analyst of many of the participants.[21] It seems that confession was the group's central activity, with the participants publicly airing their sins of masculinist thoughts and behaviors. In the words of Ringart: "The will to understand our desires . . . led us to 'work,' that is, to seek out and to confess to all traces of masculinity, or any desire for representation,' or a wish to 'take power,' etc." ("Naissance d'une secte," Rémy, Chroniques d'une imposture, 1981). Psych et po differed from the other groups in more than internal structure. It favored introspection and a certain kind of theorizing that privileged introspection over demonstrations, organizing, and the theorizing that emerged from activism of this kind. Psych et po thus absented itself from the very activities that, in the 1970s, were capturing the attention of the French media and creating among the general public a receptivity to feminist views. Even the initial decision to publicize the first small group's discussions and hold an open meeting, in order to encourage the development of a movement, was resisted by the women who would later constitute Psych et po. Attempts to confront the state through the courts or to press for different laws (for example, decriminalizing abortion) were denounced as "reformist" or, worse, "masculine." Moreover, Psych et po, alone among the MLF groups, condemned "feminism" itself, claiming that "feminists" sought simply to share in masculine power. In so doing, Psych et po divorced itself from the increasingly popular engagement with the historical legacy of feminism undertaken by others in the MLF. In its war of words with those who freely used "feminism" to describe MLF politics, it also constructed the sense of a movement that was far less diverse than we know it to have been, one that was simply bifurcated between "feminists" and Psych et po—and in which Psych et po thus seemed to have as much influence as all the other groups combined.

But in mid-decade, Psych et po dramatically changed its introspective practice. It also rather suddenly became very well financed. All the French histories question the secrecy that surrounds this funding and wonder whether there are connections that would harm Psych et po's reputation if they were known. With its newfound wealth, Psych et po launched a publishing house, des femmes, opened several bookstores throughout France, and inaugurated the mass circulation Des femmes en mouvement in a monthly and later a weekly edition.[22] Many American, British, Italian, and Spanish feminists published their works in French translation with des femmes. Cixous also published with them, although MLF women who identified with feminism published instead through Denoel-Gauthier, Voix de femmes, Feminin futur, Autrement dites, Tierce, Maspero, or Horay's series, "Femmes en mouvement."

Their well-financed publishing ventures may explain why Psych et po became the best known of the MLF groups among feminists abroad. But in France, Psych et po's struggle against feminism was apparently becoming ever more frantic, in what Picq views as "diatribes" that "lost all relation to reality." Ringart, writing of her own experience, tells us that "Antoinette ... charged the word [feminism] with everything that was wrong in the world. . . . Feminism . . . was everything that held us back and, in the guise of women's struggles, would just renew the masculine order and dominant ideology."[23] Picq quotes from Psych et po: "Socialism and feminism ... are the two Most powerful pillars of Patriarchy in decline, the final stage . . . of Phallogocentrism. . . . Feminism is radical only as root of Patriarchy."[24] It is Picq's opinion that des femmes' readers among the general public nonetheless "continued imperturbably to congratulate the magazine on its feminism. It would make no sense to them that one can be for women and not be feminist."[25]

The conflict reached its crux in 1979 when des femmes legally registered—that is, "trademarked"—both the name "MLF/ Mouvement de liberation des femmes" and the logo of the fist in the woman's sign, thereby denying other groups the right to their use. The attempt of des femmes/Psych et po to dominate the women's movement and silence French feminists now had the backing of the state legal apparatus. Their trademark of the MLF name and logo was never considered simply a symbolic move. When Tierce, the publisher of Nouvelles questions féministes and Revue d'en face, challenged it, des femmes sued for "unfair business practices" and was awarded financial "damages." The group also has not ceased its practice of suing other feminists in court: a notice in a recent issue of Nouvelles questions féministes alerts readers that des femmes has charged Christine Delphy and four others with "defamation" for circulating at a 1995 demonstration a tract critical of Psych et po. "Never has the French movement been so united," comments Judith Ezekiel, "as when it opposed Psych et po's legal registration of the logo and name 'women's liberation movement'—it brought together some 55 groups from more than 15 different cities."[26]

But in the United States, this history of French feminism is little known. Moreover, our ignorance extends beyond the split between Psych et po and French women who call themselves feminists to the history of contemporary French feminism as a theoretically grounded social movement with a broad agenda and widely disparate views and strategies. How did it happen that such a partial "French feminism" has been constructed in U.S. academic discourse? How did it happen that just when proudly self-identifying feminists in France were engaging in a struggle for existence, we in the United States were creating our own version of French feminism that, intentionally or not, put the considerable international power and prestige of U.S. academic feminists behind Psych et po and the theorists whose views are associated with them?

FRENCH FEMINISM II: MADE IN AMERICA

In my determination to trace the construction of a "made-in-America French feminism," I turned first to the earliest presentations of French writings translated and published in U.S. feminist works. These appeared in *Signs,* which published English-language translations of Julia Kristeva and Hélène Cixous in 1975 and 1976 and the first English-language analyses of the French movement in 1978. In 1980, *The Future of Difference,* edited by Hester Eisenstein and Alice Jardine, published papers from a Barnard College conference that included discussions by Jane Gallop, Carolyn Burke, and Domna Stanton, among others, of theories at work in Kristeva, Cixous, and Irigaray. In the same year Elaine Marks and Isabelle de Courtivron's *New French Feminisms: An Anthology* also appeared. In 1981, a cluster of articles presenting and dissecting French feminism was published in *Feminist Studies* and a "Special Section on French Feminist Theory" appeared in *Signs.* Toril Moi's *Sexual/Textual Politics: Feminist Literary Theory,* which opposed "French" to "Anglo-American" feminist thought and featured Cixous, Irigaray, and Kristeva, was published in England in 1985. Together these works were the foundational texts for the American—and also British—construction of the category "French feminism." This construction was a process rather than a single event. Its first stage was the introduction to American audiences of Kristeva, Cixous, and Irigaray as French writers, although not yet as "French feminists." Consider the inaugural issue of *Signs,* which included a translated excerpt from Kristeva's *Des Chinoises.* The accompanying editorial described Kristeva as "among the most provocative and respected contemporary French intellectuals"; nothing was said to connect her to feminism, and *Signs* did not then provide the biographical information about its authors that might have identified Kristeva's political affiliations. Nor did the editorial speak of the significance of *Des Chinoises* to French feminism. Readers unfamiliar with French writers—surely the vast majority of *Signs'* readers in 1975—probably read the article for the light it might shed on Chinese women, not on France. Readers introduced to Cixous in the pages of *Signs* would not have learned much that would place her in relation to a social and political movement. The editorial for the summer 1976 issue, which included Cixous's "Laugh of the Medusa"—a manifesto for what came to be called "*écriture féminine*"—described Cixous only as "a French writer, scholar, and initiator of a doctorate in women's studies at the University of Paris." A brief description of the essay, which had appeared in French the previous year, states only that it "calls for women to write a new female text." The editorial continues: "Her essay, which denies the legitimacy of 'phallic' intellectual schemes, exemplifies by its own texture the deregulation of past scholarship."

The slippage from "French writers" to "French feminists" seems to have begun with the essays by Carolyn Burke and Elaine Marks published in the summer of 1978 in *Signs.* Although both articles were still about French "writers," both also discussed the MLF. Especially in view of the absence of any other analyses of French feminism in English-language periodicals, readers would reasonably conclude from this juxtaposition of writers and the MLF that French feminist activists were all novelists, philosophers, or critics. Marks's article, a review essay on women and literature in France, most prominently discussed Kristeva, Cixous, and Irigaray, although Marks also signaled the importance of Monique Wittig and listed several other writers—Simone de Beauvoir, Nathalie Sarraute, Marguerite Duras, Marguerite Yourcenar, as well as the more junior Catherine Clément, Claudine Hermann, Chantal Chawaf, Annie Leclerc, and Christiane Rochefort. Carolyn Burke's "Report from Paris: Women's Writing and the Women's Movement" purported to cover more than the literary scene but in fact also discussed only women writers. Burke explicitly conflated writers and the women's movement: after two introductory paragraphs on the birth of the women's liberation movement in the aftermath of May 1968, she describes a feminist practice that "brings into question, and into play, the transformational powers of language." The personalities Burke singled out for attention were Cixous, Kristeva, and Irigaray; the only movement group examined was Psychanalyse et politique. She noted Cixous's association with Psych et po and especially with its publishing house and bookstores. Although Burke hinted at criticism of Psych et po on the part of some other feminists, these other feminists were not identified.

It is important to keep in mind that both Burke and Marks are French-language literature specialists who traveled frequently to France in that context and who had a sensitive ear tuned to the political implications of writing and literary criticism. Then-associate editor at *Signs* Domna Stanton is also a French-language literature specialist and most likely played the important role of obtaining, if not originating, these translations and analyses for *Signs*. Still, with only *Signs,* among feminist publications, publishing any French women at all, most U.S. readers would have lacked the knowledge to recognize the omission of other forms of politically significant practice. In hindsight, it is the conflating of writers and critics with the women's movement that is most striking, although I am not certain I noticed it at the time. True, only Burke's "Report from Paris" even claimed to be covering something larger than academic, discipline-specific concerns—something we would take for a feminist movement. And the *Signs* editorials always identified Cixous, Kristeva, and Irigaray as French "writers" or "intellectuals," never as feminists. But I doubt that I was alone in reading into these articles an analysis of French "feminism." I assumed that Cixous was a feminist simply because she, like me, identified with a "women's liberation movement." Marks, in her review essay, informed us that Cixous and Psych et po had problematized the words "feminist" and "feminism"; but then again, in *The Second Sex,* Simone de Beauvoir, accepting the position of early-twentieth-century Marxists, had also dissociated herself from "feminism," assuming it to be class-biased and narrow in its interest.[27] I think it not surprising, therefore, that in the United States the trio of already celebrated theorists—Cixous, Kristeva, and Irigaray—became identified with French feminism despite the protestations of at least Cixous and Kristeva that they were not feminists. By the end of the 1970s, the section of the Barnard College conference on "Difference" that was devoted to these particular women could be entitled "Contemporary Feminist Thought in France." This formulation in the Barnard conference papers, published as *The Future of Difference* in 1980, was reinforced by the publication in that same year of Elaine Marks and Isabelle de Courtivron's *New French Feminisms: An Anthology,* the volume I believe most significant of all for constructing "our" French feminism.[28]

It is illuminating to return to *The Future of Difference* and *New French Feminisms* with my present purpose in mind. Domna Stanton's article in *The Future of Difference,* "Language and Revolution: The Franco-American Dis-Connection," not only identifies Cixous, Kristeva, and Irigaray as the thinkers who matter but also—and in explicit contrast to the United States—identifies language as the site of feminist struggle in France. The Marks and Courtivron anthology has a broader scope, presenting pieces from diverse groups within the French movement, including writers such as Beauvoir, Françoise d'Eaubonne, Evelyne Sullerot, and Christine Delphy, whose styles and positions were more like those of American radical and socialist feminists in the 1970s. Moreover, Marks and Courtivron included a section for "Manifestoes—Actions" that focused on abortion rights and antirape work, which also would seem to belie a "Franco-American dis-connection." Still, Marks and Courtivron proclaim that "the most stimulating texts of the new feminisms are being written by women of letters, professors of literature and philosophy, [and] psychoanalysts."[29] Textually, Kristeva, Cixous, and Irigaray dominate New French Feminisms: Kristeva is represented by four pieces; Irigaray by two; and Cixous by two, one of which not only concludes the book but also runs to over 20 pages and is by far the longest piece in the anthology. Beauvoir is the only other thinker represented by multiple entries. Except for "For a Materialist Feminism" by Christine Delphy (whose initials alone are affixed to her entry, probably reflecting the custom of early movement activists to write anonymously) and a piece by Evelyne Sullerot, feminist writings by other social scientists or any historians are absent even though their work actually predominated in French feminist publishing.[30] In their introduction, Marks and Courtivron describe the basic features of a "French feminism" that confirms their selections of texts. Most striking is their elevation of Psych et po to the dominant position within French feminism: "The group now known as 'politique et psychanalyse,' [sic] one of the earliest to be formed, has become the cultural and intellectual center of the M.L.F." Elsewhere, they say that "Politique et psychanalyse [sic] is the most original of the women's liberation groups in France and perhaps in the Western world. It is also, ironically, the most dependent on male psychoanalytic and linguistic theoretical models." They go on to present Psych et po's views and models as the views of French feminists more generally. For example, Marks and Courtivron advise readers that "women concerned with the woman question in France use the words 'feminism' and 'feminist' less often than do their counterparts in the United States." They also represent French feminists as essentialists: "more convinced than their American counterparts of the difference between male and female" and thus "more imbued with notions of sexual specificity."[31] Such a claim about the supposed essentialism of French feminism would certainly have furthered a "Franco-American dis-connection," to repeat Stanton's phrase, for, as I have written elsewhere, U.S. scholars in the early to mid-1970s emphasized—indeed, overemphasized—a sharp polarity between social constructionism and essentialism and even blamed nineteenth-century feminist essentialists for the failure of First Wave feminism in adequately advancing the cause of women.[32]

And then there is the question of the legacy of earlier feminism. According to Marks and Courtivron, the new French feminisms cannot be understood diachronically as part of the history of feminism in France. The significant differences between the old and the new feminisms are best perceived by situating the new feminisms synchronically in relation to the profound changes in the orientation of French intellectual life.[33] Psych et po's antihistorical stance is thus presented as the French view, although we now know it was not widely shared in France at that time. Picq insists on this; she writes that throughout the last half of the 1970s, the address of the Bibliotheque Marguerite Durand, which constitutes an archive of feminist history, was circulating among French activists and "each one found among the 'grandmothers' one heroine who especially touched her."[34] Ironically, however, Marks and Courtivron divorce themselves from their own antihistorical view by including an invaluable chronology of historical French feminism to introduce their anthology.

The Feminist Studies and Signs special issues and Toril Moi's Sexual/Textual Politics confirmed Marks and Courtivron's characterization of French feminism. Two articles in

Feminist Studies (by Ann Rosalind Jones and Carolyn Burke) focused on Cixous, Kristeva, and Irigaray. Here one reads, for example, in Jones: "French feminists in general believe that Western thought has been based on a systematic repression of women's experience. Thus their assertion of a bedrock female nature . . . a point from which to deconstruct language, philosophy, psychoanalysis, the social practices, and direction of patriarchal culture as we live in and resist it."[35]

The *Feminist Studies* special issue did also include an article by Hélène Vivienne Wenzel that noted that Monique Wittig did not share in the "assertion of a bedrock female nature," but even in this article about Wittig, Cixous is privileged—indeed, given equal space—as the theorist whose work confers meaning on the work of Wittig.[36] The *Signs* special section on "French Feminist Theory" presented the same "French feminism," with translations of Kristeva's "Women's Time"; Cixous's "Castration or Decapitation?" and Irigaray's "And the One Doesn't Stir without the Other."[37] One of the *Signs* articles, by Lillian Robinson, attempted to alert American readers to the criticism of this "French feminism" on French soil but, in a fashion similar to the Wenzel article in *Feminist Studies*, the piece by Christine Fauré that Robinson translated still focuses, although critically, on Irigaray![38] And finally, Toril Moi's *Textual/Sexual Politics* constructs in its two parts an "Anglo-American Feminist Criticism" in opposition to a "French Feminist Theory." Simply naming the chapter titles for the "French" half underscores my point: "Hélène Cixous," "Luce Irigaray," "Julia Kristeva." In Moi's own words, "I have chosen to focus on the figures of Hélène Cixous, Luce Irigaray and Julia Kristeva . . . because their work is the most representative of the main trends in French feminist theory."[39]

FRENCH FEMINISM AND THE PROBLEM
OF NATIONAL AND DISCIPLINARY INTERESTS

What conclusions may one draw from this dissonance between two "French feminisms"? Does it matter that French feminists understand their own movement very differently from the way in which American academics define it? First, let us acknowledge that the "French feminism" known in the U.S. academy has been made in America. I would argue that this construction tells us more about ourselves than about the French. Feminists in France have tried to make this heard; most recently, Christine Delphy, in a strongly worded article in *Yale French Studies*, complained: "'French Feminism' is not feminism in France. . . . Most feminists from France find it extraordinary to be presented, when abroad, with a version of their feminism and their country of which they had previously no idea."[40] Judith Ezekiel has also addressed an American audience: "[W]hat is called 'French Feminism' in the U.S. bears little resemblance to the multifaceted social movement in which I've been active."[41] Not even Simone de Beauvoir, in writing the chapter on France for Robin Morgan's widely read *Sisterhood Is Global: The International Women's Movement Anthology*, seems to have been heard, although she makes her point perfectly clear:

> The French women's movement . . . is in constant danger, because of the existence of such groups as Psych. et Po. which pass themselves off as the women's movement . . . [and] their ideology—a convenient neo-femininity developed by such women writers as Hélène Cixous, Annie Leclerc, and Luce Irigaray, most of whom are not feminists,

and some of whom are blatantly anti-feminist. Unfortunately this is also the aspect of the French women's movement best known in the United States. Such books as Elaine Marks's New French Feminism give a totally distorted image of French feminism by presenting it, on the one hand, as if it existed only in theory and not in action and, on the other, as if the sum of that theory emanated from the school of neo-femininity.[42]

As Eleni Varikas has complained:

> To reduce "French" feminism to a few particular theoretical positions is not only to obscure the fact that the majority of feminist struggles were fought without knowledge of and sometimes against these positions; is not only to obscure the most influential theoretical positions of feminist thought in France; it is also to prevent us from reflecting on the conditions in which these multiple positions emerged [and] on their relationship with a political practice.

From this point of view, it is astonishing how little commentary there has been in the American discussion of "French Feminism" on the transformation of the Mouvement de Libération des Femmes into a trademark of one group.[43] Nor am I the first "Anglo-American" to call attention to the mismatch between "our" French feminism and "their" movement when described by French participants. Jane Gallop, a Lacanian specialist who played an important role in constructing the U.S. version of "French feminism," has written, in her recent book, Around 1981: Academic Feminist Literary Theory: "French feminism is a body of thought and writing by some women in France which is named and thus constituted as a movement here in the American academy."[44] And Nancy Fraser, in her introduction to the anthology Revaluing French Feminism: Critical Essays on Difference, Agency, and Culture, makes a similar point: "For many English-speaking readers today 'French feminism' simply is Irigaray, Kristeva, and Cixous." But then, in the endnote, she appends: "We could doubtless learn much about the working of our culture and its institutions if we could reconstruct the precise process of this synedochic reduction. It is all the more striking in that it occurred despite the strenuous protests of Monique Wittig, Simone de Beauvoir, and the editors of the journal Feminist Questions."[45] Moreover, books have been published in English that describe a broader French movement and that ought to have jarred us into questioning the "French feminism" we think we know. Claire Duchen's Feminism in France: From May '68 to Mitterrand, published in Britain in 1986, focused on the MLF as a multifaceted movement.[46] Dorothy McBride Stetson's Women's Rights in France, published in the United States in 1987, describes the sort of activism we in the United States would term "liberal" and traces the campaigns that resulted in significant new legislation in the 1970s and early 1980s.[47] Canadian Jane Jenson, writing in the New Left Review in 1990, captured the breadth of French feminism—including feminist activism in French labor unions that is ignored in the French histories discussed above.[48] Most recently, Australian Bronwyn Winter, in a 1997 Women's Studies International Forum article, decried the "(Mis)Representations" of French feminism.[49]

Translations of self-defined French feminists also exist in English. Books by Christine Delphy, Colette Guillaumin, and Michèle Le Doeuff have been published in translation;[50] and translations of Monique Wittig, Colette Guillaumin, and Nicole-Claude Mathieu have appeared in Feminist Issues. And although not well known in this country (my point exactly!), Claire Duchen's French Connections: Voices from the Women's Movement in France[51] makes available a more representative selection of

French feminists than the earlier *New French Feminisms.* Most recently, Diana Leonard and Lisa Adkins, in *Sex in Question: French Materialist Feminism,* have published translations of some of the "classic" articles originally appearing in *Questions féministes.*[52]

Why, with all this information to the contrary, do Americans insist that "'French feminism' simply is Irigaray, Kristeva, and Cixous" (to quote Fraser again)? Some of the French who have commented on the significance of what I have called a "made-in-America" version have suggested that those U.S. feminists who popularized Psych et po's ideas were themselves essentialists and/or theorists grounded in psychoanalysis who used French ideas to legitimate their own domestic agendas. Christine Delphy's recent Yale French Studies article, for example, vehemently opposes her materialist views to those of the "made-in-America French feminists":

> Only the hypothesis that these protagonists [U.S. feminists who write about "French feminism"] had an ideological and political agenda can explain the discrepancies between "French feminism" and feminism in France, the fact that these discrepancies persisted over a period of years, and, finally, that these discrepancies are not random. . . . The main reason that its inventors invented their brand of feminism as "French" was that they did not want to take responsibility for what they were saying and, in particular, for their attempt to rescue psychoanalysis from the discredit it had incurred both in feminism and through the social sciences.[53]

Gail Pheterson has also noted the compatibility between American and French essentialist views but, at the same time, the incompatibility of U.S. social constructionist and French materialist views, which she believes explains why French essentialism has been "so abundantly" imported "while its materialist critique stays home or—when in North America—in Quebec."[54]

These French "materialists" have a point: those who celebrated the three French theorists made known in the United States in the late 1970s and 1980s did focus on their essentialist aspects and their psychoanalytic approaches. But recently I have found myself looking beyond the "difference" debates to other explanations of our "made-in-America" French feminism. In locating the genesis of the U.S. version, I was struck by the key role of French literature specialists and was determined to examine not just intrafeminist politics but academic politics as well. In so doing, I was responding to reactions from the audiences, predominantly of historians, to whom I presented earlier versions of this article. The paper was well received, which was gratifying, of course; but I detected in the comments something that went deeper than respect for my scholarship—something suggesting that these audiences were hearing my paper as a defense of their interests. I recognized then that there might be something useful in exploring the disciplinary roots of "our" French feminism. Did the historians in my audiences dislike made-in-America French feminism simply because it is anti- or, at least, ahistorical? Did my audiences feel that French theory in its U.S. configuration denigrates their intellectual work?

Although feminist scholars usually pay careful attention to the implications of our intellectual work for its politics of gender, race, or class hierarchies, what about the politics of our disciplines? We rarely acknowledge the disciplinary origin of this made-in-America French feminism; indeed, in women's studies we rarely acknowledge the disciplinarity of any of our work. We claim "interdisciplinarity," but it is often the case that interdisciplinarity in women's studies is rather like the "universal" of Enlightenment discourse: seeming to be all-inclusive, our interdisciplinarity too often masks the predominance of one discipline over others. Today, the predominant discipline in women's studies is literature,[55] and especially that kind of literary studies that has been influenced by the discourses and concerns of philosophy.[56] (This is, of course, the kind of academic literary studies that does in fact come from France, where university students in literature complete a philosophy track as well.) Twenty to twenty-five years ago, women's studies programs that just as likely originated in departments of sociology or history as literature are now most heavily influenced by literature specialists. Although we know that feminist instruction can occur in a variety of settings, when we speak about "feminist pedagogy" we normally mean a format that is common even in nonfeminist literature classrooms.

A similar disciplinary specificity has affected the construction of U.S. feminist theory. On some level, we know that feminist theories are the varieties of thinking that aspire to explain women's condition and that we write and read these theories in search of the presumptions and assumptions that not only underlie masculinism but also guide feminists in developing goals and strategies. But more and more we use—or we hear others use—"theory" as a synonym for a certain kind of academic, philosophical discourse steeped in the language of current literary criticism.[57] In fact, "theory" is often used as an antonym to "history," as if historians merely list their archival findings without pondering their meanings or their contribution to understanding the human condition. Historians and social scientists are uncomfortable with and defensive about a lot of interdisciplinary women's studies scholarship, oftentimes without understanding why. I suggest that this is because there is inadequate acknowledgment that our so-called interdisciplinary field is not so very interdisciplinary after all. Those who feel excluded from that which is supposedly interdisciplinary worry that their particular contribution to the larger feminist intellectual project is diminishing.

We have set ourselves a worthy goal in aspiring to interdisciplinarity in feminist scholarship: anything less narrows and limits our understanding of women's situation in all its aspects and focuses us instead on academic agendas not shaped with women's interests in mind. Nonetheless, if we are to manage interdisciplinarity, I suggest we must begin by being more, not less, explicit in presenting our disciplinary origins, speaking carefully across our scholarly differences with care that others understand the value of our work and that we understand the value of others' work to a common project.

It was in looking at the disciplinary origins of made-in-America French feminism that I came to examine debates not only within interdisciplinary women's studies but also within the field of literature itself. Here one discovers a "French theory" that pre-existed "French feminism" in the U.S. academy, and one comes to recognize that for many American feminists in literature studies, "French feminism" was a feminist political practice, a strategy for placing both women theorists and the topic of gender centrally into their field of scholarship alongside a group of French male theorists who had already captured their colleagues' attention.[58]

Sociologist of knowledge Michèle Lamont has written about "the diffusion of French theory" in the United States, linking its increased popularity to the vacuum left in literature studies following successful critiques of New Criticism.[59] She credits a key conference, held at Johns Hopkins University in 1966, for introducing structuralist and poststructuralist theories to American scholars and also mentions a special issue of *Yale French Studies* published that same year. She explains that French theorists, many of whom made the trip to Hopkins, were introduced to American academics as a group, although were one to examine their work carefully one would quickly discover more differences among them than similarities. Even their fields differed: Louis Althusser was a philosopher, Roland Barthes a literary critic, Michel Foucault a historian of ideas, Jacques Lacan a psychoanalyst, and Jacques Derrida a philosopher whose work in France was published more often in literature journals than in philosophy journals. They became a "group," however, because in France, where they published more often in intellectual, albeit nonacademic, journals than in specifically disciplinary scholarly journals, they wrote in conversation and debate with each other. Moreover, the style of these intellectual publications encouraged a certain kind of debate that crossed disciplines easily by foregrounding theory and generalization over empirical research. The proponents of "French theory," in other words, became known to Americans as a group, were highly abstract, and presented in their writing little of the research data of interest only to specialists in their disciplines. These characteristics appear crucial to their diffusion through American academe at a moment when interdisciplinary studies were growing here. Lamont believes that the expansion of comparative literature departments in the 1970s was especially significant: "French specialists have long enjoyed a high status in comparative literature," she writes.[60] And, of course, for comparative literature departments the attraction of theory—with its foregrounding of generalizations and downplaying of specialized research-served some of the same purposes that theory serves in women's studies interdisciplinary work, because crossing the boundaries of languages and literatures presented some of the same problems as crossing disciplinary boundaries.

The diffusion of "French theory" was facilitated by—and in turn facilitated—the development of interdisciplinary studies. Outside of French literature departments, "French theory" was introduced through a number of new scholarly journals. In a later article, Lamont, writing here with Marsha Witten, identifies the following journals, all founded in the 1970s and 1980s, as collectively constituting a new interdisciplinary "subfield": *American Journal of Semiotics* (1982), *Boundary 2* (1972), *Communications* (1977), *Critical Inquiry* (1974), *Critical Text* (1983), *Cultural Anthropology* (1986), *Cultural Critique* (1985), *Diacritiques* (1971), *Feminist Studies* (1972), *Glyph* (1977), *October* (1976), *Raritan* (1981), *Representations* (1983), *Semiotext(e)* (1974), *Social Text* (1979), *Substance* (1971), and *Theory and Society* (1974).[61] It is in these journals, indeed, that the articles by Cixous and Kristeva published in *Signs* in 1975 and 1976 and, a few years later, in *New French Feminisms* were first published.

Of course, the particular theorists identified with "French theory" no more constitute the whole of French philosophy and criticism than the American-selected "French feminists" constitute the French feminist movement. But in both cases, the special interest of academic literary critics in the 1970s is obvious: the engagement with discourses, the disinterest in events. In the case of "made-in-America French feminism," what we have is "theory" without "history"—a disconnection of feminist theory from its political and social context. When U.S. scholars and students throughout the United States routinely cite Kristeva, Irigaray, and Cixous, there is little discussion of what has been happening to French women or even to French feminists.

Think of the power relationships involved here: as Jane Jenson has pointed out, there are some American scholars who have referred recently to a French "colonization" of the U.S. mind.[62] The metaphor places France in the position of power and conveys some discontent on the part of "colonized" Americans. But I'm suggesting that the reverse is at play: that it is U.S. feminists who are in the dominant position and who have expropriated one aspect of French culture for purposes here, with little regard for the French or the French context. References to the discourse of postcolonialism should lead us to this kind of understanding: as feminists, multiculturalists, or leftists, we have become aware that we abuse our power over peoples when we exoticize them, expropriate an aspect of their culture by decontextualizing it and using it for our purposes, with little interest in the people themselves. The relationship between feminists in the United States and in France is similar: the aspect that has interested U.S. feminists is the least characteristic of French feminism and the most different from ours; the more characteristic aspects of their feminism bore us. We have exoticized and even eroticized French feminism, then used it decontextualized, with little interest in French feminist activists and their concrete political struggles on behalf of very real French women. In so doing, we have abused our power, involving ourselves unwittingly in a power struggle among French women and conferring a prestige and status on one group—Psych et po—that proved injurious to the interests of those whom, I contend, we ought to have supported.

Of course, not all U.S. academic feminists celebrated "French feminism" or found it useful for their work; others reacted with vehement distaste. This may be partly because in the United States, both within and outside the academy, "French" is so often either a term of adulation or a term of derision, a site of aspiration or an anathema. The French have long been a "sign" in U.S. culture, although the meanings we have attributed to this sign have differed in different settings and different times. Most recently, the sign has been used negatively by populists as an armament in the antielitist battle. There is a kind of "nativism" at work here; the French (and sometimes more generally "Europeans") are blamed for negative aspects of ourselves (elitism, racism, classism). They (or more broadly, "Europeans") are tainted; we are pure.[63] However, that the French theorists who were popularized in the United States focused on the essential specificity of woman and "the feminine" does not explain racism or class prejudice where this surfaces in U.S. feminism. That these French theorists use an esoteric discourse does not excuse those U.S. feminists who took refuge in the academy during the 1980s and distanced themselves from the struggles of women outside.

By the same token, it seems that in France the United States is a "sign" which poorly represents our reality as well. Psych et po, for example, demonized a U.S. feminism supposedly in cahoots with the patriarchal, racist, and classist state; by playing into French resentments of U.S. cultural hegemony, they sought to secure their position as the only "true" revolutionaries. A more recent example, according to Judith Ezekiel, is the French appropriation of our "political correctness" debate. "Feminism and an alleged 'dictatorship of minorities'" are central to "the reaction against a decade of pro-American mass culture . . . the rise of antifeminism . . . and the realization that all of French immigration may not be melting down." In France, those calling themselves "anti-PC" have played on the "PC" (Parti Communiste) resonance, for example, by suggesting that supporters of Anita Hill were the "new Stalinists." And now they have targeted deconstructionist feminism for being an agent in the PC invasion of France! Ezekiel concludes: "So, French feminism colonizes America and rebounds to France under the cover of American PC, threatening French universalism and its conception of republican citizenship!"[64]

But there are also conclusions to be drawn about the French version of its own feminist history. Certainly, the recent histories describe a movement that is broader than that which we in the United States call "French feminism." Although Cixous, through her association with Psych et po, figures in that history, Irigaray does less so and Kristeva not at all. Antoinette Fouque and the group Psych et po are present but not dominant. Still, I wonder if these French histories, too, are unnecessarily narrow. To date, their accounts have focused exclusively on the 1970s' women's liberation movement. Some of the histories include the names of more reformist-oriented feminists like government ministers Simone Veil, Françoise Giroud, and Yvette Roudy or the lawyer Gisèle Halimi, who led the abortion rights struggle, or Anne Zelensky, founder of the League of the Rights of Women, or alternative socialist party leader Huguette Bouchardeau; but none describe the activities of feminists within the Left parties and unions or the influence of feminists in schools, the media, and cultural institutions. Moreover, by writing only about the 1970s, French historians have not yet provided a record of the interesting work, undertaken in the 1980s and continuing today, that focuses on antiracism, anti-Semitism, antiageism, and the many activities of solidarity with immigrant women and with the burgeoning gay liberation movement.[65]

In writing their own history so narrowly, these French feminists have diminished the impact of their struggles. At the time of their writing, they were discouraged and their movement appeared to be moribund. But their successes and failures are not unlike our own. Political representation of women in national politics is low in both countries (10.9 percent women in the French National Assembly; 11.7 percent women in the U.S. Congress), especially when compared with European Union countries like the Netherlands or the Scandinavian countries where women hold about one-third of legislative seats.[66] But in France, family law has been equalized, while our Equal Rights Amendment, covering similar aspects of the law, failed; reproductive rights are not only guaranteed but also covered by national health insurance; and feminists sustained a more radical and successful attack on marriage than occurred in the United States, perhaps because the then much more highly developed social welfare system made women's independence and single motherhood less difficult.[67] Efforts to alter work laws have seen some successes (guaranteed and paid maternity leave; equal pay for equal work) and some failures (the recent expansion of jobs for women has primarily been in temporary or part-time work, undermining the effect of equal pay laws). And although sexual violence is a controlling factor in French women's lives, as in the United States, women are generally safer in the streets of France than here. Compared with the United States, however, French feminists have been less successful in challenging the representation of women in media and cultural institutions—billboards are particularly shocking to American feminists visiting France; and feminist scholarship and women's studies in the university system is notably weak. In sum, feminism has achieved a mixed scoreboard in both our countries, and our histories are not so disconnected as they are usually described.

Finally, in both countries feminists came face to face with a significant backlash in the 1980s. Although both movements have looked for explanations in national politics, the similarities of the French and the U.S. reaction—in spite of the quite dissimilar politics of the governments in power—suggest that the cause is more likely in global cultural and economic transformations than in local power shifts. But if international factors are important, as I strongly suspect, let us respond by building an international movement to challenge the backlash. To do so, we must understand each other better—across boundaries of nation as of discipline—than we have to date.

NOTES

Versions of this paper have been presented at "Transformations: Women, Gender, Power," the Ninth Berkshire Conference on the History of Women, Vassar College, June 1993; in Lyons, France (1994); and in Adelaide, Australia (1996). I'd like to thank the many people in these audiences who offered wonderful and useful comments, many of which I've incorporated into this version. I'd also like to thank Lillane Kandel, Françoise Picq, Françoise Basch, Christine Delphy, Lisa Greenwald, Arlene McLaren, Elaine Marks, Debra Bergoffen, Paola Bacchetta, Lisa Moses, Martha Vicinus, Evelyn Beck, Debby Rosenfelt, Gay Gullickson, Sara Evans, Sharon Groves, and the editors of Feminist Studies who read earlier versions and offered me suggestions for revision. A special thanks is due to Judith Ezekiel, who not only commented on this version but also shared out-of-print books and articles generally unavailable in the United States. All translations from French sources are mine.

1. Anne Tristan and Annie de Pisan, Histoires du M.L.F. (Paris: Calmann-Levy, 1977). The authors are Anne Zelensky and Annie Sugier; the pseudonyms honor the nineteenth-century feminist and socialist Flora Tristan and the fifteenth-century writer Christine de Pisan. Pseudonyms and other forms of anonymity were typical of movement participants in the early 1970s.

2. Françoise Picq, Libération des femmes: Les Années-mouvement (Paris: Editions du Seuil, 1993); Monique Rémy, De L'Utopie à l'intégration: Histoire des mouvements de femmes (Paris: Editions L'Harmattan, 1990); Chroniques d'une imposture: Du Mouvement de libération des femmes à une marque commerciale (Paris: Association du Mouvement pour les luttes féministes, 1981); Centre Lyonnais d'Etudes Féministes, Chronique d'une passion: Le Mouvement de libération des femmes à Lyon (Paris: Editions L'Harmattan, 1989); Groupe d'Etudes Féministes de l'Université Paris VII, Crises de la société: Féminisme et changement (Paris: Editions Tierce, 1991).

3. The term "women's liberation movement" is a very historically specific word as used here and should not be read synonymously with the "women's movement." Here I'm referring to a movement that at a certain moment in the late 1960s took this term for itself in order to connect itself to the revolutionary stance of anti-imperialist "liberation" movements and at the same time distinguish itself from more "reformist" feminists associated with structured organizations like the National Organization for Women or the Women's Equity Action League. See Jo Freeman, The Politics of Women's Liberation: A Case Study of an Emerging Social Movement and Its Relation to the Policy Process (New York: David McKay, 1975), for a useful description of women's liberation at the moment when the name was used. Later, in the mid-1970s, "women's liberation movement" began to be used less as these same feminists came to identify themselves more typically as either radical feminists or socialist feminists (and identified the "reformers" as liberal feminists).

4. Nadja Ringart, "Naissance d'une secte," originally published in Libération, June 1, 1977, reprinted in Chroniques d'une imposture.

5. Françoise Picq is interesting here in viewing the insistence that feminism was wholly innovative as a stance; the pioneers of the MLF, she states, were certainly familiar with the work of writers—sometimes their professors—who in the 1960s were already researching "woman's condition." She names Marie-José Chombart de Lauwe, Anne-Marie Rocheblave-Spenle, Françoise Guelaud-Léridon, Evelyne Sullerot,

Geneviève Texier, Andrée Michel, and Madeleine Guilbert, all of whom had written important books on women in the 1960s (Picq, *Libération des femmes,* 26–27). See also Marie-Jo Dhavernas who, in her contribution to *Chroniques d'une imposture* ("Des Divans profonds comme des Tombeaux"), noted with irony that Psych et po—a group that grounded its theory in psychoanalysis—nonetheless "believes in the spontaneous generation of discourse."

6. In 1970 and 1971, before feminists had begun researching the rich, and complicated, history of earlier feminisms, Beauvoir alone seems to have stood for historical feminism. U.S. feminists who were present at a 1979 conference in New York on the occasion of the thirtieth anniversary of the publication of *The Second Sex* may remember the attack launched on Beauvoir (and on "feminism") by some French women in the audience (Hélène Cixous most notably) and the defense by others (especially Monique Wittig and Christine Delphy). What we were witnessing, without comprehending, was the split (discussed below) between Psych et po and the other groupings of the MLF. (See also Dhavernas in *Chroniques d'une imposture.*)

7. Anne [Zelensky] describes seeking out Andrée Michel after having read her *La Condition de la Française d'aujourd'hui* (1964, co-authored with Geneviève Texier). She then participated in a seminar directed by Michel; it was here that she met Jacqueline Feldman with whom she founded one of the earliest of the MLF groups. (See *Histoires de M.L.F.,* 33). A few years later, in 1972, Michelle Perrot offered the first women's history seminar in a French university, at the urging of some of her students. Françoise Basch also played a significant role in bringing together feminist activists who were then graduate students with established academics. (See Picq, *Libération des femmes,* 219–20.)

8. In her comments for a panel, "Traveling through European Feminism: Cultural and Political Practices," at the Women's International Studies Europe Conference (October 8, 1993), Judith Ezekiel states that the receptivity to U.S. and British ideas had disappeared by 1975 when she arrived in France. She traces this to the "demonization" of American feminism by Psych et po "as a component in the forging of its identity" and notes that the "cheap shots were at liberal feminism." "Psych et po even dub[bed] Rosalyn Carter a feminist in order to better criticize the capitalist nature of all U.S. feminism" (unpublished paper in my possession). Radical feminists were also criticized, according to Nadja Ringart: "Antoinette Fouque explained to [her] how she was 'wrong to believe in sisterhood . . . an illusion imported from America' and one that prevented the 'dynamic of contradictions.'" (See "Naissance d'une secte," in *Chroniques d'une imposture.*) See also Judith Ezekiel, "Antifeminisme et antiaméricanisme: Un Mariage politiquement réussi," *Nouvelles questions féministes* 17 (February 1996): 59–76.

9. "Quotidien des femmes" translates as "Women's Daily," but it was never a daily; it published irregularly between November 1974 and June 1976. *Des femmes en mouvement* appeared monthly in 1978, and then weekly from 1979 to 1982. (Thanks to Liliane Kandel [private communication] for this information, and for her comment that "quotidien/daily" in this context may have been intended to resonate with "ordinary" as in "ordinary oppression.")

10. Liliane Kandel, "La Presse féministe d'aujourd'hui," *Pénélope* 1 (June 1979): 44–71 (see esp. her listing of periodicals, 66–71).

11. Picq, *Libération des femmes,* 210–15.

12. For example, it is not always clear, from these histories, whether the amorphous MLF was the inspiration or supportive follower or critic of the strategies orchestrated by the lawyer Gisèle Halimi and Choisir, the group she organized, or the mixed-sex Movement for Abortion Liberty (MLA; later MLAC/Mouvement pour la liberté de l'avortement et contraception). The dividing points—again, in these histories—seem to be around the questions of organizing and the relationship of feminism to the liberal state: it was the MLF "groupe avortement" that gathered the signatures of 343

prominent women who affirmed, in a newspaper advertisement, that they had had abortions and should therefore be indicted under the then current laws of France. Choisir, which organized after this manifestation to defend the 343 in court (albeit never called upon to do so; but there were other celebrated court cases that Choisir did champion), and the MLA (later MLAC), which pressured the government for a new law, are not viewed as "movement" groups, even though there is clear overlap in their "membership" (recognizing, of course, that the word "membership" is inappropriate for the MLF).

13. Picq, *Libération des femmes,* 190.

14. Ibid., 275.

15. See, for example, Picq, *Libération des femmes* (183): "Women's Lib, Dolle Mina, Redstockings, Mouvement de liberation des femmes, Frauenbewegung, Movimento de liberazione della donna . . . the majority of Western countries experienced more or less the same phenomenon in the 1960s and 1970s"; or, in comparing Christine Delphy's "L'Ennemi principal" with Margaret Bentsen's "The Political Economy of Women's Liberation," where, Picq concludes, "the analysis is the same" (32).

16. In reading the feminist periodicals, one is struck by the frequency with which French feminists hurled the epithet "Stalinist" at their opponents in the movement. Clearly the existence in France of the most Stalinist of communist parties in all of Western Europe (some would say all of Europe), the Parti communiste français, handed French feminists an epithet that all would understand.

17. Judith Ezekiel, in her comments on this paper when it was originally presented at "Transformations: Women, Gender, Power," the Ninth Berkshire Conference on the History of Women, held at Vassar College in June 1993, insisted that "the social movement . . . is peopled by intellectuals, disproportionately educated, and involved in research and teaching. Let there be no doubt—we do not have an activist, nonintellectual movement on the one hand and theoreticians (the infamous French feminists) on the other." However, Paola Bacchetta, who had been intensively involved with feminism during her many years of residency in Paris and who was in the audience at that session, talked about many feminist activities and groups for and by women of color and immigrant women, arguing that it is not so much "French feminism" that is narrow in its race and class focus but rather the accounts we have of the movement, even the French accounts. Bacchetta was a founder of the ten-year-old Collectif Feministe contre le Racisme et l'Antisémitisme.

18. Christine Delphy, "Les Origines du Mouvement de libération des femmes en France," *Nouvelles questions féministes* 16–18 (1991): 146. U.S. feminists might question Delphy's statement that our movement has been free of this kind of infighting, by noting the fierce attacks posed by those such as Christina Hoff Sommers, who nonetheless call themselves feminists.

19. Compare Picq, *Liberation des femmes* (39) on the Paris scene: "Some would not return. The noisy, violent atmosphere did not suit them." In Lyons, too, at the Women's Center, dissension caused problems ("It was very conflictual"). See *Chronique d'une passion,* 104.

20. Dhavernas, *Chroniques d'une imposture.* See also Nadja Ringart's description in the same volume ("Naissance d'une secte") of Psych et po gatherings. Ringart, who was a onetime Psych et po participant and is widely quoted in others' accounts of the group, writes in the language of a deprogrammed ex-cultist. (When the publisher sent me press proofs for review of Claire Duchen's collection of French feminist documents, *French Connections,* Ringart's article was included, but by the time the book actually appeared, it had been dropped. In commenting on my presentation of a version of this article at the Berkshire conference in 1993, Judith Ezekiel stated that the publisher of Ringart's article had been threatened with a legal suit by Psych et po.)

21. According to Ringart: "Having become psychoanalyst of most of the group herself, she [Fouque] carried out her 'work' with passion and devotion. Apart from the immediate power that this position gave her, it also meant that she had an inexhaustible supply of information at her disposal" ("Naissance d'une secte," *Chroniques d'une imposture*).

22. The declared print run was 60,000 for the *Quotidien des femmes*, and 70,000 for both the monthly and weekly editions of *Des femmes en mouvement*, according to a chart published by Groupe "Notre Mouvement Nous Apartient" in *Chroniques d'une imposture*.

23. Ringart continues: "I later understood just what a fool this fight against feminism made of me: at the time, I just didn't try to get to know women who insisted on calling themselves feminists. I needed still more time before I knew that there was in this a historical fabrication about feminism, which was aided by our crass ignorance. In her hurry to point out the enemy, Antoinette had presented us with a superficial and caricatural image—a male-imposed image—of feminists" ("Naissance d'une secte," *Chroniques d'une imposture*).

24. English-language readers can get the flavor of Fouque's antifeminism from this other passage translated in Elaine Marks and Isabelle de Courtivron's *New French Feminisms: An Anthology* (Amherst: University of Massachusetts Press, 1980), 117–18: "Feminists are a bourgeois avant-garde that maintains, in an inverted form, dominant values. . . . An example: The Last Tango in Paris. A liberated young woman kills a man in order to escape from being raped. She kills a poor psychotic with her father's revolver. That's the typical feminist!"

25. Picq, *Libération des femmes*, 261.

26. Ezekiel's Berkshire conference comments. See also *Chroniques d'une imposture* for a petition signed by over sixty groups. There have been other suits, like these, usually just for writing, or signing placards or petitions, against Psych et po.

27. In "Debating the Present/Writing the Past: 'Feminism' in French History and Historiography," *Radical History Review*, 52 (winter 1992): 86, I have written that Beauvoir dissociated herself from feminism, because, in the late 1940s, she associated herself with a view of feminism's history that had been constructed prior to the First World War by socialist women. In 1907, in Stuttgart, the first international conference of socialist women had passed a resolution that "socialist women must not ally themselves with the feminists of the bourgeoisie, but lead the battle side by side with the socialist parties." From that time, socialist women began to refer to the "bourgeois feminist" movement, and they always did so disparagingly.

28. Hester Eisenstein and Alice Jardine, eds., *The Future of Difference* (Boston: G. K. Hall, 1980); and *New French Feminisms*.

29. Marks and Courtivron, *New French Feminisms*, xi.

30. Indeed, the predominance of social science research in French feminist publications has especially caught my attention, in part because this contradicts Marks and Courtivron and the U.S. image of "French feminism," but also because it is so different from the predominance of feminist literary studies in U.S. feminist publishing, which I discuss below. Government funding of feminist social science research through the Centre National des Recherches Scientifiques, and the general underfunding of the humanities in French universities may explain this difference.

31. Marks and Courtivron, *New French Feminisms*, 31, 33, x, 36.

32. Moses, "Debating the Present," 86–87. Note that 1980 was also the year of *Feminist Studies'* publication of a symposium on women's culture, with articles by Ellen DuBois, Carroll Smith-Rosenberg, Gerda Lerner, Mari-Jo Buhle, and Temma Kaplan; the essentialist debate was embedded into the sometimes acrimonious debate around a "woman's culture in women's history," too.

33. Marks and Courtivron, *New French Feminisms*, 30.

34. Picq, *Libération des femmes*, 217–19.

35. Ann Rosalind Jones, "Writing the Body: Toward an Understanding of *L'Ecriture Féminine,*" *Feminist Studies* 7 (summer 1981): 247.

36. See Hélène Vivienne Wenzel, "The Text as Body/Politics: An Appreciation of Monique Wittig's Writings in Context," *Feminist Studies* 7 (summer 1981): 264–87.

37. *Signs* also had published Irigaray's "When Our Lips Speak Together," translated by Carolyn Burke, the year prior (autumn 1980).

38. Lillian Robinson, trans. and introduction, " 'Absent from History' and the Twilight of the Goddesses: The Intellectual Crisis of French Feminism," by Christine Faure, *Signs* 7 (autumn 1981): 68–86.

39. Toril Moi, *Sexual/Textual Politics: Feminist Literary Theory* (London: Routledge, 1985), 97.

40. Christine Delphy, "The Invention of French Feminism: An Essential Move," *Another Look, Another Woman: Retranslations of French Feminism: Yale French Studies,* 87 (1995): 190.

41. Ezekiel, Berkshire conference comments.

42. Simone de Beauvoir, "France: Feminism—Alive, Well, and in Constant Danger," trans. Magda Bogin and Robin Morgan, in *Sisterhood Is Global: The International Women's Movement Anthology,* ed. Robin Morgan (Garden City, N.Y.: Anchor Press/Doubleday, 1984), 234–35. I view Beauvoir's criticisms of *New French Feminisms* as instructive, although far too sweeping: Marks and Courtivron include activist materials and writings from feminists, including Beauvoir, who did not espouse a neofemininity. But the construction of the book did lend itself to Beauvoir's reading, as I have tried to show.

43. Eleni Varikas, "Féminisme, modernité, postmodernisme: Pour un dialogue des deux côtés de l'océan," in *Féminismes au présent,* a Supplement to *Futur Antérieur* (Paris: Editions L'Harmattan, 1995), 63–64.

44. Jane Gallop, *Around 1981: Academic Feminist Literary Theory* (New York: Routledge, 1992), 41.

45. Nancy Fraser, introduction, in *Revaluing French Feminism: Critical Essays on Difference, Agency, and Culture,* ed. Nancy Fraser and Sandra Lee Bartky (Bloomington: Indiana University Press, 1992), 1, 19 n.3.

46. Claire Duchen, *Feminism in France: From May '68 to Mitterrand* (London: Routledge & Kegan Paul, 1986).

47. Dorothy McBride Stetson, *Women's Rights in France* (New York: Greenwood Press, 1987).

48. Jane Jenson, "Representation of Difference: The Varieties of French Feminism," *New Left Review* 180 (1990): 127–60.

49. Bronwyn Winter, "(Mis)Representations: What French Feminism Isn't," *Women's Studies International Forum* 20.2 (1997): 211–24.

50. See Christine Delphy, *The Main Enemy* (London: Women's Research and Resources Centre, 1977), *Close to Home: A Materialist Analysis of Women's Oppression* (London: Hutchison, 1984), and, with Diana Leonard, *Familiar Exploitation: A New Analysis in Contemporary Western Societies* (Oxford: Polity, 1992); Colette Guillaumin, *Racism, Sexism, Power, and Ideology* (London: Routledge, 1987); and Michèle Le Doeuff, *Hipparchia's Choice: An Essay Concerning Women, Philosophy, etc.,* trans. Trista Selous (Oxford: Blackwell, 1991).

51. Claire Duchen, ed., *French Connections: Voices from the Women's Movement in France* (Amherst: University of Massachusetts Press, 1987).

52. Diana Leonard and Lisa Adkins, eds. and trans., *Sex in Question: French Materialist Feminism* (London: Taylor & Francis, 1996).

53. Delphy, "The Invention of French Feminism," 196.

54. Gail Pheterson, "Group Identity and Social Relations: Divergent Theoretical Conceptions in the United States, the Netherlands, and France," *European Journal of Women's Studies* 1 (1994): 262–63. That French materialist feminism is so fiercely antibiologistic may relate to its struggles with Psych et po. For example, *Nouvelles questions féministes* has been wary of, although not completely hostile to, the recent movement for "parity" of gender representation to the French legislature. Surely there are many good

reasons for feminists to be cautious in adopting a strategy that might result only in the election of many Margaret Thatchers, but that Antoinette Fouque was an early proponent of parity must have heightened concern. See *Nouvelles questions féministes* special issues on "Parité-Pour," 15.4 (November 1994) and "Parité-Contre," 16.2 (May 1995), and Danielle Haase-Dubosc, "Liberté, Egalité, Parité," forthcoming in *Feminist Studies.*

55. Some would go so far as to claim that literature dominates the academy, or at least the human sciences. See, for example, David Simpson, *The Academic Postmodern and the Rule of Literature: A Report on Half-Knowledge* (Chicago: University of Chicago Press, 1995); and Harvey J. Kaye, *Powers of the Past: Reflections on the Crisis and the Promise of History* (Minneapolis: University of Minnesota Press, 1991). In earlier versions of this article, I have referred to "the hegemony of literature" and have therefore been interested to see terms not unlike this appear in these surveys of intellectual trends beyond women's studies.

56. It is within the discipline of philosophy that a split between "Anglo-American" and "continental" (e.g., "French") is most commonly perceived. In referring to feminism, however, the characterization of an "Anglo-American" versus "French" dichotomy makes no sense whatsoever. There are similarities and differences among all three national movements but certainly no dichotomy that links the United States more to the British experience and divides us more from the French.

57. Note in Nancy Fraser's introduction to *Revaluing French Feminism* (5): "This volume . . . concentrates on theoretical arguments—reflecting the disciplinary training in philosophy of most of the contributors." Thus, theory here equals philosophy.

58. This was certainly the case with Sue Peabody, in 1993, a recent Ph.D. recipient in history (University of Iowa), who commented at the Berkshire conference session that it was when the poststructuralists like Foucault and Derrida were introduced into her graduate courses that she turned, as a feminist, to Kristeva, Cixous, and Irigaray—searching for a way to combine the new intellectual work with a focus on gender.

59. Michèle Lamont, "How to Become a Dominant French Philosopher," *American Journal of Sociology* 93 (November 1987): 609. In contrast, Jean-Philippe Mathy believes that New Criticism prepared the way for French postmodernist ideas: "[New Criticism's] proponents had . . . prepared the ground, and the minds, for poststructuralism by stressing the autonomy of the text both from its author and the social conditions of its production, a conception of the status of literary works not unlike the views advanced by the French promoters of 'hypertextualism' and the 'death of the author.'" See "The Resistance to French Theory in the United States," *French Historical Studies* 19 (fall 1995): 335 n. 7.

60. Lamont, "How to Become a Dominant French Philosopher," 609.

61. Michèle Lamont and Marsha Witten, "Surveying the Continental Drift," *French Politics and Society* 6 (July 1988): 18. Although the authors do not mention *Signs* here, the journal—consider simply the title!—surely belongs here as well.

62. See Jane Jenson, "Ce n'est pas un hasard: The Varieties of French Feminism," in *Searching for the New France,* ed. James F. Hollifield and George Ross (London: Routledge, 1991), 139 n. 20.

63. Jean-Philippe Mathy (341–42) makes this point in his discussion of French theory more generally. He also points out that the criticism of French theory in the United States comes from both the political Right and the Left. On the Left, Mathy suggests that it is the illiberalism of French (radical) theory—its "apparent lack of faith in liberal democracy" (Mathy, citing Richard Rorty)—that bothers scholars like Rorty, Henry Louis Gates, and Cornel West. Mathy further examines the role of stereotypical views that Americans and the English have held of the French and have expressed for several centuries and how these stereotypical views are shaping the current critiques of poststructuralism. (See esp. 341–46.)

64. Ezekiel, Berkshire conference comments. See also Ezekiel's "Antiféminisme et anti-américanisme"; and Stanley Hoffman, "Battling Cliches," *French Historical Studies* 19 (fall 1995): 321–30.
65. I thank Paola Bacchetta for writing to me about these many groups, most of which are housed at the Maison des femmes.
66. According to Picq (*Libération des femmes,* 339), between 1972 and 1982, the number of marriages in France dropped by 25 percent. Also, the number of births outside of marriage multiplied from 6 percent in 1945 to 22 percent in 1987.
67. Inter-Parliamentary Union, www.ipu.org, July 25, 1998.

About the Contributors

SYLVIANE AGACINSKI is a philosopher. She has taught since 1991 at l'Ecole des Hautes Etudes en Sciences Sociales. She has published *Aparté, conceptions et morts de Sören Kierkegaard* (1977); *Volume, philosophies et politiques de l'architecture* (1992); *Critique de l'égocentrisme, l'évènement de l'autre* (1996); *Politique des sexes* (1998); and *Le passeur du temps, modernité et nostalgie* (2000).

ELISABETH BADINTER is a philosopher and a historian. She is the author of a half-dozen books including *Emilie, Emilie: l'ambition féminine au XVIIIe siècle* (1983), *L'un est l'autre: histoire des relations entre hommes et femmes en Occident* (1986), and *XY: de l'identité masculine* (1992).

PIERRE BOURDIEU was one of the most illustrious French intellectuals of the twentieth century; he died as this book was going to press. He taught at the Université d'Alger before becoming the *directeur d'études* at the Ecole des Hautes Etudes en Sciences Sociales (1964). He later became a professor of the Collège de France (1981). He was the founder and managing editor of the journal *Actes de la recherche en sciences sociales*. Among his numerous works are: *Langage et pouvoir symbolique* (1991), *La misère du monde* (1998), and *La domination masculine* (1998).

ODILE CAZENAVE is a visiting associate professor at the Massachusetts Institute of Technology, where she teaches Francophone literature and film. The author of *Femmes rebelles: naissance d'un nouveau roman africain au féminin* (1996), she has published several articles on questions of identity, migration, and globalization. Her most recent work *Nouvelle Afrique sur Seine* (forthcoming) is about the new African diaspora in Paris.

ROGER CÉLESTIN is an associate professor of French and comparative literary and cultural studies at the University of Connecticut at Storrs. He is coeditor of *Sites: the Journal of 20th-century and contemporary French studies* and the author of *From Cannibals to Radicals. Figures and Limits of Exoticism* (University of Minnesota Press, 1996). He is currently working on a cultural history of modern and contemporary France.

WHITNEY CHADWICK is an art historian who writes on surrealism, feminism, and contemporary art. She is the author of *Women Artists and the Surrealist Movement* (1985) and *Women, Art, and Society* (1990). Her most recent book is *Amazons in the Drawing Room: The Art of Romaine Brooks* (2000).

Hélène Cixous has been directing the Centre de Recherche d'Etudes Féminines at the University of Paris-VIII since 1974. She has published numerous books, novels, essays, and plays. Some of her most recent titles include: *Beethoven à jamais* (1993), *Photos de racines* with Mireille Calle-Grüber (1994), *La ville parjure ou le réveil des Erynies* (1994), *La fiancée juive* (1995), *Or, les lettres de mon père* (1997), and *Voiles* with Jacques Derrida (1998).

Catherine Cusset taught for 11 years at Yale University. She has published two essays on the libertine novel (*Les romanciers du plaisir*,1998; and *No Tomorrow: The Ethics of Pleasure in the Enlightenment*,1999). Her novels include: *La blouse roumaine* (1991), *En toute innocence* (1995), *A vous* (1996), *Jouir* (1997), *Le problème avec Jane* (1999, Grand Prix des lectrices de *Elle* 2000), and *La haine de la famille* (2001).

Eliane DalMolin is an associate professor of French and chair of the French Program at the University of Connecticut at Storrs. She is coeditor of *Sites: the Journal of 20th-century and contemporary French studies,* and the author of *Cutting the Body: Representing Woman in Baudelaire's Poetry, Truffaut's Cinema, and Freud's Psychoanalysis* (University of Michigan Press, 2000). She specializes in contemporary poetry, psychoanalysis, and cultural studies. She is currently working on a cultural history of modern and contemporary France.

Isabelle de Courtivron is a professor of French Studies at the Massachusetts Institute of Technology. She has written books on Violette Leduc and Clara Malraux and is the co-editor of *New French Feminisms,* and of *Significant Others: Creativity and Intimate Partnership* (with Whitney Chadwick). She is currently editing a collection of essays entitled "Lives in Translation: Bilingual Writers on Identity and Creativity" (forthcoming, spring 2003).

Marie Etienne is a poet. Her volumes of poetry include *Roi des cent cavaliers* (2002), *Anatolie* (1997), which won the Prix Mallarmé, and *La face et le lointain* (1986). She is also the author of several essays and articles. At present, she is writing an account of her childhood in Southeast Asia during World War II (*Sensò, la guerre*).

Eric Fassin is a sociologist in the Département de Sciences Sociales at l'Ecole Normale Supérieure in Paris. His research focuses on the politics of gender and sexuality in a comparative perspective. He has coedited with Daniel Borillo and Marcela Iacub *Au-delà du PACS: L'Expertise familiale á l'usage de l'homosexualité* (1999). His most recent work (forthcoming) is *Same Sex, Different Politics: Gay Marriage in France and the United States.*

Christine Fauré is a sociologist, director of research at the Centre National de la Recherche Scientifique (CNRS), and a member of the Centre de Recherches Politiques de la Sorbonne of the Université of Paris I. She has published works on the French Revolution, including: *Les Déclarations des droits de l'homme de 1789* (1988–1992); *Ce que déclarer des droits veut dire: histoires* (1997, Prix de l'Académie des Sciences Morales et Politiques); *Des manuscrits de Sieyes 1773–1799* (1999); and *L'Amérique des Français* (1992, with Tom Bishop). Her works on women and politics include: *Democracy without Women. Feminism and the Rise of Liberal Individualism in France* (1991), and *The Political and Historical Encyclopedia of Women* (2002).

JUDITH FEHER-GUREWICH is a Lacanian analyst and a doctor in the social sciences. She recently edited with Michel Tort *The Subject and the Self: Lacan and American Psychoanalysis* (1996) and is the editor of the Lacanian Clinic Series from Other Press. She is also the director of the Lacan Seminar at the Center for Literary and Cultural Studies at Harvard University.

GENEVIÈVE FRAISSE is a philosopher and a former "déléguée interministérielle aux droits de la Femme" during Lionel Jospin's administration. Among her books are *La raison des femmes* (1992), *Muse de la raison, démocratie et exclusion des femmes en France* (1989), and *La différence des sexes* (1996). She coedited *L'histoire des femmes en Occident,* Tome IV, *le 19e siècle,* with Michèle Perrot.

FRANÇOISE GASPARD is a sociologist and a senior lecturer at the Ecole des Hautes Etudes en Sciences Sociales. She is also France's representative to the United Nations' Commission on the Condition of Women. Her publications include: *Au pouvoir citoyennes! Liberté, égalité, parité* (with Claude Servan-Schreiber and Anne Le Gall, 1992) and *Le Foulard et la République* (with Farhad Khosrokhavar, 1995).

ANNE GILLAIN teaches film at Wellesley College. She has published books on François Truffaut, *Le cinéma selon François Truffaut* (1988); *François Truffaut: le secret perdu* (Hatier, 1991), *Les 400 coups* (1991), and, more recently, a monograph on *Manhattan* by Woody Allen (1996). She is working on a book on cinema and psychoanalysis.

BENOÎTE GROULT is a writer and an essayist. Her fiction includes *Les vaisseaux du cœur* (1988) and *Journal à quatre mains* in collaboration with her sister Flora Groult. She is well known for her feminist essays, which include *Ainsi soit-elle* (1975) and *Le féminisme au masculin*. From 1984 to 1986, she presided the "Commission pour la féminisation des noms de métier."

FARHAD KHOSROKHAVAR is a sociologist and a professor at the Ecole des Hautes Etudes en Sciences Sociales. He is well known for his research focusing on the political and social situation of Iran and the Islamic community in France. He recently published *La recherche de soi. Dialogue sur le sujet* (with Alain Touraine, 2000).

JEAN-PHILIPPE MATHY is an associate professor of French and of criticism and interpretive theory at the University of Illinois at Urbana-Champaign. He has written many articles on France as well as two books: *Extrême-Occident: French Intellectuals and America* (1993) and *French Resistance: French-American Culture Wars* (2000).

CLAIRE GOLDBERG MOSES is a professor and the chair of the Department of Women's Studies at the University of Maryland and editor and manager of *Feminist Studies*. Her books include *U.S. Women in Collective Struggle*, edited with Heidi Hartmann (1994); *Feminism, Socialism, and French Romanticism,* with Leslie Rabine (1993); and *French Feminism in the Nineteenth Century* (1984), winner of the Joan Kelly Memorial Prize for the best book in women's history or feminist theory.

JEANINE MOSSUZ-LAVAU is director of research at the Centre d'Etude de la Vie Politique Française (CNRS/Political Science, Paris), the head of course curriculum at the Institut d'Etudes Politiques in Paris, and a member of the Observatoire de la Parité. Her books include *Les lois de l'amour: les politiques de la sexualité en France de 1950 à nos jours* (1991), *Les femmes ne sont pas des hommes commes les autres* (with Anne de Kervasdoué, 1997), and *Femmes/hommes: pour la parité* (1998). In 2002 she will publish *La vie sexuelle en France*.

VÉRONIQUE NAHOUM-GRAPPE is a *chercheur* at the Ecole des Hautes Etudes en Sciences Sociales en Anthropologie des Mondes Contemporains. She has participated in *L'histoire de femmes* (1990–1992). Her publications include: *La culture de l'ivresse* (1991), *Beauté, laideur* (with Nicole Phelouzat-Perriquet, 1995), and *Le féminin* (1996).

MONA OZOUF is a historian of the French Revolution and of "l'école républicaine" and the research director at the Centre National de la Recherche Scientifique in Paris. She is the author of several studies on the French Revolution. Her works include: *Dictionnaire critique de la Révolution française* (with François Furet, 1988), *La fête révolutionnaire 1789–1799* (1976), *L'école de la France. Essais sur la Révolution, l'Utopie et l'enseignement* (1984), *La République des instituteurs* (with Jacques Ozouf, 1992), and, most recently, *Les aveux du roman* (2001).

MIREILLE ROSELLO is a professor of French and Francophone literatures at Northwestern University. Her areas of interest include cultural studies, particularly gender constructions and visual narratives, as well as postcolonial discourses. She is the author of *Infiltrating Culture: Power and Identity in Contemporary Women's Writing* (1996) and *Postcolonial Hospitality: The Immigrant as Guest* (Stanford University Press, 2001).

JOAN WALLACH SCOTT is a professor of social sciences at the Institute for Advanced Study in Princeton. Her study *Gender and the Politics of History* was awarded the American Historical Association's Joan Kelly Memorial Prize in 1989. She is also the author of *Only Paradoxes to Offer: French Feminists and the Rights of Man* (1996) and *Women, Work, and the Family* (with Louise Tilly, 1998).

GENEVIÈVE SELLIER is a *maître de conférences* at the University of Caen (Normandy), where she is director of research in film studies. Her publications include: *Les enfants du paradis* (1992), and *La drôle de guerre des sexes du cinéma français 1930–1956* (with N. Burch, 1996). She is co-editor with Odile Krakovitch of *L'exclusion des femmes, masculinité et politique dans la culture au XXe siècle* (2001). In collaboration with Odile Krakovitch and Eliane Viennot, she wrote *Pouvoir des femmes: mythes et fantasmes* (2001).

MARIETTE SINEAU is a political scientist and director of research at the Centre National de la Recherche Scientifique (CNRS). She also works at the Centre d'Etude de la Vie Politique Française in Paris. Her main fields of research are women's political attitudes and women politicians. She has written *Des femmes en politique* (1988), *Droits des femmes en France et au Québec 1940–1990: éléments pour une histoire comparée* (with Evelyne Tardy, 1993), and *Profession: femme politique. Sexe et pouvoir sous la Ve République* (2001). She coedited (with Jane Jenson) *Who Cares?: Women's Work, Child Care, and Welfare State Redesign* (2001).

Bibliography 1985–2001

Abel, Olivier, et al. "Les occasions manquées du PaCS: un débat." *Esprit* 11 (1998).

Adams, Marie-Rose, et al. "French Feminism's New Wave." *Off Our Backs* 24.3 (1994).

Adler, Laure. *Les femmes politiques.* Paris: Seuil, 1993.

Agacinski, Sylvianne. *La politique des sexes;* preceded by *Mise au point sur la mixité.* Paris: Seuil, 1998 and 2001. Translated as: *Parity of the Sexes.* Trans. Lisa Walsh. New York: Columbia University Press, 2001.

Akrich, Madeleine, and Françoise Laborie. *De la contraception à l'enfantement: l'offre technologique en question.* Spec. Issue of *Cahiers du Genre* 25 (1999).

Alezra, Claudine, Jacqueline Laufer, and Margaret Maruani, eds. *La mixité du travail, une stratégie pour l'entreprise.* Paris: Ministère de la recherche et de l'enseignement supérieur: La Documentation française, 1987.

Allison, Maggie, ed. *Women's Space and Identity.* Bradford, West Yorkshire: Dept. of Modern Languages, University of Bradford, 1992.

Allwood, Gill. *French Feminisms: Gender and Violence in Contemporary Theory.* London: UCL Press, 1998.

Allwood, Gill, and Khursheed Wadia. *Women and Politics in France 1958–2000.* London: Routledge, 2000.

Alonso, Isabelle. *Pourquoi je suis chienne de garde.* Paris: Robert Laffont, 2001.

———. *Tous les hommes sont égaux, même les femmes.* Paris: Robert Laffont, 1999.

Alonzo, Philippe. *Femmes employées: la construction sociale sexuée du salariat.* Paris: L'Harmattan, 1996.

———. *Femmes et salariat: l'inégalité dans l'indifférence.* Paris: L'Harmattan, 2000.

Amar, Micheline, ed. *Le piège de la parité: arguments pour un débat.* Paris: Hachette Littératures, 1999.

Ameziane-Hassani, Rachid, ed. *Maghrebi Women.* Cambridge, MA: Schoenhof's Foreign Books, 1993.

André, Jacques. *La sexualité féminine.* Que sais-je? Paris: PUF, 1994.

———. *Aux origines féminines de la sexualité.* Paris: PUF, 1995.

———, ed. *La féminité autrement.* Paris: PUF, 1999.

Anxo, Dominique, et al. *L'emploi du temps des hommes et des femmes et l'avenir du travail des femmes: le cas de la France:* rapport pour la Commission européenne. Paris: La Documentation française, 1997.

Appay, Béatrice, Jacqueline Heinen, and Christian Léomant, eds. *Précarisation et citoyenneté.* Spec. issue of *Cahiers du GEDISST* 23 (1999).

Ardant, Philippe, ed. *Femmes en politiques.* Spec. issue of *Pouvoirs* 82 (1997).

Assises nationales pour le droit des femmes. *En avant toutes!.* Pantin: Le temps des CeRises, 1998.

Aubert, Nicole, Eugène Enriquez, and Vincent Gaulejac, eds. *Le sexe du pouvoir: femmes, hommes et pouvoirs dans les organisations.* Paris: Desclée de Brouwer, 1986.

Aubin, Claire. *Les femmes en France, 1985–1995:* rapport pour l'ONU. Paris: La Documentation française, 1994.

Auslander, Leora, and Michèle Zancarini-Fournel, eds. *Différence des sexes et protection sociale: XIXe-XXe siècles.* Saint-Denis: Presses Universitaires de Vincennes, 1995.

———, eds. *Le genre de la nation.* Spec. Issue of *Clio* 12 (2000).

Autan, Clémentine. *Alter égaux, Invitation au féminisme.* Paris: Robert Laffont, 2001.

AVFT. *De l'abus de pouvoir sexuel: le harcèlement sexuel au travail.* Paris: La Découverte/Le Boréal, 1990.

Bachelot-Narquin, Roselyne. *Le PaCS entre haine et amour.* Paris: Plon, 1999.

Bachelot-Narquin, Roselyne, and Geneviève Fraisse. *Deux femmes aux royaumes des hommes.* Paris: Hachette littératures, 1999.

Bach-Ignasse, Gérard. "Le Contrat d'union sociale en perspective." *Les Temps modernes* 598 (1998).

Bacqué, Marie-Hélène, et al., eds. *Le méccano familial: les nouveaux enjeux de la vie privée.* Spec. issue of *Mouvements* 8 (1998).

Badgett, M. V. Lee, and Nancy Folbre. "Responsabilités familiales et sociales: les normes du comportement masculin et féminin et leurs incidences économiques." *Revue internationale du travail* 138.3 (1999).

Badinter, Elisabeth. *L'un est l'autre: des relations entre hommes et femmes.* Paris: Odile Jacob, 1986. Translated as: *The Unopposite Sex: The End of the Gender Battle.* Trans. Barbara Wright. New York: Harper & Row, 1989.

——. *XY: de l'identité masculine.* Paris: Odile Jacob, 1992. Translated as: *XY: on Masculine Identity.* Trans. Lydia Davis. New York: Columbia University Press, 1995.

Baillette, Frédéric, and Philippe Liotard. *Sport et virilisme.* Montpellier: Editions Quasimodo & fils, 1999.

Bainbrigge, Susan. "L'exception française? Utopia and Dystopia in the Debate on Parity." *French Cultural Studies* 12.2 (2001).

Ballmer-Cao, Thranh-Huyêri, Véronique Mottier, and Léa Sgier, eds. *Genre et politique: débats et perspectives.* Paris: Gallimard, 2000.

Bard, Christine. *Les femmes dans la société française au 20e siècle.* Paris: Armand Colin, 2001.

——, ed. *Un siècle d'antiféminisme.* Paris: Fayard, 1999.

——, ed. *Madeleine Pelletier: logique et infortunes d'un combat pour l'égalité: actes du colloque de Jussieu, 5–6 décembre 1991.* Paris: Côté-femmes, 1992.

Bard, Christine, and Nicole Pellegrin. "Femmes travesties: un 'mauvais' genre. *Clío* 10 (1999).

Barre, Virginie, et al. *Dites-le avec des femmes: le sexisme ordinaire dans les médias.* Paris: CFD/AFJ, 1999.

Barrère-Maurisson, Marie-Agnès, ed. *Le partage des temps et des tâches dans les ménages.* Paris: Ministère de l'emploi et de la solidarité: La Documentation française, 2001.

Barrère-Maurisson, Marie-Agnès, and S. Rivier. "Le partage des temps pour les hommes et les femmes: ou comment conjuguer travail rémunéré, non rémunéré et non travail." *Premières informations et premières synthèses* 11.1 (2001).

Barret-Ducrocq, Françoise, and Evelyne Pisier. *Femmes en tête.* Paris: Flammarion, 1997.

Barzach, Michèle. *Vérités et tabous.* Paris: Seuil, 1994.

Basch, Françoise, et al. *25 ans d'études féministes: l'expérience Jussieu.* Paris: CEDREF, 2001.

Bataille, Philippe, and Françoise Gaspard. *Comment les femmes changent la politique: et pourquoi les hommes résistent.* Paris: La Découverte, 1999.

Battagliola, Françoise. "Des femmes aux marges de l'activité, au coeur de la flexibilité." *Travail, genre et sociétés* 1 (1999).

——. *Histoire du travail des femmes.* Paris: La Découverte, 2000.

Battagliola, Françoise, Michèle Ferrand, and Françoise Imbert. *Entre travail et famille: la construction sociale des trajectoires.* Paris: CNRS/MIRE, 1990.

Battagliola, Françoise, et al., eds. *A propos des rapport sociaux de sexe: parcours épistémologique.* Paris: CSU-CNRS, 1986.

Baudelot, Christian. "Le sexe est-il un résidu?" *Les cahiers du Mage* 2 (1995).

Baudelot, Christian, and Roger Establet. *Allez, les filles!* Paris: Seuil, 1992.

Baudoux, Claudine, and Claude Zaidman, eds. *Egalité entre les sexes: mixité et démocratie. Actes du colloque, Université Paris VII, 3–4 mai 1990.* Paris: L'Harmattan, 1992.

Baulieu, Etienne-Emile, Françoise Héritier, and Henri Léridon, eds. *Contraception, contrainte ou liberté? Actes du colloque organisé au Collège de France, 9 et 10 octobre 1998.* Paris: Odile Jacob, 1999.

Beauvoir, Simone de. *Le Deuxième Sexe.* Paris: Gallimard, 1976. The title in English is *The Second Sex.* Trans. H. M. Parshley. New York: Vintage Books, 1989.

Becquer, Annie, Bernard Cerquiglini, and Nicole Cholewka. *Femme, j'écris ton nom: guide d'aide à la féminisation des noms des métiers, grades, fonctions.* Paris: INALF: La Documentation française, 1999.

Bell, David F. "Text, Context: Transatlantic Sokal." *France/USA: The Cultural Wars.* Spec. issue of *Yale French Studies* 100 (fall 2001).

Benguigui, Yamina. *Mémoires d'immigrés.* Paris: Canal + Editions, 1997.

Bensadon, Ney. *Les droits de la femme: des origines à nos jours.* Que sais-je? Paris: PUF, 1999.

Berg, Maggie. "Luce Irigaray's 'Contradictions': Poststructuralism and Feminism." *Signs* 17.1 (1991).

Berger, Anne, and Mara Negrón, eds. *Lectures de la différence sexuelle: Actes du colloque Paris VIII, CIPH, octobre 1990.* Paris: des femmes, 1994.

Berger, Denis, ed. *Féminismes au présent.* Supplement to *Futur antérieur.* Paris: L'Harmattan, 1993.

Beugnet, Martine, ed. *Marginalité, sexualité, contrôle dans le cinéma français contemporain.* Paris: L'Harmattan, 2000.

Beyala, Calixthe. *Lettre d'une Afro-Française à ses compatriotes.* Paris: Mango, 2000.

Bianchi, Marie-Thérèse. *Femmes et politique en France: un répertoire.* Chantilly: M.-T. Bianchi, 1989.

Bianchi, Marie-Thérèse, Christine Chauvet, and Laurence Douvin. *Lettre ouverte aux hommes qui ont peur des femmes en politique.* Chantilly: M.-T. Bianchi, 1990.

Bihr, Alain, and Roland Pfefferkorn. *Hommes-femmes l'introuvable égalité: école, travail, couple, espace public.* Paris: Les éditions de l'Atelier - Les éditions Ouvrières, 1996.

Bisilliat, Jeanne, and Christine Verschuur, eds. *Le genre: un outil nécessaire: introduction à une problématique thème spécial.* Paris: L'Harmattan, 2000.

Bloch, Françoise, and Monique Buisson. *La garde des enfants, une histoire de femmes: entre don, équité et rémunération.* Paris: L'Harmattan, 1998.

Blöss, Thierry. *Les rapports sociaux entre les sexes: permanences et changements.* Paris: La Documentation française, 1994.

Blöss, Thierry, and Alain Frickey. *La femme dans la société française.* Que sais-je?. Paris: PUF, 1996.

Boehringer, Monika, ed. *Simone de Beauvoir et les féminismes contemporains.* Spec. Issue of *Dalhousie French Studies* 13 (1987).

———, ed. *L'écriture de soi au féminin.* Spec. issue of *Dalhousie French Studies* 47 (1999).

Boigeol, Anne. "Les femmes et les cours: la difficile mise en oeuvre de l'égalité des sexes dans l'accès à la magistrature." *Genèses* 22 (1996).

———. "Les magistrates de l'ordre judiciaire: des femmes d'autorité." *Les cahiers du Mage* 1 (1997).

Bonnet, Marie-Jo. *Les relations amoureuses entre les femmes du XVIe au XXe siècle: essai historique.* Paris: Odile Jacob, 1995.

———. *Les deux amies: essai sur le couple de femmes dans l'art.* Paris: Editions Blanche, 2000.

Bordeaux, Michèle, Bernard Hazo, and Soizic Lorvellec. *Qualifié viol.* Genève; Paris: Méridiens Klincksieck, 1990.

Borrillo, Daniel, Eric Fassin, and Marcela Iacub, eds. *Au-delà du PaCS: l'expertise familiale à l'épreuve de l'homosexualité.* Paris: PUF, 1999.

Borrillo, Daniel, Pierre Fedida, and Geneviève Fraisse. *La sexualité a-t-elle un avenir?* Paris: PUF, 1999.

Bosio-Valici, Sabine, and Michelle Zancarini-Fournel. *Femmes et fières de l'être: un siècle d'émancipation féminine.* Paris: Larousse, 2001.

Bottari, Marianne, ed. *La citoyenneté de la femme.* Spec. issue of *La Mazarine* 4 (1999).

Bouchardeau, Huguette. "Entretien avec Margaret Maruani et Chantal Rogerat." *Travail, genre et sociétés* 2 (1999).

Bouffartigue, Paul, and Jean-René Pendaries. "Activité féminine et précarité de l'emploi." *Travail et emploi* 46 (1990).

Bourdieu, Pierre. *La domination masculine*. Paris: Seuil, 1998. Translated as: *Masculine Domination*. Trans. Richard Nice. Stanford, CA: Stanford University Press, 2001.

Bourguignon, Odile, Jean-Louis Rallu, and Irène Théry. *Du divorce et des enfants*. Paris: PUF, 1985.

Bozon, Michel, and Henri Léridon. "Les constructions sociales de la sexualité." *Population* 48.5 (1993).

————, eds. *Sexualité et sciences sociales: les apports d'une enquête*. Spec. issue of *Population* 5 (1993).

————, eds. *Sexuality and the Social Sciences: a French Survey on Sexual Behaviour*. Brookfield, VT: Dartmouth, 1996.

Bozon, Michel, and Thérèse Locoh, eds. *Rapports de genre et questions de population*. Paris: Institut national d'études démographiques, 2000.

Braconier, Alain. *Le sexe des émotions*. Paris: Odile Jacob, 1996.

Brahimi, Denise. *Maghrébines: portraits littéraires*. Paris: L'Harmattan: AWAL, 1995.

————. *Cinéastes françaises*. Villenave-d'Ornon: Fus art, 1999.

Brand, Peg Zeglin. *Beauty Matters*. Bloomington: Indiana University Press, 2000.

Bruner, Charlotte. *The Heinemann Book of African Women's Writing*. London: Heinemann, 1993.

Buhle, Mari Jo. *Feminism and Its Discontents: A Century of Struggle with Psychoanalysis*. Cambridge, MA: Harvard University Press, 1998.

Burch, Noël. "Colère des femmes/Flegme des hommes." *Tausend Auge* 21 (2001).

Butler, Judith. *Gender Trouble*. New York: Routledge, 1990.

————. *Bodies that Matter: The Discursive Limits of "Sex."* London: Routledge, 1993.

————. *Antigone's Claim*. New York: Columbia University Press, 2000.

Cacouault, Marlaine. "Prof c'est bien . . . pour une femme?" *Le mouvement social* 140 (1987).

————. "Féminisation et masculinisation des professions: approches historiques et comparatives. Introduction." *Les cahiers du Mage* 1 (1995).

Calle, Sophie, and Jean Baudrillard. *Suite Venitienne/Please Follow Me*. Trans. Dany Barash. Seattle: Bay Press, 1988.

Calle-Gruber, Mireille. *Du féminin*. Sainte-Foy, Québec: Le Griffon d'argile, 1992.

Carton, Ann, et al. *L'extrême droite contre les femmes*. Bruxelles: L. Pire, 1995.

Castelain-Meunier, Christine. *Les hommes, aujourd'hui: virilité et identité*. Paris: Acropole, 1988.

————. *L'amour en moins: l'apprentissage sentimental*. Paris: O. Orban, 1991.

————. *Cramponnez-vous les pères: les hommes face à leur femme et à leurs enfants*. Paris: Albin Michel, 1992.

————. *La paternité*. Que sais-je?. Paris: PUF, 1997.

————. *Pères, mères enfants: un exposé pour comprendre, un essai pour réfléchir*. Paris: Flammarion, 1998.

Caws, Mary Ann, ed. *Ecritures de femmes: nouvelles cartographies*. New Haven: Yale University Press, 1996.

Cazenave, Odile. "The Others' Others: 'Francophone' Women and Writing." *Yale French Studies* 75 (1988).

————. *Femmes rebelles: naissance d'un nouveau roman africain au féminin*. Paris: L'Harmattan, 1996. Translated as: *Rebellious Women: The New Generation of Female African Novelists*. London: Lynne Rienner Publishers, 2000.

————. "Vingt après Mariama Bâ: le roman africain au féminin." *Africultures* 35 (2001).

Célestin, Roger, Eliane DalMolin, and Isabelle de Courtivron, eds. *Women/Femmes*. Spec. issue of *Sites: The Journal of 20th-Century/contemporary French Studies* 4.1 (spring 2000).

Chabaud-Rychter, Danielle, ed. *Genre et techniques domestiques*. Spec. issue of *Cahiers du GEDISST* 20 (1997).

Chadwick, Whitney. *Women Artists and the Surrealist Movement*. Boston: New York Graphic Society Books, 1985.

Chadwick, Whitney, and Isabelle de Courtivron, eds. *Significant Others: Creativity and Intimate Partnership*. London and New York: Thames and Hudson, 1993.

Chaillot, Nicole, Victoria Man, and Agnès Rosenstiehl. *Europe est une femme*. Paris: La Nacelle, 1994.

Chanter, Tina. *The Ethics of Eros: Irigaray's Re-writing of the Philosophers*. New York: Routledge, 1994.

Chartier, Roger. "Différence entre les sexes et domination symbolique." *Annales: Histoire, Sciences Sociales* 4 (1993).

Choisir—La cause des femmes. *Femmes, moitié de la terre, moitié du pouvoir*. Paris: Gallimard, 1994.

Chotteau, Thérèse. *Rencontres entre artistes et mathématiciennes: toutes un peu les autres*. Paris: L'Harmattan, 2001.

Cixous, Hélène. "My Algeriance, in Other Words: To Depart Not to Arrive from Algeria." Translated by Eric Prenowitz. In *Stigmata: Escaping Texts*. New York: Routledge, 1998. 153–72.

Cixous, Hélène, and Catherine Clément. *The Newly Born Woman*. Trans. Betsy Wing. Minneapolis: University of Minnesota Press, 1996.

Cixous, Hélène, Ralph Cohen, and Ellen Messer-Davidow. "Feminist directions: articles." *New Literary History* 19.1 (1987).

Cixous, Hélène, and Susan Sellers, eds. *The Hélène Cixous Reader*. New York: Routledge, 1994.

Clément, Catherine, and Julia Kristeva. *Le féminin et le sacré*. Paris: Stock, 1998. Translated as: *The Feminine and the Sacred*. Trans. Jane Marie Todd. Basingstoke: Palgrave, 2001.

Cohen-Safir, Claude. *Cartographie du féminin dans l'utopie: de l'Europe à l'Amérique*. Paris: L'Harmattan, 2000.

Collin, Françoise, ed. *Le genre de l'histoire*. Spec. Issue of *Cahiers du GRIF* 37–38 (1988).

———. "Le sujet et l'auteur ou lire 'l'autre femme.'" *Cahiers du CEDREF* 2 (1990).

———, ed. *Le sexe des sciences: les femmes en plus*. Paris: Autrement, 1992.

———. "Parité et universalisme." *Projets féministes* 4–5 (1996). Translated as: "Parity and Universalism." *Différences* 9.2 (1997).

———. *Le différend des sexes: de Platon à la parité*. Nantes: Editions Pleins Feux, 1999.

Collin, Françoise, and Nancy Bolain, eds. *Les femmes et la construction européenne: egalité?, parité?* Paris: Les Cahiers du GRIF, 1994.

Collin, Françoise, Evelyne Pisier, and Eleni Varikas, eds. *Les femmes, de Platon à Derrida: anthologie critique*. Paris: Plon, 2000.

Colmou, Anne-Marie. *L'encadrement supérieur de la fonction publique: vers l'égalité entre les hommes et les femmes: rapport au Ministre de la fonction publique, de la réforme de l'Etat et de la décentralisation*. Paris: La Documentation française, 1999.

Combes, Danièle. "Oppression des femmes et solidarités de couple." *Les Temps modernes* 513 (1989).

Combes, Danièle, and Anne-Marie Devreux. "Les droits et les devoirs parentaux ou l'appropriation des enfants." *Recherches féministes* 7.1 (1994).

Commaille, Jacques. *Les stratégies des femmes: travail, famille et politique*. Paris: La Découverte, 1993.

———. "La construction sociale du travail des femmes." *Travail* 32–33 (1994–1995).

Concialdi, Pierre, and Sophie Ponthieux. "L'emploi à bas salaire: les femmes d'abord." *Travail, genre et sociétés* 1 (1999).

Conkelton, Sherry. "Annette Messager's Carnival of Death and Desire." *Annette Messager*, exh. cat. Los Angeles and New York: The Los Angeles County Museum of Art and the Museum of Modern Art, New York, 1995.

Conninck, Frédéric de, and Francis Godard. "Itinéraires familiaux, itinéraires professionnels: vers de nouvelles biographies féminines." *Sociologie du travail* 34.1 (1992).

Conseil d'Etat. *Rapport public 1996. Sur le principe d'égalité*. Paris: La Documentation française, 1996.

Coquillat, Michèle. *Entre elles*. Paris: Albin Michel, 1995.

Corbett, James. "Cherchez la femme! Sexual Equality in Politics and Affirmative Action in France." *French Review* 14.5 (April 2001).

Cornell, Drucilla. *The Imaginary Domain*. New York: Routledge, 1995.

———. *Freedom, Identity and Rights*. New York: Rowman and Little Field, 2000.

————. *Feminism and Pornography.* New York: Oxford University Press, 2000.

Corradin, Irène, and Jacqueline Martin, eds. *Femmes sujets d'histoire: à la mémoire de Marie-France Brive.* Toulouse: Presses universitaires du Mirail, 1999.

Cotta, Michèle. *Femmes dans les lieux de décision.* Conseil économique et social. Paris: Les éditions des journaux officiels, 2000.

Cova, Anne. *Maternité et droits des femmes en France: XIXe-XXe siècles.* Paris: Anthropos: dist. Economica, 1997.

————. "Les féministes du passé et l'apologie de la maternité." *Panoramiques* 40 (1999).

Cromer, Sylvie. *Le harcèlement sexuel en France: la levée d'un tabou, 1985–1990: d'après les archives de l'AVFT.* Paris: La Documentation française, 1995.

Cromer, Sylvie, and Marie-Victoire Louis. "Existe-t-il un harcèlement sexuel à la française?" *French Politics and Society* 10.3 (1992).

Crosson, Thierry. *Pour moi c'est elle!: enquête sur les femmes de pouvoir.* Paris: Filipacchi, 1990.

Cusset, Catherine. "Libertinage and Feminism: Interview with N. K. Miller." *Yale French Studies* 94 (1998).

————. "Libertinage and Modernity." *Yale French Studies* 94 (1998).

Czechowski, Nicole, and Véronique Nahoum-Grappe, eds. *Fatale beauté.* Paris, 1987.

Dagenais, Huguette. "Femmes au travail." *Recherches féministes* 5.2 (1992).

————, ed. *Pluralité et convergences: la recherche féministe dans la francophonie.* Montréal: Du remue ménage, 1999.

DalMolin, Eliane. *Cutting the Body: Representing Woman in Baudelaire's Poetry, Truffaut's Cinema, and Freud's Psychoanalysis.* Ann Arbor: University of Michigan Press, 2000.

Daune-Richard, Anne-Marie, and Anne-Marie Devreux. "Rapports sociaux de sexe et conceptualisation sociologique." *Recherches féministes* 5.2 (1992).

Dauphin, Cécile, and Arlette Farge, eds. *De la violence et des femmes.* Paris: Albin Michel, 1997.

Dauphin, Cécile, et al. "Culture et pouvoir des femmes: essai d'historiographie." *Annales: Histoires et Siences Sociales* 2 (1986).

Davis, Kathy, ed. *Embodied Practices: Feminist Perspectives on the Body.* London: Sage Publications, 1997.

Davisse, Annick, and Catherine Louveau. *Sports, école, société: la différence des sexes: féminin, masculin et activités sportives.* Paris: L'Harmattan, 1998.

Dekeuwer-Défossez, Françoise. *Droits des femmes.* Dictionnaire juridique. Paris: Dalloz, 1985.

————. *L'égalité des sexes.* Paris: Dalloz, 1998.

Del Re, Alisa, and Jacqueline Heinen, eds. *Quelle citoyenneté pour les femmes?: la crise des Etats-providence et de la représentation politique en Europe.* Paris: L'Harmattan, 1996.

Delas, Daniel, and Danielle Deltel, eds. *Voix nouvelles du roman africain.* Paris: Université Paris X, 1994.

Delphy, Christine. "Libération des femmes ou droits corporatistes des mères?" *Nouvelles questions féministes* 12.16–17–18 (1991).

————. "Les origines du Mouvement de liberation des femmes en France." *Nouvelles questions féministes.* 16–18 (1991).

————. "The Hill-Thomas Controversy and French National Identity." *Nouvelles questions féministes* 14.4 (1993).

————. "Rethinking Sex and Gender." *Women's International Forum* 16.1 (1993).

————. "Egalité, équivalence et équité: la position de l'Etat français au regard du droit international." *Nouvelles questions féministes* 16.1 (1995).

————. "L'invention du 'French Feminism': une démarche essentielle." *Nouvelles questions féministes* 17.1 (1996). Published in English as "The Invention of French Feminism: An Essential Move." *Another Look, Another Woman: Retranslations of French Feminism,* spec. issue of *Yale French Studies* 87 (1995).

————. "For a Materialist Feminism." *Materialist Feminism: A Reader in Class, Difference, and Women's Lives.* Rosemary Hennessy, ed. New York: Routledge, 1997.

————. *Economie politique du patriarcat.* Collection Nouvelles Questions Féministes. Paris: Syllepse, 1998. Vol. 1 of *L'ennemi principal.* 2 vols. 1998–2001.

———. *Penser le genre.* Collection Nouvelles Questions Féministes. Paris: Syllepse, 2001. Vol. 2 of *L'ennemi principal.* 2 vols. 1998–2001.

Delphy, Christine, and Diana Leondar. *Familiar Exploitation: A New Analysis of Marriage in Contemporary Western Societies.* Cambridge, MA: Polity Press, 1992.

Demichel, Francine. "A parts égales: contributions au débat sur la parité." *Recueil Dalloz.* Paris: Dalloz-Sirey, 1997.

Deschamps, Gaële. "Fragments d'une mémoire lesbienne." *Physiologie et mythologie du féminin.* Lille: Presses Universitaires de Lille, 1989.

Deutscher, Penelope. "'Imperfect Discretion': Interventions into the History of Philosophy by Twentieth-Century French Women Philosophers." *Hypatia* 15.2 (2000).

————. "Contemporary French Women Philosophers." *Hypatia* 15.4 (2000).

————. "Interview: with M. Le Doeuff." *Hypatia* 15.4 (2000).

Devreux, Anne-Marie. "Sociologie 'généraliste' et sociologie féministe: les rapports sociaux de sexe dans le champ professionnel de la sociologie." *Nouvelles questions féministes* 16.1 (1995).

Dibos-Lacroux, Sylvie. *PaCS, le guide pratique: Pour qui? Pourquoi? Comment?* Paris: Prat, 2000.

Documents du *Monde. Les femmes et la politique: Du droit de vote à la parité.* Paris: Editions Librio, 2001.

Donadey, Anne. *Recasting Postcolonialism: Women Writing Between Worlds.* Portsmouth, NH: Heinemann, 2001.

Duby, Georges, and Michelle Perrot, eds. *Images de femmes.* Paris: Plon, 1992.

————, eds. *Femmes et histoire: la Sorbonne, 13–14 novembre 1992.* Paris: Plon, 1993.

————, eds. *Histoire des femmes en occident.* 5 vols. Paris: Plon, 1992. Translated as: *A History of Women in the West.* 5 vols. Cambridge, MA: Belknap Press of Harvard University Press, 1994.

Duchen, Claire. *Feminism in France: from May '68 to Mitterrand.* London; Boston: Routledge & Kegan Paul, 1986.

————, ed. *French Connections: Voices from the Women's Movement in France.* Amherst: University of Massachusetts Press, 1987.

Dumeige, Valérie, and Sophie Ponchelet. *Françaises.* Paris: Nil, 1999.

Duroux, Françoise. *Antigone encore: les femmes et la loi.* Paris: Côté-femmes, 1993.

Duru-Bellat, Marie. *L'école des filles: quelle formation pour quels rôles sociaux?* Paris: L'Harmattan, 1990.

————. "La Découverte de la variable sexe et ses implications théoriques dans la sociologie de l'éducation française contemporaine." *Nouvelles questions féministes* 15.1 (1994).

————. "La construction sociale de la différence entre les sexes." *Revue française de pédagogie* 110 (1995).

Dutheil, Catherine, and Dominique Loiseau. "Petite contribution à la question des femmes dans l'analyse sociologique." *Utinam* 24 (1997).

Eakin, Emily. "Liberté, égalité, parité!: French Feminists Get Political." *Lingua Franca* 8.3 (1998).

Eaubonne, Françoise d'. *Féminin et philosophie: une allergie historique.* Paris: L'Harmattan, 1997.

Einhorn, Barbara, and Christine Zmroczek, eds. *Histoire/histoires: a special issue in honour of Claire Duchen.* Spec. issue of *Women's Studies International Forum* 23.6 (2000).

Elia, Nada. *Trances, Dances, and Vociferations: Agency and Resistance in African Women's Narratives.* New York: Garland Publishers, 2001.

Eliel, Carol S. "'Nourishment You Take:' Annette Messager, Influence and the Subversion of Images." *Annette Messager,* exh. cat. 55.

Ephesia, ed. *La place des femmes: les enjeux de l'identité et de l'égalité au regard des sciences sociales: colloque international de recherche, Paris, mars 1995.* Paris: La Découverte, 1995.

Etchegoyen, Alain. *Eloge de la féminité ou La nature de Sophie.* Paris: Arléa, 1997.

Etre lesbienne aujourd'hui: le MIEL enquête. Paris: Le Miel, 1988.

Ezekiel, Judith. "Antiféminisme et anti-américanisme: un mariage politiquement réussi." *Nouvelles questions féministes* 17.1 (1996).

Fabre, Clarisse, ed. *Les femmes et la politique: du droit de vote à la parité.* Paris: Librio/J'ai lu, 2001.

Fagnani, Jeanne. "Helping Mothers to Combine Paid and Unpaid Work—or Fighting Unemployment? The Ambiguities of French Family Policy." *Community Work and Family* 1.3 (1998).

———. "Lacunes, contradictions et incohérences des mesures de conciliation travail/famille." *Droit social* 6 (1998).

———. "Trente ans de politique familiale en France: l'intégration progressive du modèle de 'la mère qui travaille.'" *Regards* 18 (2000).

———. *Un travail et des enfants: petits arbitrages et grands dilemmes.* Paris: Bayard, 2000.

Farge, Arlette, ed. *Des lieux pour l'histoire.* Paris: Seuil, 1997.

Fassin, Eric. "Dans des genres différents: le féminisme au miroir transatlantique." *Esprit* 196 (1993).

———. "PaCS Socialiste: la gauche et le 'juste milieu.'" *Le Banquet: dossier Mariage, union et filiation* 12–13 (1998).

———. "The Purloined Gender: American Feminism in a French Mirror." *French Historical Studies* 22.1 (1999).

———. "'L'intellectuel spécifique' et le PaCS: politique des savoirs; Savoir c'est pouvoir: expertise et politique." *Mouvements* 7 (2000).

———. "L'avortement sous expertise (entre la France et les Etats-Unis)." *Avortement, droit de choisir et santé.* Paris: ProChoix éditions, 2001.

———. "Same Sex, Different Politics: 'Gay Marriage' Debates in France and the United States." *Public Culture* 13.2 (2001).

Fauré, Christine. *La démocratie sans les femmes: essai sur le libéralisme en France.* Paris: PUF, 1985. Translated as: *Democracy without Women: Feminism and the Rise of Liberal Individualism in France.* Trans. Claudia Gorbman and John Berks. Bloomington: Indiana University Press, 1991.

———, ed. *Le mouvement des femmes.* Paris: PUF, 1996.

———, ed. *Encyclopédie politique et historique des femmes: Europe, Amérique du Nord.* Paris: PUF, 1997. Translated as: *Political and Historical Encyclopedia of Women.* Chicago: Fitzroy Dearbon Publishers, 2002.

Fave-Bonnet, M. F. "Les femmes universitaires en France: une féminisation et des carrières différenciées." *Les cahiers du Mage* 1 (1996).

Feldman, Jacqueline. "The Exercise of Knowledge, the Difference of the Sexes; L'exercice du savoir et la différence des sexes." *Année sociologique* 42 (1992).

Femmes en migrations. Cahiers des Etudes féministes 8/9 (2000). Paris: CEDREF.

Femmes en politique. Spec. edition of *Pouvoirs* 82 (September 1997).

Ferrand, Michèle, Françoise Imbert, and Catherine Marry. "Femmes et science: une équation improbable? L'exemple des normaliennes scientifiques et des polytechniciennes." *Formation et emploi* 55 (1996).

Ferrand, Michèle, and Maryse Jaspard. *L'interruption volontaire de grossesse.* Que sais-je? Paris: PUF, 1987.

Flitterman-Lewis, Sandy. *To Desire Differently: Feminism and the French Cinema.* New York: Columbia University Press, 1996.

Folbre, Nancy. *De la différence des sexes en économie politique.* Trans. Edith Ochs and Larry Cohen. Paris: des femmes, 1997.

Forté, Michèle, et al. "De la division sexuée au partage du travail?" *Travail et emploi* 74 (1998).

Fortino, Sabine. "Le 'plaisir,' au coeur des pratiques et stratégies professionnelles féminines?" *Cahiers du GEDISST* 14 (1995).

Fougeyrollas-Schwebel, Dominique. "De la réclusion au cloisonnement: travail domestique et salariat." *Le partage du travail: bilan et perspectives.* Ed. Hervé Defalvard and Véronique Guienne. Paris: Desclée de Brouwer, 1998.

Fougeyrollas-Schwebel, Dominique, Annick Houel, and Maryse Jaspard. "Approche quantitative des violences envers les femmes au travail, quelles analyses privilégier." *Travailler* 4 (2000).

Fougeyrollas-Schwebel, Dominique, and Maryse Jaspard. "Critique féministe des statistiques: jalons pour une confrontation européenne." *Cahiers du GRIF* 45 (1990).

Fouque, Antoinette, ed. *Alliance des femmes/Women's Alliance: Journée internationale des femmes, 8 mars 1990.* Paris: Des femmes, 1992.

———. *Women in Movements: Yesterday, Today, Tomorrow and other Writings.* Trans. Anne Berger, Arthur Denner, and Nina McPherson. Paris: des femmes, 1992.

———. *Il y a deux sexes: essais de féminologie, 1989–1995.* Paris: Gallimard, 1995.

———. *Women: the Pioneer Front of Democracy.* Paris: des femmes, 1995.

Fouque, Antoinette, et al. *Women and Human Rights.* Rio de Janeiro, Brazil: IDAC Institute of Cultural Action, 1993.

Fouque, Antoinette, and Alliance des femmes pour la démocratisation. *Etats généraux des femmes: 8 mars 1989: actes.* Paris: des femmes, 1990.

Fouquet, Annie, and Claude Rack. "Les femmes et les politiques d'emploi." *Travail, Genre et Sociétés* 2 (1999).

Fourest, Caroline, and Fiametta Venner. *Les anti-PaCS ou la dernière croisade homophobe.* Paris: Pro-Choix, 1999.

Fraisse, Geneviève. *Muse de la raison: la démocratie exclusive et la différence des sexes.* Aix-en-Provence: Alinéa, 1989. Reedited with a postface, Collection Folio. Paris: Gallimard, 1995. Translated as: *Reason's Muse: Sexual Difference and the Birth of Democracy.* Trans. Jane Marie Todd. Chicago: University of Chicago Press, 1994.

———. *L'exercice du savoir et la différence des sexes.* Paris: L'Harmattan, 1991.

———. *La raison des femmes.* Paris: Plon, 1992.

———. "Sur l'incompatibilité supposée de l'amour et du féminisme." *Esprit* 5 (1993).

———. "Quand gouverner n'est pas représenter." *Esprit* 3–4 (1994).

———. *La différence des sexes.* Paris: PUF, 1996.

———. *Les femmes et leur histoire.* Paris: Gallimard, 1998.

———. "Des conditions de l'égalité économique." *Travail, genre et sociétés* 1 (1999).

———. *La controverse des sexes.* Paris: PUF, 2001.

———. *Les deux gouvernements: la famille et la Cité.* Paris: Gallimard, 2001.

France, Amérique: regards croisés sur le féminisme. Spec. issue of *Nouvelles questions féministes* 17.1 (1996).

Fraser, Nancy, and Sandra Lee Bartky, eds. *French Feminist Philosophy.* Spec. issue of *Hypatia* 3.3 (1989).

———, eds. *Revaluing French Feminism: Critical Essays on Difference, Agency, and Culture.* Bloomington: Indiana University Press, 1992.

Freedman, Jane, and Carrie Tarr, eds. *Women, Immigration and Identities in France.* New York: Berg, 2000.

Frischer, Dominique. *La revanche des misogynes: où en sont les femmes après trente ans de féminisme?* Paris: Albin Michel, 1997.

———. *A quoi rêvent les jeunes filles?* Paris: B. Grasset, 1999.

Frisque, Cégolène. *L'objet femme/Ministère de l'emploi et de la solidarité.* Paris: La Documentation française, 1997.

Gadrey, Nicole. *Hommes et femmes au travail: inégalités, différences, identités.* Paris: L'Harmattan, 1992.

———. *Travail et genre: approches croisées.* Paris: L'Harmattan, 2001.

Galceran, Sébastien. "Du CUS au PaCS: le débat n'a pas eu lieu." *Esprit* 10 (1998).

Gallop, Jane. *Around 1981: Academic Feminist Literary Theory.* New York: Routledge, 1992.

Galster, Ingrid, ed. *Cinquante ans après* Le deuxième sexe: *Beauvoir en débats.* Spec. issue of *Lendemains* 24 (1999).

———. "Fifty years after Simone de Beauvoir's *The Second Sex,* What is the Situation of French Feminism?" *The European Journal of Women's Sudies* 8.2 (2001).

Gaspard, Françoise. "De la parité: genèse d'un concept, naissance d'un mouvement." *Nouvelles questions féministes* 15.4 (1994).

———. "La fratriarcat: une spécificité française." *Après-demain* 80 (1996).

————. *La question de l'égalité des chances hommes-femmes dans le contexte de l'Union européenne.* Montréal: Chaire Jean Monnet, Université de Montréal, 1996.

Gaspard, Françoise, and Ana Coucello, eds. *Les femmes dans la prise de décision en France et en Europe.* Paris: L'Harmattan, 1997.

Gaspard, Françoise, and Jennifer Curtiss Gage. "Parity: Why Not?" *Differences* 9.2 (Summer 1997): 93–104.

Gaspard, Françoise, and Farhad Khosrokhavar. *Le foulard et la République.* Paris: La Découverte, 1995.

Gaspard, Françoise, Michèle Riot-Sarcey, and Françoise Duroux. "A propos de la parité." *Futur antérieur* 2.28 (1995).

Gaspard, Françoise, Claude Servan-Schreiber, and Anne Le Gall. *Au pouvoir, citoyennes!: Liberté, Egalité, Parité.* Paris: Seuil, 1994.

Gauléjac, Vincent de, and Nicole Aubert. *Femmes au singulier ou la parentalité solitaire.* Paris: Klincksieck, 1990.

Gautier, Arlette, and Jacqueline Heinen, eds. *Le sexe des politiques sociales.* Paris: Côté-femmes, 1993.

Gautier, Arlette, and Ilana Löwy, eds. *L'invention du naturel: les sciences et la fabrication du féminin et du masculin.* Paris: Editions des Archives contemporaines, 2000.

Gauvin, Annie, and Rachel Silvera. "Le temps des femmes: anciennes et nouvelles flexibilités." *L'économie, une science pour l'homme et la société:mélanges en l'honneur d'Henri Bartoli.* Ed. Michon François. Paris: Publications de la Sorbonne, 1998.

Génisson, Catherine. *Davantage de mixité professionnelle pour plus d'égalité entre hommes et femmes:* rapport au Premier Ministre. Paris: La Documentation française 1999.

Gillain, Anne. "l'imaginaire féminin au cinéma." *The French Review* 70 (1996).

Giroud, Françoise. *Les Françaises, de la Gauloise à la pilule.* Paris: Fayard, 1999.

Giroud, Françoise, and Bernard-Henri Lévy. *Les hommes et les femmes.* Paris: Olivier Orban, 1993.

Gisserot, Hélène. *Du côté des femmes: conférences, institutions, recherches.* Revue française des affaires sociales—Hors série 49e année. Paris: Ministère de la santé publique et de l'assurance maladie, Ministère de l'intégration et de la lutte contre l'exclusion, 1995.

Glover, J. "La faible représentation des femmes dans les sciences: les explications féministes." *Les cahiers du Mage* 1 (1997).

Godineau, Dominique. *Citoyennes tricoteuses.* Paris: Alinéa, 1988.

Goldman, Annie. *Les combats des femmes.* Paris: Castermann-Guinti, 1996.

Goldsworthy, Joanna, ed. *Reflecting on Menopause.* New York: Columbia University Press, 1994.

Grandin, Claude, Margaret Maruani, and Hélène Yvonne Meynaud, eds. *L' inégalité professionnelle dans les entreprises publiques à statut réglementaire.* Paris: Groupement d'intérêt public, Mutations industrielles, 1989.

Greer, Germaine. *The Change: Women, Aging and Menopause.* New York: Knopf, 1992.

Gregory, Abigail, and Jan Windebank, eds. *Women's Work in Britain and France: Practise, Theory and Policy.* New York: St. Martin's Press, 2000.

Gresh, Alain. "Représentant(e)s du peuple." *Manière de voir* 44 (1999).

Grosz, Elizabeth. "Philosophy, Subjectivity and the Body: Kristeva and Irigaray." *Feminist Challenges.* Ed. Carol Pateman and Elizabeth Grosz. Boston: Northeastern University Press, 1986.

————. *Sexual Subversions: Three French Feminists.* Sydney: Allen and Unwin, 1989.

Grosz, Elizabeth, and Naomi Schor. "This Essentialism which Is Not One: Coming to Grip with Irigaray." *Differences* 1.2 (1989).

Groult, Benoîte. *Pauline Roland, ou, Comment la liberté vint aux femmes.* Paris: Robert Laffont, 1991.

————. *Cette mâle assurance.* Paris: Albin Michel, 1993.

————. *Ainsi soit-elle; précédé de Ainsi soient-elles au XXIe siècle.* Paris: Grasset, 2000.

Groupe d'Etudes Féministes de l'Université Paris VII, ed. *Crises de la société: Féminisme et changement.* Paris: Editions Tierce, 1991.

Gueraiche, William. *Les Femmes et la République.* Paris: L'Atelier, 1999.

Guichard, Jean-Paul. "La mariée mise à nu par. . . ." (Women's bodies, Women's Gazes in Turn-of-the-Century Literature). Sites 6.1 (spring 2002).

Guigou, Elisabeth. *Etre femme en politique*. Paris: Plon, 1997.

———. *Une femme au coeur de l'Etat*. Entretiens avec Pierre Favier et Michel Martin-Roland. Paris: Fayard, 2000.

Guillaumin, Colette. *Sexe, race et pratique du pouvoir: l'idée de nature*. Paris: Côté-femmes, 1992.

Haase-Dubosc, Danielle. "Sexual Difference and Politics in France Today." *Feminist Studies* 25.1 (1999).

Habib, Claude. "Sur la prostitution." *Esprit* 12 (1993).

———. *Pensées sur la prostitution*. Paris: Belin, 1994.

Habib, Claude, and Irène Théry. "Conversation sur le féminisme." *Esprit* 5 (2000).

Halimi, Gisèle. *La cause des femmes; précédé de Le temps des malentendus*. Paris: Gallimard, 1992.

———. *Femmes: moitié de la terre, moitié du pouvoir: plaidoyer pour une démocratie paritaire*. Paris: Gallimard, 1994.

———. *Droits des hommes et droits des femmes: une autre démocratie*. Saint-Laurent, Québec: Fides, 1995.

———. "Où en est le mouvement des femmes?" *Krisis* 17 (1995).

———. *Rapport de la Commission pour la parité entre les femmes et les hommes dans la vie politique*. Paris: Multigraphié, 1996.

———. *La nouvelle cause des femmes*. Paris: Seuil, 1997.

———. *La parité dans la vie politique: rapport de la commission pour la parité entre les femmes et les hommes dans la vie politique*. Paris: La Documentation française, 1999.

———. "Parité, la nouvelle cause des femmes: un entretien avec Gisèle Halimi, propos recueillis par Jocelyne Praud." *Contemporary French Civilization* 24.2 (2001).

Hantrais, Linda. *Gendered Policies in Europe: Reconciling Employment and Family Life*. New York: St. Martin's Press, 2000.

Hargreaves, Alec G. *Voices from the North African Immigrant Community in France; Immigration and Identity in Beur Fiction*. Oxford: Berg, 1991.

Heilbrun, Carolyn. *The Last Gift of Time: Life Beyond Sixty*. New York: The Dial Press, 1997.

Heinen, Jacqueline, and Danièle Kergoat. *Un continent noir: le travail féminin*. Spec. Issue of *Cahiers du genre* 26 (1999).

Heinen, Jacqueline, and Josette Trat, eds. *Hommes et femmes dans le mouvement social*. Spec. issue of *Cahiers du GEDISST* 18 (1997).

Helft-Malz, Véronique, and Paule-Henriette Lévy. *Encyclopédie des femmes politiques sous la Ve République*. Paris: P. Banon, 1997.

———. *A part égale: les femmes dans la société française*. Paris: P. Banon, 1997.

———. *Les femmes et la vie politique française*. Que sais-je? Paris: PUF, 2000.

Henry, Natacha. "Gender Parity in French Politics." *Political Quarterly* 66.3 (1995).

Héritier, Françoise. *Les deux soeurs et leur mère: anthropologie de l'inceste*. Paris: Odile Jacob, 1994.

———. *Masculin/féminin: la pensée de la différence*. Paris: Odile Jacob, 1996.

Hirata, Helena Sumiko, Françoise Laborie, and Hélène Le Douaré, eds. *Dictionnaire critique du féminisme*. Paris: PUF, 2000.

Hirata, Helena Sumiko, and Danièle Sénotier, eds. *Femmes et partage du travail*. Paris: Syros, 1996.

Hitchcott, Nicki. *Women Writers in Francophone Africa*. Oxford: Berg, 2000.

———. "Gender and Francophone Writing." *Nottingham French Studies* 40.1 (2001).

Holland, Nancy, ed. *Feminism and Interpretations of Derrida*. University Park: Pennsylvania State University, 1995.

Holmlund, Christine. "I Love Luce: The Lesbian Mimesis and Masquerade in Irigaray, Freud and Mainstream Film." *New Formations* 9 (1989).

Homoparentalité: état des lieux. Paris: ESF, 2000.

Homosexualité et lesbianisme: mythes, mémoires, historiographies. Actes du colloque international, Sorbonne, Décembre 1989. 3 vols. Lille: Cahiers GKC, 1991.

Hook-Demarle, Marie-Claire, ed. *Femmes, Nations, Europe*. Paris: Publications de l'Université de Paris VII, 1995.

Houdebine-Gravaud, Anne-Marie, ed. *La féminisation des noms de métiers: en français et dans d'autres langues*. Paris: L'Harmattan, 1998.

———. "Femmes/langue/féminisation: une expérience de politique linguistique en France." *Nouvelles questions féministes* 20.1 (1999).

Huffer, Lynne, ed. *Another Look, Another Woman: Retranslations of French Feminism*. Spec. issue of *Yale French Studies* 87 (1995).

Hufton, Olwen. "Femmes/Hommes: une question subversive." *Passés recomposés: champs et chantiers de l'histoire*. Eds. Jean Butier and Dominique Julie. Paris: Autrement, 1995.

Hughes, Alex, and James Williams. *Gender and French Cinema*. Oxford: Berg, 2001.

Hurtig, Marie-Claude, Michèle Kail, and Hélène Rouch, eds. *Sexe et genre: de la hiérarchie entre les sexes*. Paris: CNRS, 1991.

Hurtig, Marie-Claude, and Marie-France Pichevin, eds. *La différence des sexes: questions de psychologie*. Paris: Tierce, 1986.

Ince, Kate. *Orlan: Millennial Female*. Oxford: Berg, 2000.

Ireland, Susan, and Patrice Proulx, eds. *Immigrant Narratives in Contemporary France*. Westport, CT: Greenwood Press, 2001.

Irigaray, Luce. *Et l'une ne bouge pas sans l'autre*. Paris: Editions de Minuit, 1987.

———. *Le sexe linguistique*. Paris: Larousse, 1987.

———. *Sexes et parentés*. Paris: Editions de Minuit, 1987. Translated as: *Sexes and Genealogies*. Trans. Gillian Gill. New York: Columbia University Press, 1993.

———. *Le temps de la différence: pour une révolution pacifique*. Paris: Librairie générale française, 1989. Translated as: *Thinking the Difference: For a Peaceful Revolution*. Trans. Karin Montin. New York: Routledge, 1994.

———, ed. *Sexes et genres à travers les langues: éléments de communication sexuée: français, anglais, italien*. Paris: Grasset, 1990.

———. *Philosophy in the Feminine*. London: Routledge, 1991.

———. *Je, tu, nous: pour une culture de la différence*. Paris: Librairie générale française, 1992. Translated as: *Je, tu, nous: Toward a Culture of Difference*. Trans. Alison Martin. New York: Routledge, 1993.

———. *Genres culturels et interculturels*. Paris: Larousse, 1993.

———, ed. *Le souffle des femmes: Luce Irigaray présente des credos au féminin*. Paris: ACGF, 1996.

———. *Democracy Begins between Two*. Trans. Anderson Kirsteen. New York: Routledge, 2001.

Irigaray, Luce, and Margaret Whitford, eds. *The Irigaray Reader*. Cambridge, MA: Basil Blackwell, 1991.

Jacoby, Eleanor. "Le sexe, catégorie sociale, Masculin-Féminin." *Actes de la recherche en sciences sociales* 84 (1990).

Jardine, Alice. *Gynesis: Configurations of Woman and Modernity*. Ithaca, NY: Cornell University Press, 1985. Translated as: *Gynésis: configurations de la femme et de la modernité*. Trans. Patricia Baudoin. Paris: PUF, 1991.

Jardine, Alice, and Anne Menke. *Shifting Scenes: Interviews on Women, Writing, and Politics in Post-68 France*. New York: Columbia University Press, 1991.

Jaspard, Maryse. *La sexualité en France*. Paris: La Découverte, 1997.

Jedryka, Joëlle. *Des femmes pour les communes*. Paris: Editions de l'Aube, 2000.

Jenny, Jacques. "Rapports sociaux de sexe et autres rapports de domination sociale: pour une intégration des rapports sociaux fondamentaux." Spec: issue of *Cahiers du GEDISST* 13 (1995).

Jenson, Jane. "Representation of Difference: The Varieties of French Feminism." *New Left Review* 180 (1990): 127–60.

———. "Ce n'est pas par hasard: The Varieties of French Feminism." James F. Hollifield and George Ross, eds. *Searching for the New France*. London: Routledge, 1991.

Jenson, Jane, and Mariette Sineau. "The Same or Different? An Unending Dilemma for French Women." *Women and Politics Worldwide.* Ed. Barbara Nelson and Najma Chowdhury. New Haven, CT: Yale University Press, 1994.

———. *Mitterrand et les Françaises: un rendez-vous manqué.* Paris: Presses de Sciences Po, 1995.

———, eds. *Qui doit garder le jeune enfant?: modes d'accueil et travail des mères dans l'Europe en crise.* Paris: LGDJ, 1998.

Kaufmann, Jean-Claude. *Corps de femmes, regards d'hommes: sociologie des seins nus.* Paris: Nathan, 1995.

———. *La femme seule et le Prince charmant: enquête sur la vie en solo.* Paris: Pocket, 2001.

Képès, Suzanne, and Michèle Thieret. *Femmes à 50 ans.* Paris: Seuil, 1986.

Kergoat, Danièle. "Les absentes de l'histoire." *Autrement* 126 (1992).

———. "A propos des rapports sociaux de sexe." *Revue M* 53–54 (1992).

———. "La division du travail entre les sexes." *Le monde du travail.* Ed. Jacques Kergoat, Henri Jacot, and Danièle Linhart. Paris: La Découverte/Syros, 1998.

Khémis, Stéphane. "Les femmes au pouvoir." *L'Histoire* 160 (1992)

Kim, Maggie, Susan St. Ville, and Susan Simonaitis, eds. *Transfigurations: Theology and the French Feminists.* Minneapolis: Fortress, 1993.

Klein, Renate, Janice Raymond, and Lynette Dumble. *RU486: Misconceptions, Myths and Morals.* North Melbourne: Spinifex Press, 1991.

Knibiehler, Yvonne. *Les pères aussi ont une histoire.* Paris: Hachette, 1987.

———, et al. *De la pucelle à la minette: les jeunes filles, de l'âge classique à nos jours.* Paris: Messidor, 1989.

———. *La révolution maternelle depuis 1945.* Paris: Perrin, 1997.

———. *Histoire des mères et de la maternité en Occident.* Que sais-je?. Paris: PUF, 2000.

Kofman, Sarah. *L'énigme de la femme: la femme dans les textes de Freud.* Paris: Galilée, 1994.

———. *L'imposture de la beauté: et autres textes.* Paris: Galilée, 1995.

Krakovitch, Odile, and Geneviève Sellier. *L'exclusion des femmes: masculinité et politique dans la culture au XXe siècle.* Brussels: Complexe, 2000.

Krakovitch, Odile, Geneviève Sellier, and Eliane Viennot, eds. *Pouvoir des femmes: mythes et fantasmes.* Paris: L'Harmattan, 2001.

Kramer, Jane. "Liberty, Equality, Sorority: French Women Demand Equal Access to Elected Office." *The New Yorker* 76.13 (2000).

Kriegel, Blandine, *Philosophie de la République.* Paris: Plon, 1998.

Kristeva, Julia. *Le génie féminin: la vie, la folie, les mots. Tome I: Hannah Arendt.* Paris: Fayard, 1999. Translated as: *Hannah Arendt.* Trans. Ross Guberman. New York: Columbia University Press, 2001.

———. *Le génie féminin: la vie, la folie, les mots. Tome II: Melanie Klein.* Paris: Fayard, 2000. Translated as: *Melanie Klein.* Trans. Ross Guberman. New York: Columbia University Press, 2001.

———. *Le génie féminin: la vie, la folie, les mots. Tome III: Colette.* Paris: Fayard, 2002.

Kristeva, Julia, and Louise Burchill. "De l'étrangeté du phallus ou le féminin entre illusion et désillusion/Experiencing the Phallus as Extraneous, or Women's Twofold Oedipus Complex." *Parallax* 4.3 (1998).

Kristeva, Julia, Alice Jardine, and Harry Blake. "Women's Time." *Feminisms: An Anthology of Literary Theory and Criticism.* Ed. Robyn Warhol. New Brunswick, NJ: Rutgers University Press, 1997.

Kruks, Sonia. "Gender and Subjectivity: Simone de Beauvoir and Contemporary Feminism." *Signs* 18.1 (1992).

Laborie, Françoise. *Divergences entre féministes françaises sur l'analyse des nouvelles technologies de reproduction humaine (NTR).* Klagenfurt: Institut für Interdisziplinäre Forschung und Fortbildung der Universität Innsbruck, 1994.

Laborie, Françoise, et al. *Evolution des droits des femmes: analyses des discours et pratiques du mouvement associatif féminin.* Paris: GEDISST-CNRS, 1994.

Laguiller, Arlette. *C'est toute ma vie: une femme dans le camp des travailleurs.* Paris: Plon, 1996.

Lamont, Michèle, and Marsha Witten. "Surveying the Continental Drift." *French Politics and Society* 6 (July 1988).

Lanzmann, Claude, ed. *Questions actuelles au féminisme.* Spec. issue of *Les Temps modernes* 594 (1997).

———. *"Différence des sexes et" "ordre symbolique."* Spec. issue of *Les Temps modernes* 609 (2000).

La parité "contre." Spec. edition of *Nouvelles questions féministes* (May 1995).

La parité "pour." Spec. edition of *Nouvelles questions féministes* (November 1994).

Lardoux, Xavier. "Le cinéma français au féminin pluriel." *Le Débat* 116 (2001).

Laronde, Michel. *Autour du roman Beur.* Paris: L'Harmattan, 1993.

Latour, Patricia, Monique Houssin, and Madia Tovar. *Femmes et citoyennes: du droit de vote à l'exercice du pouvoir.* Paris: L'Atelier, 1995.

Laufer, Jacqueline. *L'entreprise et l'égalité des chances: enjeux et démarches.* Paris: La Documentation française, 1992.

———. "Equal Opportunities between Men and Women: The Case of France." *Feminist Economics* 4.1 (1998).

Laufer, Jacqueline, and Annie Fouquet. "Les femmes dans l'entreprise: le plafond de verre est toujours là." *Revue française de gestion* 119 (1998).

Laufer, Jacqueline, Catherine Marry, and Margaret Maruani, eds. *Masculin/féminin: questions pour les sciences de l'homme.* Paris: PUF, 2001.

Le Bras-Chopard, Armelle, and Janine Mossuz-Lavau. *Les femmes et la politique.* Paris: L'Harmattan, 1997.

Le Doeuff, Michèle. *L'étude et le rouet.* Paris: Seuil, 1989.

———. "Women, Reason, etc." *Differences* 2.3 (1990).

———. *Hipparchia's Choice: An Essay Concerning Women, Philosophy, etc.* Trans. Trista Selous. Oxford, UK: Blackwell, 1991.

———. "Gens de science: essai sur le déni de mixité." *Nouvelles questions féministes* 13.1 (1992).

———. "Simone de Beauvoir: les ambiguités d'un ralliement." *Le Magazine Littéraire* 320 (1994).

———. "Simone de Beauvoir: Falling into (Ambiguous) Line." *Feminist Interpretations of Simone de Beauvoir.* Ed. Margaret Simons. University Park: Pennsylvania State University Press, 1995.

———. *Le sexe du savoir.* Paris: Aubier, 1998.

———. "Feminism Is Back in France—Or Is It?" *Hypatia* 15.4 (2000).

Le Gall, Didier, and Yamina Bettahar, eds. *La pluriparentalité.* Paris: PUF, 2001.

Le Gall, Didier, and Claude Martin, eds. *Familles et politiques sociales: dix questions sur le lien familial contemporain.* Paris: L'Harmattan, 1996.

Lefaucheur, Nadine. "Mères seules, travail et pauvreté." *Panoramiques* 40 (1999).

Legardinier, Claudine. *La prostitution.* Toulouse: Milan, 1997.

Lejeune, Paule. *Le cinéma des femmes: 105 femmes cinéastes d'expression française (France, Belgique, Suisse) 1895–1987.* Paris: Editions Atlas: Lherminier, 1987.

Lelièvre, Françoise, and Claude Lelièvre. *Histoire de la scolarisation des filles.* Paris: Nathan, 1991.

———. *L'histoire des femmes publiques contée aux enfants.* Paris: PUF, 2001.

Lemel, Yannick. "Les activités domestiques: qui en fait le plus?" *Année sociologique* 43 (1993).

Lemoine-Darthois, Régine, and Elisabeth Weissman. *Elles ont cru qu'elles ne vieilliraient jamais.* Paris: Albin Michel, 2000.

L'emploi des femmes. Paris: La Documentation française, 1993.

Leonard, Diana, and Lisa Adkins, eds. and trans. *Sex in Question: French Materialist Feminism.* London: Taylor & Francis, 1996.

Léridon, Henri, ed. *La seconde révolution contraceptive: la régulation des naissances en France de 1950 à 1985.* Paris: PUF: Institut national d'études démographiques, 1987.

Leroy-Forgeot, Flora. *Les enfants du PaCS: réalités de l'homoparentalité.* Paris: L'atelier de l'archer, 1999.

Les femmes an 2000: quel projet pour les femmes dans la société du troisième millénaire? Paris: La Documentation française, 1988.

Lesselier, Claudie, and Fiametta Venner, eds. *L'extrême-droite et les femmes.* Lyon: Golias, 1997.

Lesterpt, Catherine, and Gatienne Doat, eds. *L'ovaire dose?: les nouvelles méthodes de procréation. Actes du colloque organisé les 3 et 4 décembre 1988 par le Mouvement français pour le planning familial.* Paris: Syros-Alternatives, 1989.

Lhomond, Brigitte. "D'un antinaturalisme à un a-sociologisme: comment penser les catégories de sexe et la sexualité?" *GRAAT* 17 (1997).

Lienemann, Marie-Noëlle. *Madame le Maire.* Paris: Ramsay, 1997.

Lionnet, Françoise. *Autobiographical Voices: Race, Gender, Self-Portraiture.* Ithaca, NY: Cornell University Press, 1989.

———. "Identity, Sexuality, and Criminality: 'Universal Rights' and the Debate around the Practice of Female Excision in France." *Contemporary French Civilization* 16.2 (1992).

———. *Postcolonial Representations: Women, Literature, Identity.* Ithaca, NY: Cornell University Press, 1995.

Lipovetsky, Gilles. *La troisième femme: permanence et révolution du féminin.* Paris: Gallimard, 1997.

Lloyd, Caryl. "The Politics of Difference: French Feminism in the Nineties." *Contemporary French Civilization* 16.2 (1992).

Loiseau, Dominique. *Femmes et militantismes.* Paris: L'Harmattan, 1996.

Louis, Marie-Victoire, ed. *Actualité de la parité.* Spec. issue of *Projets féministes* 4–5 (1996).

Lovecy, Jill. "'Citoyennes à part entière'? The Constitutionalization of Gendered Citizenship in France and the Parity Reforms of 1999–2000." *Government and Opposition* 35.4 (2000).

Mahuzier, Brigitte, et al., eds. *Same Sex/Different Text? Gay and Lesbian Writing in French.* Spec. issue of *Yale French Studies* 90 (1996).

Majnoni d'Intignano, Béatrice. *Femmes, si vous saviez.* Paris: Fallois, 1996.

———. *Egalité entre femmes et hommes: aspects économiques.* Paris: La Documentation française, 1999.

———. *Le sexe médiateur.* Paris: Plon, 2000.

Makward, Christiane, and Madeleine Cottenet-Hage. *Dictionnaire littéraire des femmes de langue française: de Marie de France à Marie NDiaye.* Paris: Agence de la francophonie, ACCT, 1996.

Malaurie, Philippe. "Un statut légal du concubinage?: CUC, PIC, PaCS et autres avatars du mariage." *Commentaire* 21.82 (1998).

Malet, Emile, ed. *Les femmes aiment-elles le pouvoir?* Spec. issue of *Passages* 40 (1991).

Manassien, Michel de, ed. *De l'égalité des sexes.* Paris: CNDP Documents, actes et rapports pour l'éducation, 1995.

Mangin, Catherine, and Elizabeth Martichoux. *Ces femmes qui nous gouvernent.* Paris: Albin Michel, 1991.

Marks, Elaine, and Isabelle de Courtivron. *New French Feminisms: An Anthology.* Amherst: University of Massachusetts Press, 1980.

Martel, Frédéric. *Le rose et le noir: les homosexuels en France depuis 1968.* Paris: Seuil, 1996.

Martin, Emily. "Politique familiale et travail des femmes mariées en France." *Population* 6 (1998).

Martin, Jacqueline, ed. *La parité: enjeux et mise en oeuvre.* Toulouse: Presses Universitaires du Mirail, 1998.

Maruani, Margaret. *Mais qui a peur du travail des femmes?.* Paris: Syros, 1985.

———, ed. *Femmes, modes d'emploi.* Spec. issue of *Nouvelles questions féministes* 11.14–15 (1986).

———, ed. *La place des femmes sur le marché du travail. 1983–1990: tendances et évolutions dans les douze pays de la Communauté européenne.* Brussels: Communautés européennes, 1992.

———. "L'emploi féminin à l'ombre du chômage." *Actes de la recherche en sciences sociales* 115 (1996).

———, ed. *Les nouvelles frontières de l'inégalité: hommes et femmes sur le marché du travail.* Paris: La Découverte: MAGE, 1998.

———. *Histoire du travail féminin.* Paris: La Découverte, 2000.

———. *Histoires de pionnières.* Paris: L'Harmattan, 2000.

———. *Travail et emploi des femmes.* Paris: La Découverte, 2000.

Maruani, Margaret, and Chantal Nicole-Drancourt. *Au labeur des dames: métiers masculins, emplois féminins.* Paris: Syros-Alternatives, 1989.

Maruani, Margaret, and Emmanuèle Reynaud. *Sociologie de l'emploi.* Paris: La Découverte, 1993.

Masculin/féminin. Spec. issue of *Actes de la recherche en sciences sociales* 83–84 (1990).

Mathieu, Nicole-Claude, ed. *L'arraisonnement des femmes: essais en anthropologie des sexes.* Paris: EHESS, 1985.

———. "Différenciation des sexes; études féministes et anthropologie." *Dictionnaire de l'ethnologie et de l'anthropologie.* Ed. Pierre Bonte and Michel Izard. Paris: PUF, 1991.

———. *L'anatomie politique: catégorisations et idéologies du sexe.* Paris: Côté-femmes, 1991.

———. *Anthropologie des sexes: dossier.* Spec. issue of *Gradhiva* 23 (1998).

Mathy, Jean-Philippe. *Extrême-Occident: French Intellectuals and America.* Chicago: University of Chicago Press, 1993.

———. "The Resistance to French Theory in the United States: A Cross-Cultural Inquiry." *French Historical Studies* 19 (1995).

———. *French Resistance: The French-American Culture Wars.* Minneapolis: University of Minnesota Press, 2000.

Maure, Huguette. *La cinquantaine au féminin.* Paris: Calmann-Lévy, 1988.

Mazur, Amy. "Strong State and Symbolic Reform: The Ministère des Droits de la Femme in France." *Comparative State Feminism.* Ed. Dorothy McBride Stetson and Amy Mazur. London: Sage Publications, 1995.

Mécary, Caroline, and Flora Leroy-Forgeot. *Le PaCS.* Que sais-je? Paris: PUF, 2000.

Méda, Dominique. "Les femmes peuvent-elles changer la place du travail dans la vie?" *Droit social* 5 (2000).

———. *Le temps des femmes: pour un nouveau partage des rôles.* Paris: Flammarion, 2001.

Mehl, Dominique. *Naître? La controverse bioéthique.* Paris: Bayard Editions, 1999.

Membrado, Monique, and Annie Rieu, eds. *Sexes, espaces et corps: de la catégorisation du genre.* Toulouse: Editions Universitaires du Sud, 2000.

Merini, Rafika. *Two Major Francophone Women Writers, Assia Djébar and Leïla Sebbar: A Thematic Study of their Works.* New York: P. Lang, 1999.

Meulders-Klein, Marie-Thérèse, and Irène Théry, eds. *Les recompositions familiales aujourd'hui.* Paris: Nathan, 1993.

———, eds. *Quels repères pour les familles recomposées?: une approche pluridisciplinaire internationale. Actes du colloque international, Paris, Ministère de la Recherche, 2–3 décembre 1993.* Paris: LGDJ, 1995.

Michard-Marchal, Claire. "Humain/femelle: deux poids deux mesures dans la catégorisation de sexe en français." *Nouvelles questions féministes* 20.1 (1999).

Michaux, Agnès. *Dictionnaire misogyne.* Paris: J.-C. Lattès, 1993.

Michel, Andrée. *L'action positive pour les femmes, étude préliminaire.* Strasbourg: C.E., 1986.

———. *Non aux stéréotypes!: vaincre le sexisme dans les livres pour enfants et les manuels scolaires.* Paris: UNESCO, 1986.

———. *Citoyennes militairement incorrectes.* Paris: L'Harmattan, 1999.

———. *Le féminisme.* Que sais-je? Paris: PUF, 2001.

Mignard, Jean-Pierre, ed. *Famille, nouvelles unions, bonheur privé et cohésion sociale.* Spec. issue of *Témoin* 12 (1998).

Miller, Judith Graves. "Contemporary Women's Voices in French Theatre." *Modern Drama* 32 (1989).

Moatti-Gornet, Danièle. *Qu'est-ce qu'une femme?: traité d'ontologie.* Paris: L'Harmattan, 1999.

Moi, Toril. *Sexual/Textual Politics: Feminist Literary Theory.* London: Routledge, 1985.

———. *French Feminist Thought: A Reader.* Oxford: Blackwell, 1987.

———. *Feminist Theory and Simone de Beauvoir.* Cambridge, MA: Blackwell, 1990.

———. *Simone de Beauvoir: The Making of an Intellectual Woman.* Oxford, UK: Blackwell, 1994. Translated as: *Simone de Beauvoir: conflits d'une intellectuelle.* Trans. Guillemette Belleteste. Paris: Diderot éditeur, 1995.

———. *What Is a Woman?: And Other Essays.* Oxford: Oxford University Press, 1999.

Moi, Toril, and Janice Radway, eds. *Materialist feminism*. Spec. issue of *South Atlantic Quarterly* 93.4 (1994).

Mongin, Olivier, ed. *Masculin-féminin*. Spec. issue of *Esprit* 11 (1993).

———, ed. *L'un et l'autre sexe*. Spec. issue of *Esprit* 3–4 (2001).

Monnier, Viviane. "Violences conjugales, éléments statistiques." *Les cahiers de la Sécurité intérieure* 28 (1997).

Montreynaud, Florence. *Le XXe siècle des femmes*. Paris: Nathan, 2000.

———. *Bienvenue dans la meute: comment répondre à 100 objections adressées à ces féministes, femmes et hommes, solidaires de femmes victimes d'insultes sexistes*. Paris: La Découverte, 2001.

Morandeau-Ytak, Cathy. *Une femme, une femme: lesbiennes aujourd'hui*. Paris: Traffic, 1991.

Morganroth-Gulette, Margaret. *Declining to Decline: Cultural Combat and the Politics of the Midlife*. Charlottesville: University Press of Virginia, 1997.

Mosconi, Nicole. *La mixité dans l'enseignement secondaire, un faux-semblant?*. Paris: PUF, 1989.

———. *Femmes et savoir: la société, l'école et la division sexuelle des savoirs*. Paris: L'Harmattan, 1994.

———. "La mixité scolaire: une institution masculine." *Les cahiers du Mage* 1 (1995).

———, ed. *Egalité des sexes en éducation et formation*. Paris: PUF, 1998.

Moses, Claire Goldberg. "French Feminism's Fortune." *The Women's Review of Books* 5.1 (1987).

———. "Debating the Present/Writing the Past: 'Feminism' in French History and Historiography." *Radical History Review* 52 (winter 1992).

———. "La construction du 'French Feminism' dans le discours universitaire américain." *Nouvelles questions féministes* 17.1 (1996). Translated as: "Made in America: 'French Feminism' in Academia." *Feminist Studies* 24.2 (summer 1998).

Mossuz-Lavau, Janine. *Femmes d'Europe, miroir de l'évolution des droits des Européennes, 1977–1987.* Brussels: Communautés européennes, 1988.

———. *Femmes et hommes d'Europe aujourd'hui: les attitudes devant l'Europe et la politique*. Bruxelles: Communautés européennes, 1991.

———. *Les lois de l'amour: les politiques de la sexualité en France de 1950 à nos jours*. Paris: Payot, 1991.

———. *Women and Men of Europe Today: Attitudes towards Europe and Politics*. Brussels: Commission of the European Communities, 1991.

———. "Women and Politics in France." *French Politics and Society* 10.1 (1992).

———. "Le vote des femmes en France (1945–1993)." *Revue française de science politique* 43.4 (1993).

———. "Le vote des françaises dans les années 90." *French Politics and Society* 12.4 (1994).

———. "Les électrices françaises de 1945 à 1993." *Vingtième siècle* 42 (1994).

———. "Les Françaises aux urnes (1945–1994): bilan." *Modern & Contemporary France* 3.2 (1995).

———. "Les Françaises et la politique: de la citoyenneté à la parité." *Regards sur l'actualité* 236 (1997).

———. *Femmes/hommes: pour la parité*. Paris: Presses de Sciences Po, 1998.

Mossuz-Lavau, Janine, and Anne de Kervasdoué. *Les femmes ne sont pas des hommes comme les autres*. Paris: Odile Jacob, 1997.

Moutouh, Hugues. "Controverses sur le PaCS: l'esprit d'une loi." *Les Temps modernes* 603 (1999).

Mouvement français pour le planning familial. *Europe & elles: le droit de choisir*. Paris: MFPF, 1992.

Mozère, Liane. *Le printemps des crèches: histoire et analyse d'un mouvement*. Paris: L'Harmattan, 1992.

Nahoum-Grappe, Véronique. *Le féminin*. Paris: Hachette, 1996.

Nahoum-Grappe, Véronique, and Phelouzat-Perriquet Nicole, eds. *Beauté, laideur*. Paris: Seuil, 1995.

Naudier, Delphine. "Feminine Writing Subversive Writing?; écriture féminine écriture subversive?" *Liber* 33 (1997).

Nicole-Drancourt, Chantal. "Organisation du travail des femmes et flexibilité de l'emploi." *Sociologie du travail* 32.2 (1990).

Oliver, Kelly, ed. *French Feminism Reader*. Lanham, MD: Rowman & Littlefield Publishers, 2000.

Ollivier, Michèle, and Manon Tremblay. *Questionnements féministes et méthodologie de la recherche*. Paris: L'Harmattan, 2000.

Ozouf, Mona. *Les mots des femmes: essai sur la singularité française*. Paris: Fayard, 1995. New ed. Paris: Gallimard, 1999. Translated as: *Women's Words: Essay on French Singularity*. Trans. Jane Marie Todd. Chicago: University of Chicago Press, 1997.

Pallister, Janis. *French Speaking Women Film Directors: A Guide*. London: Associated University Press, 1997.

Pascal, Jean. *Les femmes députés de 1945 à 1988*. Paris: J. Pascal, 1990.

Perrot, Michelle, ed. *Métiers de femmes*. Paris: Editions Ouvrières, 1987.

———. "Qu'est-ce qu'un métier de femme?" *Le mouvement social: Métier de femmes* 140 (1987).

———. *Femmes publiques: réalisé à partir d'entretiens avec Jean Lebrun par Michelle Perrot*. Paris: Textuel, 1997.

———. *Les femmes ou les silences de l'histoire*. Paris: Flammarion, 1998.

———, ed. *An 2000: quel bilan pour les femmes?* Paris: La Documentation française, 2000.

———. *Le méccano familial: les nouveaux enjeux politiques de la vie privée*. Paris: La Découverte, 2000.

Perrot, Michelle, and Georges Duby, eds. *Power and Beauty: Images of Women in Art*. London: Tauris Parke Books, 1992.

Peyre, Evelyne, and Joëlle Wiels. "Le sexe biologique et sa relation au sexe social." *Les Temps modernes* 593 (1997).

Pheterson, Gail. "Group Identity and Social Relations: Divergent Theoretical Conceptions in the United States, the Netherlands, and France." *European Journal of Women's Studies* 1 (1994).

Philibert, Céline. "Memory Process and Feminine Desire in Claire Denis's *Chocolat* and Brigitte Rouan's *Outremer*." *Journal of Third World Studies* 13 (1996).

Piat, Yann. *Seule, tout en haut à droite*. Paris: Fixot, 1991.

Picq, Françoise. "Un féminisme hexagonal." *Raison présente* 100 (1991).

———. *Libération des femmes: les années-mouvement*. Paris: Seuil, 1993.

Planté, Christine. "Est-il néfaste pour qui veut lire de penser à son sexe? Notes sur une critique féministe." *Compar(a)ison* 1 (1993).

———, ed. *L'épistolaire, un genre féminin?* Paris: Honoré Champion, 1998.

Planté, Christine, Michèle Riot-Sarcey, and Eleni Varikas. "Le genre de l'histoire." *Cahiers du GRIF* 37–38 (1988).

Plantenga, Janneke, and Jill Rubery, eds. *Les femmes sur le marché du travail: rapport pour l'unité pour l'égalité des chances*, Commission européenne, 1997.

Plasman, Robert, ed. *Les femmes d'Europe sur le marché du travail*. Paris: L'Harmattan, 1994.

Pluchart, François. "Fire Sermons." Trans. Suzi Gablik. *Art and Artists* 1.5 (August 1966).

Poloni-Simard, Jacques, ed. *Femmes et histoire*. Spec. issue of *Annales: Histoire, Sciences Sociales* 4 (1993).

Ponchelet, Sophie, and Assia Benaïssa. *Née en France: histoire d'une jeune Beur*. Paris:Payot, 1990.

Powrie, Phil. *French Cinema in the 1980s: Nostalgia and the Crisis of Masculinity*. Oxford: Clarendon Press, 1997.

———. *French Cinema in the 1990s: Continuity and Difference: Essays*. Oxford: Oxford University Press, 1999.

Puaux, Françoise. "Le machisme à l'écran: entretiens avec Breillat, Cabrera, Dubroux, Ferran, Buet, Crévecoeur, Carré." *CinémAction* 99 (2001).

Rapports sociaux de sexe. Spec. issue of *La Griffe: revue libertaire* (1998).

Rausch, André. *Le premier sexe: mutations et crise de l'identité masculine*. Paris: Hachette, 2000.

Rémy, Dominique. "Le PaCS: qu'en est-il exactement?" *Lectures françaises* 500 (1998).

Rémy, Monique. *Chronique d'une passion: Le Mouvement de libération des femmes à Lyon*. Paris: L'Harmattan, 1989.

———. *De l'Utopie à l'intégration: Histoire des mouvements de femmes*. Paris: L'Harmattan, 1990.

Rétif, Françoise. *Simone de Beauvoir: l'autre en miroir*. Paris: L'Harmattan, 1998.

Riot-Sarcey, Michèle, ed. *Femmes, pouvoirs*. Paris: Kimé, 1993.

————, ed. *Femmes, pouvoirs: actes du colloque d'Albi, des 19 et 20 mars 1992, Centre culturel de l'Albigeois.* Paris: Editions Kimé, 1993.

————. *La démocratie à l'épreuve des femmes. Trois figures critiques du pouvoir, 1830–1848.* Paris: Albin Michel, 1994.

————, ed. *Démocratie et représentation.* Kimé, 1995.

Rochefort, Florence, and Mathilde Dubesset, eds. *Intellectuelles.* Spec. Issue of *Clio* 13 (2001).

Rodgers, Catherine. *Le "deuxième sexe" de Simone de Beauvoir: un héritage admiré et contesté.* Paris: L'Harmattan, 1998.

————. "Elle et elle: Antoinette Fouque et Simone de Beauvoir." *MLN* 115.4 (2000).

Rogerat, Chantal. "Femmes et syndicalistes: assimilation ou intégration? La dynamique du compromis." *La liberté du travail.* Paris: Syllepse, 1995.

————, ed. *Principes et enjeux de la parité.* Spec. issue of *Cahiers du GEDISST* 17 (1996).

Rogerat, Chantal, and Danièle Sénotier. *Le chômage en héritage: parole de femmes.* Vincennes: GREC, 1994.

Roland, René-Miguel. "Du mariage sans contrat au contrat sans mariage." *Petites affiches* 28 (1998).

Rollet, Brigitte, and Geneviève Sellier. "Cinéma et genre en France: état des lieux." *Clio* 10 (1999).

Roman, Joël. "Quotas, parité, mixité." *Esprit* 8–9 (1996).

Rosanvallon, Pierre, et al. "Parity and Universalism, I." *Différences* 9.2 (1997).

Rosello, Mireille. *Infiltrating Culture: Power and Identity in Contemporary Women's Writing.* Manchester, UK; New York: Manchester University Press; dist. St. Martin's Press, 1996.

————. *Postcolonial Hospitality. The Immigrant as Guest.* Palo Alto: Stanford University Press, 2001.

Roster, Danielle. *Les femmes et la création musicale: les compositrices européennes du Moyen Age au milieu du XXe siècle.* Paris: L'Harmattan, 1998.

Roucaute, Yves. *Discours sur les femmes qui en font un peu trop.* Paris: Plon, 1993.

Roudy, Yvette. *A cause d'elles.* Paris: Albin Michel, 1985.

————. *Mais de quoi ont-ils peur?: un vent de misogynie souffle sur la politique.* Paris: Albin Michel, 1995.

Roy, Carole. *Les lesbiennes et le féminisme.* Montréal: Saint-Martin, 1985.

Royal, Ségolène. *La vérité d'une femme.* Paris: Stock, 1996.

Rudelle, Olive. "Le vote des femmes et la fin de l'exception française." *Vingtième siècle* 42 (1994).

Sarazin, Michel. *Une femme, Simone Veil.* Paris: Robert Laffont, 1987.

Sarde, Michèle. *Regard sur les Françaises: les Françaises . . . trop aimées?* Paris: Seuil, 1985.

Sarkonak, Ralph, ed. *France/USA: The Culture Wars.* Spec. issue of *Yale French Studies* 100 (2001).

Schaeffer, Jacqueline. *Le refus du féminin: la Sphinge et son âme en peine.* Paris: PUF, 1997.

————. *Clés pour le féminin (femme, mère, amante et fille): débats de psychanalyse.* Paris: PUF, 1999.

Schemla, Elisabeth. *Edith Cresson: la femme piégée.* Paris: Flammarion, 1993.

Schor, Naomi. "French Feminism is a Universalism." *Bad Objects: Essays Popular and Unpopular.* Durham, NC: Duke University Press, 1995.

Scott, Joan. "L'ouvrière, mot impie, sordide." *Actes de la recherche en sciences sociales* 83 (1990).

————. "Universalism and the History of Feminism." *Différences* 7.1 (1995).

————. *Only Paradoxes to Offer: French Feminists and the Rights of Man.* Cambridge, MA: Harvard University Press, 1996. Translated as: *La citoyenneté paradoxale: les féministes françaises et les droits de l'homme.* Trans. Marie Bourdé and Colette Pratt. Paris: Albin Michel, 1998.

————. "'La querelle des Femmes' in the Late Twentieth Century." *Différences* 9.2 (1997).

Sebillotte, Laurent. "Vie à deux: vers un nouveau "contrat d'union": pour une adaptation du droit aux modes de vie d'aujourd'hui." *Lunes* 4 (1998).

Seligmann, Françoise, ed. *Les femmes et le pouvoir: l'exception française.* Spec. issue of *Après-demain* 380–381 (1996).

Sellier, Geneviève. "La Nouvelle Vague: un cinéma à la première personne du masculin singulier." *Iris* 24 (1997).

————, ed. *Cultural Studies, Gender Studies et études filmiques.* Spec. issue of *Iris* 26 (1998).

————. "Images de femmes dans le cinéma de la Nouvelle Vague." *Clio* 10 (1999).

————. "Masculinity and Politics in New Wave Cinema." *Sites: The Journal of 20th-Century/Contemporary French Studies* 4.2 (fall 2000).

Sellier, Geneviève, and Noël Burch. *La drôle de guerre des sexes du cinéma français: 1930–1956.* Paris: Nathan, 1996.

Sénotier, Danièle, and Nathalie Cattanéo. *Sexes et sociétés: répertoire de la recherche en France.* Paris: La Documentation française, 1998.

Serdjénian, Evelyne. *L'égalité des chances ou les enjeux de la mixité.* Paris: Organisation, 1988.

————. *Les femmes et l'égalité professionnelle: des moyens d'action.* Paris: INSEP, 1988.

————, ed. *Femmes et médias: actes du 15e congrès de l'Union professionnelle féminine, Toulon, 4–8 octobre 1995.* Paris: L'Harmattan, 1997.

Séverac, Nadège. "Comment évaluer les violences conjugales? L'approche compréhensive." *Les cahiers de la Sécurité intérieure* 28 (1997).

Shiach, Morag. *Hélène Cixous: A Politics of Writing.* London; New York: Routledge, 1991.

Siegrist, Delphine. *Oser être femme: handicaps et identité féminine.* Paris: Desclée de Brouwer, 2000.

Silvera, Rachel. "Différences, inégalités et discriminations salariales." *Les cahiers du Mage* 2 (1995).

————. "Les femmes et la diversification du temps de travail: nouveaux enjeux, nouveaux risques." *Revue française des affaires sociales* 3 (1998).

————. "Femmes et flexibilité du temps." *Mouvements* 2 (1999).

————, ed. *Les femmes et le travail: nouvelles inégalités, nouveaux enjeux: séminaire 1998–1999.* Montreuil: VO éditions, 2000.

Sineau, Mariette. *Des femmes en politique.* Paris: Economica, 1988.

————. "Pouvoir, modernité et monopole masculin de la politique: le cas français." *Nouvelles questions féministes* 13.1 (1992).

————. "Femmes et culture politique: nouvelles valeurs, nouveaux modèles?" *Vingtième siècle* 44 (1994).

————. "Les femmes politiques sous la cinquième République: à la recherche d'une légitimité électorale." *Pouvoirs* 82 (1997).

————. "L'électrice paradoxale." *Les cultures politiques des Français.* Ed. Annie Laurent and Pascal Perrineau. Paris: Presses de Sciences Po, 2000.

————. "Parité an I: un essai à transformer." *Revue politique et parlementaire* 1011 (2001).

————. *Profession, femme politique: sexe et pouvoir sous la Vème République.* Paris: Presses de Sciences Po, 2001.

Sineau, Mariette, and Jane Jenson, eds. *Who Cares?: Women's Work, Childcare, and Welfare State Redesign.* Toronto: University of Toronto Press, 2001.

Sineau, Mariette, and Evelyne Tardy. *Droits des femmes en France et au Québec: 1940–1990: éléments pour une histoire comparée.* Montréal: Editions du Remue-ménage, 1993.

Singly, François de. *Fortune et infortune de la femme mariée: sociologie des effets de la vie conjugale.* 4th ed. Paris: PUF, 1997. Translated as: *Modern Marriage and its Cost to Women: A Sociological Look at Marriage in France.* Trans. Malcom Bailey. Newark: University of Delaware Press, 1996.

Singly, François de, and Michel Glaude. "L'organisation domestique: pouvoir et négociation." *Economie et statistique* 187 (1986).

Sohn, Anne-Marie. *Chrysalides: femmes dans la vie privée (XIXe-XXe siècles).* Paris: Publications de la Sorbonne, 1996.

Sohn, Anne-Marie, and Françoise Thelamon, eds. *L'histoire sans les femmes est-elle possible? Colloque, Rouen, 27–29 novembre 1997.* Paris: Perrin, 1998.

Soral, Alain. *Vers la féminisation?: démontage d'un complot antidémocratique.* Paris: Editions Blanche, 1999.

Spivak, Gayatri Chakravorty. "French Feminism Revisited: Ethics and Politics." *Feminists Theorize the Political.* Ed. Judith Butler and Joan Scott. New York: Columbia University Press, 2001; first published in 1992 by Routledge (New York).

Steinem, Gloria. *Moving Beyond Words.* New York: Simon & Schuster, 1994.

Stetson, Dorothy McBride. *Women's Rights in France.* New York: Greenwood Press, 1987.

Stetson, Dorothy McBride, and Amy Mazur. "Women's Movements and the State: Job-Training Policy in France and the U.S." *Political Research Quarterly* 53.3 (2000).

Strauss, Frédéric. "Entretien avec Catherine Breillat." *Cahiers du Cinéma* 507 (1996).

Strauss, Frédéric, Claire Denis, and Marie-France Pisier. "Féminin colonial: mémoires d'exil." *Cahiers du Cinéma* 434 (1990).

Strauss, Frédéric, and Serge Toubiana. "Guerrières: entretien avec Solveig Anspach et Karin Viard." *Cahiers du Cinéma* 540 (1999).

Sullerot, Evelyne. *Quels pères? Quels fils?* Paris: Fayard, 1992.

Tabet, Paola. "Du don au tarif: les relations sexuelles impliquant une compensation." *Les Temps modernes* 490 (1987).

———. *La construction sociale de l'inégalité des sexes: des outils et des corps.* Paris: L'Harmattan, 1998.

Taddei, Dominique. "Les femmes et le temps de travail: vers une nouvelle conception du plein emploi." *Après-demain* 388 (1996).

Tarr, Carrie. "Questions of Identity in Beur Cinema: From *Tea in the Harem* to *Cheb.*" *Screen* 34.4 (1993).

Tarr, Carrie, and Brigitte Rollet. *Cinema and the Second Sex: Women's Filmmaking in France in the 1980s and 1990s.* New York: Continuum, 2001.

Tasca, Catherine. "Le pacte civil de solidarité: une reconnaissance responsable de la diversité des unions." *Le Banquet* 12–13 (1998).

Terrail, Jean-Pierre. "Destins scolaires de sexe: une perspective historique et quelques arguments." *Population* 2 (1992).

———. "Réussite scolaire: la mobilisation des filles." *Sociétés contemporaines* 11–12 (1992).

Terras, Christian, and Michel Dufourt, eds. *Le PaCS en question: de la croisade des réacs à l'embarras de la gauche.* Lyon: Golias, 2000.

Thalmann, Rita. *Sexe et race: discours et formes nouvelles d'exclusion du XIXe au XXe siècle: séminaires, 1990–1991.* Paris: CERG, Université Paris VII, 1992.

Thébaud, Françoise. *Écrire l'histoire des femmes.* Fontenay-aux-Roses: ENS 1998.

———. "Les féministes ont-elles raté la maternité?" *Panoramiques* 40 (1999).

Théry, Irène. *Le démariage: justice et vie privée.* Paris: Odile Jacob, 1995.

———. "Différence des sexes et différence des générations: l'institution familiale en déshérence." *Esprit* 12 (1996).

———. "Le contrat d'union sociale en question." *Esprit* 10 (1997).

———. *Couple, filiation et parenté aujourd'hui: le droit face aux mutations de la famille et de la vie privée: rapport à la Ministre de l'emploi et de la solidarité et au garde des sceaux, Ministre de la justice.* Paris: Odile Jacob/La Documentation française, 1998.

Thomas, Lyn, and Emma Webb. "Writing from Experience: The Place of the Personal in French Feminist Writing." *Feminist Review* 61 (1999).

Thomas, Yan. "L'union des sexes: le difficile passage de la nature au droit." *Le Banquet* 12–13 (1998).

Touati, Armand, ed. *Femmes et hommes: des origines aux relations d'aujourd'hui.* Marseille: Hommes et perspectives, 1995.

Toupin, Louise. "Une histoire du féminisme est-elle possible?" *Recherches féministes* 6.1 (1993).

Union européenne familiale. Unité Egalité des chances et politique. *Egalité des chances & politique familiale.* Luxembourg: Communautés européennes, 1997.

Varikas, Eleni. "Pour avoir oublié les vertus de son sexe: Olympe de Gouges et la critique de l'universalisme abstrait." *Sciences politiques* 4–5 (1993).

———. "Une représentation en tant que femme? Réflexions critiques sur la demande de parité des sexes." *Nouvelles questions féministes* 16.2 (1995).

———. "Féminisme, modernité, postmodernisme: pour un dialogue des deux côtés de l'océan." *Féminismes au présent* (a supplement to *Futur Antérieur*). Paris: L'Harmattan, 1995.

Velu, Cécile. "Faut-il 'pactiser' avec l'universalisme?: A Short Story of the PaCS." *Modern & Contemporary France* 7.4 (1999).

Venner, Fiammetta. "Le militantisme féminin d'extrême droite: une autre manière d'être féministe?" *French Politics and Society* 11.2 (1993).

Vers la parité en politique: rapport au Premier Ministre. Paris: La Documentation française, 2001.

Viart, Dominique. *Le roman français au XXe siècle.* Paris: Hachette, 1999.

Viennot, Eliane, ed. *La démocratie "à la Française" ou les femmes indésirables.* Paris: Cahiers du CE-DREF, Presses de Paris VII, 1996.

Vilaine, Anne-Marie de, Laurence Gavarini, and Michèle Le Coadic, eds. *Maternité en mouvement: les femmes, la reproduction et les hommes de science.* Grenoble; Montréal: PUG; Ed. Saint-Martin, 1986.

Vincendeau, Ginette. "Catherine Deneuve and French Womanhood." *Women and Film: A Sight and Sound Reader.* Ed. Pam Cook and Philip Dodd. Philadelphia, PA: Temple University Press, 1993.

Vincendeau, Ginette, and Bérénice Reynaud. "20 ans de théories féministes sur le cinéma." *CinémAction* 67 (1993).

Vogel-Polsky, Eliane. "Les impasses de l'égalité ou pourquoi les outils juridiques visant à l'égalité des femmes et des hommes doivent être repensés en termes de parité." *Parité-Infos,* supplemental edition to the series. Paris: Parité-Infos, 1994.

Warner, Judith. "French Benefits." *Working Mother* 24.5 (2001).

Weissman, Elisabeth. *Les filles, on n'attend plus que vous!: guide pratique et polémique à l'usage de celles qui s'interrogent sur leur engagement en politique, témoignages de Martine Aubry à Simone Veil.* Paris: Textuel, 1995.

Welzer-Lang, Daniel. *Prostitution: les uns, les unes et les autres.* Paris: Métailié: dist. Seuil, 1993.

———. *Les hommes violents.* Paris: Indigo and Côté-femmes, 1996.

Welzer-Lang, Daniel, and Jean-Paul Filiod, eds. *Des hommes et du masculin.* Spec. Issue of *Bulletin d'information des études féminines* (1992).

———. *Les hommes à la conquête de l'espace domestique: du propre et du rangé.* Montréal; Gentilly: VLB; Le Jour: dist. Inter-forum, 1993.

Welzer-Lang, Daniel, and Martine Schutz Samson, eds. *Prostitution et santé communautaire: essai critique sur la parité: colloque international, Lyon, janvier 1999.* Cabiria, 1999.

Whitford, Margaret. *Luce Irigaray: Philosophy in the Feminine.* London: Routledge, 1991.

Wilcox, Clyde. "The Causes and Consequences of Feminist Consciousness among Western European Women." *Comparative Political Studies* 23.4 (1991).

Winter, Bronwyn. "(Mis)representations: What French Feminism Isn't." *Women's Studies International Forum* 20.2 (1997).

Wittig, Monique. *The Straight Mind and Other Essays.* New York; London: Harvester Wheatsheaf, 1992. Translated as: *La pensée straight.* Paris: Balland, 2001.

Wittner, Laurette, and Daniel Welzer-Lang, eds. *Les faits du logis.* Lyon: Aléas, 1996.

Woodward, Kathleen. *Figuring Age: Women, Bodies, Generations.* Bloomington: Indiana University Press, 1999.

Yaguello, Marina. *Les mots et les femmes.* Paris: Editions Payot, 1992.

Ysmal, Colette. "Le vote des femmes depuis 1945: elles sont de moins en moins conservatrices." *Revue des deux mondes* 4 (1995).

Zaidman, Claude, and Bronwyn Winter. *La mixité à l'école primaire.* Paris: L'Harmattan, 1996.

Zarca, Bernard. "La division du travail domestique: poids du passé et tensions au sein du couple." *Economie et statistique* 228 (1990).

JOURNALS

Bulletin- C.R.I.F. Paris: Centre de recherches de réflexion et d'information féministes.

Bulletin et Actes des journées de l'ANEF—Association Nationale des Etudes Féministes.

Cahiers du CEDREF: la revue des études féministes à l'Université Paris VII. Ed. Claude Zaidmann, Liliane Kandel. Paris: CEDREF, 1989-.

Cahiers du féminisme, de la fierté lesbienne et gay. Paris: Editions de la Taupe Rouge, 1998-. Formerly *Cahiers du féminisme.* Paris: Editions de la Taupe Rouge, 1977–1997

Cahiers du Genre. Ed. Jacqueline Heinen. Paris: L'Harmattan, 1999-. Formely *Cahiers du GEDISST.* Paris: Groupe d'étude sur la division sociale et sexuelle du travail, 1991–1999.

Cahiers du GRIF. Brussels: GRIF, 1973–1997.

Clio: histoire, femmes et sociétés. Ed. Françoise Thébaud et Michèle Zancarini-Fournel. Toulouse: Presses universitaires du Mirail, 1995-.

Chronique féministe. Ed. Fanny Filosof. Brussels: L'Université des femmes, 1982-.

Femmes informations. Marseille: Centre d'orientation de documentation d'information féminin (CODIF), 1979-.

Lesbia magazine. Paris: Lesbia, 1982-.

Lettre de l'AVFT: lettre d'information de l'Association européenne contre les Violences faites aux Femmes au Travail. Paris: AVFT, 1992-.

Lunes: réalités, parcours, représentations de femmes. Ed. Anne-Françoise Khanine. Evreux: Lunes, 1997-.

Nouvelles questions féministes: revue internationale francophone (NQF). Ed. Simone de Beauvoir. Paris: Tierce, 1981- (not published between 1987–1990).

ProChoix. Ed. Caroline Fourest and Fiametta Venner. Paris: Prochoix, 1997-.

Projets féministes. Ed. Marie-Victoire Louis. Paris: AVTF, 1992-.

Prostitution et Société. Ed. Jean-Marc Bonnisseau. Clichy: Mouvement du Nid, 1989-.

Recherches féministes. Québec: GREMF, 1988-.

Travail, genre et société. Ed. Margaret Maruani. Paris: L'Harmattan, 1999-. Formely *Les Cahiers du MAGE.* Paris: GDR Mage, 1995–1997.